HOWARD ANDREW KNOX

~~~~~~

COLUMBIA UNIVERSITY PRESS - NEW YORK

PIONEER *of* INTELLIGENCE TESTING
AT ELLIS ISLAND

HOWARD ANDREW KNOX

JOHN T. E. RICHARDSON

Columbia University Press

Publishers Since 1893

New York   Chichester, West Sussex

Copyright © 2011 Columbia University Press

Library of Congress Cataloging-in-Publication Data

Richardson, John T. E.

Howard Andrew Knox : pioneer of intelligence testing

at Ellis Island / John T. E. Richardson.

p.   cm

Includes bibliographical references and index.

ISBN 978-0-231-14168-0 (cloth : alk. paper)—ISBN 978-0-231-51211-4

(ebook : alk. paper)

1. Nonverbal intelligence tests—United States.   2. Knox,

Howard Andrew, 1885–1949.   I. Title.

BF432.5.N65R53 2011

153.9'3092—dc22

2011010220

Columbia University Press books are printed on permanent and
durable acid-free paper.
This book is printed on paper with recycled content.
Printed in the United States of America

c 10 9 8 7 6 5 4 3 2 1

References to Internet Web sites (URLs) were accurate at the time of writing.
Neither the author nor Columbia University Press is responsible for URLs that may
have expired or changed since the manuscript was prepared.

CONTENTS

PART IV: THE LEGACY

ILLUSTRATIONS

TABLES

FOREWORD

Howard Andrew Knox died the year I was born—1949. So we represent two successive life spans in our efforts to understand, investigate, and measure intelligence. I first learned of Knox's work when I was a teenager. As I was doing a seventh-grade science project on mental testing, I noted some tests that I believed had really memorable and even funny names. The two that most impressed me were the O'Connor Wiggly Block Test and the Knox Cube Test, also called the Knox Cube Imitation Test. In the test an examiner knocks the Knox cubes, and the examinee must do the same. I knew what the test was, but I knew nothing of its origins. After reading John T. E. Richardson's biography of Knox, I now know much of its origins and development, as well as of the origins and development of others of Knox's tests.

In reading Richardson's book I was impressed both by how much changed in these two life spans and by how much remained the same.

One thing that changed, of course, is the centerpiece of the book, Ellis Island. It is now a museum, certainly one of the more fascinating in the United States. But even to that island I have a link, as my mother came through Ellis Island, as did my maternal and paternal grandparents. Ellis Island represented an attempt to systematize the immigration process into the United States. This book deals with one aspect of the system, the attempts to develop an intelligence test that could be used for emigrants who lacked the acculturation of the native born. The Binet tests were ill suited for use with emigrants. They required too much knowledge of a language and culture that were foreign to, well, foreigners. So Knox and others attempted to develop performance tests that would measure the intellectual skills deemed essential for successful immigration.

Do such tests truly measure intelligence in a culture-free or even culture-fair way? This question is debated even today, but the consensus is that they probably do not. Richardson points out that performance tests are not even fully nonverbal: the native language of emigrants makes a difference in their performance on both verbal and nonverbal tests. On verbal tests individuals for whom English is a second language will be at a disadvantage in answering the questions; on nonverbal tests these individuals will be at a disadvantage in understanding the instructions and perhaps in familiarity with what may seem like a strange task. These tests measure some skills that constitute part of intelligence but probably not everything. At the same time Knox's Cube Test was prescient in one respect. It is, to a large extent, a measure of spatial working memory, and research by Alan Baddeley, Randall Engle, Patrick Kyllonen, and others since the turn of the century has suggested that working memory may in fact be at the core of what has become known as general intelligence, or *g*. Moreover, different kinds of working memory, such as spatial and verbal, tend to be correlated, so the Knox Cube Test was probably a lot better as a measure of *g* than might have been expected in the early part of the twentieth century.

Moreover, it is not clear that the tests available today for measuring intelligence across cultural divides offer anything substantially better. Today's tests may be more sophisticated psychometrically, but conceptually they are not all that different.

A second thing that has changed is social attitudes toward people with intellectual disabilities. Even the terms used to refer to them have changed, as shown by the evolution of the American Association for the Study of the Feeble-Minded into the American Association on Mental Deficiency into the American Association on Mental Retardation into the American Association on Intellectual and Developmental Disabilities. They are all the same association, but the changing names reflect a changing view of the people the organization champions. Certainly terms like *idiot, imbecile,* and *moron* disappeared long ago. Richardson uses the older terms in his book, a reflection of the thinking of the times. Although the terminology has changed, it is not clear how much the tendency to discriminate has changed with it. Anthony Greenwald and Mahzarin Banaji have developed techniques for studying implicit prejudice, and it is an open question whether people's implicit prejudices have been reduced as much as the changing names suggest. I suspect that many old prejudices are still there but further beneath the surface.

The central thesis of this book is that Knox was a pioneer in the intelligence-testing movement who somehow has been largely forgotten. Richardson spends a considerable amount of the book highlighting Knox's achievements. But he never fully addresses why Knox did not quite make it into the ranks of the pantheon of the truly famous, such as Goddard and Yerkes. Was it his personal life, which was characterized by marital conflicts and even a lawsuit against him by his father? Was it the longevity of his career, which was shorter than those of some others? Was it that he simply did not get cited in the literature on psychological testing when he should have been? The last chapter of the book discusses this issue; perhaps, in the end, part of becoming a revered pioneer in a field is a matter of luck, which eluded Knox.

No one can read this book without learning a great deal about the early history of mental testing, as well as about a man who was truly a pioneer, forgotten or otherwise, of the mental testing movement. Also, no one can read the book without reflecting on the ethics of the kinds of mental testing that were done on immigrants to the United States. How, after all, should a country decide whom to allow to immigrate? As I write this foreword, there is as much debate on this issue as there was when Knox lived. I am honored to have had the opportunity to write this brief foreword, and I am delighted that I could be one of the first to read this important book.

Robert J. Sternberg

PREFACE

This book began one summer evening in 1998, when I was talking to my colleague Tomaso Vecchi in his office at the University of Padua in Italy. We had been collaborating for some time on the investigation of visuospatial short-term memory, and we were particularly interested in finding new ways of measuring people's performance in this area. Tomaso showed me a paper that had just been published by Daniel Bruce Berch of the National Institutes of Health and his colleagues Robert Krikorian and Eileen Marie Huha of the University of Cincinnati. Their paper discussed methodological and theoretical considerations raised by the block-tapping task devised many years before by Philip Michael Corsi, a research student at the Montreal Neurological Institute. Both Tomaso and I were familiar with this task: Tomaso had been using it more recently in experimental research, and I had used it back in the 1970s in assessing neurological patients as part of my postdoctoral work at the University of Oxford.

Several pages into the paper by Berch and his colleagues, we read a footnote, the most important part of which said:

> Knox (1914) developed a block-tapping task that has subsequently become known as the Knox Cubes Imitation Test. It was originally devised as part of a series of performance tests for assessing intellectual deficits in immigrants at Ellis Island. . . . It should be noted that with the exception of being included as a subtest in several intelligence scales (e.g., The Arthur Point Scale of Performance,

1947) there has been a dearth of either clinical or neuropsychological research making use of this test.

(Berch, Krikorian, and Huha 1998:322)

This was curious to us because, despite our many years of research into short-term memory, neither of us had ever heard of the "Knox Cubes Imitation Test." A quick online search of bibliographic databases soon made it clear that Berch and his colleagues had been wrong about a dearth of research: we found dozens of studies that had used the test since 1914. This led Tomaso and me to collaborate on experimental research to compare Knox's original test with Corsi's test, and we published our findings in 2001. Tomaso focused on other tasks of his own devising, but I went on to carry out a more systematic trawl of the literature, and I published a review and an experimental analysis of Knox's test in 2005.

At the same time I became intrigued about why someone involved in the assessment of emigrants at Ellis Island would have devised a simple test that modern psychologists would immediately recognize as an interesting method for evaluating short-term memory. I therefore set about gathering published material relating to Knox and his tests, and it soon became clear he had devised not just one test but several. By June 2001, I was fairly confident that I had amassed most of the literature about Knox, if not all. I had given one or two seminars about Knox and his work, and I was thinking of writing the material up into a short article. Then I received a brief message by e-mail. Headed "Subject: Howard A. Knox," it read: "He is my father and I would like to share information about him. Robert H. Knox."

It transpired that Robert's son, the vice principal of a high school in Michigan, had found on the Internet summaries of the seminars that I had given and had sent them to Robert as a Father's Day present. After a lively exchange of correspondence, I traveled to the United States in December 2001 to visit Robert in Florida and his older sister, Carolyn, in Atlanta. Both were born after their father left Ellis Island in 1916 (when I visited them, Robert was seventy-seven, and Carolyn was eighty-two), hence they had no personal memories of the events in which I was chiefly interested. Even so, they had many recollections about their father; Carolyn shared with me her father's personal correspondence from his younger days, and her son, William H. Whaley, had a collection of Knox's professional correspondence and unpublished writings. All quotations in this book not attributed to published or formally archived sources come from the letters given to me by Carolyn Knox Whaley or from other documents that remain in the family's private collection.

I wrote a short piece about Knox's military career before he worked at Ellis Island and then a longer article about his life and work. Nevertheless, it became clear that a much fuller biography was needed that would set his work at Ellis Island in the context of the public, political, and professional debates and discussions of the time. In writing this account I have been aided by many people in many different ways. Most obviously, and most important, I am grateful to the late Carolyn Knox Whaley and the late Robert Harper Knox for their personal recollections of their father and access to personal photographs and correspondence, as well as for their kindness, encouragement, and hospitality. I am also grateful to William H. Whaley for access to Knox's writings and professional correspondence; Howard Andrew Knox Jr. (whom I regret I have yet to meet) for permission to quote from his father's correspondence; Robert J. Sternberg of Tufts University for agreeing to write a foreword to this book; and three anonymous reviewers and my editor at Columbia University Press, Lauren Dockett, for their comments on earlier drafts.

Beyond this I can only list people alphabetically, since it would be invidious (not to say impossible) to try to rank them in order of importance: Greg Anderson, C. H. Stoelting Company, Chicago; Paul Anderson and Stanley Finger, Washington University, St. Louis; Michael Angelo, Thomas Jefferson University, Philadelphia; Doreen Atwood and David Prouty, Sheffield Historical Society, Sheffield, Massachusetts; Alan Baddeley, University of York; Ralph H. Baer of Ralph H. Baer Consultants; David Baker and John Popplestone, University of Akron; Tom Beardsley of Threadcity.org; Ray Bellini, Grand Lodge of New Jersey; Ludy Benjamin, Texas A&M University; Mark Berhow and Bolling W. Smith, Coast Defense Study Group; Corwin Boake, University of Texas–Houston; Ruth Brooks, formerly of Hampton, New Jersey; Margot Canaday, University of Minnesota; Eleanor Fulton Carpenter, Washington, D.C.; Marjorie Ciarlante and Suzanne A. Harris, National Archives and Records Administration; Michael Cole, University of California–San Diego; Lisa Morrison Coulthard, British Psychological Society; Stephen C. Craig, Uniformed Services University of the Health Sciences; Michel Denis, LIMSI, Université de Paris–Sud; Lois Densky-Wolff, University of Medicine and Dentistry of New Jersey; Amy Douglas, University of Missouri; Jack Eckert, Harvard University; Brent Elliott, Royal Horticultural Society; Carol Ganz, Connecticut State Library; Stephen Greenberg, National Library of Medicine; Andrew J. Harrison, Alan Mason Chesney Medical Archives of the Johns Hopkins Medical Institutions; Sarah Hartwell, Dartmouth College; Mirjam Hauck, John Oates, and Hilary E. Robertson, Open University; Ulf Hedberg, Gallaudet University; Steven Herb, Pennsylvania State University; Michelle Johnson, National Academy, New York; Russell Johnson, University of California–Los Angeles; Adam Kuper and Dany Nobus, Brunel University; David Lane, Columbia Medical Center, New York; Boleslav Lichterman, Russian Academy of Medical Sciences, Moscow; Illyce Mac Donald and Dereka Smith, National Genealogical Society; Sandra Matter, Pennsylvania State Board of Medicine; Boris Meshcheryakov, Dubna University; Erik Meyer, University of Cape Town; Brenda Milner, Montreal Neurological Institute; Barry Moreno and Diana Pardue, U.S. Department of the Interior; Betty Mueller, De Soto, Missouri; Betty Olson, De Soto Public Library, De Soto, Missouri; John Parascandola, U.S. Department of Health and Human Services; Amanda Philipp, Hunterdon County Library, Flemington, New Jersey; Lizette Royer, Archives of the History of American Psychology; Dipali Sen, Bayonne Public Library, Bayonne, New Jersey; Daniel Smith, Cleveland Public Library; Peter Smith, Cornish Colony Museum, Windsor, Vermont; Alex Stagg, Institute of Laryngology and RNID Libraries, University College London; Christopher Stanwood, College of Physicians of Philadelphia; Jason Stratman, Missouri Historical Society; the late Juliane Swiney, M.D., of Bayonne, New Jersey; David Tulsky, Kessler Medical Rehabilitation Research and Educational Corporation, West Orange, New Jersey; Jaan Valsiner, Clark University; and Tomaso Vecchi, now at the University of Pavia. Obviously, I apologize if I have inadvertently omitted someone from this list.

Finally, at various points I have used material that previously appeared in the following publications:

Richardson, J. T. E. 2001. A physician with the Coast Artillery Corps: The military career of Dr. Howard Andrew Knox, pioneer of psychological testing. *Coast Defense Journal* 15 (4): 88–93.

———. 2003. Howard Andrew Knox and the origins of performance testing on Ellis Island, 1912–1916. *History of Psychology* 6:143–70.

———. 2004. The origins of inkblots. *Psychologist: Bulletin of the British Psychological Society* 17:334–35.

———. 2005. Knox's cube imitation test: A historical review and an experimental analysis. *Brain and Cognition* 59:183–213.

CHRONOLOGY

1871   The U.S. Marine Hospital Service is created.

1876   The U.S. Supreme Court declares the regulation of immigration to be a federal responsibility.

1882   U.S. Congress imposes a tax per head on immigrants to the United States and prohibits admission to the United States of lunatics, idiots, and anyone likely to become a public charge.

1884   Francis Galton opens an "anthropometric laboratory" at the International Health Exhibition in London.

1885   Howard Andrew Knox is born in Romeo, Michigan, to Howard Reuben Knox and Jennie Mahaffy Knox.

1890   The secretary of the U.S. Treasury imposes federal control of immigration at the Port of New York.

1891   The federal government of the United States takes over the regulation of immigration and creates the Bureau of Immigration. The Marine Hospital Service is assigned responsibility for the medical inspection of arriving immigrants.

1892   The Ellis Island Immigration Station receives its first emigrants.

1897   Fire destroys the Ellis Island Immigration Station.

1900   The work of Gregor Mendel on the inheritance of traits is rediscovered.

The new immigration station at Ellis Island opens.

1901–1904　Naomi Norsworthy uses a form board to test mentally deficient children.

1902　The Marine Hospital Service is renamed the Public Health and Marine Hospital Service.

1903　Edward Thorndike expounds his theory of intelligence as a collection of special abilities.

Howard Knox graduates from Windham High School, Willimantic, Connecticut, and enters medical school at Dartmouth College, Hanover, New Hampshire.

1904　Charles Spearman expounds his theory of general intelligence.

1905　Alfred Binet and Théodore Simon publish their first "metric scale of intelligence."

1906　Henry Goddard is appointed director of research at the New Jersey Training School.

1907　Congress specifies that the categories of people to be excluded from the United States should include "imbeciles," "feeble-minded persons," and people with physical or mental defects that might affect their ability to earn a living.

1908　Alfred Binet and Théodore Simon publish their revised intelligence scale, according to which each child can be assigned to a particular intellectual or mental "level."

Henry Goddard visits Europe to learn about the new tests of intelligence and introduces Binet and Simon's 1905 scale to the United States.

Howard Knox graduates from Dartmouth College, is briefly employed at the Insane Hospital in Worcester, Massachusetts, and is then appointed to the Medical Reserve Corps at Fort Michie, New York.

1909　Knox is admitted to the Army Medical School in Washington, D.C.
Sigmund Freud and Carl Jung visit Clark University in Worcester, Massachusetts.

1910　Knox graduates from the Army Medical School and is assigned to Fort Hancock, New Jersey.
Henry Goddard coins the terms *moron* and *mental age*.
Translations of Binet and Simon's 1908 scale are published in the United States.

1911　Knox is assigned to Fort Crockett, Texas, but then resigns his commission in the Army Medical Corps and sets up private practice in Sheffield, Massachusetts.
The final version of Binet and Simon's intelligence scale is published.

1912　Knox is appointed to the Public Health and Marine Hospital Service and is assigned to work at the Ellis Island Immigration Station.

Henry Goddard visits the Ellis Island Immigration Station to test emigrants using Binet and Simon's scale.

The Public Health and Marine Hospital Service is renamed the Public Health Service.

William Stern proposes the idea of a mental quotient.

1913   Bernard Glueck uses a battery of intelligence tests at Ellis Island.

Knox develops the Ellis Island tests and publishes descriptions of the tests between September 1913 and April 1914.

1914   Knox publishes "a special scale for the measurement of intelligence."

Knox addresses the second annual meeting of the Eugenics Research Association.

1915   Knox publishes an account of the Ellis Island tests in *Scientific American.*

Lewis Terman proposes the idea of an age-scaled intelligence quotient.

Robert Yerkes proposes the idea of a point-scaled intelligence quotient.

Rudolf Pintner produces a standardization of Knox's Cube Imitation Test.

The Ellis Island tests are marketed by C. H. Stoelting Company, Chicago.

1916   Knox resigns from the Public Health Service, leaves Ellis Island, and attempts to set up a private general practice in Ashtabula, Ohio.

Henry Goddard publishes Elizabeth Pike's translations of Binet and Simon's articles.

Lewis Terman publishes the Stanford revision of the Binet-Simon scale.

Knox works for five months as acting clinical director at the State Village for Epileptics, Skillman, New Jersey, before setting up a private general practice in Bayonne, New Jersey.

1917   Rudolf Pintner and Donald Paterson produce their scale of performance tests.

The United States enters World War I; Robert Yerkes chairs the Committee on the Psychological Examination of Recruits.

Examination Alpha, Examination Beta, and the Army Performance Scale are administered to U.S. Army recruits.

1918   Federal government publishes the *Manual of the Mental Examination of Aliens.*

World War I ends, and the testing of U.S. Army recruits ceases.

1920   Robert Yerkes and Clarence Yoakum publish *Army Mental Tests*.

1923   Frances Gaw advocates the use of performance tests in vocational guidance in the United Kingdom.

1924   Knox retires to New Hampton, New Jersey, but works as a general practitioner.

1925   Grace Arthur publishes the Arthur Performance Scale.

        Paul Squires publishes *A Universal Scale of Individual Performance Tests*.

1927   Augusta Fox Bronner, William Healy, and colleagues publish *A Manual of Individual Mental Tests and Testing*.

1928   In Scotland, James Drever and Mary Collins publish *Performance Tests of Intelligence: A Series of Non-linguistic Tests for Deaf and Normal Children*.

1939   David Wechsler publishes the Wechsler-Bellevue Intelligence Scale.

1943   Immigrant reception is moved from Ellis Island to New York City.

1949   David Wechsler publishes the Wechsler Intelligence Scale for Children.

        Knox dies in Jersey City, New Jersey.

1954   The Ellis Island facility is closed.

1955   David Wechsler publishes the Wechsler Adult Intelligence Scale.

KEY PEOPLE IN THE TEXT

Anastasi, Anne (1908–2001): U.S. psychologist and author of *Psychological Testing*

Arthur, Mary Grace (1883–1967): U.S. educational psychologist, author of *A Point Scale of Performance Tests*

Binet, Alfred (1857–1911): French psychologist and developer of intelligence tests

Bronner, Augusta Fox (1881–1966): U.S. clinical psychologist

Cattell, James McKeen (1860–1944): U.S. psychologist

Davenport, Charles Benedict (1866–1944): U.S. biologist and eugenicist

Fernald, Grace Maxwell (1879–1950): U.S. educational psychologist

Freud, Sigmund (1856–1939): Austrian physician and founder of psychoanalysis

Galton, Francis (1822–1911): English anthropologist and eugenicist

Gaw, Frances Isabel (1897–1975): U.S. psychologist and educationalist

Glueck, Bernard (1884–1972): Polish-born U.S. psychiatrist

Goddard, Henry Herbert (1866–1957): U.S. psychologist

Gould, Stephen Jay (1941–2002): U.S. biologist and author of *The Mismeasure of Man*

Gwyn, Matthew Kemp (1875–1929): U.S. physician employed at Ellis Island

Hall, Granville Stanley (1844–1924): U.S. psychologist, first president of Clark University, and first president of the American Psychological Association

Healy, William (1869–1963): British-born U.S. psychiatrist

Huey, Edmund Burke (1870–1913): U.S. educational and clinical psychologist

Itard, Jean Marc Gaspard (1774–1838): French physician and author of *De l'éducation d'un homme sauvage*

Kamin, Leon Judah (1928–): U.S. psychologist and author of *The Science and Politics of I.Q.*

Kempf, Grover Andrew (1888–1982): U.S. physician employed at Ellis Island

La Garde, Louis Anatole (1849–1920): U.S. physician and president of the Army Medical School, 1910–13

Lavinder, Claude Hervey (1872–1950): U.S. physician

Leontiev (Leont'ev), Aleksei Nicolaevich (1903–1979): Russian developmental psychologist

Luria, Aleksandr Romanovich (1902–1977): Russian psychologist and neuroscientist

Meyer, Adolf (1866–1950): Swiss psychiatrist, emigrated to United States in 1892

Mullan, Eugene Hagan (1878–1965): U.S. physician employed at Ellis Island, author of *Mentality of the Arriving Immigrant*

Norsworthy, Naomi (1877–1916): U.S. psychologist

Pearson, Karl (1857–1936): English statistician

Pintner, Rudolf (1884–1942): English psychologist, emigrated to United States in 1912

Salmon, Thomas William (1876–1927): U.S. psychiatrist employed at Ellis Island

Séguin, Édouard (Edward Seguin) (1812–1880): French physician and educationalist, emigrated to United States in 1849

Simon, Théodore (1872–1961): French psychologist

Spearman, Charles Edward (1863–1945): English psychologist

Squires, Paul Chatham (1894–1958): U.S. psychologist, author of *A Universal Scale of Individual Performance Tests*

Stern, William (1871–1938): German psychologist

Stoner, George W. (1853–1932): U.S. physician, chief medical officer at Ellis Island, 1903–13

Terman, Lewis Madison (1877–1956): U.S. psychologist, author of the Stanford revision of the Binet–Simon scale

Thorndike, Edward Lee (1874–1949): U.S. psychologist

Vygotski (Vygotsky), Lev Semeonovich (1896–1934): Russian developmental psychologist

Wallin, John Edward Wallace (1876–1969): U.S. educational psychologist

Wechsler, David (1896–1981): Romanian-born U.S. psychologist and developer of intelligence tests

Williams, Louis Laval (1859–1939): U.S. physician, chief medical officer at Ellis Island, 1913–15

Woodworth, Robert Sessions (1869–1962): U.S. psychologist

Yerkes, Robert Mearns (1876–1956): U.S. psychologist and primatologist

INTRODUCTION

The history of intelligence testing has been extensively discussed in both learned and popular books and articles. People such as Francis Galton, Alfred Binet, Henry Herbert Goddard, Lewis Madison Terman, Robert Mearns Yerkes, and David Wechsler are all well known to today's students of psychology, not merely in the United States but in other countries, too. Excellent accounts have been written of their lives and work (Fancher 1998; Frank 1983; Gillham 2001; Minton 1988; J. Reed 1987; Wolf 1973; Zenderland 1998). Moreover, incisive critiques have been written of how intelligence tests have been constructed, how they have been administered, and how the results have been interpreted (Gould 1981; Kamin 1974). However, one person who has been almost completely overlooked in these accounts is Howard Andrew Knox.

Knox was a physician, not a psychologist, and his own work on intelligence testing was confined to just four years, from May 1912 to May 1916. During this period Knox worked for the U.S. Public Health Service at the immigration station on Ellis Island in New York Harbor. Among his responsibilities was the identification of mentally deficient emigrants so that they could be detained and returned to the countries from which they had embarked. To address the obvious problem of trying to assess the intelligence of people with little or no command of English, Knox and his colleagues devised a series of "performance tests" that could be administered to emigrants while making minimal use of language.

The tests that they devised were widely used between the two world wars, and some continued to be used by practitioners and researchers throughout the twentieth century. But Knox's work is also important because it led psychologists to realize that any adequate measure of intelligence must use both verbal and nonverbal tests. This idea was first articulated around 1930, was embodied in the various intelligence scales devised by Wechsler from 1939 onward, and today generally is taken for granted by psychologists around the world. In this regard Knox is a "missing link" between the early, purely verbal tests devised by Binet and the performance scales developed after World War I on which Wechsler relied.

THE STRUCTURE OF THIS BOOK

My thesis is that Knox is a neglected but key figure in the development of intelligence tests. I have pieced together what is known about his life and work from published and unpublished sources. I have provided a chronology of key events from the 1870s to the 1950s and a brief description of the main characters, or dramatis personae. I am concerned mainly with Knox's professional life, and I will mention domestic matters merely in passing. Nevertheless, Knox's personal life was relatively complicated (at least for the time in question), and figure I.1 provides a partial family tree, showing Knox and his three (or perhaps four) wives, together with their respective parents and immediate offspring. Gaps in the historical record are unlikely ever to be filled because of limitations in the available documentation or in the testimony of my informants, and this is a problem that inevitably recurs during my account.

In chapters 1 and 2, I describe Knox's childhood, his medical training, and his work as a physician with the U.S. Army from 1908 to 1911 to give an idea of what kind of person Knox was when he went to work at Ellis Island in 1912. In part 2, I describe the context of his work there. In chapter 3, I discuss the issues of immigration and intelligence that had arisen in the United States between 1880 and 1912, a period of increasing public clamor and concern that mentally deficient emigrants, particularly from countries in southern and eastern Europe, were gaining admission to the United States. In chapter 4, I discuss the attempts to measure intelligence during this period, including the introduction to the United States of the scale that had been developed in France by Binet and Théodore Simon. In chapter 5, I discuss Knox's first year at Ellis Island and how the physicians there dealt with the increasing concern about mentally deficient emigrants.

In part 3, I describe the process by which Knox and his colleagues developed their own performance tests, and I introduce the tests themselves in chapter 6. Not only did Knox and his colleagues describe these tests in regular medical

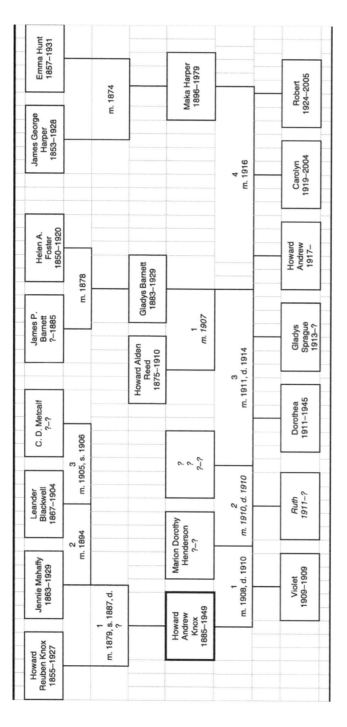

I.1 A partial family tree of Howard Andrew Knox

Note: m = married; *s* = separated; *d* = divorced. Numbers refer to successive marriages. (For example, Jennie Mahaffy was married to Howard Reuben Knox, then to Leander Blackwell, and then to C. D. Metcalf.) Information in italics is speculative and has not been confirmed. Except for the most recent generation, siblings have been omitted.

journals, but Knox in particular also brought them to the attention of a much wider audience through articles in newspapers and magazines and through presentations at conferences, as I explain in chapter 7. In chapter 8, I discuss the various practical issues in intelligence testing that Knox and his colleagues described in their various publications. These publications contain many useful and very human insights concerning the limitations of psychological testing, particularly with regard to the mental and physical state of the many emigrants whom they were called upon to examine.

As I explain in chapter 9, Knox himself played no further part in this story after he left Ellis Island in 1916. Accordingly, part 4 is concerned with the legacy of his work at Ellis Island. The tests that he and his colleagues developed constitute the first performance scale—that is, a battery or collection of performance tests that could be used to measure intelligence. In chapter 10, I describe subsequent attempts to develop performance scales, many of which incorporated tests originally developed at Ellis Island. In chapter 11, I describe the tests' wider use throughout the 1920s and 1930s until they were generally superseded by Wechsler's scales from 1939 onward. I consider what performance tests actually measure in light of current psychological research in chapter 12. My concluding appraisal in chapter 13 considers why Knox's work has been neglected and seeks to reinstate him as a key figure in the history of intelligence testing.

SOME COMMENTS ABOUT LANGUAGE

Any researcher who studies a historical figure or phenomenon has to cope with the attitudes, values, and especially language that have changed in the years since. In particular, both professionals and laypeople have in the past used different terminology to talk about individuals of limited intelligence.

In 1876, for instance, the Association of Medical Officers of American Institutions for Idiotic and Feeble-Minded Persons was established. This organization changed its name to the American Association for the Study of the Feeble-Minded in 1906, to the American Association on Mental Deficiency in 1933, to the American Association on Mental Retardation in 1987, and to the American Association on Intellectual and Developmental Disabilities in 2007. These new names reflected shifts in attitude toward people with intellectual disabilities and the rejection of pejorative or stigmatizing language. In addition, speakers and writers today are expected to use "person-first" language (in other words, "people with intellectual disabilities," not "intellectually disabled people," and certainly not "the intellectually disabled") so as to respect the integrity of the people in question and to avoid equating them with their disability.

Nevertheless, it would be anachronistic and fundamentally ahistorical to put present-day attitudes and vocabulary into the minds and mouths of people who lived one hundred years ago. Gerald N. Grob made this point well when introducing his account of a psychiatric hospital in Massachusetts between the years of 1830 and 1920:

> No doubt some readers will be offended by the constant use of the terms "insane" and "insanity" as opposed to "mentally ill" and "mental illness." Although the former two have acquired an odious connotation, they were perfectly good terms in the past. My usage, therefore, is an historical one and has no derogatory intent. After all, it is very probable that the word "mental illness" itself will in the future be looked down upon with the same disfavor as "insanity" is at present.
>
> (Grob 1966:xiii)

Similarly, I will use such terms as *mental defectiveness, mental deficiency, mental retardation, idiots, imbeciles,* and *the feebleminded,* because these were the terms used both by professionals and the general public at the time in question.

The terms *mental defectiveness, mental deficiency,* and *mental retardation* appear to have come into widespread usage toward the end of the nineteenth century. The first two terms are close synonyms (*defective* and *deficient* can both mean "lacking an essential part or quality" or "falling short") that simply describe the condition of having a limited mental capacity. However, *mental retardation* is more subtle in its meaning: It implies that people are mentally deficient simply because their intellectual development has lagged behind that of their contemporaries. (The equivalent term in French is *arriéré,* meaning *backward,* a word used colloquially in English, too.) In other words, people of limited mental capacity have followed the same course of intellectual development as everyone else but have just done so more slowly.

In the late 1800s this view of mental deficiency was encouraged by a more general idea called the theory of recapitulation. This had been first put forward by a German zoologist, Ernst Haeckel, in the slogan "Ontogeny recapitulates phylogeny." *Ontogeny* refers to the process of development in an individual organism; *phylogeny* refers to the evolutionary development of the relevant species. Haeckel's (1866) original proposal was that the development of the human embryo exactly mirrored the evolution of the human species. For instance, the early embryo has a series of clefts in each side of the throat (the pharyngeal clefts) that correspond to the gills of fish, and Haeckel claimed that this was evidence for a fishlike ancestor of modern humans. His theory proved highly influential, although his specific proposals were subsequently discredited.

One person influenced by both Haeckel's ideas and those of his contemporary, Charles Darwin, was Granville Stanley Hall. In 1892 Hall was a leading force in the creation of the American Psychological Association, and he was made its first president (Popplestone and McPherson 1999:14). In 1888 he was appointed as the founding president of Clark University in Worcester, Massachusetts. He extended Haeckel's idea of recapitulation to argue that the process of intellectual development in children was innately predetermined to recapitulate the evolution of human civilization. As he remarked:

> Realizing the limitations and qualifications of the recapitulation theory in the biologic field, I am now convinced that its psychogenetic applications have a method of their own. . . . Along with the sense of the immense importance of further coordinating childhood and youth with the development of the race, has grown the conviction that only here can we hope to find true norms against the tendencies to precocity in home, school, church, and civilization generally, and also to establish criteria by which to both diagnose and measure arrest and retardation in the individual and the race.
>
> (G. S. Hall 1904, 1:viii)

Insofar as there are similarities between the development of children and the history of human civilization, this does not in itself provide evidence for any causal mechanism that drives the former to imitate the latter. As Harry Levi Hollingworth (1927:206–13, 367–68) pointed out, it might merely show that in both cases human development is constrained by limitations of skill, knowledge, and intelligence. Even so, the recapitulation theory provided a powerful basis for conceptualizing mental deficiency in terms of mental retardation. Of course, taken literally, the recapitulation theory would simply entail that mentally deficient children were developing more slowly than normal children but would eventually reach the same stage of development. It therefore needed to be supplemented by the assumption that mentally deficient children ceased to develop at an earlier stage than normal children (see, for example, Stern 1914:84).

Mental retardation is still sometimes used as a synonym for *intellectual disability*, although it is gradually being superseded by the latter expression. Nevertheless, it is now known that intellectual disabilities can result from a wide variety of causes, many of which are likely to affect the *process* of development as well as the eventual outcome. Consequently, it is inappropriate to characterize the mental capacity of people with intellectual disabilities simply by likening it to that of normal children. In my account, then, I will use the neutral terms *mental defectiveness* or *mental deficiency* except when the original sources more specifically referred to mental retardation.

Another problematic concept is that of race. This has been used since at least the eighteenth century to refer to broad groupings of the human population. Originally, this was based on physical characteristics such as skin color and shape of the head. However, from the late nineteenth century onward, there were attempts to validate these groupings scientifically using blood group and other physiological markers as well as mental characteristics such as temperament, personality, and intelligence. The idea that different races differed in the latter characteristics—and especially in terms of intelligence—became widespread among the general public. In fact, subsequent research has shown that differences among racial groups in terms of genetic traits are relatively small in comparison with the variation in those traits among members of the same group and that racial differences in mental traits are negligible (Tobias 1996).

Because of its association with discredited theories about human behavior, character, and social organization, the term *race* is no longer acceptable in social research (Fenton 1996; Sillitoe and White 1992). Instead, researchers prefer to use the notion of ethnicity, which has been explained as follows: "Ethnicity is a fundamental category of social organization which is based on membership defined by a sense of common historical origins and which may also include shared culture, religion or language" (J. Stone 1996:260–61). Even so, this notion has come into general use only since World War II, and it would once again be ahistorical to put the term *ethnicity* into the mouths of people who lived before that time. Therefore I will use the terms *race* and *racial* where the context is appropriate.

SOME COMMENTS ABOUT PHOTOGRAPHS

Other professional practices have changed in the last hundred years. In chapter 7, I describe Knox's attempts to publicize the work at Ellis Island. These included writing an article that appeared, richly illustrated, in the popular magazine *Scientific American* in January 1915. The article included photographs of the physicians, the tests that they had developed, and apparently genuine emigrants attempting to carry out some of their tests. I have found no evidence that anyone at the time found the portrayal of emigrants in a popular magazine objectionable.

The concept of informed consent goes back to the nineteenth century, but the practice of obtaining informed consent for clinical interventions—let alone for the publication of patients' photographs—is very much a modern idea (Faden and Beauchamp 1986). Even forty years ago it was still common practice for medical textbooks and journals to include photographs of patients to illustrate particular diseases or conditions. However, the use of such photographs in the popular media would probably have caused some disquiet. Today it would be considered unethical for physicians to publish any information that would identify patients, and the publication of photographs without explicit permission from the subjects of those photographs or their relatives or guardians would be unacceptable. Since photographs of Knox and his colleagues at work are clearly of historical interest, this raises a potential problem.

One might note in passing that Knox himself seems to have become belatedly aware of a genuine ethical issue here. In chapter 7, I also mention that he wrote a contribution for a manual about the mental examination of emigrants. The manual was published in 1918 after Knox had left Ellis Island, but most of his contribution had been dropped. The full version was never published, but parts remain among his unpublished papers. They contain more photographs of apparently genuine emigrants being tested, but Knox attempted to obscure the identities of the individuals who were pictured by using black patches to mask their facial features.

Of course, some photographs of emigrants being tested are already in the public domain, either because they were included in Knox's article in *Scientific American* or because they were subsequently published in books and magazines. After discussing the matter with experienced colleagues, I decided that it would be inappropriate for me to use previously unpublished photographs of emigrants but that it would be permissible for me to reproduce photographs that had already appeared in the public domain.

The aim of this biography of Howard Knox is to locate him as a key figure in the development of intelligence tests. Readers may find it helpful to refer from time to time to the chronology of key events and the list of key people in the text, as well as to the partial family tree that appears in figure I.1. Nevertheless, I must reiterate the existence of certain inevitable gaps in the historical record because of limitations in the available documentation and in the testimony of my informants.

One particularly important gap is worth acknowledging. This book is about Knox and the intelligence tests that were developed at Ellis Island. My account is therefore told from Knox's point of view and that of other test users, rather than from the point of view of the many thousands of people who were required to take his tests. Previous writers have provided descriptions of the emigrants' experience, generously illustrated not only with photographs (ethical issues notwithstanding) but also with firsthand accounts of their treatment in general and of their medical inspection in particular (for example, Chermayeff, Wasserman, and Shapiro 1991; Jonas 1989; Reeves 2000). However, few firsthand accounts exist of what it was actually like to undergo psychological testing at Ellis Island.

HOWARD ANDREW KNOX

PART I

BEFORE ELLIS ISLAND

1

EARLY YEARS

Howard Andrew Knox was born on March 7, 1885, in Romeo, Michigan, just thirty-two miles north of the center of Detroit in northwestern Macomb County. According to the 1880 census of the United States, Romeo was then a village with just 1,629 inhabitants. Macomb County today is part of the Detroit metropolitan area, but Romeo has retained its identity and character as a village. At the time of the 2000 census the population of Romeo still numbered fewer than four thousand, and many of its nineteenth-century mansions and timber buildings survive.

Knox was the only child of Howard Reuben Knox and Jennie Mahaffy Knox (see figure 1.1). His father had been born in 1855 to Reuben and Emerette Knox in the town of Saybrook in Ashtabula County, Ohio, and worked as a traveling salesman. His mother had been born in 1863 to Irish immigrants, Andrew and Anna Mahaffy. Although Jennie had been born in Romeo, she was sent to Ireland to be brought up by other members of her family. She returned to the United States in her early teens to keep house for her father on his farm in Romeo when Andrew and Anna Mahaffy separated.

Howard Reuben Knox and Jennie Mahaffy were married in Ashtabula, Ohio, on July 14, 1879, and Howard moved in with his wife and father-in-law to help them work their farm. However, after their son, Howard Andrew, arrived, the family (grandfather, parents, and grandson) moved back to Ashtabula. This was a town with more than five thousand inhabitants on the southern shore of Lake Erie,

1.1 Howard Reuben Knox; Jennie Mahaffy Knox with Howard Andrew Knox.
Both photographs probably date to about 1890.
(Courtesy the late Carolyn Knox Whaley)

about fifty miles northeast of Cleveland. Ashtabula was already becoming a thriving port, handling mainly coal and ore. Indeed, the harbor district in Ashtabula, where the family found a house, was so well known that mail could be addressed simply to "Harbor, Ohio."

Howard Andrew Knox's parents separated when his father moved to Virginia to set up a business investing in tobacco futures. Although Jennie and Howard Reuben subsequently divorced, the latter kept an office in Ashtabula for many years, and Jennie and Howard Andrew remained in touch with Howard Reuben until he died in the 1920s. Even so, it is unlikely that he had much of an influence on his son's development. In contrast, Howard Andrew Knox had a close relationship with his mother that endured until her own death in 1929. In 1894, when he was just nine years old, Howard Andrew Knox acquired a stepfather, Leander Blackwell, who was to have a decisive influence upon the boy's choice of career.

LEANDER BLACKWELL

Leander Blackwell was born in December 1867 in the town of Blackwell Station, Missouri. The town is known simply as Blackwell today and is located in St. Francois County, about fifty miles southwest of the center of St. Louis. Leander's great-grandfather, Jeremiah Blackwell, had been born in Hopewell, New Jersey, and had fought for the United States in the War of 1812 against Great Britain and its colonies. After the war he had obtained a large grant of land in the Territory of Missouri, and the settlement that he established there was subsequently named Blackwell Station in his honor. His children intermarried with the families of other settlers and over time became prosperous (Hoelzel and Hoelzel 2000:12).

Aquilla Blackwell, Jeremiah's grandson, was born in 1844 and at first helped his father work his farm near Blackwell Station. After the Civil War Aquilla married Dolly Coleman. Following the birth of their first child, Aquilla Blackwell cleared two hundred acres of forest at Valle in neighboring Jefferson County in order to establish his own farm. According to an account published in 1888, "he now has about 300 acres in cultivation and about eleven miles of fence, making one of the best farms in Jefferson County. In all, he has about 960 acres, about 400 of which are in St. Francois County. Besides this he has considerable property in Blackwell's Station" (*History of Franklin* 1970:858). He also became a judge of the county court and "rode the circuit," presiding at various locations to hear lawsuits and other complaints or disputes.

Aquilla and Dolly Blackwell had fourteen children, of whom Leander was the oldest. The image in figure 1.2, which is taken from a tintype (ferrotype) dating from 1890, shows Aquilla and Dolly Blackwell with thirteen of their offspring. After initially working on the family farm, Leander set up as a local trader in 1888. However, in 1891 he enrolled at the Missouri Medical College (now the Washington University School of Medicine) in St. Louis. He enlisted Samuel Fulton Thurman as his preceptor (mentor for practical clinical training). Thurman was a general physician in the French colonial town of Ste. Genevieve, about fifty-five miles south of St. Louis, who had graduated from the Kentucky School of Medicine in Louisville only two years earlier. Blackwell completed the first two years of the four-year program at the Missouri Medical College, but in 1893 he transferred to the Jefferson Medical College (now part of Thomas Jefferson University) in Philadelphia, which also had a four-year program.

How Blackwell met Jennie Mahaffy Knox is not known, but by March 1894 they were planning to marry once he had taken his examinations. Blackwell did not subsequently graduate from the Jefferson Medical College. Nevertheless, completing three years of medical training would have entitled him to obtain a license by taking a state medical examination, even though he did not hold a medical degree. (Shortly afterward, in July 1894, the law in Pennsylvania was amended so that only graduates of recognized medical colleges could apply for examination by the state medical board. See *Polk's Medical Register* 1902:1648.)

That Blackwell actually passed this examination cannot be conclusively verified, because the examination records of the Pennsylvania Board of Medicine

1.2 The family of Aquilla and Dolly Blackwell, 1890. Leander Blackwell is at the top right. (Courtesy Elizabeth Mueller and Mary Myers)

were destroyed in a fire in 1994. Nevertheless, he later styled himself "Dr.," he was considered to merit an obituary in the *Journal of the American Medical Association* ("Leander Blackwell, M.D." 1904), and he was subsequently listed in the *Directory of Deceased American Physicians* (Hafner 1993:132). Indeed, it is quite clear from Howard Knox's personal correspondence that Blackwell's interest in medicine was a primary factor that determined his stepson's subsequent choice of profession.

Leander Blackwell married Jennie Mahaffy Knox in May 1894, and they set up a home in Cleveland. A newspaper report after Blackwell's death claimed that he practiced medicine in Cleveland, but this appears not to be correct. He is not listed as a physician in any local directory from the time, and he made no mention of any medical practice in his personal correspondence. There is, in fact, no evidence that Blackwell ever went on to practice medicine at all. He is not listed in the relevant editions of *Polk's Medical Register*, and his entry in the *Directory* of *Deceased American Physicians* describes him simply as an "allopath" (that is, a practitioner of conventional medicine, as opposed to a homeopath, a practitioner of homeopathic medicine) but lists no specific licenses or practices.

Indeed, although Blackwell was sufficiently motivated to undertake formal training and qualification in medicine, he seems to have always intended that his career would lie elsewhere. He was, one must remember, the oldest son of one of Missouri's established families, yet he sought to marry a divorced woman who was four years his senior and who had a nine-year-old child. It is quite probable that his family was willing to approve of this marriage and to continue to support him financially only if he secured professional status—and a potential fallback if his career plans did not work out—by qualifying as a physician.

During this time relatives in Ashtabula had looked after Howard Knox, but in July Jennie Blackwell took him to spend the summer on a farm that her mother had acquired in Romeo, and Jennie brought her father to live with her and her new husband in Cleveland. In August she spent a week dealing with legal issues in West Boylston, a town of about three thousand inhabitants in Worcester County, Massachusetts. The town had been chosen as the site for a new reservoir to supply the expanding city of Boston, and many of West Boylston's residents were displaced. Jennie Blackwell had owned property there, and she seems to have acquired a farm nearby as part of the compensation settlement. Soon afterward she brought her father, husband, and son to live on the farm.

AT SCHOOL IN WILLIMANTIC

The family lived in West Boylston for several years but in 1899 moved to another farm on Babcock Hill outside Willimantic in Windham County, Connecticut. Figure 1.3 shows Leander and Jennie Blackwell around this time. (As I will explain in a moment, that they are pictured on a horse-drawn sled is especially poignant.) The move proved to be highly fortuitous for Howard, who was now fourteen. Willimantic was a thriving manufacturing center with about nine thousand inhabitants and was part of the town of Windham, twenty-five miles or so east of Hartford. The local public high school had been created in 1888 with the merger of two existing schools, and a new school building had been opened in April 1897.

As Tom Beardsley, a local historian, said of the building in an article that ran in the *Willimantic Chronicle* in 2000, "its fine Italian Renaissance style attracted favorable comment from all visitors to the city. The new principal, S. Hale Baker (1895–1900), established a school newspaper and started an ivy-planting day to

1.3 Leander and Jennie Blackwell, ca. 1899
(Courtesy the late Carolyn Knox Whaley)

adorn the new school's walls. He also established a tree-planting program, and formed the Windham Athletic Association in the school" (14). Knox settled in well at his new school: the report that he received from the principal in June 1900 showed his grades as either H (honor work) or A (excellent) in most subjects.

The new school's second principal, Arthur Everett Petersen, replaced Baker that summer. Beardsley commented that Petersen

> laid down strict academic standards. He had an excellent record in getting students into colleges and universities across the nation. He was a history and civics teacher, who believed in education beyond textbooks. Petersen formed the school improvement society, Die Besserung, to promote culture among the students, and to encourage them to decorate their schoolrooms and corridors with pictures, statues and busts of famous men. Members of Die Besserung also entered into debating contests with the high schools of Putnam, Rockville, Stafford Springs, and Danielson.
>
> (14)

Arthur Petersen and Leander Blackwell appear to have been the major influences on the young Howard Knox. When he graduated from high school in 1903, Petersen had inspired his student to aim for a university education, while Blackwell had inspired the young Knox to take up medicine as a career. Blackwell and some of his relatives were also leading members of the Masonic Lodge in his home town, and Knox probably joined the Masons as a young man.

After high school Knox entered the medical school at Dartmouth College in Hanover, New Hampshire. (In those days the M.D. was a first degree, not a postgraduate qualification.) Like many other students Knox suffered an initial bout of homesickness, but within a month his attitude was more positive. On October 23 he wrote to his mother: "Life is just beginning to be worth living here. I am getting acquainted and coming along pretty good in my studies. This ain't half so slow a place as I thought it was." By November 20 he was positively enthusiastic: "I now have all the signs, passwords, and grips etc. of the frat and have been down there studying the skeleton today. You couldn't hire me to leave Dartmouth now." (The "frat" in question was the Alpha Chapter of the Alpha Kappa Kappa fraternity, founded in 1888.) Knox came home for the Christmas holiday and returned to Dartmouth in the New Year, but his studies were soon interrupted.

A TRAGIC ACCIDENT?

The family's farm was located on Babcock Hill Road, which linked the towns of Lebanon and Windham and overlooked the Willimantic River valley. The house was about two miles from both of the two railroad depots in South Windham, one serving the Hartford-Providence line, the other serving the Central Vermont line. The two lines converged at Willimantic station, about three miles to the north. The engineers on the two lines often raced each other to Willimantic, and accidents were common.

In the early morning of January 15, 1904, Leander Blackwell was killed by a freight train while trying to cross the Central Vermont line in his horse-drawn sled. The accident was duly reported later that day in graphic detail on the front page of the *Willimantic Chronicle*:

> Mr. Blackwell had been to the Consolidated road depot to leave milk to go to Providence on the train that leaves here at 6:15 a.m. From there he drove back to the Central Vermont depot, where he loaded his two-horse sled with several bags of grain from a box car which stood on a side track. After loading his sled he drove out from the rear of the station, and followed along beside

the track, and then turned upon the highway and started to cross the tracks just as the freight came along. No one saw the accident except the engineer, although there were several South Windham people, who were on their way to work, but all were some distance from the crossing. Some say they did not hear the engine whistle, and others say the whistle blew several times for the crossing. All agreed that they heard the train and that it was going at a high rate of speed. The engineer said that he saw the team on the crossing, but he was so close to it that he could not stop his train. He said that the man saw the train and whipped his horses and tried to get across in front of it, but the train was too close and the engine struck the sled just back of the horses, killing the man and one horse. The sled was completely demolished, and pieces were scattered all about the crossing, and the force was so great that the off horse was cut loose from the sled and pushed to one side, the only injury being shown a cut on its head. The other horse was thrown in front of the engine and disembowelled, and dragged up the track a short distance and thrown upon a sidetrack.

The *Chronicle*'s reporter speculated about the cause of the accident. An electric bell was supposed to ring at the crossing to warn of approaching trains, but this was faint and often did not ring at all. Workers at the railroad depot said that Blackwell had been careless when driving around the railroad. One suggested that he had mistaken the train's whistle for that of another train passing on the other railroad. Although Blackwell's death was generally regarded as a tragic accident, Knox had written to his mother on November 25: "Don't worry about the change which has taken place between you and the Doctor, will you dear?" The suspicion therefore remains that Blackwell's death may have been suicide. The pastor of the Willimantic Methodist Church officiated at Blackwell's funeral, which was held at the family home on January 17, and his burial was conducted later that afternoon at Windham Cemetery by a delegation from the Eastern Star Lodge of Masons.

Shortly afterward Andrew Mahaffy also died. Knox withdrew from his studies at Dartmouth College, presumably to help his mother resolve her business affairs. Nevertheless, he resumed his studies at Dartmouth in September 1904. He was required to retake an examination in physiology at the end of the second semester in June 1905, but otherwise he showed good academic progress, generally obtaining marks in the top four or five places. In the latter part of the course, he obtained clinical experience by working in various hospitals. In April 1907, for example, he took a three-week course in obstetrics at the Lying-In Hospital in New York City. ("Lying-in" referred to an extended period of bed rest both before and after giving birth.) This was housed in a brand new building constructed to

1.4 Howard Andrew Knox, upon his graduation from Dartmouth
College, March 1908. (Courtesy the late Carolyn Knox Whaley)

the highest contemporary standards on Second Avenue, along the block between
Seventeenth and Eighteenth streets (Burdette 1904).

On March 27, 1908, Knox was one of just eight students who were awarded
the degree of doctor of medicine on the basis of their performance on the
examinations held by the faculty of Dartmouth Medical School and delegates
from the medical societies of New Hampshire and Vermont (see figure 1.4).

THE GRADUATE

While her son was at Dartmouth, Jennie Blackwell had sold the farm on Babcock Hill, remarried, and moved to the town of Coventry in Orleans County, Vermont, near the Canadian border. The marriage seems to have lasted barely a year, and since the latter part of 1906 she had been living in the city of Worcester, about forty miles west of Boston in the heart of the Commonwealth of Massachusetts. When Knox graduated, he resolved to seek employment near his mother. He had specialized in psychiatry as a student, so he joined the staff of the Worcester Insane Hospital. At about this time Knox married Marion Dorothy Henderson, about whom little is known, except that she was his third cousin on his mother's side of the family. At first Howard and Marion Knox lived at his mother's house in Worcester.

The Worcester Insane Hospital was no backwater of medicine. Its history is described at length by Gerald N. Grob (1966), and the following is based largely on his account. In 1830 Worcester had been chosen as the location for an asylum for the insane by the governor and Executive Council of Massachusetts in preference to a competing bid from the city of Boston. As Grob commented, "Its healthful atmosphere, central location, and adequate medical facilities all played a role in the decision" (31). The original hospital was taken as a model for institutions elsewhere, but it had been built inexpensively and in 1877 was replaced by a completely new building. By this time Worcester itself had grown to become one of the largest cities in New England.

In 1895 the Board of State Charities resolved to appoint a state pathologist who would not be responsible for the care or treatment of patients but whose time would instead be devoted exclusively to research into mental illness. The person appointed to this post the following year was Adolf Meyer, a young Swiss neurologist who had emigrated to the United States in 1892. He had obtained an honorary post at the University of Chicago, and to support himself he had been employed as the pathologist at the Illinois Eastern Hospital for the Insane at Kankakee, about sixty miles south of Chicago. He had enhanced the space and equipment available for research there, and he introduced advanced training for the physicians in the understanding of the nervous system and mental disease.

Meyer was able to introduce even more radical reforms at the Worcester Insane Hospital, and it rapidly acquired a national reputation. Clark University was also located in Worcester, and Meyer enjoyed cordial relations with G. Stanley Hall, its president and professor of psychology. Many of Hall's students took Meyer's classes, which included demonstrations of actual clinical cases and presentations of autopsy findings. Grob quoted a contemporary source who, referring to Meyer, declared: "It is hard to overestimate the advantages which accrue to the whole institution, to physicians and patients alike, as well as to the science of psychiatry itself when a man of scientific ideals and enthusiasms becomes attached to a hospital" (1966:303–304).

Meyer undoubtedly had a major impact on the Worcester Insane Hospital, but he became disillusioned with his increasing workload and what he perceived to be lack of support from the superintendent, trustees, and State Board of Insanity. Hall had given him an appointment as docent (an unpaid teaching role) at Clark University, but Meyer's academic contribution had been chiefly confined to teaching in summer schools that Hall had arranged for schoolteachers. In 1902 Meyer left Worcester to become director of the Pathological Institute in New York City. Later in his career he moved to the Johns Hopkins Hospital in Baltimore, where in 1913 he established the Henry Phipps Psychiatric Clinic.

After Meyer's departure the Worcester hospital began a decline that lasted more than twenty years, and older work practices were resumed. The superintendent and the state authorities sought financial efficiency, not effectiveness with regard to the care and treatment of patients. The role of the pathologist was reduced to performing routine tests and autopsies, and the link with Clark University withered. In 1905 the laboratory was moved to a new building away from the wards, so that the pathologist spent little time with the patients. Working conditions for the attendants and nurses in particular were poor, leading to discontent and a high rate of staff turnover. A state law passed in 1907 to restrict the working day to eight hours specifically excluded hospital employees, and as a result they often ended up working for sixty hours over six days each week.

~~~~~~~

With the support of his mother, stepfather, and school principal, Howard Knox seems to have flourished in high school in Willimantic, and despite the deaths of both his stepfather and grandfather, he went on to do well at Dartmouth College. When he graduated from Dartmouth in 1908, he appeared to be destined for a conventional career in clinical psychiatry. By that time the Worcester Insane Hospital was hardly a promising place in which to embark on such a career. Fortunately, an opportunity arose for Knox to use his clinical skills in a quite different context, working with the U.S. Army.

2

ARMY DAYS

I n April 1908 Congress approved the reorganization of the medical department of the army. In particular, it authorized the creation of a medical reserve corps to provide a pool of several hundred medically qualified personnel who could be called to active duty to augment the regular Army Medical Corps (Stewart 2004:374). These personnel would, of course, need to be trained in the techniques of military medicine, so appointments were offered for physicians to be attached to the army through the Medical Reserve Corps.

That summer Howard Andrew Knox applied for a commission in this new body. His application was successful, and on September 23 he was appointed to the Medical Reserve Corps with the rank of first lieutenant. On September 30 he was assigned to active duty as the post surgeon in command of the Hospital Corps Detachment at Fort Michie, New York. The photograph reproduced in figure 2.1 was taken on October 1, just before Knox's departure from Worcester, Massachusetts, and was to be filed in the office of the adjutant general (the chief administrative officer of the U.S. Army) at the War Department in Washington, D.C.

Throughout his service in the U.S. Army, Knox was required to submit a written report at the end of every month to the surgeon general (the head of the medical department of the U.S. Army) in Washington, D.C. Each report specified where he had been each day of the month, what he had been doing, and which orders he had thereby fulfilled. These reports were kept in his personnel file, and this was subsequently deposited in the National Archives in Washington, D.C.

2.1 Howard Andrew Knox on October 1, 1908, in his official photograph for the War Department just after he enlisted in the Medical Reserve Corps of the U.S. Army. (Courtesy National Archives)

(AGO 1392370). As a consequence, an accurate record exists of Knox's entire military career, which extended from September 1908 to April 1911.

AT FORT MICHIE

Fort Michie had been established in 1900 on Great Gull Island in Long Island Sound, roughly twelve miles off New London, Connecticut. Its strategic role was to support the larger and more permanent post at Fort Terry on nearby Plum Island in protecting the eastern approach to Long Island Sound. Fort Michie itself was occupied by an artillery company that lived in temporary officers' quarters and barracks (Roberts 1988:566).

Until 1901 such companies had been organized into seven regiments, each containing both coast and field batteries. That year Congress had authorized the reorganization of the artillery into a single corps that consisted of thirty batteries of field artillery and 126 companies of coast artillery. In 1906 a board chaired by the secretary of war, William Howard Taft, had recommended the expansion and upgrading of the coastal defenses in order to accommodate technological developments in modern armaments and the acquisition of overseas territories from Spain. The following year Congress had reorganized the artillery into separate corps for coast artillery and for field artillery, and the Coast Artillery Corps had been increased in strength to 170 companies (McGovern and Smith 2006:13–14).

Knox's assignment was not unusual. Most coastal forts, and especially the more isolated ones such as Fort Michie, had their own hospitals. He and Marion Knox arrived at Fort Michie on October 3, 1908, and they remained there for nearly a year. Despite the isolated environment and the limited facilities, they managed to obtain accommodation on two floors in the officers' quarters (probably in a duplex apartment) with a spare bedroom for visitors. In April 1909 Marion Knox gave birth to a girl, who was named Violet at the insistence of Knox's mother. However, the baby was not healthy, and she died within a few months.

Knox remained on duty as the post surgeon, except for seven days in April when he was confined to quarters with influenza. Under army regulations an efficiency report on each serving officer had to be submitted annually to the adjutant general's office. The efficiency report that Knox received at the end of June 1909 from his commanding officer, Captain Roderick Leland Carmichael, was extremely positive. It described Knox's general bearing, military appearance, intelligence, and judgment as very good and his attention to duty and professional zeal as excellent. Knox was clearly finding a military career congenial, and it is thus not surprising that he went on to seek an appointment in the U.S. Army Medical Corps.

To proceed from the Medical Reserve Corps to the Army Medical Corps, physicians were required to undertake a year's training at the Army Medical School in Washington, D.C. Knox had applied for admission to the Army Medical School earlier in 1909, and in July he was given nine days' leave to go to Fort Jay on Governors Island in Upper New York Bay to take the entrance examination. His application was successful: he was granted ten days' leave in Washington from September 20, and he was admitted to the Army Medical School as a student medical officer on October 1.

AT THE ARMY MEDICAL SCHOOL

The Army Medical School had been founded in June 1893 by Brigadier General George Miller Sternberg, newly appointed as surgeon general by President Grover Cleveland. Sternberg's aim was to ensure that medical officers were properly trained in the techniques of military preventive medicine (Craig 2006; D. C. Smith 1994):

> Although there is no need to teach medicine or surgery to well-educated graduates of our medical colleges there are certain duties pertaining to the position of an army medical officer for which the college course of these young men has not prepared them; and certain of these duties are more important than the clinical treatment of individual cases of disease and injury because the efficiency of a command, of an army even, may depend upon their proper performance. During the past twenty years the prevention of disease has made infinitely greater progress than its cure. Recognizing this fact health officers have been appointed and health boards organized by civil communities for their own protection. A special education is needful to prepare a medical man to undertake the responsibility of protecting the public health. The army medical officer is the health officer of his command; but the young graduate seldom is equipped with the knowledge or experience necessary to efficient action in this position. The course at the Army Medical School will prepare him to cope with the questions of practical sanitation that will be presented to him at every turn in his military career.
>
> (G. M. Sternberg 1893:15)

Howard and Marion Knox found a place to live on Fourteenth Street NW, and Knox's subsequent training was apparently uneventful. He graduated from the Army Medical School, finishing forty-fourth in a class of fifty-four students. The graduation photograph in figure 2.2 was taken on April 18, 1910. The graduation

2.2 Howard Andrew Knox, April 18, 1910, shortly before his graduation from the U.S. Army Medical School. (Courtesy National Archives)

exercises were held at the Continental Memorial Hall on May 31, when diplomas were presented by the retiring secretary of war, Jacob McGavock Dickinson. Following the ceremony Knox was assigned to work as an assistant to the surgeon at Fort Hancock, New Jersey. He began his duties there on June 3, and on June 15 he received his commission as a first lieutenant in the U.S. Army Medical Corps.

During his training in Washington Knox's mother had become unwell, and she had moved in with Knox and his wife. In February this had led to a matrimonial dispute, as a result of which Marion Knox had left. Not long after Knox arrived at Fort Hancock, the adjutant general of the army, Major General Henry Pinckney McCain, received a complaint from an attorney acting for Marion Knox. She claimed that her husband had failed to provide her with financial support and that, by leaving Washington, he had deliberately abandoned her.

When the complaint was put to him, Knox insisted that, on the contrary, his wife had left *him* and, indeed, had refused to return unless he made his mother leave the house. He argued that Marion had thus forfeited any right to financial support and added that he had filed for divorce. This response satisfied the judge advocate general in the War Department that no action should be taken against Knox, and his wife's attorney was advised that this was not a matter in which the War Department could interfere. Nevertheless, the correspondence remained in his file and may well have influenced the course of his subsequent career with the army.

AT FORT HANCOCK

Fort Hancock was a primary coastal defense on the Sandy Hook peninsula on the south side of Lower New York Bay. It was first established in 1898, although the site had been used for military purposes since 1812 (Roberts 1988:516–18). (Whereas many coastal forts were dismantled after World War II, Fort Hancock has been largely preserved as part of the Gateway National Recreation Area. See McGovern and Smith 2006:26.) This was a more important posting for Knox than Fort Michie had been less than two years earlier. Despite the recent events in his domestic life, he once again received positive annual efficiency reports at the end of June 1910 from the president of the Army Medical School, Colonel Louis Anatole La Garde; from the post surgeon at Fort Hancock, Major Irving Wallace Rand; and from the chief surgeon of the Department of the East, Colonel John Van Rensselaer Hoff.

On July 9 Knox was ordered to go to Fort Ethan Allen, a large cavalry training post in Vermont, to accompany the Tenth Cavalry en route to the camp of instruction at Pine Camp, New York. This had been opened as a training center in 1908 in Jefferson County near Lake Ontario (Roberts 1988:549). The journey from Fort Ethan Allen took more than two weeks, from July 15 to July 30, and during the four weeks following their arrival Knox was on duty at the stationary hospital at Pine Camp. Stationary hospitals were temporary field hospitals that were set up near battlefields to provide immediate care for wounded personnel (see McKee

1919). In this case the stationary hospital would have helped to simulate battle conditions and would also have provided treatment for any injuries suffered during the training exercises being held there.

While Knox was at Pine Camp, he was called upon to carry out an operation on the foot of Major General Frederick Dent Grant. He was the first son of President Ulysses S. Grant, and on July 25 the major general had been given command of the Department of the East, encompassing the states of New York and New Jersey as well as the New England states. Grant apparently formed a good impression of Knox. According to Knox's family, he was given a cigar and a note describing him as Grant's favorite doctor. Knox then spent the period from August 29 to September 22 accompanying a battery of the Third Field Artillery from Pine Camp to Fort Myer, the military post at Arlington, Virginia, across the Potomac River from Washington, D.C.

Knox took ten days' leave from September 22 and reported to Fort Hancock on October 2, where he continued his duties as assistant to the surgeon for the next few months. Later in October he treated the seven-year-old daughter of an artillery sergeant who was stationed at Fort Hancock but who had previously served at a post in Florida. Her primary condition was enlargement of the inguinal glands (lymph nodes on either side of the abdomen), but Knox found that she also had a mild form of filariasis, an infectious parasitic disease that is common in tropical and subtropical regions. The girl made a prompt recovery after removal of her inguinal glands. Knox wrote up a brief report of this case that appeared in a medical journal the following June, his first publication. He concluded that the girl had probably contracted filariasis through a mosquito bite while she had been living in Florida (Knox 1911).

HELEN FOSTER BARNETT AND GLADYS BARNETT REED

In January 1911 Knox requested ten days' leave to marry Gladys Barnett Reed in Brooklyn, New York. Gladys was the third child and second daughter of James P. Barnett and Helen A. Foster, who lived in Brooklyn. James had died in 1885, leaving Helen to bring up four children alone. Hers was a nonetheless prosperous family, and in the early years of the twentieth century she acquired a reputation as a philanthropist, especially for her support of the arts. In particular, she was associated with the artists' colony that the sculptor Augustus Saint-Gaudens and his brother, Louis, founded in 1885 in the town of Cornish in Sullivan County, New Hampshire. Augustus Saint-Gaudens died in 1907, and that year Helen Foster Barnett inaugurated the Saint-Gaudens medal in his memory. This was to be awarded annually to graduating seniors from high schools in New York City "for fine draughtsmanship." It was designed by the sculptor Chester Beach and depicted a woman holding a pen and tablet against the New York City skyline. It is still awarded today by the New York City Department of Education and the trustees of the School Art League.

The following year she inaugurated the Helen Foster Barnett prize. This was to be awarded annually by the National Academy of Design (which today is called the National Academy) for a work of sculpture by an artist younger than thirty-five. The prize (worth one hundred dollars) was initially awarded to Robert Aitken for a bronze group, *Flames*. Helen Foster Barnett subsequently purchased this work, and in 1910 she loaned it to the Metropolitan Museum of Art in New York City for an exhibition. The Helen Foster Barnett prize for that year was awarded to Abastenia St. Leger Eberle for a work entitled *A Windy Doorstep*. The artist reciprocated by producing a portrait statuette of Helen Foster Barnett that was exhibited at the National Arts Club in New York in May 1912.

Louis St. Gaudens (who had adopted a different spelling of the family name) died in 1913. His widow, Annette Johnson St. Gaudens, was also an accomplished sculptor, and Helen Foster Barnett commissioned from her a large bronze sculpture in the form of a birdbath. The sculpture was exhibited in New York and Boston, and Helen then donated it to the Meriden Bird Club. This had been founded in 1910 by the naturalist Ernest Harold Baynes in Meriden, New Hampshire, not far from Cornish, for the protection and preservation of wild birds. The club was able to buy a nearby farm to establish a sanctuary for wild birds (still known today as the Helen Woodruff Smith Bird Sanctuary, after the original benefactor). Its work was supported by many local people, including members of the artists' colony in Cornish.

Baynes asked a local poet and playwright, Percy MacKaye, to write a dramatic piece to mark the formal dedication of the sanctuary on September 12, 1913. The result was *Sanctuary*, a masque (a short allegorical entertainment with masked actors) that described in speech and song the redemption of a hunter by the birds and bird spirits who had been his prey. The performance was attended by President Woodrow Wilson and his family, who had taken to spending summers near Cornish. The Wilson daughters, Eleanor and Margaret, had roles in the production, as did Helen Foster Barnett. (The performance was described in detail in the following day's editions of the *New York Times*.) The birdbath sculpture that Helen had commissioned from Annette St. Gaudens was installed at the bird sanctuary to commemorate this first performance of MacKaye's masque. (MacKaye went on to become well known nationally as a dramatist and poet.) Subsequently, Baynes illustrated the birdbath in his book, *Wild Bird Guests* (1915:230).

Gladys Barnett had married Howard Alden Reed, who was born in Philadelphia in 1875. He was a contemporary of Percy MacKaye's in the class of 1897 at Harvard

University but did not complete his degree. Reed was only thirty-four when he died in January 1910. The circumstances of his death are not known. According to the Knox family, he was an army officer who died in service (I have, however, failed to find an obituary or even a death notice in the New York newspapers), and Gladys married Howard Knox partly in order to regain access to military circles in New York and Washington, D.C.

Whatever the precise circumstances, Knox clearly entered an elevated social world when he married Gladys Barnett Reed. How or when they met is unknown. When he had taken leave in September 1910, he had given a post office box at White River Junction, Vermont, as a contact address. This was the nearest rail-road station to Cornish, which suggests that he might well have been visiting Gladys and her mother at the artists' colony. Howard and Gladys were married in Brooklyn on January 10, 1911, and they stayed for the next week or so at Gladys's family home there in Washington Park. The marriage was duly recorded in the *Army and Navy Register, Army and Navy Journal, Journal of the American Medical Association,* and *New York Times*. Knox reported for duty at Fort Hancock on January 19, while Gladys remained with her mother in Brooklyn. In March, however, Knox became involved in military maneuvers in Texas.

AT FORT CROCKETT

Mexico had seen sporadic unrest since 1908, and from time to time the United States had dispatched troops to reinforce the frontier. Indeed, between 1910 and 1912 the United States typically had almost twenty-four thousand troops stationed along the Mexican border (Hart 1987:283). Although the Mexican opposition leader Francisco Madero had called for a revolution against the regime of Porforio Díaz on November 20, 1910, the Taft administration had initially tolerated political activities and arms smuggling on U.S. soil.

By March 1911, however, Madero's forces had been joined by those of Pascual Orozco and Francisco "Pancho" Villa. They had made some gains in Mexico's northern provinces and had also caused considerable damage to U.S.-owned commercial properties. On March 7 the U.S. government announced that it was sending four battleships and a large number of troops to Texas and southern California. The official explanation was that they would be involved in military exercises, but it was widely assumed that they could be deployed to prevent any incursions from across the border and, if necessary, to invade Mexican territory itself.

Since the Civil War artillery regiments had been deployed from time to time as infantry, and from its creation in 1907 the companies of the Coast Artillery Corps had been trained in basic field techniques and infantry tactics (B. W. Smith 1993). Accordingly, orders were issued for the organization of three provisional infantry regiments from among the Coast Artillery companies that were stationed on the Atlantic and Gulf coasts. On March 9 General Grant, as commander of the Department of the East, was ordered to have all available men from the various forts in New York Harbor in readiness to leave that night by the steamship *Jamestown*.

Knox was ordered to take a sergeant and eight men and accompany a battalion from Fort Hancock. They sailed first to Fort Monroe at Hampton, Virginia, a key part of the defenses of Chesapeake Bay and home of the Coast Artillery School. There they joined battalions from other coastal forts to constitute the Third Provisional Regiment, and on March 11 they sailed for Galveston, Texas, on the U.S. Army transport *Sumner*. In all, an estimated thirteen hundred men from thirty-six companies of Coast Artillery were withdrawn from their stations along the Atlantic coast. While they were at sea, Knox was detailed as a recruiting officer to the Third Provisional Regiment. It is possible that medical personnel were used in this way because of the urgency of obtaining recruits. Indeed, on March 23 the War Department called for six to seven thousand additional recruits to bring the regiments mobilized in Texas and California to their full strength.

Knox and his men arrived in Galveston on March 17, and the following day he took up his duties as assistant to the surgeon at the infirmary of the Third Provisional Regiment in Fort Crockett. The fort had been built as an artillery installation on Galveston Island in 1897, but most of the buildings had been destroyed in a hurricane in 1900. It took several years for the site to be rebuilt and expanded, and it had just reopened as a mobilization center to respond to the unrest on the Mexican border (Roberts 1988:759). The Third Provisional Regiment was commanded by Colonel John V. White, who had been Knox's commanding officer at Fort Hancock and who was also the commanding officer of the Southern Artillery District of New York. The three regiments were organized into the First Separate Brigade under the overall command of Brigadier General Albert Leopold Mills.

On March 9 the secretary of war had issued an order that the entire command was to be immunized against typhoid as it arrived in Texas. In his report for the fiscal year ending June 30, 1911, the surgeon general of the army, George Henry Torney, maintained that this was the first time a compulsory program of immunization against typhoid had ever been attempted in any military service (54). Many personnel had previously been immunized against typhoid, but when Knox first arrived in Galveston, he would have been kept busy helping to inoculate the remainder. As a consequence, during the campaign no case of typhoid occurred among the troops stationed in Galveston, but 192 cases occurred in the civilian population during the same period.

While stationed in Galveston the three provisional regiments underwent an extended course of instruction that involved both close-order drill in camp and tactical exercises held in the surrounding Texas countryside (B. W. Smith 1993). It is unlikely that they saw any military action, since they were based at some distance from the border with Mexico. In any case, most revolutionary activity during this period took place far to the west in Chihuahua and Sonora, and the few incidents (such as those at Agua Prieta, opposite Douglas, Arizona, and at Ciudad Juárez, opposite El Paso, Texas) were easily handled by the local U.S. Cavalry. (Indeed, the correspondent of the London *Times* commented on April 16 that in Douglas most of the U.S. casualties had been local sightseers who had failed to realize that discretion was the better part of curiosity.) On May 21 Porforio Díaz relinquished power, and ten days later he left for exile in Europe. Francisco León de la Barra became interim president, pending elections to be held later in the year. In June the situation on the border eased considerably (further unrest was confined to the south of Mexico), and the Coast Artillery companies were recalled to their regular stations.

Howard Knox was on duty at the infirmary of the Third Provisional Regiment in Fort Crockett from March 18. On April 12, however, he asked to resign his commission, effective immediately. When instructed to give a reason for his request, he replied,

> My mother must soon undergo a serious surgical operation and I consider it my duty to be near her at this time. She is in New York City, near my proper Station, Fort Hancock, N.J. and while there I felt at ease regarding her condition and would feel so at the present time were I stationed there. I did not wish my personal obligations to take precedence over those owe[d] the Service, hence my resignation.
>
> (military file)

Colonel White, Knox's commanding officer, forwarded his request with these accompanying comments: "I would recommend that Lt. Knox be sent back to his station in New York Harbor, so that he could be near his mother during the critical period of her sickness. He informs me that he desires to remain in the service, but thought under the existing requirements of being ready for field service, that there was no way to be near her unless he resigned." This recommendation was duly supported by Brigadier General Mills, who forwarded Knox's request to Henry McCain, the adjutant general, in Washington, D.C.

Although the relevant paperwork was sent from Galveston on April 13, it was not received in the adjutant general's office until April 19. The adjutant general sought the advice of the surgeon general. Coincidentally, Colonel Louis La Garde, who had been the president of the Army Medical School during Knox's training, was temporarily serving as acting surgeon general. Although he had written a positive efficiency report on Knox less than nine months earlier, La Garde now commented: "Lieutenant Knox has been in the service for a year and during that time certain things have occurred that do not augur well for his future as a member of the Medical Corps. It is therefore, recommended that his resignation be accepted."

Given the apparent urgency of Knox's request and the lack of an immediate response from Washington, Brigadier Mills sent two telegrams to the adjutant general on April 19 to request authority to send Knox back to Fort Hancock. The following day McCain consulted the surgeon general's office, which replied: "If the recommendation of this office of yesterday . . . , namely, that the resignation of this officer be accepted, is approved, it is then recommended that he be returned to his station, Fort Hancock, N.J., and let his resignation take effect from that post." (The usual practice was that military personnel were discharged from the post where they had entered service.)

Accordingly, on April 21 the adjutant general sent a telegram to Brigadier Mills on behalf of the secretary of war, instructing Mills to order Knox to return to Fort Hancock and to report his arrival there. Knox duly left Galveston the following day and reported to Fort Hancock three days later. On April 26 the adjutant general sent another telegram to the commanding officer at Fort Hancock, advising that the president had accepted Knox's resignation. Later that day more formal notification was sent to both Knox and his commanding officer at Fort Hancock.

Knox's request to resign his commission was not mentioned in the adjutant general's telegram to Galveston on April 21. Indeed, it would appear that Brigadier Mills and his colleagues were not initially aware that Knox's resignation was being considered and were assuming that he would return to duty after a period of compassionate leave. Only on April 30 did Colonel White issue orders formally relieving Knox of his duties as recruiting officer for the Third Provisional Regiment and appointing his replacement. This has the further implication that Knox himself may have been unaware that his resignation had been accepted until he was notified of this by his commanding officer at Fort Hancock on April 26.

CIVILIAN LIFE

In May 1911 Howard and Gladys Knox moved to Sheffield, which was a quiet but prosperous town of about eighteen hundred inhabitants in Berkshire County, Massachusetts, near the border with Connecticut. They bought a house next door to the Methodist Episcopal Church, Knox established a general practice in their home, and his mother moved to the neighboring town of Great Barrington.

As a general physician, Knox was impressed by the new ideas of psychoanalytic theory. His interest in psychoanalysis is probably not surprising. On September 5–11, 1909, Sigmund Freud and Carl Jung had visited Worcester, Massachusetts, during the celebrations to mark the twentieth anniversary of the founding of Clark University. During their visit Freud had given five extemporaneous lectures on the origins and development of psychoanalysis, and Jung had given three lectures based more specifically on his work on word association and the case study of a four-year-old girl. Knox was not, of course, able to attend these lectures in person, because he was at the time on duty many miles away at Fort Michie.

Nevertheless, although the lectures had been given in German, they had been reported in English in several local newspapers; the *Worcester Telegram* provided the most detailed accounts (Rosenzweig 1992:199–200). Knox's mother often sent him clippings from the newspapers that were likely to be of personal or professional interest, and she probably sent him accounts of the lectures that Freud and Jung had given. In any case, authorized translations of their lectures were published in the *American Journal of Psychology* in April 1910, and these became widely known among physicians as well as psychologists.

A couple of years later Knox wrote an article advocating the use of mental suggestion in psychiatric or terminally ill patients (Knox 1913b). He referred in particular to a man who had been under his care in Sheffield:

> I discovered that he was the possessor of a well-developed system of persecutory ideas regarding a religious sect in his immediate neighborhood. He experienced great joy and relief when he could unload his imaginary troubles on me and have me take them down gravely in a notebook and promise to rectify and correct each and every one of them. He believed so firmly that I would do this that he went successfully about his business for one month at a time, when he would come back with new ideas which I handled as before. . . . The general condition of this man has steadily improved in the year he has been under treatment, although the delusions are as fixed as ever. He now pays but little attention to them.
>
> (658)

This hardly shows a sophisticated understanding of the principles of "psychanalysis," as Knox called it in this article. However, it does reveal a compassionate side. For Knox the physician must be "one in whom the patient has faith and confidence . . . a man thoroughly alive to the problems of life, its heartaches, its woes and its vagaries; and above all he must be able to paint its beauties and nobler aspects to the patient in that patient's more suggestible moments."

On October 28, 1911, Gladys Knox gave birth to a daughter, Dorothea. Otherwise, their time in Sheffield appears to have been uneventful. Indeed, quite mundane events in the Knoxes' lives warranted reports in the local weekly newspaper, the *Berkshire Courier*:

John Rock has sold a horse to Dr. Knox. (June 22, 1911)

Dr. H.A. Knox who recently located here has received a flattering offer to locate in a Minnesota community and has the matter under serious consideration. (November 2, 1911)

Fred French has bought Dr. Knox's horse. (November 9, 1911)

Dr. Knox has decided to remain in Sheffield until next summer and has bought another horse. (November 23, 1911)

Last Saturday afternoon, while attending a call near East Road, Dr. H.A. Knox left his horse standing outside the house and as has been his custom did not hitch the animal. Completing his visit the doctor was surprised to find that his horse was missing and when he arrived at the village notified several people of the disappearance of the animal. Nothing was heard from the lost horse until late Sunday morning when it was found by Charles Smith near the Graw place, and returned to its owner. (February 1, 1912)

As Doreen Atwood, a local historian in Sheffield, remarked (personal communication), it would appear that the life of a country doctor was not sufficiently stimulating for Knox. That would certainly be true for his wife, Gladys, who was used to socializing in New York City. The offer of a position in Minnesota seems to have come to nothing, but Knox was actively pursuing other possibilities. In particular, he harbored an ambition to return to the U.S. Army Medical Corps.

In September 1911 Knox's mother offered to intercede with the army on his behalf, and this aroused in him fresh hope that he might at least be allowed to return to the Medical Reserve Corps. In the absence of any clear response, Knox himself applied to the office of the surgeon general on February 14, 1912, seeking readmission to the Army Medical Corps. Moreover, he enlisted the support of a senator for Massachusetts, Winthrop Murray Crane, who the following day wrote on Knox's behalf to the assistant secretary of war, Robert Shaw Oliver.

On February 16 Lieutenant Colonel Merritte Weber Ireland wrote from the office of the surgeon general to advise Knox that there was no formal procedure for him to be reinstated in the U.S. Army Medical Corps. Consequently, he would have to reapply from scratch. Ireland added: "The Surgeon General also instructs me to say that he has carefully considered your application and that he believes it to be not for the best interest of the service to again invite you to appear for examination for reappointment in the Corps." The assistant secretary of war forwarded a copy of this letter to Senator Crane with the observation that "the [War] Department is constrained to concur in the views of the Surgeon General in this matter."

Ireland did not specify the nature of Knox's transgressions in his correspondence, so one can only speculate as to why Knox had fallen out of favor in Washington. Knox's request to tender his resignation while assigned to field duty might have raised doubts about his loyalty among his immediate superiors at Fort Crockett. There is, however, no evidence to support this idea. On the contrary, his superiors had supported the idea of Knox's simply taking a period of compassionate leave, and they seem to have been expecting him to return to duty in Galveston.

One of Knox's children suggested a different reason why his father had run afoul of the authorities. At the time venereal disease was acknowledged to be a major problem among army personnel, and Knox discovered high levels of the disease at Fort Hancock. He therefore offered treatment to both military personnel and the local prostitutes. In particular, he issued the enlisted men a prophylactic kit containing medication intended for use after intercourse. However, when he wrote to the surgeon general's office to report the success of these measures, he was apparently told that what he had done was immoral and would disgrace the U.S. Army.

In fact, the issuing of preventive medicine to army personnel was entirely in accordance with official policy. In his report to the War Department for the fiscal year ending June 30, 1909, Surgeon General Torney had advocated a variety of measures for tackling the spread of venereal disease. These included "the issue of preventive medicines for local application to such as will not be restrained by considerations of morality or prudence from exposure. . . . If such steps were taken universally throughout the army . . . , it is believed that the evil record of the American Army might be greatly bettered" (58). Torney's report the next year was even more adamant:

The venereal peril has come to outweigh in importance any other sanitary question which now confronts the army and neither our national optimism nor the Anglo-Saxon disposition to ignore a subject which is offensive to public prudery can longer excuse a frank and honest confrontation of the problem. There is no reason to think that these diseases are beyond the reach of preventive medicine any more than other contagious diseases and their immunity from restriction must be attributed to the public disinclination to discuss them and legislate concerning them.

(Torney 1910:59)

Torney again advocated various strategies, including "approved measures of personal prophylaxis of those who will, contrary to advice, expose themselves to venereal infection" (60).

In January 1911 Torney had asked the adjutant general to seek information from all commanding officers and post surgeons concerning the measures being adopted to control the spread of venereal disease, and he presented the results in his report for that year (54–64). He discovered a great variation in practices and—not surprisingly—in the incidence of venereal disease. Fort Hancock emerged well, with only three-fifths of the overall national rate. He concluded the relevant section of his report with a number of practical recommendations to the secretary of war, including that of selling prophylactic kits at cost in military canteens.

Indeed, Torney mentioned that the army was already distributing prophylactic kits to a large number of military posts (60). In the circumstances Knox's superiors can hardly have had any objection to his dispensing such kits to enlisted personnel. Torney also noted that low rates of venereal disease had been achieved at some posts with the cooperation of the local authorities in the medical supervision of prostitutes, either requiring them to submit to medical inspection or removing those found to be infected (60–61). Nevertheless, he seems to have regarded this as the responsibility of civilian authorities. If Knox had indeed been treating the local prostitutes at Fort Hancock, this may have been seen as going far beyond his duties.

However, the most obvious explanation for the antipathy expressed by both Torney and Louis La Garde toward Howard Knox is that his private life (in particular, his separation from his first wife, Marion, and his prompt betrothal to Gladys Barnett Reed) had led him to be seen as unreliable and undesirable as an army officer at a time when officers were expected to observe strict standards of propriety. One additional consideration should be mentioned. Knox's marriage to Gladys Reed lasted barely three years, and in 1916 he married for the final time. When I interviewed two children from this final marriage in December 2001, both were adamant that their father had had a second wife *before* Gladys Barnett Reed. They described his second wife as a European woman from an aristocratic family who had been taken ill with appendicitis while her ship was entering New York Harbor. They reported that Knox had been called from his post at Fort

Hancock to operate on her and that their marriage had resulted in a daughter called Ruth.

It is hard to reconcile this with Knox's military records, which account for his activities from the day that he announced his intention to divorce Marion Knox (June 14, 1910) to the day that he married Gladys Barnett Reed (January 10, 1911). This is a limited window of time for him to have met, married, and divorced another wife, let alone to have had a child with her. The only time that he was away from his post was the period of ten days from September 22 to October 2, 1910, and, as I mentioned earlier in this chapter, the evidence suggests that he spent this time with Gladys Reed and her mother in Cornish. There is no record of any marriage during this time nor of any later divorce. (In contrast, his marriage to Gladys was announced in both the *Army and Navy Register* and the *Army and Navy Journal*.)

One might be inclined to dismiss the idea of a fourth wife as family mythology. After all, my informants were not born until some years after these events had supposedly taken place. Yet both recalled at first hand the funeral of Knox's mother in 1929, and both recalled that the daughter, Ruth, turned up at this occasion, to Knox's apparent displeasure. One possibility is that her mother had been an unmarried woman who was in reality suffering complications in pregnancy, that Knox had married her as an arrangement so that her child would not be born out of wedlock, and that he had endeavored to keep these circumstances from his superiors.

The truth of the matter is unlikely ever to be resolved, given the remoteness of the events in question and the lack of documentary evidence. Thus any speculation is fairly idle. Nevertheless, if Knox's superiors discovered that something of this sort had indeed happened, it might account for their conclusion that "certain things have occurred that do not augur well for his future as a member of the Medical Corps."

~~~~~~

Howard Knox had enjoyed a successful start to his military career at Fort Michie in 1908–1909 and had satisfactorily completed a period of training at the Army Medical School in Washington, D.C., leading to his commission in the Army Medical Corps. By April 1911, however, after less than a year's service, he was not sufficiently well regarded by his superiors for them either to discourage him from resigning his commission or to allow his subsequent readmission to the corps. Instead, he was forced to seek alternative employment elsewhere and opened his general practice in Sheffield in May 1911.

In October 1911 he applied for an appointment as assistant surgeon in the Public Health and Marine Hospital Service, a different branch of the U.S. government, where little or nothing would be known of his supposed transgressions in the Army Medical Corps. In April 1912 his application was accepted, and this resulted in his assignment to the immigration station at Ellis Island in New York Harbor. The next three chapters are concerned with the background and significance of that appointment to provide a context for understanding the nature of Knox's subsequent contribution to the field of intelligence tests and intelligence testing.

PART II

THE CONTEXT

3

IMMIGRATION, INTELLIGENCE, AND THE PUBLIC HEALTH SERVICE

For many years the immigration policy of the United States had been largely permissive and not contentious. The main concern had simply been the cost of supporting destitute immigrants. Many seaboard states had initially addressed this concern by requiring a bond or tax to be paid by any immigrant who was likely to become a public charge. However, during the first half of the nineteenth century the states in question tended to supplement or replace this bond with a head tax on all immigrants. This was not popular with commercial interests, especially in inland states that received many immigrants but did not benefit from the taxes levied at their point of entry.

In 1876 the U.S. Supreme Court held that such arrangements were unconstitutional and that the regulation of immigration should be a federal responsibility (see Klebaner 1958). The situation was eventually rectified in 1882 by Congress, which passed a law that imposed a tax of fifty cents on each immigrant to meet the cost of any need for relief and protection. The act also prohibited outright the admission of lunatics, idiots, and anyone likely to become a public charge. The individual states remained responsible for implementing these restrictions, acting on behalf of the secretary of the treasury.

Nevertheless, under the Immigration Act of 1891, the federal government took over the regulation of immigration by adding the Bureau of Immigration to the Treasury Department. The act also extended the categories of people who would be refused admission to the United States to include "persons suffering from a loathsome or a dangerous contagious disease." The officials of the new Immigration Service were not medically qualified and were therefore not competent to determine which individuals fell within the last category. Consequently, it was necessary to assign the medical inspection of arriving emigrants to some other federal agency.

THE MARINE HOSPITAL SERVICE

A separate division of the Treasury Department had evolved from a program originally set up in 1798 to provide health care for merchant seamen (see F. Mullan 1989). In 1871 this division had been formalized as the Marine Hospital Service. Its physicians had adopted uniforms and ranks (assistant surgeon, passed assistant surgeon, surgeon, and senior surgeon) modeled on those of the military. For instance, the rank of assistant surgeon was equivalent to that of lieutenant, and the rank of passed assistant surgeon was equivalent to that of captain. (*Passed* referred to the physician's having passed the test for promotion to surgeon.) In 1889 the physicians were legally constituted as a commissioned corps appointed by the president.

After the demise of the short-lived National Board of Health in 1883, the Marine Hospital Service progressively took on the responsibility for matters relating to public health. To reflect this, it was renamed "the Public Health and Marine Hospital Service" in 1902 and then just "the Public Health Service" in 1912. One public health responsibility that it had acquired was the quarantine inspection of ships arriving from foreign countries. It was, accordingly, appropriate and convenient for the Marine Hospital Service to be assigned the medical inspection of arriving emigrants under the 1891 Immigration Act.

In 1903 the Bureau of Public Health and Marine Hospital Service produced *Book of Instructions for the Medical Inspection of Immigrants*. This manual instructed physicians on the various conditions constituting "dangerous contagious diseases" (pulmonary tuberculosis and trachoma, a chronic condition affecting the conjunctiva) and "loathsome diseases" (syphilis, gonorrhea, leprosy, and favus, a type of ring worm) that, along with insanity and idiocy, would warrant mandatory exclusion. The manual also listed other conditions that might warrant exclusion on the ground that the person was likely to become a public charge, but it advised that it was the role of the inspectors of the Immigration Service to make the final judgment in these cases. In the same year the Bureau of Immigration was transferred to the new Department of Commerce and Labor. One result was that officials of the Immigration Service and the physicians of the Public Health and Marine Hospital Service were accountable to different branches of the U.S. government.

THE ELLIS ISLAND IMMIGRATION STATION

The most important point of arrival in the United States was the Port of New York. Until 1855, however, no attempt was made to process emigrants arriving there. That year the State of New York established a processing facility at Castle Garden on the southern tip of Manhattan Island. This had originally been a military battery (Castle Clinton) built on an artificial island, but it had subsequently been absorbed into Manhattan Island by the expansion of the adjacent Battery Park. (Today the site is a national monument once again known as Castle Clinton.)

As I mentioned earlier, the 1882 Immigration Act made individual states responsible for the regulation of immigration on behalf of the U.S. Treasury. In particular, New York State authorities were under contract to continue to process emigrants through Castle Garden. Nevertheless, in light of the significance of this gateway to the United States, the secretary of the treasury terminated the contract in April 1890 and imposed federal control of immigration at the Port of New York, thus anticipating the terms of the 1891 Immigration Act. New York State authorities retaliated by refusing to allow the federal government to use their processing facility at Castle Garden.

The federal government temporarily established its own immigration processing facility in the old Barge Office, a building just east of Castle Garden. After passage of the 1891 Immigration Act, this facility became accountable to the Bureau of Immigration in the Treasury Department. In the meantime, however, the House Committee on Immigration resolved to commission the construction of an entirely new immigration station. The location chosen was Ellis Island, close to the New Jersey shore in Upper New York Bay. This had originally been a small area of mud flats that had acquired its name from Samuel Ellis, its owner at the time of the American Revolution. In 1808 the federal government had bought it for construction of another coastal battery.

Terrance McGovern and Bolling Smith (2006) describe the development of such defenses:

> While virtually every nation recognized the superiority of forts over ships and relied on fortifications to protect their harbors, America took to them with particular enthusiasm. They particularly suited the American character. It required little manpower except during time of war and did not threaten the liberties

of a people raised to distrust standing armies. Equally important, coastal forts, rather than encouraging international conflicts, would deter them.

(4)

Accordingly, three waves of fortifications were put in place after 1794 (in light of wars in Europe and tension with France), 1807 (in response to the threat from Britain), and 1816 (in the aftermath of the War of 1812). After the American Civil War, however, these fell into decline until 1886, when a board chaired by the secretary of war, William Crowninshield Endicott, recommended the establishment of a new generation of coastal defenses (which would include Fort Michie and Fort Hancock, where Howard Knox later served with the U.S. Army).

The fate of the coastal battery on Ellis Island followed this pattern. It was completed in 1812, and in 1814 it was named Fort Gibson. Although its armaments were improved during the 1840s and 1850s, its strategic significance declined, and by the 1880s the site was being used mainly as a munitions store by the U.S. Navy. In 1890 these munitions were removed to nearby Fort Wadsworth on Staten Island, which, following the Endicott board's recommendations, was being developed as a key part of the defenses of New York Harbor (see Roberts 1988:554–55). Fort Gibson was thus militarily redundant, and Ellis Island became available for alternative use.

Although some military buildings were retained, the central building for the new immigration station was built from scratch on fill, mainly obtained from the construction of the New York subway system. The building was two stories high and constructed of Georgia pine with slate roofs. The first emigrants were received there on January 1, 1892. However, the building was completely destroyed by fire on June 15, 1897. The fire was discovered soon after midnight and was believed to have broken out in the furnace (Moreno 2004:85). At the time 191 emigrants were housed in the hospital and the detention dormitories; those in the hospital were transferred to Bellevue Hospital in New York City, and those in the detention dormitories were accommodated in large rental houses near Battery Park (Unrau 1984, 2:580).

The Barge Office was brought back into service while the immigration station was rebuilt (this time using steel, brick, and concrete) between 1897 and 1900. Detained emigrants were held aboard the steamship *Narragansett* moored off Ellis Island, and hospital services were contracted out to the New York City Health Department and the Long Island College Hospital in Brooklyn. The new immigration station was completed on December 17, 1900. However, it was subsequently enlarged by the addition of a third floor, and the area recovered by fill was extended to permit the construction of hospital facilities and an administration

3.1 The immigration station at Ellis Island, New York Harbor, 1912.
(Courtesy Photography Collection, Miriam and Ira D. Wallach Division
of Art, Prints and Photographs, The New York Public Library,
Astor, Lenox and Tilden Foundations)

building. Figure 3.1 shows the main building of the immigration station at Ellis
Island in 1912.

THE INSPECTION OF EMIGRANTS AT ELLIS ISLAND

Emigrants who were traveling in first-class or second-class accommodations received a cursory examination in their cabin before their ship docked in Manhattan. However, those who were traveling in steerage (or third class) were not
inspected on board. Instead, following their debarkation they were taken by barge
to Ellis Island to receive a more detailed inspection and interrogation. Because of
the sheer numbers of people to be examined, the primary form of assessment

used was the line inspection, from which only selected emigrants were detained for individual examination.

In 1906 the assistant surgeon general of the Public Health and Marine Hospital Service, Henry Downes Geddings, was instructed to "make an inspection of all the operations connected with the medical examination of aliens" at Ellis Island. His report took the form of a long letter to the surgeon general dated November 16, and it gave a detailed firsthand account of the procedures in place:

> The scrutiny of the second [i.e., second-class] cabin passengers is close, they passing in review on the ship, and being subjected to inquiry, and with special attention paid to examination for trachoma and favus, and also for tuberculosis. . . . The first [i.e., first-class] cabin inspection is limited except in certain instances to circulating among them, and thus observing them. Cases exciting the suspicions of the officers are sometimes examined on the ship, sometimes sent to the Island. If a passenger is seen in the first cabin, but his appearance stamps him as belonging in the steerage or second cabin, his examination usually follows.

However, the experience of the passengers who were taken to Ellis Island was quite different:

> The examinations take place in a large room which by means of structures of pipe standards and wire gratings is divided into numerous compartments on either side of a central gangway. Into the end of this gangway there opens a stairway from the lower floor of the immigration building, and the passing up these stairs constitutes a presentation of the aliens for medical examination. At the head of the stairway the arrivals are met by an attendant who stamps the ship card borne by each arrival with the date. The immigrants pass along the gangway at a uniform gait, attendants being stationed to keep the line moving, to prevent congestion on the one hand, and to prevent breaks in the line and a waste of time on the other. Arrived at the end of the gangway, the immigrants are deflected to the right or left as the case may be into a narrow railed alley, of which two are in use at all inspections, and in busy times three, each of the alleys constituting *a line*. Crowding is prevented by attendants, and the arrivals [are] as equally distributed as possible into the various alleys. Immediately upon entering the alley, the immigrant is confronted by a medical officer, who rapidly looks into the condition of his scalp, the general physique, make up and gait of the individual, the presence of deformities, etc. and any defects presenting are indicated by a sign in chalk on the clothing of the individual, usually in the nature of the word "ex," which indicates that further inquiry is desirable. Pass-

ing on the immigrant is confronted by another officer, and undergoes a further scrutiny, with possibly the addition of other chalk marks, as "c" signifying an ocular condition requiring inquiry, "s" for senility, a letter for poor physique, another for hernia, for deformity, paralysis, lameness, etc., so that it is not infrequent to see an individual bearing sometimes as many as three or four chalk marks, when he or she arrives at the end of the alley, where is met the medical officer who is examining eyes for the detection of trachoma. The degree of skill and celerity with which this last operation is performed is remarkable. The more expert of the officers evert a lid with each hand, and that without pain or inconvenience in normal eyes. Instruments for the eversion of lids are seldom used, and then only as a relief for tired fingers, etc. . . .

The immigrant having arrived at the end of the alley, if without chalkmarks, now turns sharply to the right or left, and the formality of the medical examination is over for these individuals. Those with chalkmarks, are diverted in the opposite direction, and are kept in a compartment, until opportunity presents to make a more critical examination into discovered defects, in one of the numerous examination rooms. These rooms are of course separate for the sexes, and female attendants attend in the female rooms. These critical examinations are largely conducted in the intervals between the arrivals of the steerage from different ships, or between the barge loads from the same ships. While upon the line, there has been a scrutiny for the detection of mental disorders discoverable by appearance, demeanor or action. Two officers skilled in the detection and diagnosis of mental and nervous disorders have been on duty at various points on the lines, and when the suspect reaches the examination rooms, which are specially reserved for this class of cases, these two are joined by a third, and a searching inquiry is entered into. . . . In the examinations in the rooms some of course pass successfully and join their shipmates; others have their disabilities confirmed and the process of verification for deportation or exclusion is entered into. The sick are sent to hospital as a measure of humanity and with a view to cure. Some of those treated however come within the classes debarred by law, as trachoma, vagus, and those likely from physical causes to become a public charge, and are held until they can be put on board ship to be returned. Treatment in hospital of course terminates the disability of others, and the treatment concluded they take up their interrupted passage.

(Geddings 1906)

Similar firsthand accounts were given by Acting Assistant Surgeon Joseph G. Wilson (1911), Surgeon Eugene Hagan Mullan (1917a), and a visiting researcher, Bertha May Boody (1926:49–58). The implication is that essentially the same form of line inspection was used from the 1890s to the 1920s. This used a traditional diagnostic approach based on the careful examination of an individual's appearance and demeanor. Wilson did acknowledge that "all symptoms must have their relative value interpreted in the light of a full knowledge of the peculiar conditions under which they are observed, and with due regard to the racial characteristics of those who present them" (95). Nevertheless, he claimed that the following conditions could be detected simply by observation of a person's gait:

> Dislocation of hips; hipjoint disease; rheumatism; wooden legs; all the various paralytic affections; ankylosis of knee, ankle, or hip; locomotor ataxia; paresis, paranoia; flat feet; club feet; acute local infections; phlebitis; epididymitis; scrotal tumors; neuritis; rectal inflammations; gonorrhœa; rickets; muscular dystrophies; idiocy; corns; cerebral and cerebellar tumors; the intoxications of drugs or alcohol; elephantiasis; acute abdominal pains from any cause.
>
> (96)

There were, of course, major developments in the forms of assessment used in the examination rooms, and some are the main focus of this book. Nevertheless, the duality gave rise to tension between the arduous, even monotonous, work of line inspection and the far more interesting work of individual examinations.

In particular, in his report to the surgeon general Geddings commented on the conduct of one assistant surgeon, Thomas William Salmon, who had insisted on carrying out individual psychiatric examinations to the complete exclusion of any duty on line inspection. Geddings's opinion was that Salmon had willfully misinterpreted the orders of his seniors, he had outlived his usefulness at Ellis Island, and he should be transferred elsewhere. As a result, Salmon was reassigned to the Marine Hospital at Chelsea, Massachusetts (Bond 1950:33, 35). However, he was invited back to Ellis Island in 1913 to assist in the dissemination of the work on mental testing that had been carried out there. He subsequently became an eminent psychiatrist; indeed, in 1923 he was elected president of the American Psychiatric Association.

MENTAL DEFICIENCY

Until this time the physicians' interest in "mental disorders" among emigrants had been mainly focused upon psychiatric illnesses. For example, Salmon had contributed a section to the 1905 annual report of the Public Health and Marine Hospital Service that was concerned with the diagnosis of insanity in emigrants; it contained an ambitious proposal for the building of an observation pavilion at Ellis Island where suspected cases could be safely and efficiently cared for and adequate facilities for diagnosis provided (Salmon 1905). However, there was an increasing professional and public concern with regard to the identification of mental deficiency among emigrants: not only were mentally defective people likely to become a public charge themselves—the argument went—but if such people were allowed to enter the United States and later had children, their off-spring would almost certainly constitute an additional burden.

There have always been popular assumptions that intelligence is at least partly inherited, but this was first proposed as an explicit scientific hypothesis by the English anthropologist Francis Galton in the 1860s. His cousin, Charles Darwin, had published *The Origin of Species* (1859), in which he envisaged that the principle of natural selection would apply to both physical traits and patterns of behavior. Inspired by these ideas, Galton studied the prevalence of "eminence" in the various relatives of eminent men. This led him to conclude that eminence—or, more specifically, "genius"—was a hereditary trait (Galton 1869). This view was adopted by Darwin too, in *The Descent of Man*:

> So in regard to mental qualities, their transmission is manifest in our dogs, horses, and other domestic animals. Besides special tastes and habits, general intelligence, courage, bad and good temper, etc., are certainly transmitted. With man we see similar facts in almost every family; and we now know through the admirable labours of Mr. Galton that genius, which implies a wonderfully complex combination of high faculties, tends to be inherited; and, on the other hand, it is too certain that insanity and deteriorated mental powers likewise run in the same families.
>
> (Darwin 1871, 1:106–107)

Galton later coined the term *eugenics* (from the Greek *eugenes,* meaning well-born) to describe the application of social engineering to enhance the endowment of hereditary qualities in human beings (Galton 1883:17). These ideas became more widespread in the early 1900s following the rediscovery of the work of Austrian monk and botanist Gregor Mendel on the inheritance of traits. (His work had been overlooked when it was published in 1865.) In particular, the biologist Charles Benedict Davenport (1910:14–16) postulated that the inheritance of mental deficiency followed Mendelian principles. In 1910 Davenport established the Eugenics Record Office at Cold Spring Harbor on Long Island, New York, for the promotion of eugenics and eugenics research.

These sentiments gathered ground even among members of Congress, who in 1907 passed a further immigration act that added to the categories of people to be excluded from the United States "imbeciles," "feeble-minded persons," and people with physical or mental defects that might affect their ability to earn a living. The significance of the first two categories was that they reflected varying levels of mental deficiency: "idiots" were the most severely impaired, "imbeciles" were less impaired, and "feeble-minded persons" were only mildly impaired. Thus the terms of the 1882 Immigration Act were radically extended to encompass any individual who might be regarded as mentally deficient to even the slightest degree.

The third category was formally stated as "persons not comprehended within any of the foregoing excluded classes who are found to be and are certified by the examining surgeon as being mentally or physically defective, such mental or physical defect being of a nature which may affect the ability of such alien to earn a living." In other words, medical evidence could be used to support exclusions because the person was likely to become a public charge. This was argued to be a reasonable prescription, given that immigrants could pay a bond against their subsequently becoming a public charge ("New Immigration Law" 1907). Nevertheless, medical evidence was increasingly used to justify exclusions in the years that followed.

Some physicians were reluctant to become involved in such cases and endeavored to maintain their independence from the immigration process (Kraut 1988; 1994:68–69). Fitzhugh Mullan (1989) described their position:

> The practice of Service officers was to segregate their role as doctors examining and treating individuals from the requirements of the nation for social control over those arriving on its shores. . . . The job of the Service officers was to make medical diagnoses for the use of the Immigration Service and those who made immigration policy but not to function as arbiters themselves. In this spirit, Service physicians never sat on the Boards of Special Inquiry that made the final decision on exclusions and, at a number of points, the Service resisted pressure from the Immigration Service to find more of the arrivals physically or mentally unfit.
>
> (46, 48)

Indeed, the senior surgeon at Ellis Island, George W. Stoner, felt that, although many people were excluded because physical or mental defects might affect their ability to earn a living in particular occupations, the relevant defects would not necessarily prevent them from earning a living in different occupations. In other cases the person would not need to earn a living, because she or he was of independent means or could rely upon the financial support of friends or family. Either way, too many people were being excluded (see Fairchild 2003:33, 36).

Nevertheless, despite the reservations of the Ellis Island physicians, eugenic assumptions were finding widespread acceptance in the United States. When Sigmund Freud gave his series of extemporaneous lectures at Clark University in 1909, he mentioned eugenics in the fifth lecture on September 11. Saul Rosenzweig (1992) paraphrased the account that appeared in the following day's issue of the *Worcester Sunday Telegram* in the following manner: Freud "discussed 'race suicide' in terms of the difference between fertility rates in the Occident and in the Orient, and the devastations of warfare in eliminating the best and the strongest young men as future fathers. He referred, in particular, to the loss of 2,500,000 men in the Napoleonic Wars. Freud spoke of eugenics as essential for the future of society" (131).

In his commentary on these lectures Rosenzweig noted that this material was omitted from the authorized translation that was published six months later in the *American Journal of Psychology* (Freud 1910). This suggests that Freud was rather diffident about leaving a permanent record of these remarks in a journal with an international readership. Nevertheless, he seems to have felt that an American audience would be especially receptive to such ideas (Rosenzweig 1992:132).

<hr />

By the time Howard Knox sought an appointment in the Public Health and Marine Hospital Service in October 1911, it was widely held, both by the general public and by political figures in the United States, that feebleminded people were degenerate individuals responsible for social problems, that they were endangering the biological fitness of the nation, and that their numbers were being boosted by feebleminded immigrants, especially from southern and eastern Europe. This led to pressure to restrict immigration further and to widespread complaints that the immigration authorities—and by implication the physicians who advised them—were failing to prevent mentally defective people from entering the country. (For a contemporaneous account of the political and public debate during this period, see P. F. Hall 1913.)

When Knox submitted his application, the entire Public Health and Marine Hospital Service had only 135 officers, and the selection of new officers took place just twice a year (F. Mullan 1989:35). As a consequence, several months elapsed before Knox was instructed to present himself to the board of examiners in Washington, D.C., on April 8, 1912. Victor Heiser, a physician who had been examined in July 1898, made it clear in his subsequent recollections that the process was an exceedingly thorough and arduous affair:

> I was somewhat startled to find I was one of forty-two candidates for only three vacancies. . . .
>
> The preliminary physical examination was so rigid that twelve aspirants were promptly ruled out. Thirty began the week's ordeal of writing. Each day's paper contained only four questions, and, since eighty was the minimum

passing mark, whoever failed in a single one was automatically eliminated. The Board read the papers at night, and just before nine o'clock of the second day the announcement was made, "The following gentlemen will be excused," and five disappointed young men filed out. . . .

I grew more and more excited as our numbers dwindled. However, I still did not see how I could face the humiliation of walking out. I observed each morning the precaution of placing my hat within easy reaching distance, so that, at the sound of my name, I could make my exit as speedily and inconspicuously as possible.

Happily I was spared, and found myself among the ten who finished the written part of the examination. But the pre-medicals were still to come. We were to be orally examined in history, philosophy, economics, literature, and kindred subjects. . . .

After the pre-medicals, each of the survivors was taken to a hospital and requested to examine and diagnose six patients. Although they had been told to mislead us if possible, the clinical signs were theoretically so obvious that we should be able to make correct diagnoses. The same technique was followed in the laboratory, where we were required to analyze specimens and identify bacteria and parasites under the microscope; many of the slides had been specially prepared to confuse us.

At the end of a grueling two weeks, eight were left from whom the lucky three were to be chosen.

(Heiser 1936:11–12)

Two weeks later it was announced that three candidates, including Heiser, had passed their examination and would receive commissions in the service.

Knox too was successful: he attained an overall average of 84.99 percent, and this was sufficient to earn him an appointment with the Public Health and Marine Hospital Service in New York City. He took up a temporary post with the service on April 29, 1912, while awaiting his commission as an assistant surgeon. This was duly issued on May 13, and he was assigned to work under the direction of Senior Surgeon Stoner in the immigration station at Ellis Island, effective May 24. This placed him at the center of the controversy about whether the island's physicians were capable of identifying mentally defective emigrants.

4

THE MEASUREMENT OF INTELLIGENCE

B oth researchers seeking to demonstrate the heritability of intelligence and practitioners seeking to classify people as mentally normal or deficient clearly needed some procedure for measuring intelligence. Accordingly, in step with the developments in the conceptualization of intelligence that I mentioned in chapter 3 came developments in the measurement of intelligence.

GALTON AND CATTELL

In Britain, France, and Germany scholars and practitioners alike had discussed different ways of measuring intelligence since early in the nineteenth century (see Young 1924). However, Francis Galton was one of the first to implement these methods in a practical way.

In 1851 a royal commission had organized the Great Exhibition in the Crystal Palace in Hyde Park in London to celebrate contemporary industrial technology. The event was a financial as well as a cultural success: the London *Times* reported that the exhibition had had six million visitors between its opening on May 1 and its closure on October 15. However, the success of the foreign exhibitors suggested that Britain was lagging behind its European competitors. The royal commissioners therefore decided that the profits from the exhibition should be used to establish a scientific, educational, and cultural center on an area of land in nearby South Kensington. In future years this site was progressively occupied by the Royal Albert Hall, Natural History Museum, Royal College of Music, Imperial College, and the Science Museum, all of which remain today.

In the meantime the royal commissioners temporarily leased a large area in the middle of the site to the Royal Horticultural Society to accommodate its gardens and offices. This area was surrounded with Italianate arcades to separate the horticultural gardens from the temporary structures that were built from time to time to house subsequent exhibitions. However, relations between the royal commissioners and the society soured, and in 1882 the commissioners successfully pursued legal proceedings to have the society evicted. Even so, they allowed the society to remain until 1888 so that it could maintain the horticultural gardens while a series of international exhibitions with different scientific themes was held. On these occasions the temporary buildings housing the exhibits often encroached upon the gardens themselves (Hobhouse 2002).

The second of these exhibitions was held to acknowledge advances in the scientific study of health and, more specifically, in the fields of sanitation and hygiene. The exhibition opened on May 8, 1884, and was sponsored by Queen Victoria and her oldest son, the Prince of Wales (the future King Edward VII). The centerpiece of the event was the reproduction of an entire medieval London street, presented to demonstrate the role of environmental factors (and especially the design and construction of domestic buildings) in the spread of disease. Other exhibits were concerned with improvements in diet, dress, furniture, plumbing, and sewerage. The event was a considerable success and attracted four million visitors (Adams 1996:9–35).

Francis Galton was a scholar and researcher of independent means, and he had obtained permission to set up an "anthropometric laboratory" at the international health exhibition. (*Anthropometric* means "relating to the measurement of human beings"; it was originally used to refer to the measurement of physical characteristics, but Galton extended it to refer to the measurement of psychological performance.) For a small fee visitors to Galton's laboratory were measured physically in a wide variety of ways, and they then carried out a series of tasks, including tests of hearing, eyesight, reaction time, and visual estimation. More than nine thousand visitors had been assessed by the time the exhibition closed in 1885 (Galton 1885). Galton moved his anthropometric laboratory to the nearby South Kensington Museum (now the Victoria and Albert Museum) and continued to collect data there. As a result the project yielded an enormous amount of information concerning the participants' physical characteristics and their performance in simple tests (see Gillham 2001:211–14).

Galton was initially interested in evaluating the associations among the various measures that he had collected. To render the different measures commensurable, he proposed that they be transformed into standard scores (that is, distributions of scores that have a mean of zero and a standard deviation of one), and that the resulting pairs of scores should be plotted against each other as a scatter diagram. The regression line is the straight line that provides the best fit to the points in such a diagram. Galton defined a new index of the "co-relation" between two variables as the slope of the regression line between them when they had been transformed into standard scores, and he labeled this index with the letter r (apparently for "regression") (Galton 1888). Subsequently, his colleague Karl Pearson (1896) showed that this was mathematically equivalent to a different formula using the products of the standard scores that had originally been derived by a French scientist called Auguste Bravais (1846). Today r is usually described as the "Pearson product-moment correlation coefficient" or simply "Pearson r," although patently both Bravais and Galton had made significant contributions to its development (Denis 2001). This measures the magnitude and the direction of the relationship between two sets of scores obtained from the same individuals.

Galton originally focused on the relationships among purely physical characteristics of his participants. However, he also discussed his work with James McKeen Cattell, an American student who was working for a doctoral degree under the supervision of Wilhelm Wundt at the University of Leipzig in Germany. Cattell (1886) had devised new techniques for measuring reaction times, and Galton's research encouraged him to use the same techniques to investigate variations in performance across different people. Cattell spent two years in England between 1886 and 1888, during which he visited Galton's Anthropometric Laboratory and also collected further data from students at the University of Cambridge (Sokal 1987). On returning to the United States, Cattell established a psychological laboratory at the University of Pennsylvania, where he envisaged a program of research on "mental tests and measurements" (J. M. Cattell 1890).

Nevertheless, in 1891 Cattell moved to Columbia College in New York (it became Columbia University in 1896), and it took another three years before he could implement this research program. Cattell and his student Livingston Farrand (1896) published preliminary findings based on just one hundred participants, but these were descriptive and provided no new insights into the nature of human intelligence. In the meantime the American Psychological Association had set up a committee to consider whether different laboratories might collaborate in the collection of anthropometric data (Sanford 1896). The committee set out to construct a standard set of tests that could be administered to college students, but its members failed to reach any consensus on whether they should include tests of higher mental processes such as memory rather than simpler tests such as measures of reaction time (Baldwin, Cattell, and Jastrow 1898).

Eventually, Clark Wissler (1901) published results from Cattell's program based on data from more than three hundred students. These results showed only weak correlations among their scores on different mental tests and only weak correlations between their scores on the mental tests and the average marks that they obtained in their courses. Edward Lee Thorndike had been another of Cattell's students, and after obtaining his doctoral degree in 1898 he worked for a year at Western Reserve University (now Case Western Reserve) in Cleveland before joining the faculty at Columbia University in 1899. Thorndike carried out a similar study in collaboration with Herbert Austin Aikens, the head of the psychology department at Western Reserve. They argued, "A priori it is more rational to look on the mind as a multitude of particular capacities, all of which may be highly independent of one another" (Aikens and Thorndike 1902:374), and their findings tended to support this view. Thorndike (1903:23–39) later expounded this theory of "special abilities" in an influential textbook on educational psychology.

In fact, Cattell's research suffered from two problems. First, the participants were all college students, which limited the scope for variation. Consequently, his attempts to establish correlations between academic attainment and performance on mental tests were subject to "restriction of range," and he would have systematically underestimated their true magnitude. Second, his tests of reaction time required a single response to a single stimulus. Recent research using participants who are representative of the general population has found a much more substantial relationship between general intelligence and reaction time in tasks where different responses have to be given to different stimuli (Deary, Der, and Ford 2001).

However, a British psychologist, Charles Edward Spearman, took quite a different view. Patricia Lovie and Sandy Lovie (1996) provided a definitive account of Spearman's life. He had been an officer in the British army but retired in 1898 when, like Cattell, he decided to study for a doctoral degree in Leipzig under the supervision of Wilhelm Wundt. Following the outbreak of the South African War in 1900, Spearman was recalled to the army from Germany and was assigned to serve in Guernsey, one of the Channel Islands off the northwest coast of France. He returned to England after being released from military service in 1902, and he and his family resided in the Berkshire village of Appleton. There he took the opportunity to administer various combinations of psychological tests to sixty children from the local village school, thirty-three boys from a local private school, and twenty-six adults. Later that year Spearman resumed his studies in Leipzig, where he completed his doctoral degree (on the somewhat different topic of spatial localization) in 1906, and he returned to England in July 1907 to join the faculty of University College London.

On his return to Leipzig in 1902 Spearman analyzed the data that he had collected in Appleton, and he published the findings in a paper in the *American Journal of Psychology* in 1904. He claimed that performance on a particular test depended on both on a central trait or factor that he called "general intelligence" and a specific trait or factor that was unique to tests of that kind. Wissler had actually found fairly high correlations among the marks that Cattell's students had obtained in different courses. This led Spearman to infer that academic assessments were better measures of general intelligence than were Cattell's tests. Nevertheless, Spearman also argued that Cattell's tests were often fairly unreliable. Spearman claimed that, if the relevant correlation coefficients were adjusted for this poor reliability, children's scores on those tests showed strong relationships with academic assessments.

BINET AND SIMON

Researchers in other countries were also questioning the value of simple tests of the sort that had been devised by Galton and Cattell. In France, Alfred Binet and Victor Henri (1896) published a manifesto for an approach to "individual psychology" in which they proposed that differences in higher mental functions such as memory, comprehension, and imagination could be measured in the same way as more basic sensory processes. They suggested the kinds of test that might be used, and Binet spent the next few years evaluating a wider range of tasks.

Binet and Henri's work came to the attention of Stella Emily Sharp, a doctoral student working under the supervision of Edward Bradford Titchener at Cornell University. She decided to give some of the tests suggested by Binet and Henri to several other graduate students on several occasions to check the reliability of their results. Although there seemed to be consistent differences among the students in their performance on particular tests, these did not show the same pattern across different tests. Sharp herself drew the inference that the various mental functions being measured were relatively independent of one another. Even so, she concluded, "There can be little doubt that the method of procedure employed by M. Binet is the one most productive of fruitful results" (1899:390).

Joseph Peterson (1926:109) commented that the studies by Sharp and Wissler led to a decline of interest in mental testing in the United States through the next decade. However, he also pointed out severe flaws in Sharp's study. Her participants were even more highly selected and more homogeneous than Wissler's, and they would not have been likely to show consistent individual differences. They were also just seven in number. Titchener had attempted to collect comparative data from the students who were taking his undergraduate course, but these data were unusable because not all the tests could be administered in the time available and because some students skipped classes from time to time. Finally, Peterson argued that several tests used by Sharp would be tapping particular abilities, not complex mental functions (1926:106–107).

By the early 1900s, Binet himself had amassed a large amount of evidence about the probable value of different kinds of test in the measurement of intelligence (Peterson 1926:117–62). At this time, the French government introduced laws prescribing universal education, and the minister of public instruction appointed a commission to establish the measures that would be needed to ensure that mentally deficient children benefited equally from this provision. The commission resolved that children should be assigned for special education only if it were shown that they were unable to benefit from the instruction given in ordinary schools. However, the commission did not specify the nature of the examination that might warrant this conclusion. With another colleague, Théodore Simon, Binet set about constructing a series of tests that could be used to identify mentally deficient children who were in need of special education.

In their first report Binet and Simon (1905b) presented the series of thirty tests listed in table 4.1. The labels in the table are not direct translations of those used by Binet and Simon but more accurately reflect their content in modern terminology. These tests were supposed to constitute a "metrical scale of intelligence" (échelle métrique de l'intelligence) in that they comprised a series of increasing difficulty, "starting on the one hand from the lowest intellectual level that can be observed, and ending on the other hand with the level of average normal intelligence" (194). By comparing the performance of mentally deficient children with that of normal children, the former performance could be categorized as exhibiting idiocy, imbecility, or feeblemindedness (débilité) (195). In a separate paper Binet and Simon (1905a) presented data from both normal and mentally deficient children on their scale, and they showed how it might be used to classify mentally deficient children as idiots, imbeciles, or feebleminded.

Binet and Simon were at pains to point out that their scale was essentially a classification scheme rather than a "measure" in any strict sense:

This scale does not, strictly speaking, provide the measure of intelligence— because intellectual qualities are not measured like lengths, they cannot be superimposed—but a ranking, a hierarchy among diverse intelligences; and for practical purposes this ranking is equivalent to a measure. We will therefore be able to know, after having studied two individuals, whether one rises above the other, and by how many degrees; whether one rises above the average of other individuals regarded as normal, or whether he remains below; knowing the normal progress of intellectual development in normals, we will be able to tell by how many years such an individual is retarded or advanced.

(Binet and Simon 1905b:194–95; my translation)

TABLE 4.1 BINET AND SIMON'S 1905 SERIES OF TESTS

1. Tracking a moving object with the eyes
2. Grasping and manipulating a tactile stimulus
3. Grasping and manipulating a visual stimulus
4. Recognizing an item of food
5. Searching for a concealed item of food
6. Responding to simple commands and imitating simple gestures
7. Identifying parts of the body and familiar objects
8. Pointing to objects in a pictured scene
9. Naming of objects in a pictured scene
10. Comparing two lines of unequal length
11. Repeating a sequence of three spoken digits
12. Comparing two objects of different weight
13. Responding to suggestion
14. Defining familiar objects
15. Repeating sentences of fifteen words
16. Comparing familiar objects from memory
17. Remembering an array of pictured objects
18. Reproducing a design from memory
19. Repeating sequences of spoken digits
20. Identifying similarities between familiar objects from memory
21. Comparing pairs of lines of unequal length
22. Arranging five similar objects in terms of their weight
23. Identifying a missing object from the previous sequence
24. Finding rhymes
25. Finding the missing word in a sentence
26. Making up a sentence containing three words
27. Replying to an abstract question
28. Telling the time when the hands of a clock are reversed
29. Imaginary paper folding and cutting
30. Comparing abstract concepts

Source: Compiled from Binet and Simon 1905b:199–223 (my translation).

Later Binet and Simon (1908) presented a more elaborate version of their scale of intelligence. This version was structured according to age, and they assigned different subtests to the ages at which most children performed them successfully. For instance, their original scale included tests of memory for sequences of spoken digits. (Today these would be called tests of memory span or, more specifically, tests of digit span.) In the 1908 version sequences of two, three, five, and seven digits were to be administered to children aged three, four, seven, and twelve, respectively. The full classification of the tests is shown in table 4.2.

Each child was to be tested at a number of different age levels, beginning with the one corresponding to their chronological age; their intellectual level (*niveau intellectuel*) or mental level (*niveau mental*) was defined as the highest age level at which they could pass all or all but one of the subtests. However, they were also to be credited with one additional year if they passed five subtests beyond that level and with two additional years if they passed ten subtests beyond that level (Binet and Simon 1908:65). The classification of the subtests was based on the performance of children aged three to thirteen. Even so, Binet and Simon argued that their scale could also be used to classify mentally deficient adults:

> We shall keep the common terms, idiot, imbecile, and feebleminded, while giving them a precise definition and a possible application through the tests in our scale. An idiot is a being who cannot communicate with his fellow creatures through language; he does not speak and he does not understand; he corresponds to the normal level of intelligence that arises between birth and the age of two years. To establish a differential diagnosis between the idiot and the imbecile, it is therefore sufficient to use the following tests: first, to give verbal commands such as to touch his nose, mouth, eyes; second, to make him name some easy familiar objects that he will find and pick out in a picture. These are our tests for the age of three; in reality they belong equally well to two years as to three.
>
> The boundary between imbecility and feeblemindedness is no more difficult to establish. An imbecile is someone who is incapable of communicating with his fellow creatures through written language; so he can neither read nor understand what he has read, nor write to dictation or spontaneously in an intelligible way. One will apply to him our tests corresponding to the age of eight. Since it is possible that sometimes one is faced with someone who is illiterate due to poor school attendance, one will use several other tests for seven years and eight years, such as describing pictures, counting the value of a pile of five- and ten-centime coins, comparing two objects from memory; all these supplementary tests provide a robust boundary between imbecility and feeblemindedness.

There remains one last boundary to draw, that which separates feeblemind-edness from a normal state. This is more complicated; we believe it to be not fixed but variable, just according to the circumstances. The most general formula that one can adopt is this: an individual is normal if he behaves in life without needing other people's supervision, if he succeeds in a job that is sufficiently remunerated to meet his personal needs, and lastly if his intelligence does not lower his status below that of his parents.

(87–88; my translation)

Binet and Simon had administered their scale to twenty mentally deficient adults in different Parisian hospitals, and they found that none achieved a mental level higher than ten years of age. Within this range they proposed that idiocy constituted a mental level less than two years, imbecility constituted a mental level between two and seven years, and feeblemindedness constituted a mental level between eight and ten years. They also argued that their scale had a potentially wide application:

Let us point out the very great usefulness to humanity that there would be in carrying out an intellectual examination of young recruits before enlisting them. Many feebleminded, that is, young people whose intellectual weakness renders them incapable of learning and understanding the theory and drill of arms and of submitting to regular discipline, report for medical examination; and they are declared "fit for service" because it is not known how to examine them from an intellectual point of view.

(94; my translation)

However, according to Peterson (1926:289–94), Binet's efforts to induce the French government to use mental testing in the recruitment of army personnel were largely frustrated.

Simon left Paris in October 1908, but Binet continued to develop their scale until he died in 1911. In 1909 he published a critical review of what had been learned from the previous thirty years of educational research, including one chapter devoted to intelligence. The first half of this chapter is concerned with the measurement of intelligence; he presented an elaborated scale for measuring intelligence in children from three months to fifteen years and discussed the strengths and limitations of his approach. In the second half of the chapter Binet described his idea of intelligence and the scope for improving intelligence through education.

He began by attacking those who maintained that intelligence could not be increased: "Some recent philosophers seem to have given their moral support to

TABLE 4.2 BINET AND SIMON'S 1908 MEASURING SCALE OF INTELLIGENCE

Three Years

Point to the nose, the eyes, the mouth.

Name the objects in a picture.

Repeat a sentence containing six syllables.

Give one's family name.

Four Years

Give one's sex.

Name a key, a knife, a penny.*

Repeat three digits.

Compare two lines of different length.

Five Years

Compare two boxes of different weights.

Copy a square.

Repeat a sentence containing ten syllables.

Count four pennies.

Put together two triangles to make a rectangle.

Six Years

Repeat a sentence of sixteen syllables.

Compare two figures from an aesthetic viewpoint.

Define familiar objects in terms of their use.

Carry out a sequence of three tasks from memory.

Give one's age.

Say whether it is morning or afternoon

Seven Years

Identify objects missing from pictures.

Say the number of fingers on both hands.

Copy a written sentence.

Copy a triangle and a diamond.

Repeat five digits.

Describe a picture.

Count thirteen pennies.

Name four common coins.

Eight Years

Read a short news item and recall two facts from it.

Add up three pennies and three nickels.

Name four colors.

Count backward from twenty to zero.

Compare two objects from memory.

Write a short phrase from dictation.

Nine Years

Give the complete date (day, date, month, year).

Recite the days of the week.

Define familiar objects in terms beyond just their use.

Read a short news item and recall two facts from it.

Give correct change from a selection of coins when offered a quarter in payment for an item costing five cents.

Arrange five weights from the heaviest to the lightest.

Ten Years

Recite the months of the year.

Name all the different coins.

Use three words in two sentences.

Answer five less difficult comprehension questions.**

Answer five more difficult comprehension questions.

Eleven Years

Explain the absurdities in nonsense sentences.

Use three words in one sentence.

Say more than sixty different words in three minutes.

Define three abstract words.

Rearrange nine words to make a proper sentence.

Twelve Years

Repeat seven digits.

Find three rhymes for a word.

Repeat a sentence containing twenty-six syllables.

Interpret the scenes shown in different pictures

Explain the events described in a short passage.

Thirteen Years

A piece of paper is folded twice and a small piece is cut out of one of the folded edges. What would the piece of paper look like if it were unfolded?

Draw from memory an arrangement of triangles presented by the tester.

Compare two abstract concepts.

* Binet and Simon used the word *sou* (the colloquial term for a five-centime piece) as a basic unit of currency with which even small children would be familiar. Here I have substituted *penny* and other common forms of U.S. currency.

** The "comprehension" questions, presented in two series of different levels of difficulty, were concerned with appropriate behavior rather than linguistic understanding. For example, one question was: "When a friend accidentally hits you, what should you do?"

Source: Compiled and adapted from Binet and Simon 1908:3–59 (my translation).

these deplorable verdicts in asserting that an individual's intelligence is a fixed quantity, a quantity that cannot be increased. We must protest and react against this brutal pessimism" (Binet 1909:141). He argued quite the opposite:

> Nowadays, if one considers that intelligence is not a single function, indivisible and with a distinctive essence, but that it is formed through the combination of all those lesser functions of discrimination, observation, retention, etc., whose plasticity and extensibility have been noted, it will seem incontestable that the same law governs the whole and its elements, and that consequently someone's intelligence is open to development; with practice and training, and especially method, one succeeds in increasing their attention, their memory, their judgment, and in becoming literally more intelligent than they were before.
>
> (143; my translation)

To achieve this, he suggested that teachers should introduce exercises in "mental orthopedics": "Just as physical orthopedics puts right a crooked spine, likewise mental orthopedics puts right, cultivates, strengthens attention, memory, perception, judgment, willpower" (150).

In 1911 Binet and Simon published the final version of their scale, amending, replacing, or assigning certain subtests to slightly different ages. They assigned five subtests for administration to each of seven age levels: six, seven, eight, nine, ten, twelve, and fifteen. A separate set consisting of the five most difficult subtests was proposed for use with adults. Binet (1911) published a similar account as sole author. He now proposed another scoring scheme in which a child's mental level was calculated as the age at which she had passed all five subtests, plus one fifth of a year for each subtest passed beyond that level. He concluded this article by looking forward to the wider application of these methods to the study of aptitudes of character and the psychological condition. (For more extensive accounts of Binet's contribution to psychology, see Peterson 1926; Siegler 1992; and Wolf 1973.)

I should add that Binet and Simon were not the only European psychologists who were developing scales for measuring intelligence. In particular, Sante de Sanctis, working in Rome, devised a graded series of tests for identifying the level of mental deficiency in children aged seven to sixteen. According to Kimball Young (1924), de Sanctis's initial account was published in several languages simultaneously, although the French version is the one most commonly cited (de Sanctis 1906). Later de Sanctis arranged for an English summary of two of his lectures at the University of Rome to be published in an American journal, and this contains essentially the same account of his tests (de Sanctis 1911):

I. *Give me a ball.* (Present five balls, each of a different color. Note the time of response. As soon as this is given, even by a simple gesture, drop the screen between the experimenter and the subject.)

II. *Which is the ball you just gave me?* (Show the same five balls arranged in a row. Note the time of response, and as soon as there is a sign of recognition, drop the screen.)

III. *Do you see this block of wood?* (Show a wooden cube such as is used in the kindergarten.) *Pick out all the blocks like this from the pile on the table.* (Show five cubes mixed with three cones and two parallelopipeds. Note the time required for selecting and arranging the cubes, and replace the screen.)

IV. *Do you see this block?* (Show a cube.) *Point out a figure on the form chart that looks like it.* (Show the form chart, and note the figure to which the subject points. If he points to one of the small squares, proceed as follows:) *Take this pencil (or pointer) and point out all the squares on the chart as fast as possible without missing any, taking the figures line by line.* (Note the time, the mistakes and omissions, and drop the screen as soon as the subject has finished.)

V. *Here are some more blocks like those you have pointed out on the chart.* (Spread the blocks out on the table in such a manner that the distance between the cubes is not more than two centimeters. Each cube should be just one-half centimeter longer on each side than the next smaller one. To make the test more difficult one may (a) increase the number of cubes scattered on the table or (b) decrease the differences in size.) *Look at them carefully and tell me 1. How many there are. 2. Which is the largest? 3. Which is the farthest away from you?* (Note the time, the errors, and the omissions, and replace the screen as soon as the questions are answered.)

VI. *Do large objects weigh more or less than small objects? Why does a small object sometimes weigh more than a large one?* (The second question is put if the first has been answered correctly.) *Do distant objects appear larger or smaller than near objects? Do they only seem smaller or are they really smaller?* (This question will show whether the subject is aware of optical illusions.)

(505–507)

(The "form chart" measured 15.5 inches by 11.5 inches and contained ten rows, each with fourteen triangles, oblongs, and squares.)

According to de Sanctis, failing the second test was a sign of severe mental deficiency, failing the fifth test was a sign of moderate mental deficiency, failing the sixth test was a sign of slight mental deficiency, and passing all six tests was a sign of no mental deficiency. However, he argued that it was not sensible to define these categories using Binet and Simon's scale:

The application of the scale in these cases would imply that the degrees of intellectual defect in idiots or in dements correspond to the degrees of intellectual development in ages of growth. It would assume that the laws of intellectual regression and involution are the same as those of progression and evolution. This is yet to be proven; rather, we have good reason to believe that it is not true for all idiots and imbeciles, and that it is still farther from the truth with dements. Illness rarely produces retardation, arrest, or destruction of the intelligence as a whole. And in any case how can we assume so lightly that psychic correlations maintain their rhythm in intellectual decay?

(503–504)

In other words, de Sanctis rejected the idea that mental deficiency was simply a matter of mental retardation. On the contrary, he argued that the causes of intellectual disability were likely to affect the process of intellectual development as well as the eventual outcome. De Sanctis's tests were used for some years in both Europe and the United States, but they were largely superseded by Binet and Simon's scale, and within twenty years the tests themselves had been forgotten (Peterson 1926:190–91).

GODDARD AND THE INTRODUCTION OF BINET AND SIMON'S TESTS TO THE UNITED STATES

As Robert Stuart Siegler (1992) pointed out, many other countries had introduced universal public education toward the end of the nineteenth century, and they too confronted the problem of how best to educate children with a highly diverse range of capabilities. In particular, the introduction of compulsory education in the United States had raised the issue of how to deal with children who seemed to be ineducable. At the very least these children demanded a disproportionate amount of time and attention from their teachers (Zenderland 1998:58–59). The most common response to this problem was to broaden the range of facilities and institutions that provided additional support for mentally deficient children.

Some states already had institutions to educate children who had such special needs. The best-known institutions were at Vineland, New Jersey, at Faribault, Minnesota, and at Lincoln, Illinois, but the staffs at these schools had great difficulty identifying and classifying mentally deficient individuals so that they could provide them with the most appropriate forms of support and training (Peterson 1926:225). As I mentioned earlier, and as Binet too had found in Paris, simple sensory tasks did not seem to provide valid measures of intellectual ability. In any case, sensory tasks also seemed to be inappropriate for testing mentally deficient children, because many did not understand the test instructions, and many were simply unable to cope with the relevant apparatus or equipment (Popplestone and McPherson 1999:67).

The New Jersey Training School at Vineland had a well-established reputation for its positive approach to the education and training of mentally deficient people. In 1906, however, its superintendent, Edward Ransom Johnstone, decided to appoint a director of research to bring a more scientific approach to the understanding of mental deficiency (Zenderland 1998:60–67). In seeking candidates for this post, Johnstone sought the advice of G. Stanley Hall, the president of Clark University in Worcester, Massachusetts. Hall recommended Henry Herbert Goddard, who had worked for his doctoral degree under Hall's supervision between 1896 and 1899.

Once appointed to the new position, Goddard set about constructing a psychological laboratory at the Vineland Training School, complete with all the latest equipment. However, administering tests to the students at the training school proved to be difficult, and Goddard lacked comparative data from normal individuals. Moreover, consistent with Wissler's (1901) findings in college students, the Vineland students' performance on laboratory-based tasks showed little or no relationship to their teachers' assessments of their intellectual abilities (Zenderland 1998:89–91).

Because of this disappointment Goddard decided to spend two months in 1908 visiting physicians, educationalists, and psychologists in Europe to see whether he could find a better approach to the study and measurement of intelligence. Although he met de Sanctis and learned about his series of tests, Goddard did not seek out Binet, partly because of the disparaging comments made about Binet's work by others whom Goddard consulted. For his own part, Binet made few personal contacts in his professional life, and he and his wife were in poor health and probably not receiving visitors (Wolf 1973:34–35, 196–97). While he was in Brussels, however, Goddard was shown Binet and Simon's 1905 scale by Ovide Decroly, who had been using the scale with both normal and mentally deficient children (see Decroly 1908).

Goddard returned to the United States and began to use the 1905 scale in a tentative way with students at his own institution. He also published in the training school's house journal short accounts of both Binet and Simon's scale and of de Sanctis's series of tests (Goddard 1908a, 1908b). The following year he received Binet and Simon's (1908) account of their revised scale. Some years later, in correspondence with Young (1924:35), Goddard described his reactions on seeing the scale: "When I read Binet's 'Measuring Scale,' I rejected it as too formal and exact. I thought 'mind' could not be measured in that way. A second thought showed me that my impression or feeling was of no value compared to the serious declaration of a man like Binet. I accordingly set about trying out the scale on our children. The more I used it the more amazed I was at its accuracy." Goddard (1910b) published a short account of the 1908 scale and then used his own translation of the scale to evaluate students at the Vineland Training School.

For Goddard, Binet and Simon's scale solved the problem of how to identify and classify mentally deficient people in a precise, objective, and reliable manner (Zenderland 1998:74–75). This was becoming an urgent problem because of slippage in the vocabulary that was being used. In particular, the term *feebleminded*, which had previously been used to refer to the mildest form of mental deficiency (and thus the hardest to diagnose), was by this time becoming used as a generic term to cover mental deficiency of all levels of severity. Goddard raised this specific issue at the 1909 annual meeting of the American Association for the Study of the Feeble-Minded (now the American Association on Intellectual and Developmental Disabilities).

The association convened a small committee to investigate different ways of classifying mental deficiency, and Goddard was appointed to serve on it. The committee seems to have made little progress during the subsequent year, although its chair, Walter Elmore Fernald, made it clear that he supported Goddard in advocating a system based upon measures of intelligence rather than upon the presumed underlying pathology (Zenderland 1998:99). At the association's annual meeting in 1910, Goddard was the only member of the committee present, so he was asked to make a report. His report formed the basis of a paper published later that year, "Four Hundred Feeble-minded Children Classified by the Binet Method" (Goddard 1910a).

Although Goddard referred consistently to "children" in this and many other articles, the mentally deficient people whom he had tested were aged twelve to fifty years (392). It would therefore probably be more accurate to refer to them as students instead. In terms of their performance on Binet and Simon's 1908 scale, however, none achieved better than twelve years. Following Binet and Simon's earlier classification, Goddard proposed that those whose mental capacity was between zero and two years should be regarded as idiots; that those whose mental capacity was between three and seven years should be regarded as imbeciles; and that those whose mental capacity was between eight and twelve years should be regarded as feebleminded (394–95). Although this seemed to be a purely practical suggestion, it implied that the identification and classification of cases of mental deficiency should henceforth be the professional responsibility of psychologists, not physicians.

Goddard then turned his attention to the matter of nomenclature and the specific point that *feebleminded* had come to be used as a generic term. Indeed, many institutions set up to provide support for mentally deficient people had names containing the word *feebleminded*. Goddard felt that it was necessary to devise some new name to refer to children and adults who were only slightly mentally deficient, partly to focus the attention of professionals and the public upon the task of identifying this group, who to untrained observers might appear to be of normal intelligence. He suggested the term *moron*, the neuter form of the Greek *moros*, meaning foolish (395). The association accepted both his proposed classification scheme and this new term.

In referring to a child's performance on their scale, Binet and Simon had always used the expression "mental level" to recognize that this was not something that was fixed but something that was subject to change through development or training. Moreover, although the use of this term was intended to reflect the broad level at which the individual was functioning, they did not subscribe to the view that mental deficiency was only a matter of mental retardation:

> The exact nature of this inferiority is not known, and in the absence of other evidence it is very prudent to refuse to liken it to an arrest in normal development. It does seem that the intelligence of these beings has undergone a certain arrest; but it does not follow that this arrest (that is, the disproportion between their degree of intelligence and their age) is the only characteristic of their condition. In many cases, there is probably also a deviation in their development, a perversion. The fifteen-year-old idiot who is still taking the first verbal steps of a three-year-old baby cannot be completely likened to a three-year-old child, because the latter is normal whereas the idiot is impaired. Necessarily, therefore, there are differences, either visible or hidden, between them.
>
> (Binet and Simon 1905b:192; my translation)

Nevertheless, in his presentation to the American Association for the Study of the Feeble-Minded, Goddard diverged from this by using the expression "mental age." This has at least two implications. First, bearing in mind that he was actually talking about mentally deficient *adults,* it implies that this was a fixed characteristic. He expressed this view elsewhere: "One of the greatest joys that I got from the Vineland experience was a knowledge which enabled me to say to teachers, 'Do not burn the midnight oil, do *not* worry about these children that you cannot bring up to grade. They are feebleminded and *no one* can bring them up to grade'" (1933:26; emphasis in the original). Second, "mental age" implies that mental deficiency is essentially a matter of mental retardation: mentally deficient children acquire particular forms of behavior later than other children, but the order in which they acquire them is the same (Tuddenham 1966). The fifteen-year-old idiot with a mental age of three really is just like a normal three-year-old child in terms of intellectual capabilities.

In other words, as Siegler (1992) noted, Goddard championed the idea of intelligence testing for reasons that were quite antithetical to Binet's own thinking (see also Fancher 1998; Wolf 1973:216–17). One reason that Goddard assumed intelligence to be fixed was that he had come to believe that mental deficiency was an inherited characteristic. In 1909 he had met the biologist Charles Davenport, who introduced Goddard to eugenic research (Zenderland 1998:153–58). As a consequence, Goddard was encouraged to carry out his own studies to demonstrate the inherited nature of mental deficiency.

He began with a report based upon two male students at the Vineland Training School. In both cases he claimed to have found ten feebleminded relatives in the students' family histories (Goddard 1911a). This was followed by a book written for a general readership about the family history of another student who was given the pseudonym of Deborah Kallikak (Goddard 1912e). However, this was simply part of a much more extensive investigation that involved the family histories of 327 Vineland students (Goddard 1914). In all these works Goddard endeavored to show that feeblemindedness was a recessive trait inherited according to Mendelian principles. (For a detailed account of Goddard's work on this subject, see Zenderland 1998:143–221.)

At the same time Goddard continued to champion the use of Binet and Simon's scale for measuring intelligence in both normal and mentally deficient individuals. In the fall of 1910 with the help of five assistants he used the scale to test all the children in a single school system. He obtained results from 1,547 children and presented comparisons of their chronological ages (which ranged from four to fifteen years) and their mental ages (which ranged from two to thirteen years) (Goddard 1911b). He also commissioned one of his main fieldworkers, Elizabeth Kite, to translate into English the principal articles by Binet and Simon describing the evolution of their scale, and he published Kite's translations as a single volume (Binet and Simon 1916).

HUEY, TERMAN, AND THE STANFORD-BINET SCALE

Nevertheless, Goddard was by no means the only person considering Binet and Simon's scales. From 1903 to 1905 Lewis Madison Terman had worked for his doctorate at Clark University on a comparison of boys of high and low intelligence (Terman 1906). Like Goddard, Terman had been supervised at first by G. Stanley Hall. However, Hall disapproved of mental testing, and Terman had completed his investigation under the supervision of Edmund Clark Sanford, even though the latter specialized mainly in laboratory-based research (Terman 1930).

Terman had read Binet's early work and had sent Binet a copy of his doctoral thesis. Indeed, Binet and Simon may well have taken Terman's findings into account when they developed the 1908 version of their scale (Peterson 1926:189). The 1905 version had been reviewed in a major U.S. journal, the *Psychological Bulletin,* yet Terman was initially not aware of the scale's existence. Nevertheless, in the summer of 1907 Edmund Burke Huey, a friend and fellow student of Henry Goddard's at Clark University, brought it to Terman's attention. Huey had returned to Clark University in 1904 after spending time in Europe, and he had made a point of keeping in touch with European developments in mental testing (Minton 1988:24, 33, 276).

Huey's main interest was in the teaching of reading, and today he is best known for the book on this subject that he published in 1908. However, he was also interested in mental deficiency, and in 1909–10 he worked at the Illinois School for the Feeble-Minded before moving to work with the psychiatrist Adolf Meyer at the Johns Hopkins University and Hospital in Baltimore. Huey was particularly familiar with the writings of Binet and Simon, and in 1910 he published his own translation of their 1908 scale (Huey 1910a). Elsewhere he advocated the use of the scale to identify mentally deficient children in the school system (Huey 1910b).

By 1910 Binet and Simon's research had become the subject of lively discussion and debate in the United States and in many other countries. One commentator remarked that the majority of publications on psychological testing that had appeared that year had been related specifically to Binet and Simon's scale (Freeman 1911). Binet and Simon were alert to the various comments and criticisms that other writers had made, and they attempted either to rebut or to accommodate them when they devised the 1911 revision of their scale (for reviews and discussion, see Huey 1912; Peterson 1926:215–40). Moreover, Huey's translation of Binet and Simon's scale was shortly joined by others.

In the latter part of 1910 Guy Montrose Whipple of Cornell University published the *Manual of Mental and Physical Tests* in which he included translations and commentary on de Sanctis's series of tests and on both versions of Binet and Simon's scale (469–517). He substituted new material for some of the nonsense sentences intended for eleven-year-old children in the 1908 scale because he considered them to be "rather blood-curdling" (509):

Yesterday on the fortifications they found the body of an unfortunate girl cut into eighteen pieces. They think she killed herself.

Yesterday there was an accident on the railroad, but it wasn't serious: There were only forty-eight deaths.

Someone said: If I kill myself in despair some day, I won't choose a Friday, because Friday is a bad day that would bring me bad luck.

Binet was unimpressed: "It would appear that these stories seem frightening to young Americans. Our young Parisians laughed at them" (1911:145). Indeed, Whipple had retained a question that was just as "blood-curdling" in one of his tests for twelve-year-olds:

> A person who was going for a walk in the forest of Fontainebleau suddenly stopped, very frightened, and ran to the nearest police station to report that they had just seen hanging from the branch of a tree a . . . (After a pause.) A what?

According to Binet and Simon, "The only correct response, as the context indicates, is: *a person hanged*" (1908:55; emphasis in the original).

John Edward Wallace Wallin was another psychologist who had obtained his doctoral degree at Clark University. In 1910 he had substituted for Goddard at a summer school held at the New Jersey Training School, and he had been inspired by seeing Binet and Simon's scale being used there (Wallin 1962). The superintendent, Edward Johnstone, helped Wallin to obtain a position as the first psychologist at the State Village for Epileptics at Skillman, New Jersey. (It later became the New Jersey Neuro-Psychiatric Institute.) Wallin prepared his own translation of the 1908 version of Binet and Simon's scale and reported the results of administering the scale to epileptic patients (Wallin 1911, 1912).

The following year Frederick Kuhlmann of the Minnesota School for the Feeble-Minded produced an amended English translation of the 1908 scale that he later used to evaluate thirteen hundred mentally deficient children (Kuhlmann 1912, 1913). Finally, Clara Harrison Town of the Illinois School for the Feeble-Minded translated Binet and Simon's 1911 account of the final version of their scale (Binet and Simon 1912). Her translation went through two further editions in the next three years. Town also published a commentary based upon her own experience with the 1911 version of the scale (Town 1912).

Between 1905 and 1910 Terman had restricted his daily activities because of poor health, and he had been in no position to carry out academic research of any kind (Minton 1988:30–37). By the summer of 1910, however, his health had improved. He was appointed to a position in the education department at Stanford University and was encouraged to resume his research. Terman (1930) subsequently recalled that Huey had visited him once again just before the beginning of the new school year and had urged him to investigate Binet and Simon's 1908 scale. The research project that Terman undertook as a result was a highly ambitious one.

Working with a graduate student, Hubert Guy Childs, and two research assistants, Katherine Kip and Edith Bushnell, Terman administered Binet and Simon's scale to nearly four hundred children at schools in the Stanford, Long Beach, and

Palo Alto areas between February and May 1911. Later that year he published an account of his initial impressions of the scale: The results suggested that it was a feasible tool but that certain tests needed to be assigned to different ages (Terman 1911). He also thought it would be useful to add a number of other tests, including one on the interpretation of fables that he had devised in his doctoral research several years before. Accordingly, Terman and his colleagues obtained data on these additional tests from the same population of children.

They published the results of the project in a series of four papers that culminated in a revision and extension of Binet and Simon's scale but also suggested ways in which this revision could be yet further developed (Terman and Childs 1912a, 1912b, 1912c, 1912d). Huey was initially used as the chief consultant on the project, but he died in 1913 and was replaced by Henry Goddard (Minton 1988:57). Terman then completed the final version of the scale and arranged for a team of research assistants (Grace Lyman, George Ordahl, Louise Ordahl, Neva Galbreath, and Wilford Talbert) to administer the scale to a thousand children. They published the results in 1915 and described their new instrument as "the Stanford revision of the Binet-Simon scale" (Terman et al. 1915).

The following year Terman published a detailed account of the new scale, setting it in the context of the wider literature on intelligence testing and giving advice and instructions on its proper use. The new scale became generally known simply as the "Stanford-Binet scale," and it was probably the most widely used intelligence test for children between the two world wars. From 1927 Terman worked with another colleague, Maude Amanda Merrill, on a further revision and extension of the scale; this was published in 1937 and was used throughout the second half of the twentieth century (Terman and Merrill 1937). Thus it was Terman's version of Binet and Simon's scale, not Goddard's, that had a lasting impact on mental testing. Even so, like many researchers of the time, Terman shared Goddard's assumptions about the nature of intelligence.

First, although Terman had earlier believed that intelligence was a collection of diverse capabilities, he was influenced by Goddard and other researchers to adopt Spearman's (1904) view that it was a single trait (Minton 1988:49). Second, although Binet and Simon (1905b) had explicitly warned that their scale did not provide a formal measure of intelligence, Terman and Child described it as a "measuring scale of intelligence" (1912:61). Elizabeth Kite used the same phrase in her own translation, which Goddard endorsed (Binet and Simon 1916:40, 275). Third, in common with Goddard, Terman believed that intelligence was determined largely by inheritance rather than by upbringing or environment. (Even so, Terman believed that he himself was an exception to this rule. As he commented in his autobiography, "I know of nothing in my ancestry that would have led anyone to predict for me an intellectual career" [Terman 1930:298].)

The implication was that mental deficiency also was determined largely by inheritance rather than by upbringing or environment. Moreover, for both Goddard and Terman a commitment to hereditarian views about the nature of human intelligence extended to an active endorsement of the eugenics movement. Terman focused on reducing opportunities for reproduction among the feeble-minded people who were already in the United States:

> It is safe to predict that in the near future intelligence tests will bring tens of thousands of . . . high-grade defectives under the surveillance and protection of society. This will ultimately result in curtailing the reproduction of feeble-mindedness and in the elimination of an enormous amount of crime, pauperism, and industrial inefficiency.
>
> (Terman 1916:6–7)

> If we would preserve our state for a class of people worthy to possess it, we must prevent, as far as possible, the propagation of mental degenerates. . . . The one hopeful method of curtailing the increasing spawn of degeneracy is to provide additional care for our higher-grade defectives during the reproductive period.
>
> (Terman 1917:165)

However, it was Goddard who took the lead in arguing that Binet and Simon's tests could be administered to emigrants at Ellis Island to establish how successful the physicians were in identifying those who were mentally deficient. He first made this proposal in May 1912, only a few days before Howard Knox joined the team of physicians there.

5

AT ELLIS ISLAND

When Howard Knox was appointed to the Public Health and Marine Hospital Service in April 1912, he gave up his general practice in Sheffield, Massachusetts, and he, Gladys, and their daughter, Dorothea, moved to a new home
in the neighborhood of Tompkinsville in the northeastern part of the Borough of
Richmond. The borough encompassed the whole of Staten Island (and indeed
was renamed the Borough of Staten Island in 1975). Today the area is part of the
New York metropolis. However, when Knox and his family moved there, it was a
very different environment. To begin with, according to the 1910 census, the population of the Borough of Richmond was only 85,969 (compared with 4.77 million
for the city of New York as a whole). A roughly contemporary source described
Richmond thus:

> The population of the island is largely collected in a series of villages which lie
> along the coast—New Brighton, West Brighton, Port Richmond, and Mariners
> Harbor on the north; Tompkinsville, Stapleton, Clifton, Rosebank, Fort Wads-
> worth, and South Beach on the east; and Tottenville on the southwest shore. The
> villages which lie along the north and northeast shore are in reality continuous
> and form one unit of population. The interior of the island contains a few small
> hamlets but for the most part is essentially rural. . . .
>
> Staten Island is to a great extent a residential section. Even in the villages
> most people live in detached houses. Apartment houses and tenements are

rare. There are spots in some of the villages where considerable congestion oc-
curs and where the population live under poor sanitary conditions. Outside of
the villages the conditions of life are practically rural.

(Lavinder, Freeman, and Frost 1918:138–39)

Knox's appointment to the Public Health Service (as it was renamed in August
1912) was noted in the 1914 edition of the *American Medical Directory*, where he is
shown as a Fellow of the American Medical Association and a member of affili-
ated societies at the state and county level, specializing in neurology and psychiatry (American Medical Association 1914:1034).

His first few months at Ellis Island seem to have been fairly uneventful. In October the surgeon general of the Public Health Service wrote to all commissioned
officers to say that "the Secretary [of the treasury] wishes to have published, for
the use of the public, articles relevant to hygiene and the public health." Each
officer was asked to nominate three subjects on which he would write, although
only articles selected by the surgeon general would be published. Knox suggested
the following titles:

"Human Carriers of Disease"
"Fingers, Food and Flies"
"The Role Played by Milk in the Transmission of Disease"

There is no evidence that these articles were ever written. Indeed, it quickly
transpired that more pressing issues needed to be addressed if Knox and his colleagues were to venture into print.

MENTAL DEFICIENCY AMONG EMIGRANTS

By 1910, there was widespread concern in the United States that the immigration authorities were failing to prevent mentally defective people from entering
the country. To try to respond to this concern, toward the end of that year the
immigration officials at Ellis Island invited the superintendent of the New Jersey
Training School, Edward Johnstone, and his director of research, Henry Goddard,
to visit the immigration station and advise them on current practices (Zenderland 1998:266). As Goddard subsequently recalled, they were specifically asked
"to see if we could offer any suggestion as to how the service could be improved
in the direction of recognizing and detaining more of the mental defectives"
(1912b:110). Johnstone and Goddard spent a day at Ellis Island early in 1911, but
they were unable to offer any constructive suggestions:

At the end of the day we both felt ourselves overwhelmed by the size of the problem and the general situation. The physicians seemed to be doing wonderful work in the recognition of physical defect and insanity. The number of immigrants passing thru was so vast; the methods then known of detecting mental deficiency were so slow and cumbersome that it seemed hopeless to make any improvement in the method and while we felt sure that from a statistical standpoint, there must be many defectives who were passing thru, yet we saw no way in which it could be stopped without enormous outlay on the part of the government.

(110)

The admission of mentally deficient immigrants also came to be of interest to the State Charities Aid Association. This organization had been established in 1872 to coordinate the activities of public charities in the state of New York. Initially, the association had focused on conditions in county poorhouses, but since 1900 it had been concerned with conditions for the care of people who were mentally ill. In 1906 Homer Folks, the secretary of the association, had submitted to the surgeon general of the Public Health and Marine Hospital Service recommendations regarding the detention and deportation of insane emigrants at Ellis Island. This broadened to include a concern about the identification of both insane and mentally defective emigrants. The board of managers of the association adopted the following resolution at a meeting on February 16, 1912:

1. WHEREAS, It has been shown by the State Commission in Lunacy that there are at the present time 8,000 aliens, one fourth of all the insane supported at public expense in the New York State Hospitals; the support of these aliens costing the State approximately $2,000,000 annually; and

2. WHEREAS, It has been shown that insanity, feeble-mindedness and other mental defects prevail to a very great degree in recent immigrants resulting in their becoming public dependents; and

3. WHEREAS, It is more humane as well as more effective to reject insane and mentally defective immigrants at the time of their arrival than to deport them after they have gained a residence in this country and have brought their families here; and

4. WHEREAS, The federal statutes contemplate the exclusion of insane and mentally defective immigrants although the facilities for the mental examination of arriving immigrants are inadequate, and the safeguards for the humane care of those deported are insufficient; therefore be it

RESOLVED, by the BOARD OF MANAGERS OF THE STATE CHARITIES AID ASSOCIATION that Congress be urged to provide for the mental examination of arriving immigrants by physicians trained in the diagnosis of insanity and mental defect; for adequate facilities for the detention and examination of immigrants in whom insanity or mental defect are suspected; and for the safe and humane return to their own homes of those whom it is necessary to exclude.

("Resolutions" 1912)

As a result of Goddard's visit to Ellis Island, the commissioner for immigration asked him for evidence of how many mentally deficient emigrants were escaping detection. Goddard considered how many children at the Vineland Training School and other institutions had been born abroad, and he published his findings in October 1912. First, he outlined his own position:

> There seems to be a rather prevalent opinion that an undue percentage of the immigrants are mentally defective or, to put it the other way, an unduly large percentage of our mental defectives have come from foreign countries. In the opinion of the writer this is grossly overestimated and the actual number, if it could be obtained, would be found to be far less than is supposed. Of three large families of defectives in three different sections of the State which we have investigated at Vineland, neither one is made up of recent immigrants. The Kallikak family, an account of which has just been published, is of good English stock of the Colonial period. The nameless feeble-minded girl who brought the feeble-mindedness into the family is not referred to anywhere as being a foreigner. She may have been one of the class that was indentured to this country in Colonial times.
>
> (Goddard 1912c:91)

Goddard then asked the superintendents of other institutions how many of their charges had been born outside the United States. He obtained data from sixteen institutions (including his own) that housed a total of 11,292 individuals. The country of birth was not known in the case of 263 individuals, leaving "a trifle over 11,000. Of these 11,000 inmates the total number who were foreign born was 508, or about 4½ percent., a surprisingly small number as it seems to the writer. When we consider that many of these admissions are for quite a large number of years, so that this 508 may be all of the aliens that have gotten into the institutions in the past ten years" (94). As Leila Zenderland (1998:267) observed, of more than three hundred feebleminded individuals at the Vineland Training School, only twenty-two had been born abroad.

Goddard concluded, "From this there is practically nothing on which to base a conclusion that any large proportion of clearly defective persons are escaping our immigration officers and entering the country" (94). He summarized these results in another article that was published shortly afterward and added: "Incomplete as these figures are they are a sufficient answer to that large group of people who are inclined to think of our problem of the feeble-minded as closely related to that of immigration" (Goddard 1912b:109).

Nevertheless, even certain physicians of the Public Health and Marine Hospital Service contributed to the sense of moral panic that schools and hospitals were being swamped by extreme numbers of mentally deficient immigrants. In an article that was published in a popular magazine in April 1912, Assistant Surgeon Alfred Cummings Reed paraphrased the annual report of the commissioner for immigration for the fiscal year ended June 30, 1911:

> He finds that the present medical quarters are not large enough for the proper execution of the laws relating to physical and mental defectives. Expansion to an appropriate size is prevented by the failure of Congress to appropriate the funds requested. He notes the large number of feeble-minded children in the schools of New York City who have passed [through] Ellis Island, and gives as one reason, lack of time and facilities for thorough examination as to mental condition. The result is that the law in this particular is practically a dead letter. According to the law, the feeble-minded as well as idiots and imbeciles are absolutely excluded. It is of vast import that the feeble-minded be detected, not alone because they are predisposed to become public charges, but because they and their offspring contribute so largely to the criminal element. All grades of moral, physical and social degeneracy appear in their descendants, and it is apparent how grave is the social and economic problem involved.
>
> (A. C. Reed 1912a:389)

In May 1912 Henry Goddard returned to Ellis Island with some assistants from the Vineland Training School. He reported later that year that the physicians appeared to have better facilities and that the whole situation was no longer so new and overpowering as it had seemed on their previous visit. They therefore asked to be allowed to carry out an experiment:

> The request was this, that two of the Vineland Laboratory workers should be allowed to spend the day there, the one standing on the line and selecting such of the persons who came thru as seemed to her mentally defective, her sole method of determining this being by her observation of them as they passed, based on her experience with mental defectives at the Institution at Vineland. The other assistant was to be in a nearby room with the Binet tests and without

knowledge of whether the persons sent in were normal or defective, was to apply the test with the aid of an interpreter and see what the result might be. This was done.

In the course of the day, twelve immigrants were selected for testing. Nine of these were picked out because it was thought they were mentally defective. Three were selected as control cases, the opinion of the selector being that they were normal. The result as found by the Binet Scale was as follows:

Of the nine suspects, every one was from at least four to nine years backward. Of the three controls, one was seven years old and tested six; one was nine years old and tested ten; one was adult and went entirely thru all of the Binet tests.

(Goddard 1912b:110)

These results simply showed that Binet and Simon's scale largely confirmed the judgments of Goddard's assistants. His account implied that all the emigrants tested were children, and he did not mention the decisions made about these emigrants by the physicians of the Public Health and Marine Hospital Service. However, he resolved to return to Ellis Island to compare the effectiveness of his own procedures with those of the physicians for an entire week.

Goddard was unable to arrange this third visit until the following September. When he arrived, he found that the conditions for testing emigrants were not the most favorable: "There were many interested observers of every test: the interpreters were unused to the tests and many delays were encountered" (Goddard 1912b:111). Even so, he felt that the results that he obtained were still remarkable:

Forty-four persons were tested. Thirty-three of these were selected by the regular medical inspectors of the department. Of these thirty-three, *fifteen* proved to be defective while *eighteen* were normal. Eleven cases were selected by the Vineland experts in feeblemindedness: of these eleven, *only two* were *not* defective, and one of these had been taken to compare with a very defective sister rather than because the case itself seemed defective.

It is thus seen that of those selected by the physicians less than half were correctly selected, while of those selected by the experts seven-eighths were rightly chosen.

(111; emphasis in the original)

On the last day of their visit Goddard carried out a further experiment. His assistants stood by the line and simply tallied every person whom they considered to be mentally defective, without calling them out of the line. The physicians continued as usual and called out of the line anyone whom they considered to be mentally defective for further investigation.

> The results were, of something more than 1,260 who passed in line, Misses Bell and Mateer [Goddard's assistants] recorded 83 as defective; the physicians selected 18. If the above ratio of correct selections holds, then there were about 72 defectives in that line of whom the physicians recognized about 8—approximately 10 per cent.
>
> It is hardly necessary to say that this is no disparagement of the physicians. They do not pretend to be experts on feeblemindedness. The comparison simply shows what experts can do.
>
> On this basis then, experts would detect at least ten times as many mental defectives as are now recognized by physicians who are experts in other lines but not in feeblemindedness.
>
> (111)

Goddard suggested that his findings shed light on the validity of the judgments made by trained observers and on the validity of Binet and Simon's scale:

> I am now entirely convinced and satisfied that persons trained for a year or two in institutions for the feeble-minded where they have had opportunity to see and study these people as these two assistants have had, can go to Ellis Island or any Immigration Station and standing by the line as the immigrants pass, pick out with marvelous accuracy every case of mental defect in all those who are above the infant age. . . .
>
> One other point was practically settled. The objection and fear had arisen that it would not be possible to give the Binet test by the aid of an interpreter, since in so many cases the value of the tests stands upon the question of being exactly right. . . . There is no doubt that a carefully trained psychologist who was conversant with the principal languages would be the ideal person to make this examination. Nevertheless, even with the non-psychological interpreters whom we used, the results were remarkably satisfactory.
>
> (112–13)

Goddard concluded by proposing that Congress should appropriate the funds to provide for the appointment of six suitable people who would be trained at institutions for mentally deficient people and then be sent to work at Ellis Island. Goddard's studies were reported in detail in an editorial in the January 18 edition of the *Journal of the American Medical Association,* which concluded with a similar call for more resources to "relieve the country of an enormous and continuing burden of expense and responsibility, to say nothing of the deleterious effect of this defective stock on the entire social fabric" ("Problem of the Feeble-minded among Immigrants" 1913:210).

RESPONSE OF THE ELLIS ISLAND PHYSICIANS

Goddard had two different criticisms to make of the Ellis Island physicians. First, their use of diagnosis by inspection was not a reliable means of detecting those emigrants who might be mentally deficient. Second, traditional medical procedures did not provide a reliable way of identifying mental deficiency even in those emigrants who had been detained for individual examination. In 1906 the assistant surgeon general of the Public Health and Marine Hospital Service, Henry Geddings, had been asked to report to the surgeon general regarding the medical examination of emigrants at Ellis Island. His report had provided a detailed account of the procedures of the line inspection, but it was remarkably vague when it came to describing the "critical examinations" that were carried out on those emigrants who had been called out of the line.

At least one contemporary account suggests that these examinations were both arbitrary and unreliable. Archibald Willingham Butt was the military aide at the White House from 1908 until his death in the sinking of the *Titanic* in April 1912. It was Butt's custom to write letters to his sister-in-law describing the events of each day, and on October 18, 1910, he accompanied President William Taft on a visit to Ellis Island, where they were shown around by the commissioner for immigration, William Williams. That evening, he wrote:

> This morning we went to Ellis Island, where we tramped around for several hours—without learning much, I fear, for this cut-and-dried inspection is never very illuminating.
>
> We spent one hour in the room where special cases were being considered. I should hate, myself, to be forced to decide whether immigrants should be deported or whether some members of a family should be admitted or sent back. But I believe I would be able to do it with more intelligence than was shown this morning. One incident was very amusing. A Welshman with his seventeen-year-old daughter and five small children were brought in. He had a slight hernia, and it was therefore recommended that he be returned. The pathetic picture of the young girl taking care of all these young brothers and sisters rather appealed to the President. But the Commissioner, in order to make his case good, proceeded to ask a lot of stock questions to indicate that the immigrant was too ignorant

to be admitted even if he had sound health. He asked him if he knew what form of government we lived under, and the immigrant said he did not know. He then asked him if it was a monarchical form, to which he also got an ignorant reply. The President, evidently thinking that even the majority of Americans did not know what "monarchical" meant, began to interrogate the immigrant himself, and the first question was:

"Do you know who is the chief of this country?"

And the reply was promptly given: "The President."

"Do you know who the President is?" asked the President.

"Yes sir; Mr. Taft," answered the immigrant.

The President then turned, laughing, to the Commissioner, and said:

"Mr. Commissioner, you cannot convince me of this man's total ignorance. He seems to know more than a good many Americans I have met. I think you might admit this family."

(Butt 1930:548–49)

Consequently, although the physicians at Ellis Island insisted on the validity of diagnosis by inspection as the most appropriate tool for identifying those emigrants who might turn out to be mentally deficient, they were probably not in a strong position when it came to defending the techniques that they used in their follow-up examinations. It is therefore not surprising that they did not dismiss Goddard's approach immediately.

Indeed, in an article published in January 1914, Surgeon Ezra Kimball Sprague mentioned that he had tried out various tests, including both the de Sanctis tests and Binet and Simon's scale, "early in the last fiscal year" (Sprague 1914:466). The fiscal year ran from July 1 to June 30, and this would imply that Sprague was using these tests during the summer of 1912. In fact, it appears to be the same investigation as that described in an article published in the fall of 1912 by Assistant Surgeon Reed:

Under the direction of men specially trained in the diagnosis of mental disorders, a unique investigation is being conducted at Ellis Island, which promises a means of recognizing feeblemindedness in aliens, where now such recognition is attained with the greatest difficulty. The principle employed is that of the well-known Binet-Simon system of tests for intelligence, or of tests for mental age as compared to physical age, which in a modified form has been so successfully used by Dr. Goddard. Each group of tests furnishes an index of the mental status of the normal child of a corresponding age. Those who fall below the test group of appropriate age, are rated as feebleminded, imbecile or idiot, according to the degree of deficiency.

This system is not applicable to immigrants because of the different conditions under which they have lived, which vary greatly with different races. Hence it is sought to determine a standard of normal intelligence for the adult of each race. The investigation is being conducted on normal illiterates only, in order to establish a minimum standard of normal-mindedness for each race. Obviously all who fall below this standard of mentality can be classed as defective.

(A. C. Reed 1912b:542)

Despite having been so scathing about his colleagues only a few months before, when he had described the law on the exclusion of feebleminded emigrants as "practically a dead letter" (1912a:389), Reed was now almost ecstatic in his praise for their efforts:

There is very thoro [sic] routine examination of all cases which on the primary inspection show any evidence or suspicion of defect or disease. . . . Officers are detailed from time to time for special courses of instruction at various large institutions especially for the study of insanity and mental defectiveness. . . . As the sole national agency operating to combat epidemic disease, and to promote preventive medicine, the Public Health Service stands high in the medical profession, and deserves its hearty sympathy and support.

(544)

Nevertheless, the initial piloting of Binet and Simon's scale at Ellis Island does not seem to have been successful. It threw up problems that were not simply about the adequacy of the norms (the standards or levels of performance that were supposed to be typical of normal children) but about the appropriateness of the tests themselves.

One week before the editorial about Goddard's investigations, an article by Assistant Surgeon Howard Knox appeared in the *Journal of the American Medical Association*. He began by referring to Binet's criteria for classifying people as idiots, imbeciles, or feebleminded, except that he used the term *moron* that had been introduced by Goddard. However, Knox then insisted that it would be "manifestly absurd" to use tests such as Binet's with uneducated people, because these tests assumed a particular culture and language. Apparently with Goddard in mind, he continued: "To the uninitiated using routine tests for defectives nearly all the peasants from certain European countries appear to be of the moron type: but of course this is a fallacy. If these peasants are questioned about conditions existing in the land from which they come most of them will show average intelligence" (Knox 1913a:105).

In the course of the same article Knox also claimed that both physical and mental defects were inherited according to Mendelian principles:

A drop of ink in a barrel of water does not make ink, but the greater the number of drops of ink in that barrel of water the more inky it becomes. Likewise every defective, both mental and physical, that enters this country or is born in it is another drop of ink and may become a parent who will fulfill one of the many theoretical expectations of Mendel and will surely produce defective progeny. . . .

With special reference to the examination of immigrants it may be said that the detection of morons or higher defectives is of vastly more importance than the detection of the insane, for the reason that the insane or potentially insane will soon be recognized after landing and placed in an asylum or deported so that in either event they cannot propagate and affect the race adversely. On the other hand, the moron will not be recognized and will immediately start a line of defectives whose progeny, like the brook, will go on forever, branching off here in an imbecile and there in an epileptic, costing the country millions of dollars in court fees and incarceration expenses.

(105–106)

Clearly, Knox shared the views about intelligence and mental deficiency that were prevalent at the time among politicians, professionals, and the public.

Knox's article in the *Journal of the American Medical Association* was immediately followed by a complementary piece by Assistant Surgeon Carlisle P. Knight. Knight agreed that the identification of mentally deficient emigrants was a major social problem: "Census statistics show that 30 per cent. of the feeble-minded children in the general population of the United States are the progeny of aliens or naturalized citizens. The financial outlay for caring for this class of people is enormous" (1913:106). Referring to the classification of mentally deficient people as idiots, imbeciles, and feebleminded, he continued:

The idiot is a type which is usually easily recognized. The physician with the ordinary medical training or the layman will detect one when seen. . . . The imbecile is a step further up the scale from the idiot, ranging from the low-grade imbecile nearest the idiot through degrees to the high-grade imbecile in whom there is some power for receptive education. The stigmata of degeneration in these cases are generally well marked, the articulate speech being defective and the vocabulary limited. The hardest problem with which we have to deal is that class of feeble-minded commonly known as the "school dunce," with feeble attentive powers, unable to give his attention to abstract matters from which to build up the concrete and being easily confused even with the simplest questions.

(Knight 1913:106–7)

Nevertheless, the experience and expertise of the physician on line inspection would enable him to make these difficult judgments:

> The duties of the medical officer detailed for the medical inspection of immigrants make of him an expert in the system of diagnosis by inspection, in that he must decide quickly the advisability of holding a case for further physical diagnosis or mental observation. An officer with experience, becoming familiar with the different races, studying closely their characteristics, knowing something of their language, can tell at a glance the abnormal from the normal as they pass him on the line, on being presented for examination. . . . As the person approaches, the gait, stature and expression are quickly noted so that by the time he is ready to engage in conversation with the alien, the medical inspector's general impressions have been made and so within a few seconds he is able to determine the course to pursue in either passing or detaining.

(107)

In contrast, a physician without proper training and experience "would be absolutely useless in the detection of the feeble-minded on primary inspection, because his vision is too finely focused on the refinements of diagnosis to give sufficient perspective in eliminating in a general way the defectives from the normal and also because of his lack of knowledge of the racial characteristics" (Knight 1913:107). In short, the main response of the physicians of the Public Health Service to Goddard's findings at Ellis Island was to explain the difficulty of the task facing them but also to insist on the importance of traditional diagnostic procedures.

Nevertheless, as a defense of working practices at Ellis Island, the impact of these pieces was considerably weakened by an editorial that followed them in the same issue of the *Journal of the American Medical Association*. The journal had regularly published editorials expressing concern about the admission of insane and feebleminded emigrants (see Zenderland 1998:420). On this occasion the author criticized Goddard's (1912c) finding that in sixteen institutions for mentally deficient people only about 4.5 percent had been born abroad; the *JAMA* writer claimed that, according to other surveys, the proportion of feebleminded people in such institutions was four times higher among people born abroad than among those born in the United States. The author continued: "Since the examining physicians at Ellis Island with manifestly inadequate facilities and by the most cursory sort of inspection are able to pick out on an average from forty to fifty cases of mental defect each month, it seems highly probable that large numbers of the higher grades of mental defect must pass unobserved" ("Feeble-mindedness and Immigration," 1913:129)

Even the chief medical officer at Ellis Island, Senior Surgeon George W. Stoner, wrote an article in defense of practices at the immigration station; it appeared in the New York Medical Journal in May 1913. First, he claimed that many physicians had visited to find out about the work at Ellis Island and that "the expressions and comments of such visitors are usually very complimentary to the medical officers thus engaged." He acknowledged "that the results might be improved, that among the thousands arriving every day there are probably many more physically and mentally diseased or defective persons than can possibly be detected by the necessarily hurried examination that must be given to most of them, on the line." However, he argued that the solution would be for the Public Health Service to increase the number of officers available for duty (Stoner 1913:957).

Stoner went on to claim that the alleged cost of supporting insane or mentally deficient immigrants in state institutions was being exaggerated by people who resented the federal government's having responsibility for the medical inspection of emigrants. In any case, he argued, many of these immigrants had become insane three years or more after their entry into the United States, and under the relevant immigration laws they were therefore not liable to be deported. He also suggested that immigrants with mental diseases were more likely to come to the attention of public institutions than were people born in the United States, because the latter were often looked after in their communities by their families or friends.

Stoner observed that the New York State Commission in Lunacy had appointed a board of inspectors who had visited Ellis Island on a number of occasions and were always "very free in expressing themselves to the effect that everything seemed to be going on very well" (958). Conversely, physicians from Ellis Island were often called on to support state or municipal work. He concluded that a more careful inquiry into practices at Ellis Island "would probably convince any fairminded person that remarkably good work is being done there, in behalf of the immigrant as well as for the good of the State" (960). Even so, the Treasury Department needed extra funds so that it could supply the necessary number of medical officers and so that the Department of Commerce and Labor could supply a sufficient number of interpreters.

A CHANGE OF LEADERSHIP

Unfortunately, these articles did little to quell the public and professional disquiet concerning the admission of mentally deficient emigrants. Although Assistant Surgeon Alfred Reed had previously welcomed the attempt to test Binet and Simon's scale at Ellis Island, he continued to write articles criticizing the administration there. In the summer of 1913, for example, he argued that the issue was not being addressed because "the staff is too small and the administrative policy is passive, rather than aggressive, reactionary rather than progressive" (A. C. Reed 1913:172). Indeed, according to Elizabeth Yew (1980), a physician at the Cabrini Medical Center in New York City who researched the medical inspection of emigrants at Ellis Island, Reed eventually resigned his commission with the Public Health Service in protest.

Assistant Surgeon Thomas William Salmon had been removed from his post at Ellis Island in 1906 for insubordination. His subsequent conduct at the Marine Hospital at Chelsea, Massachusetts, was evidently satisfactory, and he was promoted to the rank of passed assistant surgeon. Moreover, in 1911 the New York State Commission in Lunacy asked that Salmon be given leave of absence to serve as the chief medical examiner of the Board of Alienists (Bond 1950:39). (Alienist is an old word for psychiatrist. It derives from the sense of alienation as "derangement of the mental faculties" and has no direct link with the sense of alien as foreign.) The role of the State Commission was to ensure that legislation regarding the care and treatment of mental patients was being observed and to make recommendations concerning the management of asylums.

Salmon was given the task of investigating the numbers of insane immigrants who were to be found in New York hospitals. In his subsequent report he argued that the facilities at Ellis Island should be improved; in particular, there should be adequate provision of detention wards and interpreters, and medical officers who were specially trained in psychiatry should be detailed at the main ports of entry into the United States. He also suggested that the medical inspection of emigrants could be carried out instead either at the ports of embarkation or while the emigrants were aboard their ships. Nevertheless, he also argued for a better standard of care for patients who were deported and those who returned voluntarily (Salmon 1911).

As a result of this work, in February 1913 Salmon was granted a further leave of absence from the Public Health Service to carry out a national survey of mental health provision for the National Committee for Mental Hygiene. This organization had been set up by Clifford Whittingham Beers in 1909 to promote the prevention of mental illness and improved standards of care for mentally ill patients. (It became the National Association of Mental Health in 1950, and today it is known as Mental Health America.) Salmon's work on behalf of the national committee proved so valuable in enhancing the public awareness of mental illness that it continued to employ him for several years with the support of grants from the Rockefeller Foundation (Bond 1950:50–59).

Salmon contributed a chapter about immigration to a book on the treatment of nervous and mental diseases, and he took the opportunity to express concern about the entry of mentally deficient immigrants. Even with the best facilities, Salmon maintained, "many mentally defective immigrants must escape detection in the examination at the ports of entry." As a result, *nearly all the mentally defective children in the ungraded classes in New York City are the children of immigrants*" (Salmon 1913a:275–76; emphasis in the original). He concluded by advocating increased resources for identifying mental disease and mental defects at the ports of entry.

Salmon also contributed a chapter on mental diseases to a book on preventive medicine and hygiene. Having considered a variety of other factors in the causation of insanity, he turned to the topic of immigration. Here he insisted that "no measures for the prevention of insanity which have yet been suggested can prove so efficacious as artificial selection of accretions to our population" (Salmon 1913b:307), and he claimed that existing immigration laws should be enforced and tightened. However, he also pointed out that immigration itself should be seen as a likely cause of mental disease and distress in large numbers of immigrants:

These crowds of immigrants, 30 per cent. of the adults illiterate and less than 20 per cent. with any trade, are, practically without mental examination or selection, projected into our most congested centers of population, to bear, during their first year in America, as severe stress as any group of population can be called upon to endure. One result is that they flood our hospitals for the insane. . . .

We have been far too careless of the welfare of recently landed immigrants. There seems to be a general impression that, however unsanitary their surroundings or however heavy may be the burdens placed on them, immigrants are, in some way, fitted for such hardships, either by nature or through previous experiences in their homes. Of course, this assumption is wholly without justification, and it is time that the social, economic, physical, and moral welfare of these newcomers be given the earnest attention of the federal and state governments and of societies and individuals. By so doing something may be done to lessen the terrible prevalence of mental disease in this large group of our population.

(307, 308)

A particularly blunt attack on the leadership at Ellis Island came in a letter from Homer Folks, the secretary of the State Charities Aid Association. On March 14, 1913, Folks wrote to William Gibbs McAdoo, who had been appointed secretary of the treasury in the administration of the newly elected president, Woodrow Wilson. After congratulating McAdoo on his new appointment, Folks turned to the identification of mentally defective emigrants at Ellis Island:

> It seems an extraordinary fact, but it nevertheless seems to be indubitably true, that the medical service at Ellis Island has consistently and persistently, though often subtly and invisibly, opposed the establishment of any adequate system for the detection of insane and feebleminded immigrants, and when by sheer force of public opinion specialists in mental diseases have been secured, their work has been so circumscribed with difficulties, and hedged about, that it has been only partially effective. My experience has lead [sic] me to believe that the one man directly responsible for this is the medical head of the Ellis Island medical service, Dr. Stoner. He may be professionally competent, may have many admirable qualities as to which I am not informed, nor do I attempt to offer any explanation of why he has pursued this policy. I only say that it seems to be absolutely clear that this has been his policy.
>
> Dr. Stoner's assignment to Ellis Island is, I believe, about to expire, and the question of his reassignment for another term of years in the ordinary course of events would, I believe, be acted upon almost immediately. I do not write to ask you to accept the view of the case I have stated above, but to ask you to take steps to see to it that the reassignment is not made until you can assure yourself, in whatever way you may deem wise, that the best interests of the Ellis Island Service indicate such a reassignment. The State Hospital Commission of the State of New York has, I believe, whole areas of information bearing on this matter. Some of the men who have had special training in mental disease and who have served on Ellis Island might state their experiences. . . . New York State is being asked to spend $11,000,000.00 this year in the care of the insane. I am confident that the reduction from this sum that would have resulted from an adequate inspection of immigrants for mental defect, which would have been in operation but for Dr. Stoner, would be reckoned by the millions and not by hundreds of thousands.
>
> (Folks 1913)

McAdoo sought the advice of the surgeon general of the Public Health Service, Rupert Blue. Blue had been appointed by President Taft in November 1911, and he had a reputation as an able and effective leader. (In 1916 he was the only surgeon general ever to be elected president of the American Medical Association; see F. Mullan 1989:58.) In his reply dated March 21, Blue observed that Stoner had just completed three terms of service at Ellis Island, having been the chief medical officer since 1901. In the normal course of events officers were assigned for further terms of service if it were deemed to be in the service's interest. However, Blue reported, it had already been determined that Stoner would be transferred elsewhere.

It took a few weeks to find Stoner's replacement, so McAdoo waited until May 9 to respond to Folks's letter. He was then able to report that, on the recommendation of the surgeon general, orders had been signed that day by which Stoner would be taking charge of the Marine Hospital at Stapleton on Staten Island. (In an ironic coincidence Stoner's paper defending the practices of the medical staff at Ellis Island was published as the lead article in the *New York Medical Journal* the day after he left his post. The position to which he was moved was in fact the one that he had held before his appointment as chief medical officer at Ellis Island, so this was scarcely a promotion. He later worked in the surgeon general's office in Washington, D.C., before retiring to Stapleton in 1931.) McAdoo also reported that Stoner's duties at Ellis Island were being assumed by Surgeon Louis Laval Williams, who had served there as chief administrative officer of the medical division from 1899 to 1901 (Unrau 1984, 2:581–82).

While these events were taking place, Howard Knox was ordered to attend an appraisal meeting at the Public Health Service in Washington, D.C., to review his work during the previous year. He had expected to be transferred to a post in one of the service's laboratories and trained for a research career. Instead, he was temporarily assigned to work in a psychiatric hospital so that he could study mental diseases. He took this to mean that he was likely to be based at Ellis Island for some time. As a relative newcomer to the Public Health Service, he may well have been seen as being more open to new ways of identifying mentally deficient emigrants than his colleagues who had served under Senior Surgeon Stoner.

In the spring of 1913 Goddard obtained funding for a more extensive project at Ellis Island. He sent three assistants and some interpreters to administer the 1908 version of Binet and Simon's scale and a number of other tests to six groups of emigrants who had been passed by the physicians of the Public Health Service. Two groups (consisting of twenty Italians and nineteen Russians) were picked out by Goddard's assistants because they considered them to be feebleminded; and four groups (thirty-five Jews, twenty-two Hungarians, fifty Italians, and forty-five Russians) were picked out because they appeared to be represent average emigrants.

At first, Goddard was not sure how the results of this study should be interpreted. Zenderland (1998:279) notes that Goddard did not mention this study at all in his major work, *Feeble-Mindedness* (Goddard 1914). He did eventually present some of his findings in December 1916 at the annual meeting of the American Psychological Association, where he gave only a tentative conclusion: "The problem is a difficult one on account of the conditions under which the immigrants arrive in this country, but the conclusion seems warranted that mental tests have at least a limited application to the problem and undoubtedly with more study this might be increased until they become fairly satisfactory" (Goddard 1917a:69). Nevertheless, he published a full account the following year (Goddard 1917b).

Assessed according to their performance on Binet and Simon's scale, all but one of the emigrants in the first two groups were judged to be feebleminded. Nevertheless, the same was true of more than four-fifths of the emigrants in the other four groups. Even when he tried out various ways of adjusting the results (for instance, by discounting tasks with which they might not be familiar), the proportion of "average immigrants" identified as mentally deficient seemed remarkably high. Although he emphasized that the study had been based on "six small highly selected groups," he nevertheless concluded: "One can hardly escape the conviction that the intelligence of the average 'third class' immigrant is low, perhaps of moron grade" (243).

Two other aspects of this study are worth mentioning. First, the other tests that he used included three that appeared to depend less on linguistic competence and cultural knowledge. Goddard did not feel that these had been particularly helpful, but the physicians at Ellis Island may have been encouraged to try them out for themselves. I will discuss the results of their endeavors in chapter 6. Second, two years after the immigrants had been assessed, Goddard sent his fieldworkers to try to locate them to see how they were coping despite apparently being feebleminded. Few of them could be found, and even they were generally unwilling to cooperate with the fieldworkers. Goddard nonetheless concluded that they "make good after a fashion" (269).

Finally, Goddard asked whether the high prevalence of mental deficiency in emigrants was the result of heredity or an environmental deprivation. Given his assertions elsewhere about the nature of intelligence and mental deficiency, his conclusion was rather surprising:

We know of no data on this point, but indirectly we may argue that it is far more probable that their condition is due to environment than that it is due to heredity. To mention only two considerations: First, we know that their environment has been poor. It seems able to account for the result. Second, this kind of immigration has been going on for 20 years. . . . If the condition were due to hereditary feeble-mindedness we should properly expect a noticeable increase in the proportion of the feeble-minded of foreign ancestry. This is not the case. Some years ago the writer made a study [(Goddard 1912c)] in which it was shown that only 4½ per cent of inmates of institutions for feeble-minded were of foreign parentage.

(270)

Whether the criticisms of Senior Surgeon Stoner were justified or not, his successor as chief medical officer, Surgeon Williams, took a more active approach in encouraging his physicians to rebut the criticisms of Goddard and others. As I mentioned earlier, these criticisms were twofold: their use of diagnosis by inspection was not a reliable means of detecting emigrants who might be mentally deficient, and traditional medical procedures were not a reliable way of identifying mental deficiency in emigrants who were detained for individual examination.

To address the latter criticism the physicians sought ways of testing intelligence that were more appropriate for use with emigrants than was Binet and Simon's scale. The tests that they constructed are the main focus of this book, and I will discuss them in later chapters. It would, however, be totally impracticable to use these tests in the initial screening of emigrants: this would continue to depend on diagnosis through inspection. Goddard had maintained that his staff at Vineland was more proficient at detecting mentally deficient emigrants because of its greater experience with observing mentally deficient people. However, the physicians at Ellis Island maintained that they were more proficient at detecting mentally deficient emigrants because of their greater experience with observing emigrants. It would be necessary to keep making this argument in the pages of leading medical journals.

Accordingly, in June 1913 Knox published an article in the *New York Medical Journal* entitled, "A Diagnostic Study of the Face." He began by emphasizing his qualifications and experience: "After having scrutinized some fifty thousand faces during the past year, and after having examined the five thousand most interesting of these with some care, I have arrived at the conclusion that in the physiognomy and external anatomy of the face we have a field for diagnostic study that cannot profitably be eliminated from the consideration of any medical, surgical, or mental case" (Knox 1913c:1225). He then presented "the following somewhat heterogeneous group of conditions and diseases [that] present facial signs with considerable regularity":

Nationality, temperament, occupation, sexual relations and habits, sensuality, drug addictions, alcoholism, emotional excitement, loss of sleep, hereditary syphilis, intracranial syphilis, paresis, tabes dorsalis, brain tumor, psychopathic predisposition, psychogenetic disorders, sane and insane paranoiac systems, dementia præcox, epilepsy, hypomania, cyclothymia, paralysis agitans, exophthalmic goitre, hysteria, neurasthenia, melancholia, manic depressive insanity, chorea, hydrocephalus, idiocy, imbecility, feeblemindedness, higher feeblemindedness (moron), moral obliquity, local and other paralyses and atrophies, acromegaly, cretinism, myxedema, osteitis deformans, torticollis, lupus, local epithelioma, and malignant tumors of other parts, herpes zoster, erysipelas, anthrax, glanders, purpura, hemophilia, leprosy, rhachitis, acne, goundou, menstruation, pregnancy, menorrhagia, fatigue, severe pain, exhausting diseases in children, iritis, glaucoma, conjunctivitis, keratitis and its sequelæ, trachoma, recession of the eyeball, psoriasis and other skin diseases, sarcoma of superior maxilla, tetanus, actinomycosis, phosphorus, silver, lead, arsenic, and opium poisoning (chronic poisoning by the first four), acquired and congenital heart disease, simple cardiac hypertrophy, pseudoleucemia, both varieties of true leucemia, chlorosis, pernicious anemia, malaria, Addison's disease, parasitosis, chronic atrophic rhinitis, nasal obstruction, sprue, chronic gastrointestinal diseases, hepatic congestion, cirrhosis and abscess of the liver, cholecystitis and acute catarrhal jaundice, arthritis deformans, rheumatic fever, typhoid fever, scarlet fever, measles and German measles, smallpox, varioloid, varicella, yellow fever, pneumonia, tuberculosis and other febrile affections, atheroma, renal disease, appendicitis, peritonitis, pancreatitis and acute yellow atrophy of the liver, local reaction to irritant cosmetics and applications, such as oil of cade, hernia and weak abdominal walls, fibroid tumors and ovarian cystoma in fair complexioned people, gout, lithemia and intestinal toxic absorption, parasitic affections of the face and scalp, such as ringworm, sycosis barbæ, and favus, and impending death.

(1226)

The rhetorical aim of presenting this huge list was undoubtedly to inspire confidence in the reader that the physicians of the Public Health Service were well equipped to identify a wide range of diseases in emigrants purely by means of "diagnosis through inspection."

At the same time Knox commented that some physical signs could mislead an untrained observer. He described a facial appearance found in certain white people that he called "simian reversion" (that is, reverting to an apelike ancestor). He characterized this as follows: "The nostrils are more or less circular in outline; even though the skin be white, there is usually a certain kinky appearance of the hair, especially over the temporal bones [the temples]" (1227). He illustrated this with a photograph of an emigrant who had a number of other physical blemishes, including malformation of the helix (the fold of skin around the edge of the ear). The photograph's caption went on to say: "This case was selected by a lay worker from a school for the feebleminded as a mental defective. Competent examination revealed the fact that this subject was of normal mental balance, above the adult average for his race, and spoke three languages fluently" (1226).

In 1913 the immigration station at Ellis Island received another new physician, Bernard Glueck. He had graduated from Georgetown University Medical School in Washington, D.C., in 1909 and then spent four years in Washington as a junior physician at the Government Hospital for the Insane. (This had for many years been known colloquially by the name that it was given officially in 1916, St. Elizabeths Hospital.) Glueck was temporarily assigned to work as a psychiatrist at Ellis Island with the rank of acting assistant surgeon, and in October 1913 he published an article about his work there in the *New York Medical Journal*. This showed an astute awareness of the problems involved in the assessment of mentally deficient emigrants.

He began by distinguishing two "modes" of defining intelligence and feeblemindedness: "A social one, having as its criterion the individual's ability for a proper fulfillment of his tasks as a member of a given society, and an artificial one having as its criterion the individual's ability to solve a certain set of artificial problems" (763). He insisted that "primarily any definition of feeblemindedness must be a social one. . . . The feebleminded are individuals who on account of incomplete cerebral development are unable to perform their duties as members of society in the position of life to which they were born" (761). In contrast, an artificial definition ignores the social context:

> Viewed from the standpoint of the average normal intelligence of the American, whole tribes of African savages might easily be considered feebleminded, yet if we consider the situation from the standpoint of [the] social definition of feeblemindedness the average normal individual of these same tribes of savages is able to perform his duties as a member of society in the position of life to which he was born. At best any artificial definition of feeblemindedness can only serve to augment the social one. It can never supplant it. It can only be relied upon when employed within the limits of its usefulness.
>
> (761–62)

By way of example, Glueck focused on the 1908 version of Binet and Simon's scale. He noted that it was originally intended to represent the average intelligence of French children, and he acknowledged that Goddard and others seemed to have been successful in adapting it for use with American children. In contrast, the emigrants who arrived at Ellis Island had come from nearly all parts of the world, so the norms on which it was based were not appropriate:

> Does the Binet-Simon measuring scale of intelligence or its American modification, evolved as these were from French and American children, represent the average normal intelligence of practically the entire human race? Assuredly not. . . . The Binet-Simon scale was never intended to assume such wide spheres of usefulness and application. Binet, to my knowledge, never

stated that it represented anything but the average normal intelligence of the French child.

(762)

Glueck went on to point out that the responsibilities of the physicians at Ellis Island fell into two parts: "The first is the primary picking out of those suspected of being defective, while the second consists in the final diagnostication of those so put aside." The former relied upon the efficiency of diagnosis through line inspection. Existing scales of intelligence were of no use for the latter, but these scales pointed out "the *modus operandi* whereby we might establish some dependable standard by which to measure the immigrant. We must create for these people an artificial environment, with its artificial complexities and problems, and observe what is the average normal way in which the immigrant should solve these problems" (763).

In consultation with Passed Assistant Surgeon Eugene Hagan Mullan, Glueck devised the battery of tests listed in table 5.1, and he set out to collect normative data for these tests (that is, data from normal individuals to establish the standards or levels of performance to be expected in people who were not mentally deficient):

At the outset it was felt that if a correct idea was to be gained of the average normal intelligence of a given race, only such individuals should be tested who were as far as possible free from the benefits of artificial, purposive education. It was the average native ability which was sought. For this reason fifty individuals, who in their outward appearance suggested nothing abnormal, were picked off at random from the inspection line. None of them had ever attended school or knew how to read or write. They were between the ages of eighteen and forty, and, in this instance, of the Polish race.

(764)

Glueck did not explain the significance of choosing Polish emigrants, and he did not mention the language in which the tests were administered. In fact, he had been born in Poland in 1884 and had come to the United States in 1900 (Lebensohn 1973). As a fluent native speaker of Polish, he was able to administer the tests himself, without an interpreter.

Series A consisted of "questions intended to bring out the mental stock of the individual tested"; Series B consisted of "tests of pure intellectual capacity"; Series C consisted of "tests intended to bring out the individual capacity to grasp a rather unusual experience by means of new mental associations"; Series D consisted of "tests of ability to acquire new knowledge"; Series E contained tests of

TABLE 5.1 GLUECK'S SERIES OF TESTS

Series A

1. Number of months in the year
2. Names of the months
3. Number of days in the year
4. Number of days in the week
5. Name the days of the week
6. Number of weeks in a month
7. Name of the capital of native country
8. Name of the ruler of native country
9. Names of native coins and units of currency
10. Number of God's commandments
11. Significance of Easter
12. Ability to tell time by a watch

Series B

1. $5 + 4$
2. $7 + 9$
3. $2 + 3 + 4$
4. $15 + 17$
5. 5×3
6. 4×7
7. $10 - 7$
8. $12 - 5$
9. $18 - 7$
10. What number added to 2 makes 15?
11. Divide twenty apples into four equal parcels.
12 How many legs do three horses have?

Series C

1. Count the days of the week backward.
2. Count backward from twenty to one.

Series D

1. Name of the ship on which passage was made
2. Port of embarkation
3. What force drives the ship?

Series E

1. Name of the current month
2. Date
3. Day of the week

Series F

1. Repetition of four digits
2. Repetition of five digits
3. Repetition of six digits
4. Repetition of seven digits

Series G

1. Give three physical differences between a horse and an ox
2. "Healy" rack puzzle

Source: Glueck 1913:764–66.

orientation; Series F contained tests of recent memory; and Series G contained tests of discriminative ability and the ability to perceive differences in size and form (764). The "Healy" rack puzzle was probably a "form board" test devised by William Healy in which five rectangular blocks had to be fitted into a rectangular frame (see Healy and Fernald 1911:14–15). I will discuss this kind of test in more detail in chapter 6.

5.1 Doctors Howard A. Knox, Charles W. Vogel, Bernard Glueck, Harry Laughlin, and Matthew Gwyn at Ellis Island, ca. 1913. (Courtesy National Archives)

Glueck himself was struck by the tremendous variations in performance that he found: "Here we have fifty individuals who were as near alike in most respects as is possible among human beings. Under circumstances which were as near alike as possible, these individuals were given the same thirty-eight problems for solution, and the results of correct answers varied all the way from eighteen to the full thirty-eight." Although he thought that the choice of tests could be much improved upon, "it is my firm belief that a set of tests could be evolved which would represent, as near as is possible, what the average immigrant of a given race should be able to accomplish mentally, if he is to be considered normal" (766).

Many items in Glueck's series of tests were either taken from or were similar to those in Binet and Simon's scale. Indeed, Series F is more akin to the corresponding task in the 1905 version of their scale, insofar as it consists of a sequence of items of increasing difficulty. Many are tests of specific cultural knowledge, and nearly all rely on language for their administration. Eugene Mullan had encouraged Glueck to use these tests, but the set of tests that Glueck believed might be developed would be of a rather different nature:

The hundreds of thousands of immigrants which come to our shores annually speak an untold number of languages and dialects, and practically the only route through which access may be had to an individual's mentality, language, is closed to the examiner unless he is able to speak the alien's language. Dependence upon interpreters is very undesirable in the carrying out of this work, I am convinced of that. The tests, therefore, should be as far as possible performance tests so as to eliminate to the greatest possible extent the element of language.

(764)

This notion of a "performance test" was to prove central to the work at Ellis Island. It refers to a test that involved the measurement of performance, or overt nonverbal behavior, on the part of the person being examined, as opposed to the recording of her written or spoken responses.

Figure 5.1 shows Howard Knox and some of his colleagues at Ellis Island around the summer of 1913. By this time the physicians had essentially acknowledged Goddard's argument that they needed to use formal tests to assess the intelligence of emigrants, but they had come to realize that the only appropriate instruments would be performance tests that did not rely on competence in spoken English or on specific cultural knowledge. However, the only example of such a test that Glueck had incorporated in his investigation was the "Healy rack puzzle." It was clear that further tests of this sort would need to be devised. In fact, Knox and the other physicians had in the meantime been developing a wide range of performance tests for use at Ellis Island, and in the next chapter I describe the process by which they were developed.

PART III

DEVELOPING THE ELLIS ISLAND TESTS

6

THE ELLIS ISLAND TESTS

H oward Knox (1913a) and Bernard Glueck (1913) had identified two major flaws in the notion of using the scale devised by Alfred Binet and Théodore Simon (1908) to identify mental deficiency among emigrants. On the one hand, the scale was effectively testing knowledge of a particular culture and language, and people from countries with different customs, practices, and languages simply would not possess this knowledge. On the other hand, the only comparative data for assessing whether a particular emigrant was mentally deficient had been obtained from French or American schoolchildren, and these data were wholly inappropriate for determining whether people from other countries were capable of earning their living in the United States.

The second problem could be addressed by obtaining more appropriate comparative data. The physicians at Ellis Island had immediate access to large numbers of emigrants whom they had deemed *not* to be mentally deficient and who might therefore provide them with just such data. However, the first problem was more difficult. They would need to find tasks that did not rely on specific cultural knowledge and tests that could be administered with minimal use of language, ideally by means of pantomime alone on the part of both examiner and examinee. By 1913 some tasks of this nature already had been devised, and these had come to be known as performance tests in that they relied on the measurement of overt performance.

FORM BOARDS

Such tasks already had a long history, although they had initially been used only as devices for training both normal and mentally deficient children rather than as assessment tools. The earliest person who is recorded to have used such a task was a French physician, Jean Marc Gaspard Itard, of the Institution Nationale des Sourds-et-Muets (the National Institution for the Deaf and Dumb) in Paris. In 1798 a boy of about eleven or twelve years was found to be living in the woods in Aveyron, a *département* (administrative area) in southern France. Although he initially resisted attempts to capture him, he was eventually restrained and sent first to local hospitals in Saint-Affrique and then Rodez. A local priest obtained permission for the boy to be sent for evaluation at the Institution Nationale, where he was brought to Itard's attention. The boy had apparently been living in a totally feral state, he seemed to have no command of language, and his behavior was similar to that of children who had been diagnosed as idiots.

The boy became known as *le jeune sauvage de l'Aveyron* or "the wild boy of Aveyron." The director of the Institution Nationale exhibited the boy at learned and scientific gatherings but in other respects did nothing whatsoever to help him. Philippe Pinel, the chief physician at the Salpêtrière Hospital in Paris, declared that the boy was indeed an idiot, which had the practical implication that he was totally ineducable. However, Itard disagreed with this diagnosis; he argued that the boy was simply uneducated and might well be capable of learning new skills and information. To test this hypothesis Itard was allowed to take the boy to live with him and his housekeeper. He named the boy Victor and set up a number of experiments, including the following:

> I attached to a board two feet square three pieces of paper of very distinct forms and of highly contrasting colors. One was circular and red, another triangular and blue, and the third was square and black. I attached nails to the board in the same pattern and pierced holes in the middle of three pieces of cardboard of the same colors and shapes. I placed the pieces of cardboard on top of the corresponding shapes and left them for a few days. I then removed them and presented them to Victor, and he put them back without any difficulty. By turning the board around and thereby changing the order of the shapes, I made sure that these initial results were not just coincidental but the result of genuine comparison.
>
> (Itard 1801:80–81, my translation)

Itard obtained similar results when the three shapes differed in form but not in color and vice versa. Using more shapes and more similar forms and colors led to "some mistakes and signs of uncertainty, but these disappeared after a few days' exercise." Perhaps not surprisingly, "in the end the multiplicity and complications of these little exercises strained his attention and his docility," giving rise to expressions of impatience and fury on Victor's part (82). Itard's results did show that even someone who was mentally deficient and who had no language could acquire new mental associations. Nevertheless, Victor failed to learn any social or practical skills, and after six years he was sent to live in an asylum, where he died in 1828.

In 1837 Itard was asked to look after another child who had been diagnosed as an idiot. Itard considered that he was by this time too old to take on such a task, but he suggested that, if someone else were prepared to do so, he would supervise that person. Édouard Séguin, whose father had studied medicine with Itard, agreed to work with him and learned from Itard about the causes of mental deficiency and the possibility of training mentally deficient people. In 1839 Séguin set up a school for mentally deficient children, and in the 1840s he wrote two books on the education of children who were mentally deficient (Séguin 1843, 1846).

Following the French revolution of 1848, Séguin emigrated to the United States, where he lived until his death in 1880. He anglicized his name to Edward Seguin and helped to establish several schools for mentally deficient children. He advocated the use of physical and mental tasks to develop independence in mentally deficient people (Seguin 1856), and his ideas proved to be highly influential. In 1876 he became the founding president of the Association of Medical Officers of American Institutions for Idiotic and Feeble-Minded Persons (today the American Association on Intellectual and Developmental Disabilities).

During the course of his work Seguin made more permanent versions of the apparatus that Itard had used in seeking to develop Victor's intellectual abilities, and Seguin used these "form boards" in the training of mentally deficient children. According to Reuel Hull Sylvester (1913), who had visited the schools that Seguin established and who had interviewed his widow,

One consists of an inch board about one foot square into the surface of which are cut four circular recesses a half inch deep and varying between an inch and three inches in diameter. Corresponding to these are four circular blocks one inch thick. Board and blocks are soft wood and are not stained or painted. Another Seguin board is of hard wood, is considerably larger than the kind just described and has a dozen variously shaped symmetrical forms. In a third kind the blocks are of light colored wood on one side and of dark colored wood on the other. (2)

Sylvester further reported that Seguin had envisioned and had partly constructed a series of such boards of increasing levels of difficulty, but that Maria Montessori (the Italian physician and psychologist) was the first person to use such devices for training normal children. The boards were indeed incorporated into the Montessori method of education (Montessori 1912:195).

From 1900 to 1902, Joseph Hershey Bair carried out research for a doctoral degree at Columbia University on the acquisition of new skills and how learning new skills interfered with the retention of old ones (Bair 1902). He focused mainly on typewriting skills, but he also used a task similar to Seguin's with children aged two to five. He described the apparatus only in vague terms: "The method used to make this test was to see how many trials were necessary for the child to put ten blocks of various shapes into their respective holes in a board. The blocks and their holes were all about the same size, and no block could be put into any but its own hole. Each block had a handle to it so that the child would always get the right side of the block on the board" (34). His apparatus was subsequently used by Naomi Norsworthy, who from 1901 to 1904 worked toward her doctoral degree at Columbia under the supervision of Edward Lee Thorndike. She called it a block test, and she described the apparatus and test procedure as follows:

A board 42.5 cm. by 30.5 cm. and 2 cm. [16¾ in. by 12 in. by ¾ in.] thick had holes of the shapes shown in Fig. 5 cut in it to a depth of 8 mm. [5/16 in.]. Blocks provided with convenient handles and fitted snugly into these holes were placed beside the board. The child was told to fit each block into its own proper hole as fast as possible, after having watched it done once. A second trial was allowed after a considerable interval. The time taken was noted in seconds.

(Norsworthy 1906:25–26)

An illustration of the apparatus showed outlines of ten shapes in three rows: a regular hexagon, a triangle, and a semicircle; a circle, an oblong, and an elongated hexagon; and a diamond, a regular octagon, an oval, and a square. Norsworthy used the block test in a battery of tasks for assessing mentally deficient children and adults, and she found that most performed less well than normal nine-year-old children.

In 1904 a world's fair was held in St. Louis, Missouri, to commemorate the centennial of the Louisiana Purchase. This was the natural successor to the Great Exhibition that had been held in London in 1851 and a series of subsequent events designed to celebrate European and American industrialism and imperialism (for a detailed account, see Parezo and Fowler 2007). Robert Sessions Woodworth, Thorndike's colleague at Columbia University, was allowed to set up a laboratory on the campus of Washington University in St. Louis for the purpose of administering a variety of perceptual and mental tests to fairgoers. The fair ran from April 30 to December 1, and during that time about eleven hundred people were tested. The fair included the Congress of Races, which featured displays by many different national and ethnic groups, and Woodworth focused on collecting data from these different groups in order to compare performance across people from different races. He published a brief summary of the tests and the main findings some years later (Woodworth 1910; see also Benjamin 2004).

Woodworth suggested that "two important features of intelligent action are quickness in seizing the key to a novel situation, and firmness in limiting activity to the right direction, and suppressing acts which are obviously useless for the purpose in hand." He went on to describe a simple test that called for these qualities and that he described as "the so-called 'form test'":

> There are a number of blocks of different shapes, and a board with holes to match the blocks. The blocks and board are placed before a person, and he is told to put the blocks in the holes in the shortest possible time. The key to the situation is here the matching of blocks and holes by their shape; and the part of intelligence is to hold firmly to this obvious necessity, wasting no time in trying to force a round block into a square hole. The demand on intelligence certainly seems slight enough; and the test would probably not differentiate between a Newton and you or me; but it does suffice to catch the feebleminded, the young child, or the chimpanzee, as any of these is likely to fail altogether, or at least to waste much time in random moves and vain efforts.
>
> (180–81)

From this vague description it is not possible to tell where Woodworth obtained his board, although it would clearly have been convenient for him to have used Bair's apparatus.

Henry Goddard (1912d) constructed an apparatus similar to Bair's for use at the Vineland Training School, but he introduced a number of modifications:

His board was a little larger (twenty inches by fourteen inches by one inch).

He replaced the hexagon and the octagon with a five-pointed star and a cross.

He changed the proportions of the blocks so that no block could be fitted into the wrong recess.

He used blocks that were twice as deep as the recesses, which enabled him to dispense with the handles that Bair had used.

This apparatus became variously known as the Seguin Form Board, the Seguin-Goddard Form Board, and the Vineland Form Board. Figure 6.1 shows an example of this form board subsequently used by Howard Knox at Ellis Island.

At the University of Pennsylvania Edwin Burket Twitmyer devised a more elaborate version of Goddard's apparatus in which the order of the blocks was reversed. This apparatus was used by one of his students, Reuel Sylvester (1913), in a detailed experimental analysis of the form board test as used with both normal and mentally deficient children. Sylvester proposed a standard procedure

6.1 The Seguin Form Board. (Courtesy William H. Whaley, M.D.)

for administering the test, and he made an interesting observation: "Form board time records do not correlate well with Binet Test results, children who are considerably retarded according to the Binet scale usually being more successful at the form board test than are normal children of the corresponding Binet age" (54). Even though Sylvester was responsible for standardizing the procedure for administering the Seguin Form Board, it is Goddard's apparatus and not Sylvester's that has been used in research and practice ever since, notably in the Tactual Performance Test of the Halstead-Reitan Neuropsychological Test Battery (Reitan 1966).

PICTURE FORM BOARDS AND CONSTRUCTION TESTS

There were other circumstances in which performance tests seemed to be more appropriate than conventional verbal tests. William Healy was born in the United Kingdom, and his family emigrated to the United States while he was a child. He graduated from Harvard and then obtained his degree in medicine at Rush Medical College in Chicago in 1900. After five years of general practice in Chicago, he studied neurology and psychiatry in Vienna, Berlin, and London. In 1909 he was appointed director of the new Juvenile Psychopathic Institute (now the Institute for Juvenile Research) in Chicago.

Healy argued that many attempts to treat juvenile delinquents were unsuccessful because they did not take account of the offenders' mental capabilities (Healy 1910). However, many of the children and young people that Healy came across in his work had little formal education and only a poor grasp of English. Indeed, some came from homes where English was not spoken, and others had only limited language skills because they were deaf. The mental capability of these individuals would need to be assessed in ways that avoided the use of language as far as possible.

Healy appointed as his assistant Grace Maxwell Fernald, who had completed her doctoral degree at the University of Chicago in 1907. They set about the task of compiling a collection of tests that could be used with the diverse population that they encountered (Healy and Fernald 1911). First, they thought that form boards of the sort devised by Seguin could be made more interesting, and thus more motivating, if they were based on pictures of real-life scenes. They devised three such picture form boards (11–13). For instance, one was a jigsaw based on a picture of a mare and her foal taken from a child's picture book. Figure 6.2 shows an example later used by Howard Knox at Ellis Island. (The actual picture was

6.2 The Mare-and-Foal Picture Form Board.

(Courtesy William H. Whaley, M.D.)

6.3 Healy and Fernald's Construction Puzzle (A).
(Courtesy William H. Whaley, M.D.)

roughly eight inches by eleven inches and was colered.) Some pieces were taken from arbitrary areas of the picture, but other pieces followed the natural lines of the two animals, and hence the examinees could be guided by both the shapes of the pieces and the fragments of the scene that they contained. Healy and Fernald noted that by far the most common difficulty encountered by their examinees was that of fitting the two right-angled triangles together to make the equilateral triangle in the top left-hand corner.

Next, Healy and Fernald presented two construction puzzles. In the first the examinee had to fit five rectangular pieces into a rectangular frame whose internal dimensions were four inches by three inches. Figure 6.3 shows an example

subsequently used by Howard Knox at Ellis Island. Whereas Goddard had adjusted the size of the blocks in his form board to ensure that they would not
fit into the wrong recesses, Healy and Fernald designed this puzzle so that the
pieces were partially interchangeable. As they commented, "The significance
of the results obtained largely hinges upon this interchangeableness. This test
brings out perception of relationships of form and also the individual's method
of mental procedure for the given task—particularly his ability to profit by the
experience of repeated trials, in contradistinction to the peculiar repetition of
impossibilities characteristic of the subnormal and feeble-minded groups" (14–
15). Healy and Fernald reported that most twelve-year-olds could complete this
puzzle in two minutes. They called it Construction Puzzle (A), but it became more
generally known as the Healy Puzzle "A" or the Healy Frame Test.

In their second construction puzzle both circular and semicircular pieces and
rectangular pieces with square or rounded ends had to be fitted into recesses
in a board. Figure 6.4 shows an example subsequently used by Howard Knox at

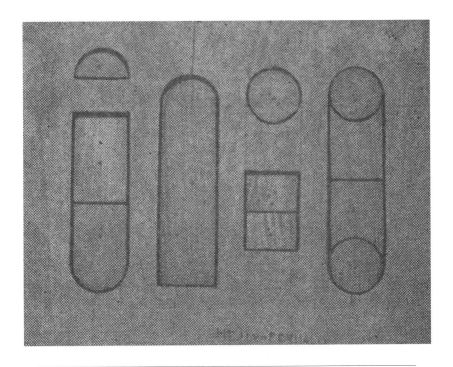

6.4 Healy and Fernald's Construction Puzzle (B), as depicted in Knox's
article in the January 9, 1915, issue of *Scientific American*.

Ellis Island. All the pieces were one and three-eighths inches wide; the spaces with only one rounded end were five inches long; and the rectangle was two inches long. Once again, the puzzle was designed so that the pieces were partly interchangeable. Healy and Fernald reported that most twelve-year-olds could complete the puzzle in three minutes but that their choice of strategy was more informative than the time that they required to complete it. They called this Construction Puzzle (B), although, since Fernald was responsible for the design, it is sometimes called the Fernald Test.

Healy and Fernald described a number of other tests, including mechanical puzzle boxes; remembering pictures and geometric figures; learning associations between numbers and symbols; remembering a short text; and tests of writing, arithmetic, and motor coordination. However, their picture form boards and construction puzzles are of most relevance to the present discussion. Surgeon Ezra Sprague had tried out various tests at Ellis Island during the summer of 1912. In addition to the de Sanctis tests and Binet and Simon's scale, he used the Seguin Form Board and Healy and Fernald's construction puzzles (see Sprague 1914). Moreover, in the summer of 1913 Bernard Glueck had constructed a battery of tests, including what he called the "Healy" rack puzzle (Glueck 1913), which was probably the Healy Frame Test.

In January 1914 Surgeon Matthew Kemp Gwyn published a short article in the *Medical Record* reporting on the use of Healy and Fernald's tests at Ellis Island:

> A great deal of work has been done during the past two years in detecting the feebleminded among aliens arriving at Ellis Island. The Simon-Binet tests were tried out but found to be impractical on a large scale. They required too much time in the first place, and in practice were not found suited to illiterates. It was necessary to secure tests which could be used in common among a mass of people of various races, or varying school advantages, together with a large number who were utterly illiterate.
>
> The most hopeful method appeared to be a series of performance tests. What may be called the Healy frame, and the Fernald test, and the Healy Picture Puzzle, taken from the series of tests devised by Healy and Fernald have been found of great value.
>
> (Gwyn 1914:198)

"The Healy Picture Puzzle" was the Mare-and-Foal Picture Form Board. (Curiously, the picture of a mare and her foal used by Gwyn was not the same as the picture in Healy and Fernald's original article. In Gwyn's version the two animals were depicted facing each other, and the pieces were taken from different parts of the scene.) Gwyn claimed that mentally normal emigrants would usually complete this puzzle in two minutes, whereas feebleminded emigrants would take longer or would fail to complete it at all. (Once again, this was often because they could not work out how the two right-angled triangles fitted together to make an equilateral triangle.) By way of illustration he presented data from twenty-two emigrants who had been diagnosed as feebleminded.

Although Gwyn reported that Healy and Fernald's tests were "found of great value" (198), Sprague (1914) mentioned that Howard Knox "had recently introduced other performance tests" (466). Before turning to look at those tests, I think it is important to clarify when Knox's tests were devised. Knox described these tests in a series of articles published in a variety of journals between September 1913 and April 1914. However, it was not customary (as it is now) for journals to declare the dates when articles were accepted for publication. Knox might well have been keen to publicize his new tests (I will describe his efforts to do so in chapter 7), but his articles may have been subject to a publication lag of many weeks or months.

Fortunately, there exists contemporary evidence to establish the chronology of his work. In the summer of 1913 he was visited by Professor Walter Dill Scott of Northwestern University. Scott brought a letter of introduction dated July 22, 1913, written by Harry Levi Hollingworth. In 1909 Hollingworth had completed his dissertation under the supervision of James McKeen Cattell at Columbia University and had obtained a post there as an instructor at Barnard College. He had carried out an important study on the effects of caffeine on mental and motor efficiency (Hollingworth 1912) that had been funded by the Coca-Cola Company and used in its defense against the federal government's claim that its product contained a harmful ingredient (caffeine) that caused mental deficiency (Benjamin 2003; Benjamin, Rogers, and Rosenbaum 1991).

In this research Hollingworth had used simple psychological tests of the sort that Cattell had used previously. However, Hollingworth became interested in the more complex tasks used in intelligence tests and in the new performance tests being devised at Ellis Island. The letter of introduction that Hollingworth wrote for Scott said: "I have been telling my friend, Prof. Walter Dill Scott, head of the department of psychology in Northwestern University, about our recent interesting visits to your mental test rooms, and about some of the ingenious tests you have yourself devised. He wants to see too. He is the bearer of this note, and is one of the leading workers in applied psychology. I'm sure you'll be glad to welcome him." Scott's interest in the Ellis Island tests was not a superficial one. As an industrial psychologist, he was interested in developing new kinds of tests that could be used in personnel selection (in particular, to recruit effective salespeople). A few years later Scott was able to put his knowledge to a different use in the selection of officers during World War I.

The letter of introduction that Hollingworth produced for Scott demonstrates two things. First, Knox's work was becoming known to psychologists, not simply in the New York area but across the United States. Second, many of his "ingenious tests" had already been developed by July 1913. In April of that year Knox had been briefly assigned to work at a psychiatric hospital so that he could study mental diseases. In a letter that he wrote to his mother toward the end of May, he mentioned that he had worked on line inspection for only two short spells since leaving the hospital and that, instead, "mental work" had been occupying most of his time. This suggests that many of his performance tests were devised in May and June of that year. Nevertheless, the only evidence concerning the process of their development comes from the sequence of Knox's publications from September 1913 until the following April, and the account that follows adopts that chronology.

THE VISUAL COMPARISON TEST AND THE DIAMOND FRAME TEST

The first of these publications appeared in the *New York Medical Journal* on September 13. It described "two new tests for the detection of defectives" that were "given to the profession for what they may be worth in the special lines of work in which they may be used." Knox continued:

> In the detection of alien illiterate morons they have been found to be of considerable value when used in conjunction with our other performance tests, and it is of interest in this connection to note that in May, 1913, one hundred and eight mentally defective aliens were detected by the medical officers of the United States Public Health Service at Ellis Island, and that the great majority of these were of the moron or higher defective class. This number is about four times the number of mental defectives certified during the month of May, 1912, before our performance and other tests were developed and standardized for time, etc., to suit our special needs. In other words, we have broken new ground, as no one else seems to have worked with alien illiterate defectives and nowhere in the literature are these defectives described.
>
> (Knox 1913e:522–23)

This statement is interesting for several reasons:

1. Knox was providing a resounding affirmation of the importance of performance tests in the identification of mental deficiency among emigrants (and, by implication, an equally resounding rejection of Binet and Simon's

scales). (Incidentally, this appears to have been the first time that the phrase "performance test" was used in an academic or medical publication. Even so, Knox clearly thought he was using a phrase that was in common use rather than coining a new technical expression.)

2. Knox was responding to the professional and public demand that the physicians of the Public Health Service should find effective ways of excluding mentally deficient emigrants (and those of "the moron or higher defective class" would be the hardest to identify).

3. The claim to have "broken new ground" overlooks Goddard's (1912b, 1912c) accounts of his work with emigrants, but these were published in the house magazine of the Vineland Training School, not in the conventional medical literature. Knox might have been genuinely unaware of Goddard's papers— or the slight might have been intentional.

Knox then presented his Visual Comparison Test, which had five sections (figure 6.5). First, the examinee was shown a display containing ten line drawings of leaf clusters. These consisted of five identical pairs presented in two rows of

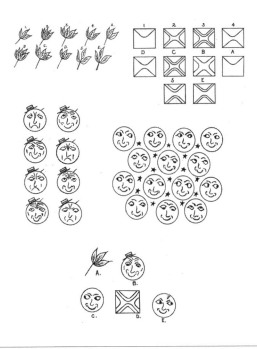

6.5 The Visual Comparison Test.
(Courtesy William H. Whaley, M.D.)

five leaf clusters in a random order. "After the subject's attention is surely directed he should be able to designate or 'pair' the five pairs in twenty-eight seconds." The second display contained ten line drawings of envelopes, and these similarly consisted of five identical pairs. "These envelopes should be 'paired' in eighteen seconds after the attention is directed" (523).

The third display contained eight line drawings of faces:

> To normal illiterates over twelve years of age (the entire test being standardized for illiterates over twelve years of age) four of these faces appear depressed or "sad" and four appear elated or "happy." Once the subject thoroughly understands, and his attention is directed, he should point out the "sad" ones in twenty seconds. If in any of these tests it appears that the subject does not understand what is wanted the test should be repeated twice for him, and time taken with the stop watch at each repetition. If after the three trials the subject cannot be made to understand what is wanted by the examiner or a competent interpreter, then the fact is evidence that he is defective.
>
> (523)

The fourth display contained fourteen line drawings of the man in the moon. The eyes were looking to the left in four drawings, to the right in four drawings, upward in three drawings, and downward in three drawings. "The subject should be able to point out the four moons that are looking to the left in fourteen seconds." In the final section of the test the examinee was shown a leaf cluster, a face, a rightward-looking moon, an envelope, and a leftward-looking moon and in each case was required to find the same drawing in the original display. "The time element has not been worked out for this section, but it is hardly the less valuable" (523).

The second new test was actually a variation of the Healy Frame Test. Healy and Fernald (1911) had found that their original test (in which five rectangular pieces were to be fitted into a rectangular frame) could be completed by most normal twelve-year-olds in two minutes. Knox and his fellow physicians had decided that fifty-five seconds would be a more appropriate standard for emigrants. Even so, they were concerned that the test was still too easy for their purposes; indeed, it was often completed by accident. To avoid these problems Knox used six blocks cut on the bias that fitted into a diamond-shaped frame measuring four and three-quarter inches on each side. As he commented, "The 'bias' does away with the element of luck, and, while easy to accomplish, it requires constant thought and attention" (523). He later described this as the Diamond Frame Test (figure 6.6).

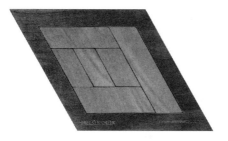

6.6 The Diamond Frame Test.

(Courtesy William H. Whaley, M.D.)

THE CUBE IMITATION TEST AND THE GEOGRAPHICAL PUZZLE

Knox published another article in the following week's issue of the *New York Medical Journal* titled "The Differentiation Between Moronism and Ignorance" (Knox 1913f). This was the main issue confronting the physicians at Ellis Island: Did some emigrants perform poorly on tests such as those in Binet and Simon's scale because they were mentally deficient or because they simply lacked the relevant cultural knowledge? Knox began by arguing that there was no genuine diagnostic problem in assessing children at schools for the feebleminded, since their mental deficiency had already become apparent to their teachers or relatives. At Ellis Island, however, accurate standardized tests were needed to identify mental deficiency in emigrants, because the physicians had no such insights into their background and personal history.

In this paper Knox introduced two more performance tests. One was the Cube Imitation Test (figure 6.7). Knox's original caption for this figure read:

> The author's "Cube Imitation" Test. This consists of four large and one small black cube. Beginning on the left, the examiner moves the small cube, as shown by the dotted lines, and the subject is asked to do what the examiner did. The examiner's movements are slow and deliberate. A study of a large series of cases has shown that high grade imbeciles can imitate line (a) but not (b), that feebleminded can imitate line (b) but not (c), that morons or higher feebleminded imitate line (c) but not (d), that normal persons can imitate line (d) and that only bright persons can imitate line (e). This test was developed at Ellis Island, and is one of the most valuable single performance tests. This standardization is

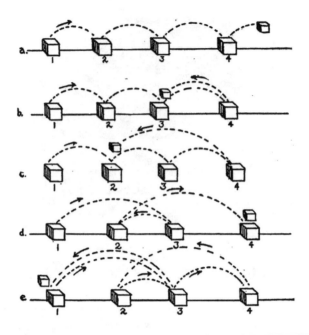

6.7 Knox's Cube Imitation Test.

for illiterates over twelve years of age. a. High grade imbecile; b, feebleminded; c, moron; d, normal; e, bright.

(564)

This description neglected to mention some crucial information concerning the apparatus used in this test. The four large cubes were actually mounted on a single strip of wood, and each cube and the section of the strip on which it was mounted were painted in a distinctive color. Toward the end of 1915 Knox arranged for many of his tests to be produced commercially, and the publisher's sales leaflet provided this more detailed account of the apparatus for the Cube Imitation Test: "Consisting of a board carrying 4 colored one-inch cubes (red, blue, green and yellow) fastened 4 inches apart, and a smaller black cube for tapping" (Knox 1915d:3).

The second test was a new form board (figure 6.8). Knox commented: "It is a valuable test since in attempting to fit the pieces into their proper places the defective demonstrates that muscular incoordination, limited sense of adaptability, and lack of decision which are often seen in defectives, and hence aid in their detection" (1913f:564). He called this test the "G" test, or Geographical Puzzle, presumably because the pieces resembled different regions on a map.

Knox claimed that these tests provided the physicians at Ellis Island with the means to differentiate between moronism and ignorance:

> It is probably now possible to say in every case whether an alien is defective or whether he is simply ignorant. The ignorant who are not defective possess among other attributes, the following: Didacticality, originality, ingenuity, the power of prolonged attention, and the ability to cooperate intelligently if not accurately with the examiner. They also possess a natural moral tone and finesse, regardless of whether these have been taught or not. The tests evolved and made use of at Ellis Island at the present time are intended to, and probably do, show a presence or absence of these characteristics.
>
> (564–65)

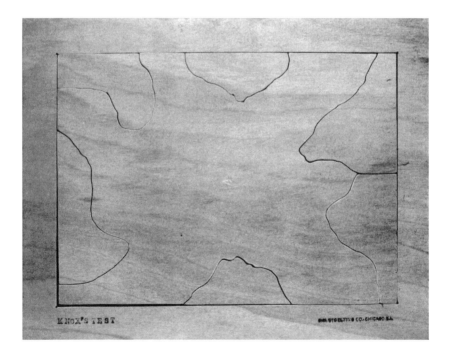

6.8 The Geographical Puzzle.

(Courtesy William H. Whaley, M.D.)

Knox went on to sketch out "a general method of examination" that could be used to identify feeblemindedness in emigrants older than twelve (although he also added, "Educated persons, of course, should be tested by means of the ordinary Simon–Binet scale"):

1. The first point to determine is whether or not, in dealing with foreigners, the subject and the interpreter understand each other perfectly. When this is determined to the satisfaction of the examiner, he should question the subject with a view to finding out, what he knows and remembers of the ordinary occurrences and everyday duties of his previous environment; for instance, if he was a farmer, ask about the farm, if a tailor, ask technical questions about that trade, and so on, suiting the questions to the calling and method of living. Further than this, ask about conditions in the place from which the subject came.

2. Determine what the subject remembers about his journey, whether he knows the names of the large cities through which he passed, and whether he knows the name of the ship he came on.

3. Is he well oriented for time, person, and place?

4. Has he ordinary facts of common knowledge, such as the number of days in a week and months in a year, with their names?

5. Can he meet the ordinary little emergencies of life? What would he do if tempted in various ways? Would he avoid trouble and questionable things? These points should be determined by special questions suited to the age, sex, and standard of living in each case.

6. If he can count forward from one to twenty, he should be able to count backward from twenty to one.

7. He should be able to remember and repeat, after ten seconds, five figures.

8. He should be able to obey three simple commands, and he should be able to touch with a pencil, after the examiner, four like objects such as dice or cubes, skipping any one and jumping back to any one; this latter is the "C. I.," or cube imitation test. . . .

9. After looking at an ordinary picture containing a dozen objects for thirty seconds, he should be able to name six of them from memory.

10. He should be able to copy a diamond or a square with a lead pencil.

11. He should be able to arrange in the order of their weight five cubes of different weights.

12. He should be able to do the "G" test or geographical puzzle in two minutes and twenty seconds. Defectives nearly always attempt the impossible in doing this puzzle, and they thereby show that they possess but a small sense of the "fitness of things." Clumsiness and incoordination are also shown, and these are important since nearly all defectives possess them to some degree. . . .

13. The "F" or Healy-Fernald test [Healy and Fernald's (1911) Construction Puzzle (B), the Fernald Test] should be accomplished in three minutes, and the "H" or the Healy puzzle [Healy and Fernald's Construction Puzzle (A), the Healy Frame Test] in fifty-five seconds.

These thirteen elements of the examination can be gone through within twenty minutes, and repeated on the following or subsequent days if desired, and when this is done the examiner is quite well acquainted with his subject and is in a good position to give him a mental rating. If he makes a total failure of four thirteenths of the examination as given here, he should be considered in the moron class, provided a reasonable attempt has been made to instruct him, in points that could not be accomplished at the primary examination.

(565)

The first two elements are clearly questions of general and more recent factual knowledge. The third element is a standard clinical assessment that is still used today to rule out brain damage and disease, toxic drug states, and concussion: examinees are expected to be able to say roughly what time of day it is, what their name is, and where they are. With the exception of the Cube Imitation Test, the next eight elements were taken from Binet and Simon's scales, and the last element was obviously taken from Healy and Fernald's (1911) collection.

Knox (1914d) gave exactly the same account of the "general method of examination for aliens over twelve years of age" in an article that was published in March 1914 about subnormal mentality in emigrants. However, it is likely that he wrote this article at about the same time as his paper on the differentiation between moronism and ignorance—in other words, during the summer of 1913— and simply added some data concerning the numbers of emigrants who had been identified and deported as mentally deficient during September and October 1913 to make it appear more topical. As I will show later in this chapter, by the following February Knox had abandoned the approach he had adopted in these two articles. Instead, he separated the verbal tests from the performance tests, and he structured the performance tests to reflect the levels of achievement to be anticipated in children of different ages.

THE IMBECILE TEST AND THE MORON TEST

In November 1913, Knox (1913g) published a brief account of two additional tests that he had developed for use at Ellis Island. He introduced his account as follows:

We say that a brain with insufficient ability to solve a problem (without previous training) of the proper complexity for its physical age is a defective one, and we classify the possessor according to the point in life where his mental development was arrested. Thus, if he develops not at all or but little, he falls into the idiot class; if he reaches one year of mental life and stops, he is a low grade imbecile; if he reaches six or thereabouts, he is said to be an imbecile, or, as some say, a high grade imbecile; if he stops at eight, he is said to be feebleminded; and if he does not pass the age of twelve mental years and he is in body four or more years older, he is said to be a moron or higher feebleminded.

(1017)

Clearly, Knox's view was that mental deficiency was tantamount to mental retardation, a view that others (including de Sanctis, Binet, and Simon) would have disputed.

The first test that he presented was a form board measuring six inches by eight inches that contained nine pieces. Knox had found that this could be com-

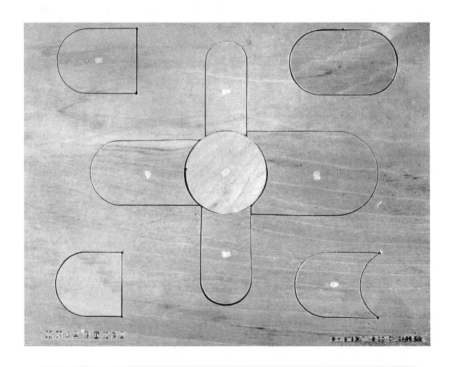

6.9 The Imbecile Test. (Courtesy William H. Whaley, M.D.)

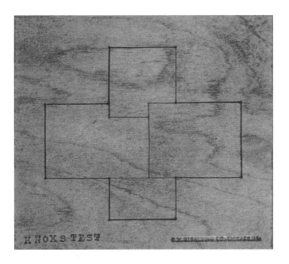

6.10 The Moron Test. (Courtesy William H. Whaley, M.D.)

pleted by normal six-year-olds in less than ninety seconds. He argued that adults who failed to complete it within ten minutes should be regarded as having a mental age of less than six and classified as an imbeciles unless they had some physical disability that might interfere with their performance of this test. He therefore described it as the Imbecile Test (figure 6.9).

The second test was a form board measuring four inches by five inches that contained just four pieces. Knox had found that this could be completed by normal children ten years or older in less than three minutes, and he described it as the Moron Test (figure 6.10). Although he did not make it explicit, the argument was presumably that an adult who failed to complete it should be regarded as having a mental age of less than ten and classified as a moron. However, even if the examinee completed the test, Knox suggested that it should be given several times to ensure that it had not been completed by accident.

THE CONSTRUCTION BLOCKS TEST, THE CASUIST TEST, AND THE FEATURE PROFILE TEST

In January 1914 Knox (1914a) published an extended account of the rationale for the procedures being used at Ellis Island. First, he described the detailed taxonomy of mental deficiency that was used "for scientific purposes and for our own personal satisfaction" (215), although he acknowledged that for legal purposes people with mental deficiency had to be classified simply as "idiots," "imbeciles," and "feebleminded." Next, he discussed various factors (both prenatal and postnatal) that appeared to predispose people to mental deficiency. Third, he discussed the personal qualities needed in the examiner as well as the physical and behavioral signs of mental deficiency in individuals of different ages. Fourth, he provided a detailed critique of the 1908 version of Binet and Simon's scale when applied to illiterate emigrants, focusing on the tests used by Binet and Simon to assign the mental levels of six, seven, eight, and nine years.

In this article Knox was at pains to emphasize that the diagnosis of mental deficiency was not simply based on a cursory visual inspection. For one thing, the line inspection usually involved explicit interrogation that could incorporate questions about personal history or simple tests of arithmetic. Any emigrants who showed suspicious signs could be referred for a more thorough physical and mental examination. The latter could involve a number of tests, but Knox reported that when the officers were under pressure they had found that three tests were the most useful. One was a simple addition test based on counting piles of cards, which had been devised by the former assistant surgeon Eugene Mullan. The second test was counting backward from twenty to one, and the third was the Cube Imitation Test. Of course, this stage of the procedure was simply a preliminary screening to decide who should be held for further examination and who should be allowed to continue the immigration process.

Knox illustrated the procedures used at Ellis Island by depicting a record card used to summarize the performance of emigrants in a test protocol developed from the one described in his previous paper (Knox 1913f). The first stage of the evaluation involved four tasks. These included the immediate recall of a short story describing five actions with which the examinee would be familiar, the Cube Imitation Test, and Mullan's addition test. They also included the Construction Blocks Test in which the examinee watched the examiner building a structure using five three-inch cubes and then had to re-create the structure from memory. Knox did not illustrate this test; figure 6.11 is taken from his unpublished papers.

The second stage of the evaluation consisted of the Seguin Form Board, Imbecile Test, Geographical Puzzle, Healy Frame Test, Fernald Test, Mare-and-Foal Picture Form Board, Moron Test, and Diamond Frame Test. Knox referred to the work that Surgeon Matthew Gwyn had been doing with the Mare-and-Foal Picture Form Board, and Knox emphasized the need to design new performance tests. In this paper (1914a) he took the opportunity to present two such tests.

One was a form board that Knox had designed. It measured eight inches by twelve inches. He called it the Casuist Test (figure 6.12) and described it as fol-

6.11 The Construction Blocks Test. (Courtesy William H. Whaley, M.D.)

lows: "A test of native ability and ingenuity. Normals of eleven years or older should put the sections of this test in place in less than five minutes with not over five false moves" (219). He mentioned that a colleague in the Public Health Service, Dr. Henry C. Cody, was using the test in experimental work with both normal and mentally deficient individuals. However, Knox did not explain the choice of name. *Webster's Third New International Dictionary* (1961) defines a casuist as (a) "one skilled in or given to ... reasoning about or resolution of questions of right or wrong in conduct" or (b) "one skilled in or given to ... sophistical, equivocal, or specious reasoning."

The second test was a picture form board that Knox had devised in collaboration with Assistant Surgeon Grover Andrew Kempf. It consisted of a jigsaw of a

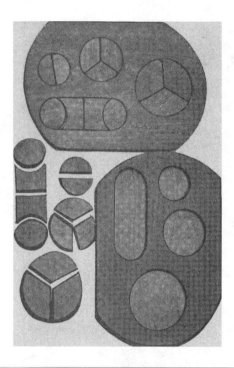

6.12 Two models of the Casuist Test, as depicted in Knox's 1915 *Scientific American* article.

person's head viewed in profile (figure 6.13). Knox called it the Knox-Kempf profile test, but it became widely known as the Feature Profile Test. Knox reported that Kempf was using this test in research with both normal and mentally deficient people and that his findings suggested that it could readily be performed by normal nine-year-olds. Subsequently, Knox gave a more detailed account:

> The "feature-profile" test requires a degree of intelligence rarely found in the feeble-minded: a 12-year-old child or an adult with corresponding mentality may be expected to put it together in five minutes or less. The profile head is made of wood, half an inch thick, and its greatest measurements are six by ten inches. There are seven pieces exclusive of the main one, the eye, nose and mouth each comprising one, while the ear is made up of four sections which can only be fitted together in one way. Successfully to pass this test shows that the subject possesses ability to read a diagram; however, it is an entirely fair test, because the object is familiar to everyone.
>
> (Knox 1914b:128)

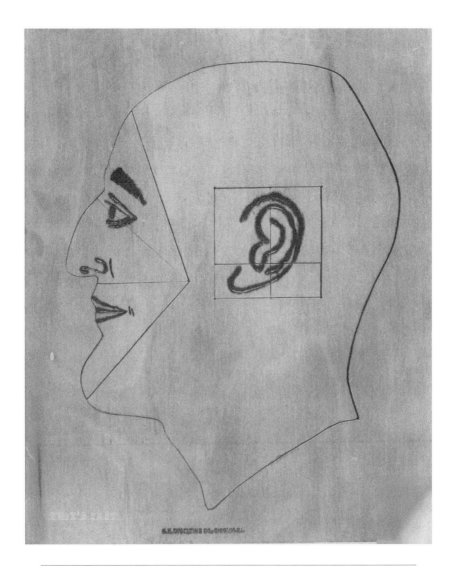

6.13 The Feature Profile Test. (Courtesy William H. Whaley, M.D.)

"A SPECIAL SCALE FOR THE MEASUREMENT OF INTELLIGENCE"

In February 1914 Knox published another account of the procedures used at Ellis Island in the *Journal of Heredity*, the monthly journal of the American Genetic
Association, which had strong links with the eugenics movement. (Knox's article
[1914b] began with the following editorial commentary: "How the Public Health

Service Prevents Contamination of Our Racial Stock by Turning Back Feeble-Minded Immigrants—General Characteristics Noted and Progressive Series of Tests Applied to Determine Exact Mentality.")

Knox began by summarizing the temperamental peculiarities and mental characteristics by which "mental enfeeblement" could be recognized:

(1) Dullness and stupidity and an inability to make use of such knowledge as they may have acquired.

(2) Faulty reasoning and judgment and an inability to correctly estimate sizes, shapes and forms. . . .

(3) Lack of ingenuity and native ability. Defectives are usually only capable of performing work that they have already learned after painstaking training. . . .

(4) Faulty attention and memory. The first of these renders it practically impossible to learn anything complicated. The second makes it unsafe to depend upon such persons to perform necessary acts with which they may be entrusted. . . .

(5) Exaggerated egotism, which gives them confidence in their own abilities, often at the expense of others. . . .

(6) Selfishness and absence of the altruistic sense are common attributes. . . .

(7) Emotional instability and hysterical outbursts are seen in various degrees. Illtimed [sic] mirth and grief and unusual reactions to minor excitations are common.

(8) Exaggerated susceptibility which causes them to be easily led and misdirected by more gifted persons.

(9) Inability to withstand temptation. . . .

(10) Early brain fag [fatigue] and absence of the power of sustained energy. Such people are incapable of consistent efficient work for any great length of time.

By way of explanation he added:

By this it is not meant that all defectives are possessed of all the above mentioned characteristics but it is true that every defective who is certified by the United States Public Health Service is possessed of a certain group of them and perhaps in some cases all of them. These ten are not all the peculiarities by which defectives in general are distinguished, but the elements and mental spheres enumerated here will serve to give a clear idea of what constitutes mental enfeeblement in the aliens who are presented for examination.

(125)

The purpose of the Ellis Island tests was to identify people with these char-acteristics: "Knowing the signs and manifestations, how may they best be eluci-dated and brought out in order to make a proper diagnosis and certificate? This is probably best accomplished by a graduated system of performance tests, ac-curately standardized, and a system of test questions of increasing complexity suited to the age, education and previous environment of the subject" (125–26). In other words, the tests were designed to identify mental enfeeblement through the demonstration of impaired performance across a diverse range of intellectual capabilities (see also Groszmann 1917:182). Knox emphasized at this point that the functions of the officers of the Public Health Service were advisory rather than legal in nature: "Their duty is done when the proper certificate has been rendered; the people should not hold them responsible therefore if defectives are often admitted notwithstanding adverse certificates" (1914b:126).

In this account Knox divided the procedures for detecting mentally defi-cient emigrants into three parts. The first part was the line inspection, which was based on detailed observation of the emigrants' appearance and demeanor. However, Knox acknowledged that some mentally deficient emigrants showed no outward signs, in which case they might be asked questions on the following subjects: "The journey, experience during the trip, simple concrete addition and the ability to count backward, facts of common knowledge that the immigrant should know and his grasp of his surroundings. This examination must be brief, rapid and to the point because from three to five thousand people must be ques-tioned in this way each day" (128).

Those who were detained would receive a more thorough examination. The first part was similar to the procedure that he had described the previous Sep-tember (Knox 1913f), but here he described it in more detail and with some amendments:

1. First question the subject about the ordinary occurrences and every-day duties of his previous environment. If he claims to have been a farmer ask about that vocation, if a tailor ask about that, framing the questions to the calling and previous style of living. Further than this ask about conditions as they exist in the town or locality from which the alien came.

2. Does he know the day of the week, the date, the month of the year, where he is, who he is, and who and what the examiner is? This set of questions deter-mines his orientation and grasp on his surroundings.

3. Common knowledge comes next; the number of hours in a day, days in a week, weeks in a month, months in a year with their names, the differ-ence between certain animals with which he is familiar, the names of flowers,

musical instruments, etc., with which he is familiar, and brief descriptions of each.

4. Immigrants should be able to do simple addition although they have never attended school and all normal immigrants over eight years old can do it. After adding like numbers, they should be asked to add unlike numbers, when one of the previously used like numbers is increased or decreased by 1, for instance, 4 and 4 =, 4 and 5 =, 4 and 3 =, 6 and 6 =, 6 and 5 =, 6 and 7 =, or 8 and 8 =, 8 and 7 =; rapidly and without difficulty. They should be able to add the following numbers rapidly, realizing in each case that each succeeding problem is but 1 greater than was the previous one; 7 and 1 =, 7 and 2 =, 7 and 3 =, 7 and 4 =, 7 and 5 =, 7 and 6 =, 7 and 7 =, 7 and 8 =, etc. The vast majority of defectives excepting mathematical savants will go through a most laborious mental process in attempting to do this latter set of problems only to emerge with a most absurd answer, for instance, they may give the answer to 7 and 2 as more than the sum of 7 and 8. . . .

5. Ask questions which tend to show the moral tone as "Why is it wrong to kill?" and "How should one regard his parents as compared to other people?" and "Is it wrong to steal?" and if so, "Why?" Determine whether he would try to resist temptation, how he would meet evil suggestions and other questionable things. Some most astonishing answers have been obtained to these questions as in the case of a boy who, while he professed a love for his parents, wished them dead that he might inherit their property; he was 17 years old and was found defective by the other tests.

6. Construct as nearly as possible miniature problems and incidents of life as the alien has lived it in his country and ask what he would do in each position.

7. If he can count from 1 to 20, as all normal aliens usually can, he should be able to count from 20 to 1 without hesitation; he should have no difficulty in naming the days of the week backward.

8. He should be able to repeat six, or at least five, figures after the examiner, as 2-9-8-7-5-6-4, or 5-2-9-7-3. The figures should be given slowly and distinctly, not repeating each set more than twice.

9. The subject should be able to obey three or more simple commands as "open the door, bring me that book, and put this penny on the table."

10. After looking at a picture for thirty seconds, the picture containing 12 objects with which he is familiar, he should be able to name six of them from memory, without much hesitation.

11. A diamond or a square should be copied with a lead pencil even though he has never attempted this before.

12. The alien should be able to arrange in the order of their weights four
cubes of the same size, weighing respectively 12, 15, 18, and 21 gms.

(1914b:129–30)

As with Knox's previous assessment protocol, many items were taken or
adapted from those in Binet and Simon's scale. The inclusion of simple addition
questions may have been influenced by the study that Glueck (1913) had carried
out. However, the most obvious difference between this assessment protocol and
its predecessor is that it contains no performance tests. These were reserved for
the final part of the examination and presented as a "special scale for the measurement of intelligence." Knox explained: "Just as Binet has evolved questions of
increasing complexity for his French school children, so the United States Public
Health Service has evolved a set of performance tests of increasing complexity.
These are applicable to every age from three years upward and the point in the
scale where an adult stops determines his mental age and the grade of defectives
under which he will be classified" (130). The scale specified the levels of achievement to be anticipated in children of different ages on appropriate selections of
tests (see table 6.1).

A SCALE FOR ESTIMATING MENTAL DEFECTS

Except for the final test, based on "the picture of a ship," all the procedures in
table 6.1 had been described previously. The Ship Test was depicted in an alternative account that was presented one week later in the *Journal of the American Medical Association* in an article titled "A Scale, Based on the Work at Ellis Island, for Estimating Mental Defect" (Knox 1914c). In this article Knox presented his "special
scale" as a self-contained instrument that included tests taken from Binet and
Simon's 1908 scale. Indeed, Knox even retained the nonsense sentences that Guy
Whipple had found "rather blood-curdling" (1910:509). The Ship Test (figure 6.14)
was a picture puzzle of a ship that had been devised by Bernard Glueck before he
returned to his permanent position at the Government Hospital for the Insane.
The original picture had been cut up into ten rectangles that a normal emigrant
older than twelve was expected to assemble within ten minutes, on the assumption that a steamship was something he or she should readily recognize (see Anastasi 1954:240; Zenderland 1998:271). The complete scale for estimating mental
defects is shown in table 6.2.

Knox also described seven tests that he referred to as "make-up tests for
adults" (742). These were intended for use with adults whose mental ages

TABLE 6.1 KNOX'S PERFORMING TEST EXAMINATION

At three years a child should be able to

Recognize toys and simple objects as such.

At four years a child should be able to

Put some pieces in the Seguin Form Board, and do line *a* of the Cube Imitation Test or touch any two of the blocks.

At five years a child should be able to

Put all the pieces in the Seguin Form Board in three minutes or do line *b* of the Cube Imitation Test or touch any three of its blocks.

At six years a child should be able to

Do the Imbecile Test in five minutes with no more than six errors. Line c of the Cube Imitation Test is easy for normal children at this age. The Construction Blocks Test may be started now; tell the child to take three blocks all the same shape and build a figure with them. Demonstrate this for the child for twenty-five seconds, then break up the structure and ask the child to build the same thing. . . .

At seven years a child should be able to

Do the Geographical Puzzle in three to five minutes, the Seguin Form Board in thirty seconds, and the Imbecile Test in less time and with fewer mistakes than at six years. Add one block to the Construction Blocks Test.

At eight years a child should be able to

Do the Healy Frame Test in five minutes and imitate line *d* of the Cube Imitation Test.

At nine years a child should be able to

Do the Diamond Frame Test in five to ten minutes; the Mare-and-Foal Picture Form Board in less than four minutes, the Seguin Form Board in twenty seconds. The complexity of the Construction Blocks Test may be increased to work with five blocks.

At ten years a child should be able to

Do the Moron Test in less than ten minutes and all the details of the Visual Comparison Test within ten minutes.

At eleven years a child should be able to

Do the line *e* of the Cube Imitation Test after no more than five demonstrations. The eight-, nine-, and ten-year tests should be performed in less time and with fewer mistakes.

TABLE 6.1 KNOX'S PERFORMING TEST EXAMINATION (*continued*)

At twelve years a child should be able to

Do the Casuist Test in five minutes; any mistakes must be sensible and not absurd.

At thirteen to fifteen years a child should be able to

Do the Casuist Test in less time and with fewer mistakes than at twelve years, with no demonstration beforehand, and the Feature Profile Test in five minutes with no mistakes. The youngster should be able to assemble within ten minutes a picture of a ship pasted to a board and cut into ten equal-sized pieces of the same shape (all cut vertically).

Source: Adapted from Knox 1914b:130.

6.14 The Ship Test. The picture of the ship used in the puzzle was colored.
(Courtesy William H. Whaley, M.D.)

according to the previous tests had been estimated at between eight years and twelve years. Analogous to makeup examinations in school, they gave examinees the opportunity to produce normal performance in alternative assessments. The first three tests were form boards. One was described as Gwyn's "triangle" and was to be completed three times in forty-five seconds; the second was described

TABLE 6.2 SCALE FOR ESTIMATING MENTAL DEFECTS

At three years a child should be able to

1. Recognize toys and simple objects.
2. Point to ear, nose, or lips.
3. Repeat two figures, such as seven, five.
4. Recognize objects in child picture books with which the child is familiar.
5. Know her or his own name.

At four years a child should be able to

1. Put some of the pieces in the Seguin Form Board.
2. Do line a of the Cube Imitation Test or touch any two blocks.
3. Repeat three figures, such as seven,. nine, five.
4. Recognize ring, pencil, shoe, hat.
5. Know his or her own sex.

At five years a child should be able to

1. Put all the pieces in the Seguin Form Board in three minutes.
2. Do line b of the Cube Imitation Test or touch any three blocks.
3. Count any number of the examiner's fingers.
4. Copy a square and circle.
5. Obey two commands, as "Shut the door and hand me the pencil."

At six years a child should be able to

1. Do the Imbecile Test in five minutes with fewer than six mistakes.
2. Do line c of the Cube Imitation Test.
3. Build a structure with four blocks after seeing the same structure for twenty-five seconds.
4. Know right from left.
5. Know her or his own age.
6. Obey three commands, "Open door, shut window, and bring book."
7. Know the purpose of familiar domestic animals.

At seven years a child should be able to

1. Do the Geographical Puzzle, after being shown, in five minutes.
2. Do the Imbecile Test with more facility than at six years of age.
3. Imitate the structure in the Construction Blocks Test, using five blocks.
4. Copy a diamond with a lead pencil.

TABLE 6.2 SCALE FOR ESTIMATING MENTAL DEFECTS (*continued*)

5. Repeat four figures, such as nine, three, seven, four.

6. Count readily from one to twenty.

7. Name the action shown in simple picture, such as "driving horses."

At eight years a child should be able to

1. Do the Healy Frame Test in five minutes.

2. Do line d of the Cube Imitation Test.

3. Count from twenty to one with not more than two errors.

4. Know the difference between water and milk, horse and cow, if these are familiar to the child.

5. Repeat five figures, such as seven, three, five, nine, two.

6. Recognize the primary colors, red, blue, green, and yellow.

At nine years a child should be able to

1. Do the Diamond Frame Test in five or ten minutes.

2. Do the Mare-and-Foal Picture Form Board in five minutes.

3. Do the Seguin Form Board in twenty seconds.

4. Know the date.

5. Name the days of the week and tell the approximate time.

6. Arrange five cubes in the order of their weight.

At ten years a child should be able to

1. Do the Moron Test in less than ten minutes.

2. Do the Visual Comparison Test.

3. Name the months of the year.

4. Do simple addition of unlike and like numbers: 5 and 4 = ? 5 and 5 = ? 6 and 5 = ? 6 and 6 = ? up to and including 8 and 7 = ? 8 and 8 = ?

5. Do simple addition of two numbers, one of which is increased each time by 1: 7 and 1 = ? 7 and 2 = ? 7 and 3 = ? 7 and 4 = ? 7 and 5 = ? etc., to 7 and 8 = ?

6. Recite the days of the week backward.

At eleven years a child should be able to

1. Do line e of the Cube Imitation Test after no more than five demonstrations.

2. Repeat six figures, such as six, nine, two, five, seven, three.

3. Remember at least three of five details from a simple story.

4. Distinguish between ice and glass; the feet of horses from those of cows and dogs; or among other objects familiar to the child.

(*continued on next page*)

TABLE 6.2 SCALE FOR ESTIMATING MENTAL DEFECTS (continued)

5. Give an intelligent account of what she or he has been doing for the past year.

6. Perform simple subtraction from ten when given a concrete example, such as
10 eggs − 3 eggs = ?

At twelve years a child should be able to

1. Do the Casuist Test in five minutes with only sensible mistakes.

2. See absurdities, for example, "A man walked down the street swinging a cane with his hands in his pocket."

3. Solve syllogisms, such as "I am taller than my brother, and my brother is taller than my father. Which of us is the tallest?"

4. Provide a solution to a story, such as "A man was walking in the woods, and he saw something hanging from a tree that frightened him; he ran back to the village and told the police. What did he see?"

5. Perform simple subtractions from twenty, such as 20 cents − 4 cents = ?

6. Divide twenty apples into four equal groups; how many will be in each?

Children thirteen and older should be able to

1. Do the Feature Profile Test in ten minutes.

2. Do the Ship Test.

3. Obey four commands.

4. Solve a problem: "My head is to my hat as my hands are to my ———?"

5. Define justice, pity, truth, goodness, and happiness.

6. Combine factors in concrete addition, such as one horse and one man have how many legs? One horse and one man and one chicken? Two horses and one man and two chickens?

Source: Adapted from Knox 1914c:741–42.

as Kempf's "diagonal" and was to be completed once in three minutes (figure 6.15). The implication of their names, of course, is that they had been devised by Surgeon Matthew Gwyn and Assistant Surgeon Grover Kempf, respectively. The third test was Healy and Fernald's (1911) Construction Puzzle (B) (the Fernald Test), to be completed in five minutes (see figure 6.4).

The fourth test required the examinee to count sixty dots, each about an eighth of an inch in diameter, arranged in ten parallel rows of six dots. The fifth test required examinees to "give an intelligent and connected account of the technicalities of the[ir] previous occupation." The sixth test required examinees to discourse at length on a topic with which they were familiar. Knox added: "If

6.15 Gwyn's Triangle Form Board and Kempf's Diagonal Form Board, as depicted in the 1915 *Scientific American* article.

this is done well and the subject uses more than fifty words in his description the examiner should be particularly sure of his ground before certifying the case." The seventh test was described as "the ink-blot imagination test" (742); Knox gave no information about this test but promised that it would be described in a forthcoming article in another journal. (I discuss Knox's detailed account in the next section.)

Knox explained that, as with Binet and Simon's scale, it was not appropriate to start at the beginning. Rather, the examiner should start with an estimated mental age and then move to higher or lower ages until finding the level for which the examinee met all the requirements. Using a scoring scheme analogous to that proposed by Alfred Binet (1911), Knox suggested that mental age should be calculated as the age at which the examinee passed all the subtests with credit for subtests passed beyond that level. For instance, if an examinee passed all six subtests for the age of seven years, only one of the six subtests for the age of eight years, but four subtests beyond that level, the examinee's mental age would be calculated by counting the five additional subtests against the six subtests needed to attain a mental age of eight, leading to the assessment of seven and five-sixths years.

Finally, Knox presented data that had been obtained from Italian, "Hebrew," Polish, and Russian children and adults aged three to fifty, all of whom had subsequently been classified as having normal intelligence. For instance, he described performance on the relevant lines of the Cube Imitation Test in 567 children aged four to eleven and performance on line d of the test in 3,735 people aged thirteen to fifty. Unfortunately, the data were collected before it was decided that a single measuring scale would be developed, and different examinees had carried out different subtests.

It would not, in any case, have been appropriate to use these data to construct a single set of norms for the measuring scale as a whole, because the examinees had not been sampled at random from the emigrants arriving at Ellis Island. As Knox explained in his introduction:

> I present this paper, based on tests which I have made on over 4,000 suspected defectives in the last eighteen months and many more made by my associates. It must be remembered that our cases were suspected of being deficient and were therefore not representative of the normal, although all were considered sufficiently near the required standard to be allowed to pass, except about 400 certified as feeble-minded and (in a few cases) as imbeciles.
>
> (1914d:741)

The actual data presented in this paper appear to have come from emigrants who were initially suspected of being mentally deficient but who were subsequently admitted to the United States (that is, excluding those who were certified as mentally deficient). Knox's reference to "the last eighteen months" implies that he had begun to collect these data as early as September 1912. Moreover, only four hundred emigrants had been classified as feebleminded or as imbeciles out of more than four thousand who had been suspected of being mentally defective; this is clearly at variance with the view of Goddard and others that the physicians at Ellis Island were failing to detect large numbers of people with mental deficiency.

THE INKBLOT IMAGINATION TEST

In the *Medical Record* for April 25, Knox presented the promised account of his Inkblot Imagination Test (1914f). He constructed a set of six inkblots and asked his participants, "What do these spots look like and what do they remind you of?" His description was accompanied by an illustration that contained the shapes shown in figure 6.16. The six inkblots were numbered clockwise beginning with the one at the top, and the caption read:

> Blots used for testing the imaginative faculties. These ink blots were designed for the purposes of a comparative study of the associative and constructive

6.16 The Inkblot Imagination Test. (Courtesy William H. Whaley, M.D.)

imaginative powers of normals and defectives among aliens. Each was intended to resemble vaguely a number of common objects, for instance (1) might cause one to recall a snake, a pennant, a rope, or a river (depending on his experiences); (2) an animal or a map; (3) a lizard, a mouse, or a rat; (4) a leaf, a flower, or a cloud; (5) a house or a hay stack; (6) a strawberry, butterfly, or an umbrella.

(751)

His main study was concerned with fifty Italian emigrants aged fifteen to thirty. Half had been found to be mentally deficient according to his measuring scale, and the other half had been found to be of average intelligence. The first group tended to take nearly twice as long to provide interpretations of the inkblots, and the quality of their interpretations was impoverished (in the sense of being less logical or sensible) compared with those of the normal participants. Knox concluded that the quality and speed of the responses given in tests of imagination might be useful in identifying cases of mental deficiency. Nevertheless, this is patently not a performance test, because it demands both verbal instructions on the part of the examiner and verbal responses on the part of the examinee.

Knox never acknowledged any particular source for this test, so where might the idea have come from? Two weeks earlier, on April 12, an article about the Inkblot Imagination Test had appeared in the *World Magazine*. The article was neither signed nor titled, but the author (probably Knox himself) commented: "It is an old game, this of making blots with ink on paper and trying to find out what ideas they arouse in the minds of different people." In fact, toward the end of the nineteenth century, games that involved the construction and interpretation of inkblots were played by children on both sides of the Atlantic.

In Europe such games were known as klecksography, after a work by Justinus Kerner, a German poet and physician. Because of failing eyesight toward the end of his life, Kerner sometimes dropped blots of ink on writing paper, and he would fold up the sheets of paper, intending to throw them away. However, if he unfolded the paper, he often found that the inkblots had made intriguing shapes. He elaborated these shapes into intricate cartoons and used them to illustrate his poems. These became popular, so in 1857 he put together a collection of inkblots and poems. Kerner died in 1862, and his collection was eventually published in 1890. In the United States a similar game was described in 1896 by Ruth McEnery Stuart and Albert Bigelow Paine in their book titled *Gobolinks, or Shadow-Pictures for Young and Old*. This book explained how to make inkblots and use them as prompts for making up imaginative verse: "The Gobolink . . . is a veritable goblin of the ink-bottle, . . . a self-made eccentric creature of a superior imagination" (ix).

The first suggestion that inkblots might be used in psychological research was made by Alfred Binet and Victor Henri (1896). They suggested that the interpretation of inkblots could be used to study variations in what they called "involuntary imagination" (443–44). Binet (1903:225) went on to use the description of inkblots in a standardized test, although he found this to be less useful than asking for descriptions of everyday objects (Wolf 1973:126). Binet's research subsequently led Fedor Egorovich Rybakov, a professor of neuropsychiatry at the Imperial Moscow University, to include inkblots in what he called an atlas of procedures to be used in investigations of personality that was published in 1910.

The first person actually to use inkblots in psychological research appears to have been George Van Ness Dearborn of Harvard. He published a short note recommending the use of inkblots in research on perception, memory, and imagination (Dearborn 1897), and in a separate paper he presented preliminary results from a study in which sixteen participants each gave their interpretations of ten inkblots (Dearborn 1898). Similar studies were carried out by Stella Sharp (1899) at Cornell University and by Edwin Asbury Kirkpatrick (1900), a teacher at the Fitchburg Normal School in Massachusetts who had been one of the first students to graduate in psychology from G. Stanley Hall's department at Clark University.

At about this time Edmund Burke Delabarre, one of Dearborn's colleagues at Harvard, compiled a collection of inkblots, apparently for use in experiments investigating the effects of hashish. In December 1898 he described some of his results at the annual meeting of the American Psychological Association, which was held at Columbia University. In his abstract Delabarre mentioned that small doses of hashish in solid extract form increased the richness of his imagery and thought, but he did not refer to their specific effects on his interpretations of inkblots (Delabarre 1899; see also Delabarre and Popplestone 1974). John Armstrong Popplestone and Marion White McPherson (1999:140) of the Archives of the History of American Psychology at the University of Akron reproduced examples of Delabarre's inkblots.

At the University of Iowa, Carl Emil Seashore (1908:144–49) published a manual of experiments for psychology students. One experiment involved the construction and presentation of six inkblots to demonstrate the interpretative nature of perception. However, one problem with these early studies was the lack of standardized material, which made it hard to compare the results obtained by different researchers. In his *Manual of Mental and Physical Tests,* Guy Whipple (1910:430–35) referred to this lack of standardized material and described a series of twenty inkblots that he had published commercially. In a test manual that was intended for use by schoolteachers, William Henry Pyle (1913:33–35) of the University of Missouri also included the Imagination or Ink-Blot Test, which used Whipple's collection of inkblots.

There is thus no shortage of sources from which Knox might have obtained the idea for his own Inkblot Imagination Test. To narrow the search, however, one might consider that there are two ways to make inkblots. Dearborn (1897) suggested taking a rectangular piece of paper that had previously been folded in two, leaving a crease; if a blot of ink is dropped on one side of the crease and the two halves are pressed firmly together until the ink has been absorbed, this leaves an inkblot that is symmetrical. In his subsequent article, however, Dearborn (1898) suggested a different method using two separate squares of paper: if a blot of ink is dropped on one piece of paper and the other piece is rubbed gently against it, this leaves an asymmetrical inkblot.

Most researchers whom I have mentioned either described how they had made their inkblots or provided actual examples. Table 6.3 classifies the researchers according to whether they used symmetrical or asymmetrical inkblots. Kerner's klecksography and the Gobolinks of Stuart and Paine were constructed using the first method described by Dearborn, and all were symmetrical. The inkblots used by Binet, Delabarre, Sharp, Seashore, and Rybakov were all asymmetrical and presumably constructed using the second method described by Dearborn (or, conceivably, merely by dropping ink onto a single sheet of paper). Kirkpatrick did not say how he had made his inkblots, but his participants' interpretations suggest that they were probably asymmetrical. Whipple's collection included both symmetrical and asymmetrical inkblots.

This exercise suggests a number of conclusions. Figure 6.16 shows that Knox's inkblots were all asymmetrical. It is reasonable to assume that Knox did not have access to Rybakov's *Atlas*. Even by the 1940s, only one copy had traveled as far from Russia as western Europe (Baumgarten-Tramer 1943). The right-hand column of table 6.3 shows that Seashore's 1908 manual of psychology experiments was published only six years before Knox's Inkblot Imagination Test and may therefore have been Knox's source of inspiration. Of course, given both the passage of time and the absence of any documentary evidence, it is highly unlikely that this could ever be substantiated conclusively.

Of course, the most famous inkblot user was the Swiss psychiatrist Hermann Rorschach. The most authoritative biography of Rorschach is probably that of Henri Ellenberger (1954), and what follows is largely based on his account. Rorschach appears to have arrived at the idea of using inkblots in a psychological test in about 1911, while he was a physician at the asylum in Münsterlingen, a town on the shore of Lake Constance in northeastern Switzerland. A former school friend, Konrad Gehring, was a schoolteacher in a neighboring town, and he and Rorschach had remained close friends. Rorschach had thought of using inkblots to elicit interpretations from his patients for comparison with their responses in tests of word association. He and Gehring decided to carry out an informal study using Rorschach's inkblots to investigate whether gifted children gave more imaginative interpretations than did less gifted children.

However, Rorschach never published the results of this study and instead adopted a more psychoanalytic approach to the diagnosis and treatment of psychiatric patients. In the meantime Rorschach's former teacher and the head of the psychiatric clinic in Zurich, Eugen Bleuler, was supervising a young Polish student, Szymon Hens. In 1917 Hens submitted a dissertation that featured an inkblot test, and this prompted Rorschach to undertake work on the diagnostic role of inkblots in clinical patients. He focused on the interpretations given to a particular set of ten inkblots; five were monochrome, the other five were colored, but all were symmetrical. Rorschach reported the results of this research in his 1921 book, *Psychodiagnostik*.

The evidence in table 6.3 tends to corroborate Ellenberger's suggestion that Rorschach and his friend Gehring probably knew about inkblots because they had played klecksography as children, an idea also supported by Rorschach's high school nickname: "Klex." Moreover, Saul Rosenzweig (1944) commented that the inkblots and interpretations provided in Stuart and Paine's book *Gobolinks* (1896) would lend themselves fairly readily to the scoring procedure devised by Rorschach. Franziska Baumgarten-Tramer (1943) noted that Rorschach had worked in Moscow in 1913–14, and she speculated that he might have come across Rybakov's *Atlas*. However, the evidence in table 6.3 tends to support Ellenberger's contention that Rorschach probably did not know about the earlier

TABLE 6.3 SOURCES OF SYMMETRICAL AND ASYMMETRICAL INKBLOTS

Symmetrical	Asymmetrical
Kerner 1890	Binet and Henri 1896
Stuart and Paine 1896	Dearborn 1898
Dearborn 1897	Delabarre 1899
Rorschach 1921	Sharp 1899
	Binet 1903
	Seashore 1908
	Rybakov 1910
	Knox 1914f

work using inkblots that had been carried out in France, the United States, and Russia.

Finally, someone who encountered Knox's paper on the Inkblot Imagination Test without being aware of its historical and scientific context might be led to entertain the notion that the work of Howard Knox and that of Hermann Rorschach were somehow connected. It is certainly true that they had a common interest in the use of inkblots in tests of the imagination. However, Rorschach dealt with symmetrical inkblots, Knox with asymmetrical ones, and the histories of both researchers indicate there probably was no connection between them.

FAMILY MATTERS

While Knox was developing his tests and writing up accounts of his work for publication, there were also significant developments in his domestic life. The Knoxes' second daughter, Gladys Sprague Knox, was born in Tompkinsville in January 1913. (Although it is possible that she was named partly in honor of Surgeon Ezra Sprague, Knox's colleague, Sprague was also the family name of Gladys Knox's maternal grandmother.) Within the family Dorothea and Gladys were known as Tweet and Hap, respectively. For a while life in New York City had gone smoothly. In May 1913 Knox had written to his mother, "The work is going well and I am very happy with it. . . . The children are looking fine and Tweet does much talking. . . . Gladys and I have been to a couple of good shows lately but I didn't care so awful much about them, I would rather have gone to some good vaudeville and we may go to some tomorrow night."

Nevertheless, early in 1914 Howard and Gladys Knox divorced. Gladys took the girls to live with her mother, Helen Foster Barnett, in Brooklyn. Helen continued to support the development of the arts in New York. For instance, in April 1915 the Friends of Young Artists' Society organized a competition of works of sculpture on the theme "What is war?" to encourage young and impecunious artists, and Helen Foster Barnett donated the first prize of two hundred dollars. Three years later she was among members of the Club of Lace who contributed items to an exhibition of lace held at the Brooklyn Museum. In 1920 she donated a four-manual, seventy-two-stop pipe organ to the Church of the Messiah in Brooklyn in memory of her son, Seymour, who had been well known in the borough as a painter of landscapes and portraits.

By 1917 Helen Foster Barnett was planning for the continuation of her work after her death. She set up the Barnett Foundation, which subsequently paid for the annual award of Saint-Gaudens medals to graduates of New York City high schools "for fine draughtsmanship," a tradition that continues today. She increased the value of the Helen Foster Barnett prize to $200, and, when she died in July 1920, she bequeathed $5,000 to the National Academy of Design to be invested so that the income could fund the award of the prize annually thereafter. Her bequest was evidently invested wisely: in 2008 Helen Foster Barnett prizes of $5,000, $4,000, and $3,000 were awarded to different sculptors at the 183rd Annual Invitation Exhibition of Contemporary American Art.

She had also set up two trust funds of $100,000 each to "support, maintain and educate" Tweet and Hap "according to their position in life." Gladys and the girls continued to live in Brooklyn, and they spent their summers in a cottage, "Pessapuncke," at Mattituck in Suffolk County on Long Island. Gladys Knox died in February 1929 when her daughters were still in their teens. Dorothea attended the Finch School in Manhattan (which was then a finishing school but later became the degree-granting Finch College) and Vassar before marrying in 1932. Hap attended the Masters School at Dobbs Ferry in Westchester County, New York; studied for a time in Lausanne, Switzerland; and then graduated from the Packer Collegiate Institute, a private girls' school in Brooklyn Heights, before marrying a U.S. Army lieutenant in 1933.

Howard and Gladys Knox's divorce had been acrimonious. Howard Knox agreed to have no further contact with his two daughters, and they in turn were brought up to believe that he was dead. Indeed, when Hap's forthcoming marriage was announced in the New York Times in December 1932, he was described as "the late Dr. Howard Andrew Knox," although he was alive and well and living little more than sixty miles away in New Jersey. Dorothea and Hap did not learn that he was still alive until the spring of 1945, and Dorothea died soon afterward without seeing her father again.

Following the breakdown of his marriage, Knox took an apartment in Brooklyn. His mother, who had been living in the Knoxes' former home in Sheffield, Massachusetts, moved in with him soon afterward. In April 1914 they were unexpectedly visited by his father, Howard Reuben Knox, who had retained a home in Ashtabula, Ohio, but who had been working and living in Florida. He stayed for a month, but his visit resulted in litigation between father and son. On March 2, 1915, the *Brooklyn Times* reported what it called "the bare legal announcement" of the events that had transpired in court that day:

> Along in April, 1914, the elder Knox became alarmed at his physical condition and decided to come North. He knew his son was a practising physician. Although he had never seen him since the divorce action [with Jennie Knox], he sought him out.
>
> In his complaint the father says he came to visit his son at the latter's request. The son had always lived with his mother. His son examined him and to his father's intense alarm, said he was dangerously ill. This was on April 21,

6.17 Howard Knox testing a female emigrant at Ellis Island, ca. early 1914.© 2009 by Brown Brothers. Reprinted by permission.

of last year. This, says the elder Knox, effected [sic] his powers of reason. Induced by "various arts and wiles," he alleges, he signed a transfer of mortgages amounting to $20,000 to his son. He says there was an agreement whereby he was to receive his property back if he changed his mind as to its ultimate disposal. By chance he declared he found that the agreement relative to the return of his property had disappeared from his other papers.

He had lived in his son's home for more than a month when he determined to leave. His former wife also lived in the same house.

He hurriedly packed his belongings and went to his home in Ashtabula. There he consulted a physician, he asserted in the complaint, who told him he was well and might look forward to a long life. His heart trouble was pronounced a trifling affliction.

On June 22, 1914, the *Brooklyn Times* reported, Judge Frederick E. Crane of the New York Supreme Court (which in New York is a lower court) had signed an order that directed Howard Andrew Knox to show cause why he should not be

6.18 Howard Knox testing a male emigrant at Ellis Island, ca. early 1914.© 2009 by Brown Brothers. Reprinted by permission.

restrained from selling or transferring the notes and mortgages in question. Nevertheless, at the proceedings on March 2, 1915, Judge William J. Kelly set aside that order, effectively wiping all litigation in the case from the slate. The *Brooklyn Times's* reporter wryly commented that this formal announcement acted "as an effective screen to one of the most interesting cases ever developed in the Brooklyn courts." The newspaper added that the parties had apparently arrived at some agreement outside court, but it interpreted the outcome as a victory for the doctor over his father. After the hearing Knox seems to have had no further dealings with his father. Howard Reuben Knox subsequently joined a consortium of investors building hotels in Florida, but he is believed to have committed suicide following the loss of his investments during a crash in the Florida real estate market in 1926.

By the end of April 1914 Knox's account of the performance tests that he and his colleagues had devised at Ellis Island was complete. By modern standards his account was a relatively informal one. This chapter contains essentially all the information that Knox provided concerning both how the tests should be administered and how the examinees' performance should be evaluated. Not surprisingly, researchers and practitioners who subsequently wished to make use of the tests felt it necessary to standardize both their administration and the scoring procedure. I will discuss this in later chapters, where I will also consider the impact of these tests both on practices at Ellis Island and on intelligence testing in general. Figures 6.17 and 6.18 show Knox at work at Ellis Island, probably early in 1914.

Both photographs depict Knox testing apparently genuine emigrants. In the introduction I mentioned that I would be reproducing such photographs only if they were already in the public domain. Figure 6.17 was used to illustrate an article in *Life* magazine that marked the opening of the Ellis Island immigration museum in September 1990 (Kinney 1990:30). Figure 6.18, which shows Knox being assisted by an interpreter named Isaac Prussin, has been published on several occasions. The complete photograph was included in two illustrated books about Ellis Island (Chermayeff, Wasserman, and Shapiro 1991:141; Jonas 1989:76), in a book chapter concerning the assessment of intelligence in non-English speakers (Harris, Tulsky, and Schultheis 2003:360), and in the official guide, *Ellis Island & Statue of Liberty*, for 2010–11 (10). It was, however, cropped, removing the interpreter, in a National Geographic Society publication, *We Americans* (1975:267), and in my own article about Knox's life and work (Richardson 2003:157).

7

POPULARIZING THE WORK AT ELLIS ISLAND

P rodded by the office of the surgeon general, Knox and his colleagues began
to popularize their work through articles in newspapers and magazines, presentations at conferences and to local medical associations, and finally through
a manual for the mental examination of emigrants. Nothing had come of the
letter Knox had received in October 1912 asking him to suggest three articles
on matters relating to hygiene and the public health. The surgeon general had
sent the form letter to all commissioned officers in the Public Health Service.
Knox had duly suggested three titles, but there is no evidence he ever wrote the
articles.

Less than a year later Knox received a personal letter in July 1913 from the
assistant surgeon general, William Colby Rucker, suggesting that Knox write a
popular article based on his paper that had just appeared in the *New York Medical Journal*, "A Diagnostic Study of the Face" (Knox 1913c). Rucker proposed that it
"might be of great value to the reading public, and might also serve as a scheme
for bringing before the people in concrete form, an evidence of the splendid work
which our corps is now doing at Ellis Island. . . . If you will forward me the manuscript, . . . I will endeavor to get some of my magazine friends in this city to place
it." Once again, there is no evidence that Knox ever wrote this article, but he appears to have taken this as encouragement to disseminate the work at Ellis Island
more widely.

Two months later Knox published "The Differentiation Between Moronism and Ignorance" in the *New York Medical Journal*. This was the article that featured his account of a "general method of examination" and the Geographical Puzzle. The following day, September 21, the *New York Herald* carried an article about the puzzle and a summary of the method of examination. The article was unsigned but was probably written by Knox himself. The headline read "Jig Puzzle Used at Ellis Island to Test Intelligence of Aliens," and the article itself began: "Suppose yourself landed on the shores of a foreign country and asked to solve a puzzle in two minutes and twenty seconds just to tell whether you were feeble minded!" Accompanying it was the picture of the Geographical Puzzle that had appeared in the *New York Medical Journal*.

On October 13 Knox was one of the speakers at an event in support of a campaign to set up a "clearing house" for monitoring mentally defective people, and the *New York Times* reported his remarks the next day. Knox described the procedures being used at Ellis Island and emphasized the need for the physicians to be absolutely certain in their diagnoses of mental deficiency. As a result, some emigrants were given the benefit of the doubt, with the risk that they and their progeny might become a social and financial burden. As an example, he cited an Englishman aged twenty-four who was asked a question based on one of Binet and Simon's tests: "A man walked into the woods. He saw something hanging from a tree that frightened him, and he ran back to notify the police. What did he see?" The emigrant, apparently a London cockney, answered, "A brawnch" (branch). According to Binet and Simon (1908:55), the only correct response to this question was "A person hanged." Nevertheless, Knox reported that the man had been permitted to land under bond.

Two weeks before Knox described his Inkblot Imagination Test in the *Medical Record* on April 25, 1914, the *World Magazine* had carried an article about the test, including illustrations of the inkblots that Knox had used and a photograph of Knox himself. The article was both unsigned and untitled, but it gave an accurate idea of the use of the test:

> Have you got an imagination? If not, read no further on this page or you may scare yourself into believing you are mentally defective.
>
> These are splashes of ink—just such blots as you make when writing with a tired hand or with a rusty pen. They mean nothing, but if you have an imagination each of them will suggest something to you.
>
> It is an old game, this of making blots with ink on paper and trying to find out what ideas they arouse in the minds of different people. It is no longer a

mere game, for in the hands of psychologists and specialists in mental diseases it has become a scientific test of the intelligence of persons suspected of being below normal.

"What does this splash suggest to you?" is the question they ask. And they time the response with a stop watch, for the speed with which the mind acts is as important to them as is the nature of the reply.

Dr. Howard A. Knox, assistant surgeon, United States Public Health Service, is using this—with several other tests, of course—as a gauge of the intelligence of immigrants at Ellis Island. Getting suspected defectives to play the game of ink blots and making a record of how they succeeded was his own idea. . . .

If you are fond of self-analysis and do not fear the results, try the game yourself. You will not only get some fun out of it, but may learn something about your own mind.

Even so, claims that the physicians at Ellis Island were admitting large numbers of mentally deficient immigrants were frequent. The Medical Society of the State of New York discussed the issue in the closing session of its annual meeting on April 30. The following day the *New York Times* reported the outcome:

Congress was appealed to yesterday by the Medical Society of the State of New York to provide more stringent measures for the enforcement of the immigration exclusion law against insane and mentally defective immigrants. The physicians who ended their annual meeting in the Hotel Astor said that the present system of admitting immigrants was a menace to the public health of the country and placed an unjust burden upon the State for the care of the mentally defective.

The physicians adopted unanimously a resolution urging congress [sic] to provide for the mental examination of all arriving immigrants by physicians of the United States Public Health Service; for adequate facilities for the detention and mental examination of immigrants by experts in the diagnosis of insanity and mental disease at all the large ports of entry, with a detail of American officers on all immigrant ships, and for an equitable share by the Federal Government of the cost of maintenance of insane immigrants who are now cared for by the State. Expeditious deportation methods are asked for to relieve the State institutions of the care of insane aliens.

By this time, however, the chief medical officer at Ellis Island, Surgeon Louis Williams, seems to have thought that he could mount a more aggressive defense against such claims. In late May 1914 he addressed the annual meeting of the American Medico-Psychological Association (now the American Psychiatric Association) in Baltimore. He began by emphasizing the sheer scale of the task confronting his physicians, that of "examining daily, between the hours of 9.30 a.m. and 4.30 p.m., from 2000 to 5000 immigrants" (Williams 1914:259). Next, he reminded his audience of the procedure that was followed:

> As the immigrants pass through the primary inspection line each is inspected by two physicians, one of whom takes special note of any indication of mental defect or disorder and addresses to each alien a few questions in his own language. All who in appearance or behavior excite suspicion, or who give irrelevant or stupid replies, are set aside for further inquiry. The suspects thus turned aside are at once given a brief preliminary examination for the purpose of sifting out and discharging those among them who are obviously of sound mind. Of those who remain each one appears before a board of at least two medical officers, who examine him by every available test which experience has proved to be useful and prepare a record of their findings.
>
> (260)

Williams went on to report with evident satisfaction that the proportion of emigrants who had been identified as mentally deficient had increased from 18 per 100,000 in the fiscal year ending June 30, 1912, to 50 per 100,000 in the fiscal year ending June 30, 1913, and to 91 per 100,000 in the first ten months of the fiscal year ending June 30, 1914. More specifically, a total of 555 people had been deported from the United States as mentally defective during the fiscal year ending June 30, 1913, which represented a threefold increase in the number of people who had been excluded in each of the previous five years. Moreover, in April 1914 alone, 157 in every 100,000 emigrants had been identified as mentally deficient. Most of this increase was a result of the increased number of emigrants who had been classified as feebleminded rather than as idiots or imbeciles.

In fact, a short item in the *New York Times* of April 19 had reported that the officers of the Bureau of Immigration were finding it hard to accommodate the numbers of emigrants who were being detained as mentally defective. However, instead of attributing this to the increased efficiency of Surgeon Williams's staff, an immigration official was quoted as blaming European families who wished to get rid of mentally deficient relatives or unscrupulous immigration agencies that were busy booking mentally deficient people in increasing numbers in anticipation of the introduction of more draconian immigration laws.

THE SECOND ANNUAL MEETING OF THE
EUGENICS RESEARCH ASSOCIATION

In May 1914 Knox submitted a paper for presentation at the second annual meeting of the Eugenics Research Association. William F. Blades, the association's secretary-treasurer, then wrote to the surgeon general of the Public Health Service to request that Knox be allowed to attend the meeting to describe his work at Ellis Island, and permission was duly granted. The meeting was held at Columbia University on June 19 and 20.

The program was made up largely of individual presentations, including contributions from two professors in the department of psychology at Columbia, James McKeen Cattell and Robert Woodworth. However, the main event was a symposium, "The Most Pressing Topics for Research in Eugenics," introduced by the association's first president, Charles Davenport. A subsequent report identified four main points that emerged from the discussion:

> That more emphasis must be placed on the study of the mental traits of the individual;
> That the psychologist is not willing to grant the proof of the existence of unit characters or traits now used in describing the mental activities of man;
> That tests for intelligence need closer standardization;
> That a better definition of feeble-mindedness, or, as Dr. C. B. Davenport suggested, "feeble-mindness," must be made.
>
> ("Trend of the Science of Eugenics" 1914:388)

The first point simply acknowledged that much previous work in eugenics had been based on the study of physical rather than mental traits. The last two points recognized that intelligence tests were still evolving and that definitions of feeblemindedness based on performance in intelligence tests needed to be improved. However, the second is a more subtle point.

Davenport was influenced by the German biologist, August Weismann, who argued that the inheritance of traits was mediated by specific kinds of cells that he called the germ-plasm. Gregor Mendel's findings on the inheritance of physical traits, especially as they had been interpreted by the British geneticist William Bateson, had indicated that traits should be regarded as independent unit characters carried by different "determiners" (or what today are called genes) and that the determiners inherited from different parents remained distinct and did not blend with one another. Davenport put these ideas together into three principles:

The principle of independent unit characters states that the qualities or characteristics of organisms are, or may be analyzed into, distinct units that are inherited separately. . . . The principle of the determiner in the germ-plasm states that each unit character is represented in the germ by a molecule or associated groups of molecules called a *determiner*. . . . The principle of segregation of determiners in the germ-plasm states that characteristics do not blend.

(1910:6–7)

Davenport talked in terms of the presence or absence of determiners that in themselves might be dominant or recessive. For instance, on the one hand, he claimed that the determiner for brown eyes was dominant, so inheriting it from *one* parent would be sufficient to yield brown eyes, and only children who failed to inherit it from either parent would have blue eyes. On the other hand, the determiners for certain congenital abnormalities were recessive, so these conditions would be apparent only in those children who had inherited them from *both* parents (10–14). (Today these would simply be referred to as different forms, or alleles, of the same gene rather than the presence and absence of a single form.) Davenport's view was that this latter analysis applied to the inheritance of mental deficiency (14–16), but this depended critically upon the assumption that feeblemindedness was a "unit character." If that assumption were false, it would be harder to establish whether mental deficiency was inherited.

Charles Spearman (1904) had of course concluded that intelligence tests defined a central trait or factor that he called general intelligence. In his book *Feeble-Mindedness: Its Causes and Consequences*, Goddard (1914:556–57) interpreted Spearman's results as consistent with his own ideas about the nature of intelligence. As Goddard asserted in the preface, "Normal intelligence seems to be a unit character and transmitted in true Mendelian fashion" (ix). However, some psychologists had already cast doubt on this assumption. Edward Thorndike (1903) had argued that intelligence was simply a multitude of specific capacities. Subsequently, some researchers obtained evidence for Spearman's position (Burt 1909; see also Krueger and Spearman 1907), and others obtained evidence for Thorndike's (W. Brown 1910; see also Thorndike, Lay, and Dean 1909).

Binet's (1909) view had been similar to Thorndike's: "Intelligence is not a single function, indivisible and with a distinctive essence, but . . . the combination of all those lesser functions of discrimination, observation, retention, etc." (143). By the time of the Eugenics Research Association's meeting, the matter was still far from resolved. In a brief report of the meeting the *Journal of Heredity* observed that considerable dissatisfaction had been expressed with the idea that feeblemindedness was a unit character. Indeed, Woodworth had gone so far as to declare that eugenics could not hope to gain the support of psychologists until it had either proved or abandoned this hypothesis.

In the formal business of the meeting, Cattell was elected as association president to succeed Davenport, and William Blades was reelected as the secretary-treasurer. Knox presented his paper on current methods for detecting mental defectiveness among emigrants. During his talk he digressed to talk about an emigrant whom he described as closely resembling the "missing link." The *New York Times* reported this part of his presentation the following day:

> "This man was a Finn, 39 years old, and his occupation was linesman for a telephone or telegraph company," he [Knox] said. "One familiar with the reconstruction of the man of the Stone age could not help but note the close resemblance. The head was one, the external anatomy of which I will never be likely to forget. The forehead was low and receding. The supra-orbital ridges [above the eyes] were sharp and prominent. The eyebrows were long and shaggy. The eyes were sharp and piercing. The nose was saddle-shaped, with a prominent tip. The lips were thick and protruding, while the chin was massive and heavy.
>
> "The teeth articulated at an outward angle and the canines were particularly well developed. The ears were almost entirely below the line drawn horizontally backward from the external cantle of the eye. The arms were unusually long, and the olecranon processes [i.e., the bony points of the elbows] were largely prominent. The hands were remarkable. Each little finger was virtually a thumb that could be used with any other finger. The little fingers were consequently very short.
>
> "The body was round and short. The feet were large, and flat with prehensile toes. If you will exercise your imagination, you will see that the man's occupation was particularly well chosen for his physical make up, since he may have inherited the characteristics of his ancestors who perhaps often found it necessary to climb to the tree tops to escape some giant animal of their time. The man's mentality was of a low order, although he was able to read and write.
>
> "I simply mention this case here for the reason that it is one of a great class who possess atavistic features, indicative of a physically retrogressive make-up that is not good for our racial type and from the presence of which we must sooner or later suffer. The waste basket diagnosis of constitutional inferiority applies quite well, but this is not a mandatorially excludable condition, and all or any of such cases may be admitted at the discretion of the immigration officials who are not themselves physicians.
>
> "At this point it might be well for me to state, for it is not pertinent to the rest of the paper, that the people from certain countries who are coming here at the present time are almost all physical inferiors, and with the present laws we are

absolutely powerless to stop them, and that it would be a very simple matter to do this if we had different physical standards."

Knox's presentation was also reported by the *New York Tribune,* and the *Daily Express* of London carried an interview with Knox the next day. Despite Knox's insistence that "constitutional inferiority" was "not a mandatorially excludable condition," both these accounts confirmed that the man had in fact been deported two weeks earlier on precisely those grounds.

"Constitutional inferiority" was a "waste basket diagnosis" because it was used by physicians of the time to cover a wide variety of conditions of which antisocial behavior was a common feature. In the 1890s Julius Ludwig August Koch, a German physician, suggested the alternative terms *psychopathic inferiority* and *psychopathic personality* in order to avoid the implication that the underlying cause was necessarily constitutional in nature. The latter of these terms was progressively adopted by other German physicians, including the eminent psychiatrist Emil Kraepelin. Kraepelin's writings became influential in English-speaking countries, so that by the end of the 1920s *psychopathic personality* had replaced *constitutional inferiority* in those countries, too (Sass and Felthous 2008). However, even *psychopathic personality* later proved to be unsatisfactory (Karpman 1948), and the preferred expression among physicians in the United States today is *antisocial personality disorder.*

Even so, it seems to have suited Knox and his colleagues to use the term *constitutional inferiority* to justify the exclusion of emigrants on the ground that they were likely to become a public charge. On May 14, 1914, Knox had made the following statement at a board of special inquiry that was held to determine whether a female emigrant should be admitted:

> The constitutional inferiority is aside from the psychopathic personality—is apart from it. The constitutional inferiority implies that the entire organism, physical and mental, is below par, below what it ought to be. That the resistance to insanity and the resistance to physical diseases is less than that of the normal person. The normal individual will go through life with health upon which the ordinary disease or sickness and various infectious diseases of childhood suffers very little permanent harm, but the health with any difficulty of these kind of individuals, will succumb to these diseases. They fall down more commonly than normal people. It is used in Germany a great deal and we are going to use it in this country more than formerly. . . . They designate it as an inferior make up of tissues, both the nerves and physical. That is, the individual is not made up of good stock, the physical make up is not what it should be. The brain is made up of cells and those cells from their lack of functionating, lack of proper formation,

or lack of proper development—that enters into it more—these cells are not as fully developed as they might be and consequently they cannot be expected to functionate as normal cells would. . . . The psychopathical personality implies that while the individual is not insane she has many of the characteristics of the insane person. Now certain individuals are inclined to believe that the world is down on them. That hard luck seems to follow them around more than the ordinary individual. Now these people are not insane, but that characteristic is a characteristic of insanity, one type of insanity, so that they cannot be considered normal, and that would be one kind of psychopathic person. Now there are other people who are non-responsive—who are unsociable, who stick around by themselves. They may not be exactly insane, but those are the characteristics of dementia praecox. The lack of ability to beget normal offspring—that is the fundamental characteristic of the individual. It is absolutely a hereditary thing. They will often beget individuals worse than themselves.

(I will discuss the significance of the term *dementia praecox* later in this chapter.) Knox's deposition was considered sufficiently authoritative that it was cited at subsequent boards of inquiry to justify the deportation of other emigrants.[1]

Immediately after the meeting of the Eugenics Research Association, William Blades wrote to Knox: "Permit me to say that I considered it a very excellent paper and I have heard a great deal of comment all of which was very flattering to me for having secured you for the program. I have the honor also to inform you that you have been elected a member of the Eugenics Research Association." Subsequently, Knox exchanged publications with the superintendent of the Eugenics Record Office, Harry Hamilton Laughlin, and entertained visiting parties of trainee fieldworkers that Laughlin brought to Ellis Island.

In September 1914 the secretary of the Mississippi Valley Medical Association asked the Public Health Service to send an officer to its next meeting to deliver a twenty-minute presentation titled "Mentally Defective Aliens: A Medical Problem." The surgeon general asked Knox to undertake this task. The meeting was held in Cincinnati on October 27–29, and on the way Knox stayed for the night of October 26 at Army and Navy Headquarters in Washington, D.C. According to a letter that he sent his mother that evening, he was still writing his paper. Nevertheless, it was of a sufficient standard to be accepted by a local medical journal and was published the following year (Knox 1915b).

---

1. Knox's deposition may be found in the records of the Immigration and Naturalization Service, Record Group 85, Accession 60A600, box 679, file 53791/126, National Archives, Washington, D.C.

In his presentation Knox reviewed the legal authority for requiring emigrants to undergo mental examination, described his scale for measuring intelligence, and talked about the results of administering such tests at Ellis Island. He mentioned that 1,114 people had been detained at Ellis Island during the fiscal year ending June 30, 1914, of whom 1,064 had subsequently been deported. Of this number, 957 had been classified as mentally defective, reflecting a substantial increase on the figure of 555 people that Surgeon Louis Williams (1914) had reported for the previous fiscal year. This was partly the result of an increase in the number of emigrants examined at the Port of New York (more than one million in 1914) but partly also because by this time nearly one emigrant in a thousand was being deported as mentally defective.

KNOX'S *SCIENTIFIC AMERICAN* ARTICLE

In January 1915 Knox published yet another account of his scale in *Scientific American* (1915a). Then as now *Scientific American* was aimed at a general readership interested in scientific matters. Knox's article was accompanied by a column of classified advertisements as well as advertisements for scientific and technical books, the *National Sportsman* magazine, real estate gold bonds, Sanatogen vitamins, and *Whitaker's Peerage, Baronetage, Knightage and Companionage*. (The last advertisement was aimed at Americans related to prominent families in Britain or its colonies who might even inherit such titles as the result of the deaths of the incumbents in "the present great but sad war in Europe.")

Knox began by explaining the purpose of his instrument:

The measuring scale to be given further on only determines the intellectual power, that is, the ability to think, to reason, to judge, to adjust one's self to the social requirements of the world around him and to exist harmoniously in it, in conformance to its laws and customs. . . .

The purpose of our mental measuring scale at Ellis Island is the sorting out of those immigrants who may, because of their mental make-up, become a burden to the State or who may produce offspring that will require care in prisons, asylums, or other institutions.

Or, as the article's subtitle put it, the scale contained "a progressive series of standardized tests used by the Public Health Service to protect our racial stock" (52).

Knox pointed out that the scale included questions and tests appropriate for different ages from three to thirteen and that older people should be able to meet the requirements for thirteen-year-olds:

In other words, for the purposes of examination 13 years is adult or maximum development so far as the scale is concerned. The "mental" age of a given individual is the point in the scale beyond which he can go no farther; suppose for example that a man of 40 years could only do the things that a 9-year-old should do, we would say that this man was but 9 years old mentally, and this is a very common place for the mentally retarded to stop, in fact, a great many tramps such as the ones that go to make up the "hobo" armies that travel about the country and annoy church gatherings are actually less than this age mentally. They are easily led and influenced.

(53)

As he had in one of his earlier papers (Knox 1913g), Knox was again expressing the view that mental deficiency was tantamount to mental retardation.

He then presented "a scale for estimating mental defects in illiterates and others." This was essentially the same as the original account published in the *Journal of the American Medical Association* almost a year before (Knox 1914c; see table 6.1) and included the seven "make-up tests" for adults whose mental ages

TABLE 7.1 ADDITIONAL TESTS FOR EDUCATED EMIGRANTS

Age	Test
Seven years	Repeat a spoken sentence of ten words.
Eight years	Write from dictation a sentence of ten words.
Nine years	Make a sentence using the words man and dog. Give the opposites of good, right, white, wise, giving an illustration such as "tall—short."
Ten years	Make a sentence of not less than ten words, using the words man, dog, and gun. The answer must show some thought and not be simply, "I saw a man, dog, and gun the other day." This would be almost a failure.
Eleven years	Make a sentence using the words man, dog, gun, and rabbit, showing each of these taking an active part.
Twelve years	Test the person in the spelling of such words as he commonly uses. Then have him give the multiplication tables from 4 to the table of 8, inclusive.
Thirteen years onward	The degree of education must be ascertained and questions improvised that will tend to show how much the man profited by his education and, in short, whether he knows as much as he ought to.

Source: Adapted from Knox 1915a:57–58.

7.1 Surgeon Louis L. Williams (seated) and his staff at Ellis Island.
From left: Howard A. Knox, James G. Townsend, Grover A. Kempf,
Harry Laughlin, Walter L. Treadway, Samuel B. Brooks, Harry F. White,
Robert L. Wilson, Henry C. Cody, Ezra K. Sprague, Eugene H. Mullan, and
Charles W. Vogel, in a photograph that accompanied the 1915
Scientific American article. (Courtesy National Archives)

had been estimated at between eight and twelve years, according to other tests. However, Knox also included additional tests for "educated" emigrants between the ages of seven and thirteen, that is, those who could read and write. These tests, listed in table 7.1, were all verbal and hence were not performance tests.

As was (and still is) common for articles published in *Scientific American*, Knox's piece contained copious illustrations. These featured all the performance tests and included a group photograph of the physicians at Ellis Island (figure 7.1). The original caption read:

Surgeon L. L. Williams and staff of the United States Public Health Service, at Ellis Island, N.Y. These officers stand guardian to our national health, and the colossal piece of preventive medicine carried on by them saves the country untold millions of dollars each year and helps to maintain the high physical and mental standard of our race. The officers of the United States Public Health Service are commissioned by the President in the same manner as are the officers of the Army and Navy, and the scheme of the Service as regards rank, pay, duties, and social life is in general the same.

(52)

Perhaps most strikingly, however, Knox's *Scientific American* article was illustrated with photographs of apparently genuine emigrants attempting to carry out some of the performance tests. For instance, the original caption to figure 7.2 read:

A mentally defective immigrant woman attempting to perform the fourth, or *d*, line of the cube test, with which she had but little success, having failed in three out of four trials. She was the mother of three children, one of which was defective also, and the other two, while normal intellectually, were, of course, capable of transmitting feeblemindedness and neuropathic tendencies to their offspring.

(53)

7.2 Dr. Harry White testing a female emigrant, another illustration
for the 1915 *Scientific American* article.

7.3 Dr. Harry White testing a male emigrant, also in the
1915 *Scientific American* article.

Similarly, the original caption to figure 7.3 read:

> There is practically nothing in the physiognomy of this immigrant that indi-
> cates the gross mental defect that he possesses. The alien is performing, with
> considerable difficulty, the Seguin formboard, a task which should not require
> more than 20 seconds in normal adults; this alien required anywhere from
> 45 seconds to 4½ minutes, and his performances did not improve with practice
> and repeated trials.

(53)

AT THE PSYCHIATRIC INSTITUTE

In the summer of 1915 Knox was temporarily detailed to work as an assistant
physician at the Psychiatric Institute of the New York State Hospitals (today part
of the Columbia University Medical Center), which was located in Manhattan
State Hospital on Ward's Island. He took the opportunity to write a paper, "A
Broader View of Mental Deficiency in Aliens," which was published in the *New*

York *Medical Journal* that October (Knox 1915c). He commented that the physicians of the U.S. Public Health Service had adopted "a constantly broadening view of what really constitutes mental deficiency" (755) and that this explained the drastic increase, from 25.1 per 100,000 in 1908 to 50.8 per 100,000 in 1913, in the proportion of emigrants who had been certified as mentally deficient.

This much broader conception of mental deficiency included the feeble-minded, paupers, inebriates, criminals, epileptics, the insane, those with congenital asthenia (i.e., weakness) and poor physique, "the diathetic class" (those predisposed to acquire certain diseases), and "persons possessing stigmata and deformities" (752–54). Knox seems to have been especially interested in congenital deformities of the hands as signs of mental deficiency. He later wrote to the *Journal of Heredity*, enclosing two x-ray photographs to illustrate a case of polydactylism (having extra fingers or toes) in an Italian emigrant. The journal used these in an unsigned editorial ("Extra Fingers and Toes" 1916), but its author considered that the condition had no link with mental deficiency and consequently "possesses no eugenic significance" (324).

While he was at the Psychiatric Institute, Knox also wrote a short paper about dementia praecox. This was eventually published in late 1917 in a series of articles (referred to as a "medical symposium") that was appended to a book by Maximilian Paul Eugen Groszmann, *The Exceptional Child* (Knox 1917e). The term *dementia praecox* had been adopted near the end of the nineteenth century by the German psychiatrist Emil Kraepelin to refer to a disorder seen in late adolescence or in early adulthood that was characterized by progressive intellectual deterioration. Kraepelin believed that the disorder was organic in nature and probably caused by some kind of hormonal abnormality following puberty.

The visit of Sigmund Freud and Carl Jung to the United States in 1909 had prompted an interest among American physicians in psychoanalytic accounts of such diseases. In particular, many were influenced by the view of the Swiss psychiatrist, Eugen Bleuler. Bleuler argued that the notion of dementia praecox was too narrow, and he put forward the new term of *schizophrenia*. He also suggested that the disease had psychodynamic origins. Other American physicians, such as Adolf Meyer, argued that schizophrenia resulted from a complex interplay of biological, social, and psychological factors.

Knox himself had published a paper advocating the application of psychoanalytic ideas in general medical practice (Knox 1913b). It is not particularly surprising, then, that in the paper that he wrote at the Psychiatric Institute Knox took a view similar to Meyer's. As Knox put it, "Dementia præcox has a toxic [i.e., organic] origin with a superimposed psychosis of psychogenic derivation" (1917e:650). However, he also felt that once the disease was established, any attempt at treatment was "a more or less useless endeavor"; the only hope was to spot the disease before its full onset, in what he called the stage of "predementia præcox" (649).

In some cases, Knox argued, dementia praecox was mainly an organic disease, in which case hormone therapy might be needed. In other cases it was particularly a problem of psychic maladjustment, in which case it would be necessary to investigate its psychological origins by a variety of means, including psychoanalysis. Knox commented: "It is in this direction that I have already made some endeavors. It will take years to determine whether or not these have been effective, and even then I shall not know with certainty that the cases would have developed dementia præcox if it had not been for my efforts" (650).

Subsequently, the expressions *dementia praecox* and *schizophrenia* have tended to be used interchangeably, but American clinicians define them more broadly than their counterparts elsewhere in the world, and *schizophrenia* is more commonly used by those who maintain that the primary origins of the disease are psychodynamic (as the etymology of the term—"splitting of the mind"— would suggest). Nevertheless, research using brain imaging and other modern technology has identified neurological abnormalities not only after but even before the onset of the disease. This has led to calls to drop use of the term *schizophrenia* altogether and to reinstate Kraepelin's original notion of dementia praecox (Adityanjee et al. 1999).

MARKETING THE ELLIS ISLAND TESTS

Knox's paper in *Scientific American* attracted a good deal of interest from academic researchers, clinical practitioners, and educationalists. He received not only numerous requests for reprints but also a number of requests for copies of the actual apparatus used in his performance tests. Knox seems to have originally assumed that others would simply make their own copies. For instance, he advised that the various form boards should be backed with a thin sheet of wood or cloth to stop the pieces from slipping through (Knox 1915b). However, at some point during 1915 he arranged for copies of the Ellis Island tests to be produced and distributed by C. H. Stoelting Company of Chicago, an established and well-known supplier of laboratory equipment and test materials. The leaflet describing the "Apparatus and Supplies for 'A Scale for Estimating Mental Defects'" bears the date November 15, 1915 (Knox 1915d).

The cost of a complete set of the materials, including a "Book of Instructions" and fifty blank record cards "used by the U.S. Public Health Service at Ellis Island, N.Y.," was $41.69. "Book of Instructions" was, however, something of a misnomer. It was officially entitled *Alien Mental Defectives: A Collection of Papers Descriptive of* the *Tests and Methods Employed by the United States Public Health Service, Ellis Island, N. Y.* (Knox 1915e). In fact, it consisted simply of a set of reprints of three of Knox's previously published papers (Knox 1913e, 1914c, 1914f). These had been reset and repaginated to fit on statement-size paper (5.5 inches by 8.5 inches), and each set of reprints was presented in a "Photomount Pamphlet Binder" supplied by Gaylord Brothers of Syracuse, New York.

One can assume that Knox's superiors were content with the idea of his work's being made available in this way, because they subsequently arranged for copies of the commercial versions of the performance tests to be purchased for use at Ellis Island. Illustrations of the tests, many bearing Knox's name, were included in the *Manual of the Mental Examination of Aliens* (1918), which I discuss next. In chapters 10 and 11, I describe how the tests were used by many other researchers and practitioners between the two world wars.

THE *MANUAL OF THE MENTAL EXAMINATION OF ALIENS*

This project had a tortuous history and took more than five years to come to fruition. Although new medical officers had long received a book of instructions for the inspection of emigrants, this did not take into account the increased interest in mental examination. In February 1913 the Public Health Service therefore agreed that there should be a new manual specifically on this topic. Senior Surgeon Stoner assigned passed assistant surgeons Eugene Mullan and Marshall Crapon Guthrie to take the matter forward. However, Guthrie left Ellis Island soon afterward, and little work appears to have been done in the next six months.

In August 1913 Mullan went to Surgeon Williams, who by then had replaced Stoner as the chief medical officer, with a rather different proposal. He suggested that an officer should be detailed to administer mental examinations to normal emigrants in order to build up a body of normative data with which the performance of other emigrants might be compared. Mullan reported that a small start had already been made, in that he had tested eighteen Italian emigrants, while his colleague Bernard Glueck had tested fifty Polish emigrants. Their other responsibilities had prevented them from doing more than this; however, if an officer were assigned to this task as a sole responsibility, two thousand emigrants could be tested in a year, Mullan claimed.

He justified his proposal on two grounds. First, the physicians were currently in a position to identify those emigrants who were patently mentally deficient. However, the only normative data available were from children in France or the United States and were inappropriate for use with emigrants. In the absence of valid normative data, the physicians were unable to make more subtle decisions and exclude those emigrants who were only moderately deficient. Second, if the Public Health Service did not take the initiative in this area, physicians and psychologists elsewhere (he mentioned the New York State Psychiatric Institute and the Vineland Training School, in particular) might well do so, Mullan argued.

Surgeon Williams forwarded Mullan's proposal to the surgeon general in Washington, saying that it had his "cordial approval" and that, if approved, Mullan should be designated to take on the work. Moreover, Williams suggested that it would form an important part of the proposed manual of mental examinations and that all the physicians at Ellis Island engaged in carrying out mental examinations should be asked to contribute material to this project. He added that he had asked Passed Assistant Surgeon Thomas Salmon to assist in editing the work. Salmon was at this time on leave of absence from the Public Health Service and was working for the National Committee for Mental Hygiene, but he had nevertheless agreed to help with this project.

The surgeon general, Rupert Blue, replied that he approved the plan as a whole, and he wrote to Salmon to invite him to chair a board to be responsible for preparing the manual. In his letter Blue referred to the proposed manual as a pamphlet, implying that he was not expecting a substantial piece of work. He added that Salmon's role would have to be an unofficial one since there would be no remuneration. He then asked Williams to meet Salmon to discuss the membership of the board but added that he, Blue, would be unable to spare anyone to replace Mullan while he was engaged in testing normal emigrants. Williams replied that he could manage without a replacement for Mullan but needed four or five additional interpreters.

Members of the initial board convened to prepare the manual for the mental examination of emigrants were

Passed Assistant Surgeon Thomas W. Salmon (chair)
Passed Assistant Surgeon Eugene H. Mullan
Assistant Surgeon Grover A. Kempf
Assistant Surgeon Howard A. Knox
Assistant Surgeon George Parcher
Acting Assistant Surgeon Bernard Glueck

They did not meet as a board until the beginning of December 1913, when they came up with two recommendations. First, they endorsed Mullan's proposal for the collection of normative data "to enable us to formulate adequate standards for determining mental deficiency in different types of immigrants." They suggested that this work could be carried out while other portions of the proposed manual were being prepared. Second, they requested that Assistant Surgeon

Walter Lewis Treadway be appointed to the board to replace Bernard Glueck, who had returned to his regular position at the Government Hospital for the Insane in Washington. Knox mentioned the board's work in an article that he published in the *New York Medical Journal* in January (Knox 1914a).

Mullan had previously sought advice on the selection and administration of tests from Robert Woodworth and one of his colleagues at Columbia University, Henry Alford Ruger, and in early January Mullan embarked on the collection of data. He worked with an interpreter who spoke Italian, Spanish, and German, and Mullan initially proposed to focus on emigrants of those nationalities. After spending a week developing their procedures, Mullan and his interpreter selected cases from among the emigrants who had been detained for at least twenty-four hours in the detention rooms or from the ambulatory cases in the hospital on Ellis Island. (It is unclear what inducements, if any, the emigrants were given to participate.) However, Mullan and the interpreter excluded emigrants who had been detained as possible cases of mental deficiency.

Toward the end of May 1914 Surgeon Williams mentioned Mullan's study during his address to the annual meeting of the American Medico-Psychological Association in Baltimore. He explained that the study's aim was to "aid in standardizing the tests in use, and assist in establishing at least approximately a practical standard upon which certification may be based" (Williams 1914:266). With the outbreak of World War I in Europe in September 1914, finding suitable examinees became difficult. However, Mullan concluded that they already had collected sufficient data, and he discontinued the study with a total of 296 emigrants examined. Three turned out to be mentally deficient, so their data were dropped from the analysis.

The tests that Mullan had used were predominantly verbal. They seem to have been based on the test battery that Mullan had previously advised Glueck (1913) to use in his work with Polish emigrants (see table 5.1) and included tests taken from or similar to those in Binet and Simon's 1908 scale. However, they also included the Healy Frame Test and the Geographical Puzzle, as well as a version of the Cube Imitation Test, modified in certain respects:

The cubes were tapped with a spool instead of a block "so as to draw the subject's attention from the exact way in which the cubes were struck and to the essential nature of the problem, the order in which the different cubes were touched by the examiner" (E. H. Mullan 1917b:39).

After six trials in which each of a line of four cubes was tapped once, a fifth cube was added to the line, and the examinee underwent four trials in which each of the five cubes was tapped once (see figure 7.4).

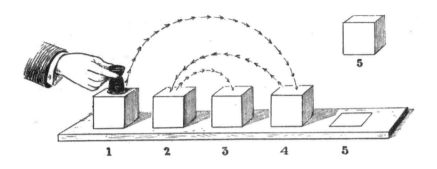

7.4 The modified version of the Cube Imitation Test,
as described by Mullan in his 1917 report.

A contemporary account by one of Mullan's colleagues, Milton Hugh Foster (1914),
implied that in this version of the test all five cubes were the same color: "The
cube test . . . consists in placing four or five ordinary wooden blocks of the same
size and color in a row on the table before the subject" 1069). However, neither
Mullan nor Foster specified the color.

The examinee was allowed two attempts in the first trial but only one attempt in all
other trials. Although the cubes were generally tapped at a constant rate of one per
second, a longer pause (between one and a half and two seconds) was interposed
after the second or third item in each sequence. Mullan found that 75 percent of
examinees could copy four trials with four cubes and one trial with five cubes.

In September 1914 Knox received a request for reprints from Adolf Meyer
at the Johns Hopkins Hospital in Baltimore. Knox sent some reprints but commented in a cover letter that "they do not, however, represent our advanced work
or findings." He explained that "a complete report of our work will be published
by the Public Health Service in the near future in the shape of a manual for the
mental examination of immigrants." It would be based on the research that Eugene Mullan had been carrying out during the previous year "and also upon the
practical work done by myself and others." At least two sections had already been
written, one on psychiatry by Walter Treadway and another on working with interpreters by Grover Kempf.

Early in 1915 Thomas Salmon resigned as chair of the board that had been
convened to prepare the manual. This may have been because of the pressure of
his work for the National Committee for Mental Hygiene, where he was responsible for commissioning surveys of mental health provision in particular states

and, indeed, was carrying out some of these surveys himself (Bond 1950:55–58). Nevertheless, he may also have been dissatisfied at the lack of progress on the manual. To try to speed matters up Surgeon Williams, the chief medical officer at Ellis Island, wrote to the surgeon general on March 1 to suggest that surgeons Ezra Sprague and Milton Foster should be added to the board and that, as the senior officer, Surgeon Sprague should be asked to replace Salmon as its chair.

During this time, of course, Howard Knox had not been idle. His article had appeared in *Scientific American* less than two months before and had attracted a good deal of attention. On March 1 he wrote to the surgeon general, offering to prepare a brief monograph describing the use of his intelligence tests. The assistant surgeon general, Leland Eggleston Cofer, replied by asking whether it would be feasible for him to prepare such a monograph for publication in the Public Health Service journal, *Public Health Reports*. Knox agreed to prepare this publication, and Surgeon Williams forwarded Knox's reply to Washington with the following comment:

> A monograph of this kind, if published by the Bureau, would be regarded as an authoritative statement of the settled practice in the examination of defective aliens and should therefore represent the concensus [sic] of opinion of the officers engaged in such work. It would also be, to some extent, a forecast of the manual the preparation of which is now being pushed. For these reasons it is suggested that Dr. Knox's article, before publication, be submitted for criticism and discussion to the board detailed by the Bureau to prepare a manual for the examination of mental cases.

The surgeon general, Rupert Blue, approved the preparation of the monograph on this basis. Knox did indeed prepare such a monograph, but it was never submitted to the Public Health Service for publication and was never, indeed, formally published at all.

The board met on May 26, 1915, to discuss the preparation of a manual for the mental examination of immigrants and agreed an outline of contributions together with the names of authors who would take responsibility for each chapter. On June 18 Surgeon Sprague forwarded to the surgeon general a contribution from Eugene Mullan with the title "Psychology of the Arriving Immigrant." Sprague pointed out that it contained results from 293 subjects, or one and a half times as many as Binet and Simon had tested in devising their 1908 scale. Sprague thought that the contribution was not too long for the proposed manual but that, if the work were regarded as too voluminous to be included, he recommended "that it be published separately as a valuable original contribution to the subject and for use of others engaged in work along the same lines."

In July the chapters by Knox ("Mental Deficiency and the Use of Certain Intelligence Tests in the Examination of Immigrants") and Treadway ("A Guide to the Psychiatric Examination of Immigrants") were also forwarded to the surgeon general's office. Like Mullan's chapter both were longer contributions, and Sprague thought the board would need extra time to consider them. After a further exchange of correspondence with the surgeon general's office, the remaining chapters were completed in August and early September. Nevertheless, Assistant Surgeon General Cofer was not entirely satisfied with the manuscripts that he received, and he turned for advice to Surgeon Claude Hervey Lavinder.

Lavinder had graduated from the University of Virginia in Charlottesville in 1895 and had initially trained as a radiologist. However, he had been assigned to a variety of locations after he joined the Marine Hospital Service in 1897, and his most recent work in New York City had been mainly concerned with the epidemiology of pellagra. This disease is manifested in lesions of the skin, but it also gives rise to alimentary and neurological symptoms and eventually death. Previously, it had been relatively rare in the United States, but it had become increasingly prevalent, especially in the South, since 1907. Lavinder had written about the prognosis and treatment of pellagra, and in 1913 he had produced a report on its prevalence and geographic distribution. Even so, the task of investigating the cause of pellagra was given to his colleague in the Public Health Service, Joseph Goldberger, who eventually showed that it resulted from a dietary deficiency of the vitamin niacin in people who subsisted chiefly on maize.

In September 1915 Lavinder was appointed to work in the laboratories at Ellis Island. It is not clear whether the true purpose of his appointment was for him to advise on the manual for the mental examination of emigrants, but immediately on his arrival he was appointed chair of the board responsible for the manual, replacing Sprague. Soon afterward Surgeon Williams left Ellis Island, and Senior Surgeon James Clifford Perry was appointed as chief medical officer in his place. The membership of the board was now reduced to Lavinder, Mullan, and Treadway. By December, however, Treadway had left the Public Health Service, and Mullan had temporarily been assigned elsewhere, leaving Lavinder in sole charge of the project. On December 18 Lavinder wrote to Assistant Surgeon General Cofer in a personal rather than an official capacity:

I have gone over all of the manuscripts. If all is published it will make book (octavo size) of not less than 500 pages, profusely illustrated, both with cuts and charts etc. Some of the mss. are all right, some are indifferent and some I do not think suitable as they now are. I do not feel sure from the language of our instructions as to whether the board is expected or permitted to express any opinion as to the quality of the material, or whether it is simply expected to arrange the material submitted for the printer. I am sure however that this book, when issued, will be closely scrutinized by many outsiders, and of course the Bureau desires to get out a creditable publication. Hence I take the liberty of offering some opinions. Besides the quality of the mss. there is an evident lack of consistency and coherence in the whole thing. The various articles do not hang well together. I think this is necessarily the case in any book written in this manner, that is the assignment of a subject to various writers without any editorial supervision. An editor in chief would have had in mind the completed book and required things so arranged as to make a coherent and consistent whole.

I venture to suggest the advisability of appointing some man editor in chief with full powers to do whatever is necessary to get out the book, even to the extent of selecting some other man to write an article if necessary. In no other way will the thing be satisfactory, I fear. Of course the selection of such an editor in chief should be done with care, and if necessary he can have an advisory board, but he must have broad powers.

Cofer referred the matter to Blue, the surgeon general, who wrote to Senior Surgeon Perry, the new chief medical officer, on December 22:

The Bureau is desirous of expediting in every way possible the completion of this manual, and it has been suggested by Surgeon Lavinder that the whole mass of MSS. should be put in the hands of an editor in chief, who could arrange the material to the best advantage so far as economy and efficiency are concerned. The Bureau, having special confidence in Surgeon Lavinder's abilities along these lines, is desirous of making him the editor in chief, but before doing so it was thought that you should state, as a result of a conference with him, whether this work would necessitate his giving his whole time to it, or whether by assistance of some kind, his laboratory duties could be carried out at the same time he was arranging and editing the manuscript. In this connection the desires of the Bureau are as follows:

The book or manual should be arranged as if it were written by one person, but due notice should be given on the covers and in the press that the material has been contributed by the officers who have done so. In other words, it is not desired that it should be simply a collection of articles, for various reasons not necessary to mention here.

Again, while the Bureau desires illustrations, and believes them to be necessary, it must be borne in mind that every illustration adds distinctly to the expense attending the publication of the book, and also adds to the size of the latter, which so far as general utility is concerned, should be kept as small as possible.

Lavinder was duly appointed editor-in-chief of the proposed manual, but within a few months his work was interrupted, not by his laboratory duties but by a major epidemic of poliomyelitis in the northeastern United States.

In the early years of the twentieth century, poliomyelitis had been endemic throughout the United States. It had been estimated that, across the entire country, there were between five thousand and twelve thousand cases per year, roughly one-fifth of which proved fatal. There had been sporadic peaks in its incidence, but these had been mainly local. However, in May 1916 an epidemic of poliomyelitis began in Brooklyn and spread to the other boroughs of New York City. The number of new cases peaked in the second week in August, then declined to normal levels by the end of October. Altogether, 9,345 individuals were affected, 80 percent of whom were children younger than five. Twenty-four percent of all people affected—98 percent of whom were younger than fifteen—died. Moreover, the disease spread to the surrounding states, affecting New York, New Jersey, Pennsylvania, Delaware, Maryland, Connecticut, Massachusetts, Rhode Island, Vermont, New Hampshire, and Maine, so that the total number of cases attributed to the New York epidemic was put at twenty-three thousand.

In early July the Public Health Service offered to monitor the progress of the epidemic. Lavinder was ordered to suspend his other duties and was assigned the task of investigating its epidemiology, together with two colleagues based in Cincinnati and with the support of a team of experienced physicians. Although Lavinder and his colleagues gathered a substantial amount of evidence, the distance between them impaired their collaboration. It was disrupted yet further when the United States entered World War I in April 1917. After one or two brief meetings Lavinder was left with the task of completing their report, which he submitted on September 8. It was eventually published the following July (Lavinder, Freeman, and Frost 1918) and is today regarded as a major work on the epidemiology of poliomyelitis (see, for example, Trevelyan, Smallman-Taynor, and Cliff 2005).

Once the epidemic was past its peak, Lavinder was able to devote time to working once more on the proposed manual for the mental examination of emigrants, and Senior Surgeon Perry submitted a revised manuscript to the surgeon general on January 31, 1917. After explaining the reason for the further delay, he commented:

> The editor does not believe the manuscript is ideal and it may be stated that an ideal result could not be expected under the conditions. It is believed, however, that the publication will provide a book not discreditable to the Service, and one that will be highly useful.
>
> It can be improved in a second edition as experience with it, no doubt, will suggest many changes of importance. However, immediate publication of the

present manuscript is recommended, and it is believed that the work will produce a satisfactory working manual.

Much modification has been made in the material, and a considerable portion of manuscripts has been rejected in order to prevent overlapping, and to provide a suitably sized book.

The article of Dr. Treadway and that of Dr. Knox has not been used, except in a very small part. They were rejected not on account of their quality, but simply for lack of space, as it was the desire of the Bureau to reduce the size of the manual. I have returned the manuscripts of Doctors Treadway and Knox so that they may use it in some other publication if they should so desire.

As part of the revision, it was also agreed to use Sprague's suggestion that Mullan's chapter be published as a separate report: It appeared in October 1917 in the Public Health Service series Public Health Bulletins, entitled *Mentality of the Arriving Immigrant* (Mullan 1917b). Perry also enclosed a memorandum stating, among other things, that the various sections of the manual would not be described as "chapters" and that no credit would be given to any particular officer: The introduction would simply state that the manual was the result of a process of evolution in which all the officers who had served at Ellis Island had had a part.

Despite Lavinder's work, the manual was not yet complete. The surgeon general referred the revised manuscript for further editing, and Passed Assistant Surgeon Lawrence Kolb was given the task of producing the final version. He made further extensive changes aimed at removing any repetition and ensuring that the text was current. He rewrote the section on performance tests, which in the final manual ran only six pages (30–35). Photographs of eight tests were provided, and readers were referred to Mullan's (1917b) report for further information. The Cube Imitation Test was mentioned but was not described in detail nor listed as a performance test (29). Senior Surgeon Perry submitted the final manuscript on August 20, 1917. The surgeon general sent it to the Government Printing Office three days later, but, under wartime conditions, it was not published until the following year, when the anonymous *Manual of the Mental Examination of Aliens* appeared as "Miscellaneous Publication No. 18" of the Public Health Service.

By modern standards *manual* is once again a misnomer. It did not prescribe when or how to use particular tests or how to evaluate an emigrant's performance. Instead, it left considerable discretion to individual examiners. For instance, it only was suggested that "each immigrant should be given one or two performance tests" (30). Elsewhere, Mullan (1917a) recommended that initial screening of individual emigrants should include tasks such as counting, addition, and the Cube Imitation Test, but thereafter he commented,

There is individuality in each officer's method of conducting a mental examination. There is also a great deal in common about the various examination methods. Some tests and questions are used by all, while individual preference obtains in regard to other tests. As time goes on, new tests and methods are tried, and the ones that are found to be of value are adopted by all. Other tests are tried, found to be useless, and are given up.

(746)

Mainly as a result of Knox's own endeavors, the Ellis Island tests soon became widely known among physicians, psychologists, and educationalists across the United States, and copies of the tests were readily available from C. H. Stoelting Company. Nevertheless, Lavinder dropped Knox's chapter from the *Manual of the Mental Examination of Aliens*, and only a brief description of the Ellis Island tests remained. According to Knox's family, this engendered in Knox a lifelong resentment toward Lavinder.

Knox considered turning his chapter into a book. In January 1916 the superintendent of the Eugenics Record Office, Harry Laughlin, wrote to ask whether Knox had made any progress in this regard, suggesting that such a book would be a valuable contribution to the field, and Knox sent him the manuscript of the rejected chapter. With Knox's agreement Laughlin submitted it to Warwick and York, a publishing house in Baltimore, and Laughlin promised to seek another publisher if they did not wish to take it. However, nothing seems to have resulted from these efforts on Knox's behalf. His unpublished papers do contain parts of a manuscript, but these are mainly photographs of the Ellis Island tests, together with photographs of emigrants arriving at Ellis Island and being interviewed and tested by the physicians.

8

PRACTICAL ISSUES IN INTELLIGENCE TESTING

In their various publications Knox and his colleagues raised a number of interesting issues about intelligence and intelligence testing in the particular
context of the inspection of emigrants. The primary issue was the validity of the
process of line inspection. Both Knox (1913c, 1914b) and Assistant Surgeon Carlisle Knight (1913) had written in defense of the validity of line inspection as carried out by experienced physicians. Whether they were genuinely convinced of
this is not entirely clear. When Assistant Surgeon Grover Kempf was interviewed
many years later in 1977, he recalled: "The mental examination of immigrants
was always haphazard. It couldn't be any other way because of the time given
to pass immigrants along the line. Some questioning—if the immigrant did not
respond or looked abnormal he was sent in and given a further examination"
(Kraut 1994:71).

The physicians at Ellis Island were in a no-win situation. If they insisted that
they were identifying most, if not all, mentally defective emigrants, they would
never be given additional resources. If they argued for additional staff, they
would be criticized for failing to protect the nation. When their chief medical officer, Surgeon Louis Williams, spoke at the 1914 annual meeting of the American
Medico-Psychological Association in Baltimore, he sought to achieve a middle
way between these two alternatives:

> At present the point of maximum error in the examination is the primary in-
> spection. . . . The most potent factor, however, in fixing the amount of time given

each alien is the necessity for passing them fast enough to avoid blocking the work of the immigration officials. . . . A few additional seconds devoted to each alien would be of great value, but, for the reasons given, these additional seconds can be secured only by a substantial increase in the medical personnel and a corresponding increase in the working space. . . . The possibilities of the present law cannot be fully realized until a sufficient number of medical officers, a sufficient force of competent interpreters and an adequate working space shall have been provided.

(Williams 1914: 266–67)

Knox (1913c) had provided a long list of clinical conditions that he maintained could be identified through "a diagnostic study of the face." In his account, "Mental Examination of Immigrants," Eugene Mullan (1917a:737–38)—by this time promoted to the rank of surgeon—adopted a similar rhetorical ploy when listing the wealth of symptoms that the physicians could detect on line inspection:

Various kinds of dementia, mental deficiency or epilepsy would be suggested by: Stigmata of degeneration, facial scars, acneiform rashes, stupidity, confusion, inattention, lack of comprehension, facial expression of earnestness or preoccupation, inability to add simple digits, general untidiness, forgetfulness, verbigeration, neologisms, talking to one's self, incoherent talk, impulsive or stereotyped actions, constrained bearing, suspicious attitude, refusing to be examined, objecting to have eyelids turned, nonresponse to questions, evidences of negativism, silly laughing, hallucinating, awkward manner, biting nails, unnatural actions, mannerisms and other eccentricities.

In diagnosing mental deficiency, Knight (1913:107) had observed (as others had before him) that the identification of feebleminded people was "the hardest problem with which we have to deal." Nevertheless, the Ellis Island physicians were at the same time deeply aware of the implications of such a diagnosis and the responsibility that was thereby imposed upon them. As Surgeon Williams commented:

The law places a heavy responsibility upon the medical officers who perform this work, a responsibility which should and does make for conservatism. Because of this conservative attitude the medical inspection of mentally defective aliens at Ellis Island has been criticised at times and the claim made that it does not go far enough, and that many persons are passed by our examiners who should be excluded. That the examination is still far from perfect is readily conceded; we hope to make it better. But much of the criticism thus far has been based upon the opinions of observers without medical knowledge; lay workers who have learned the usual tests employed in examining school children, or else upon the dicta of persons who may be otherwise qualified to express an opinion, but who have not taken into consideration either the practical difficulties which confront the medical examiner, or the gravity of a certificate of feeble-mindedness under the immigration law. We cannot afford to make many mistakes in examining aliens. While failure to recognize a feeble-minded individual results in his admission into the country to the detriment of the state, on the other hand a certificate based on insufficient grounds means unnecessary and painful separation of families and the sending back an alien to the ends of the earth regardless of the hardship involved. . . . For these reasons it is not surprising that we cannot concede the justice of criticisms based upon work in a widely different field, and which are made without a knowledge of the legal aspects of this work and the discouraging array of practical difficulties which surround it.

(Williams 1914:264–65)

Just as Williams stressed the need to be conservative because of the serious consequences of an incorrect diagnosis of mental deficiency, Knox claimed that the tests provided a fair assessment of the emigrants who were being tested. In his article in *Scientific American* he remarked that, in obtaining normative data for their tests, "the majority of the cases examined were somewhat below their racial and social average, so that the only criticism of the measuring scale is that it is too easy, at any rate it is eminently fair to anyone tested by it" (Knox 1915a:53).

THE ROLE OF LANGUAGE, CULTURE, AND EDUCATION

The Ellis Island physicians had criticized the use of Binet and Simon's scale to evaluate emigrants because it depended upon linguistic communication and cultural knowledge. In principle, interpreters could address the matter of language, and the physicians did use interpreters provided by the Department of Commerce and Labor. Knox (1913a) had emphasized that interpreters needed to be properly selected and trained, but even so problems could still arise. Surgeon Ezra Sprague discussed some of the issues:

It must also be remembered that the alien can rarely be addressed in his native tongue by the examiner. Though several of the public health officers at present engaged in the examination of immigrants at Ellis Island are capable of conducting a primary mental examination in one or more foreign languages, it is considered unsafe to make a final decision without the assistance of an official interpreter. In cases in which the interpreter must be depended upon entirely the alien is at a decided disadvantage, especially in cases of suspected insanity when shades in expression carry much weight.

Interpreters will at times give voice to their own mental interpretation of the subject's answer rather than a literal translation. For instance, to the question "What is your occupation?" the reply was, "He is a farmer." The actual statement was, "I use a pick and shovel." The interpretation may or may not have been correct and though it may appear unimportant, it may have determined a line of questioning to gauge the subject's intelligence, and to him it may have made a decided difference whether he was called upon to discuss farms and farming or some other occupation with which the pick and shovel could be legitimately associated. Again, the attitude of the interpreter may be such as to excite or even frighten the subject, placing him in such a state that he is far from able to do himself justice.

(1914:466)

Moreover, in formal test situations interpreters sometimes went beyond simple translations of an emigrant's responses, particularly when these appeared to be inept or illogical (see Popplestone and McPherson 1999:77). It would then become unclear whose intelligence was being evaluated, the emigrant's or the interpreter's. The unreliability of interpreters was one of the main reasons for trying to develop performance tests of intelligence (Glueck 1913).

Even with a perfectly competent interpreter, however, tests such as those in Binet and Simon's scale took for granted certain cultural knowledge. Knox had reproached Henry Goddard and his assistants for their uncritical use of Binet and Simon's scale during their visits to Ellis Island in 1911 and 1912: "To the uninitiated using routine tests for defectives nearly all the peasants from certain European countries appear to be of the moron type: but of course this is a fallacy. If these peasants are questioned about conditions existing in the land from which they come most of them will show average intelligence" (Knox 1913a:105). Elsewhere, Knox (1914a) noted in detail the cultural demands of the tests used to assign mental levels of six, seven, eight, and nine years in Binet and Simon's scale. If it were used routinely to screen emigrants, he suggested that about 75 percent would appear to be defective.

In his survey, *Mentality of the Arriving Immigrant,* Eugene Mullan provided a particularly clear example of the role of cultural knowledge (1917b:123–24). One of his tests presented the examinees with several pictures, and they had to describe what each depicted. One picture was called "Last Honors to Bunny," and it showed three children grieving over the body of their pet rabbit: One child was holding a bunch of flowers, another was digging a hole with a small spade, while the third looked on mournfully. This test caused problems even for literate adults, and Mullan discussed why this might be:

> It is obvious that the result obtained from the "Last Honors to Bunny" picture is entirely different from the result which would be obtained in the case of people other than arriving immigrants.
>
> In order to interpret a picture correctly, the immigrant must be familiar with pictures of various kinds. He must also be experienced in the customs or events portrayed in a picture. In addition he must possess the power of constructive imagination. In other words, he can arrive at a situation portrayed in a picture only after analyzing and separately considering all the picture elements in the light of past experiences, then combining all these findings into the interpretation. . . .
>
> The poor interpretations of the last picture were partly due to some of the following causes: Mistakes of details; took the rabbit for a cat, dog, goat, pig, etc. They had never seen pets treated well. They had never seen them treated with signal honors. Many are not accustomed to seeing rabbits used as pets. . . . In certain places it is not customary to cover the grave of the dead with flowers. Even if an immigrant has had some experience with pictures, pictures of this kind are hard to interpret.
>
> (1917b:123–24)

Of course, those emigrants who came from wealthier families might have acquired the relevant cultural knowledge through their education or training, but in that case the tests would be measuring educational level rather than intelligence. On the contrary, the aim of the Ellis Island physicians, according to Knox, was to devise "tests that demonstrate native ability and which presume no previous instruction" and which could therefore be used even "with those in whom no scientific effect at teaching has been previously attempted" (1913g:1017). Surgeon Matthew Gwyn made the same point: "It was necessary to secure tests which could be used in common among a mass of people of various races, or varying school advantages, together with a large number who were utterly illiterate" (1914:198).

Surgeon Milton Foster, their colleague, discussed the role of education and training as contaminating factors, while taking care to acknowledge the importance of Binet and Simon's scale so long as it was used in appropriate situations:

> It would be impossible to discuss this subject without some reference to the Binet-Simon scale. The work of these investigators was very complete and the results extremely valuable for the population which they examined. A critical examination, however, of the tests employed will show that many of them de-

pend on the ability to use words in definition and in stating comparisons. Such a power depends largely on training and not solely on native ability. In this respect the scale is clearly not applicable to illiterates, and experience in applying it literally to ignorant immigrants has amply demonstrated this fact.

A careful study of the Binet-Simon scale is extremely useful, and every one who undertakes to make examinations of mental defectives should be thoroughly familiar with it, as it forms an important foundation on which to build up a plan of examination suitable and especially devised for those who have had no educational training or the advantage of association with educated persons.

(1914:1070)

Knox (1913f) had made the specific observation that, by relying on cultural knowledge, tests of the sort included in Binet and Simon's scale confounded the distinction between "moronism" and mere ignorance. He argued that assessing children at schools for the feebleminded presented no genuine diagnostic problem, because their deficiency had already become apparent to their teachers and families through their poor ability to acquire new knowledge. Consequently, the tests used in educational contexts were not required to distinguish between children who were mentally defective and those who were simply ignorant. However, by the same token, such tests were wholly unsuitable for assessing emigrants who lacked the necessary background knowledge (including literacy) to tackle such tests.

Foster made a similar point:

The examination of an illiterate person for the purpose of determining his mental capacity is often difficult. To distinguish between ignorance and feeblemindedness is by no means easy. Many of the elaborate and complicated tests for measuring the intellectual ability are clearly inapplicable and we cannot use them. All mental processes which obviously depend on education or special training for their development are at once ruled out, and by a careful analysis we find that many of the usual tests recommended require these educated and trained faculties on the part of the subject.

(1914:1068)

Foster pointed out that the amount of cultural knowledge that a person could acquire would vary not just across races and countries but across different social groups within the same country. Hence, if tests of this nature were used to identify mental deficiency, the criteria of deficiency would need to vary in the same way: "Thus in determining feeble-mindedness in foreign races by measuring the amount of their acquired knowledge, a great deal of time and energy must be expended in deciding what are normal standards for each race and also for the various social and geographical classes in each country; and at best such standards are only relative" (1068).

In his *Scientific American* article Knox suggested that the Ellis Island tests would be particularly valuable in industries that employed large numbers of emigrants. On the one hand, the tests would enable employers to identify employees who were mentally defective and hence more likely to cause accidents in the workplace:

> To illustrate the working of this measuring scale of intelligence and to demonstrate how an American business man could weed out the worthless and very often dangerous mental weaklings from his service the writer will cite the case of an immigrant picked at random from the thousands of defectives that have been handled by the United States Public Health Service at Ellis Island. It is to be supposed that this scale should be of particular value in the industries at this time when alien labor is being so widely employed, especially since it was founded scientifically upon work done upon aliens. Investigation has shown that they are frequently the cause of serious and expensive accidents, and the immigrants immediately connected with these accidents have often been grossly lacking mentally. The fact that mental defectives are generally inefficient is well known.
>
> (1915a:58)

On the other hand, the tests would also enable employers to identify applicants who might prove to be efficient employees even though they tended to perform poorly on more conventional tests, such as those contained in Binet and Simon's scale:

> This same measuring scale could, however, be used in industrial enterprises to determine the intelligence, and hence the probable efficiency of illiterate or poorly educated aliens seeking employment, and on all others of equal intelligence, such as the negro population of certain parts of the South. One must remember that ignorance is not feeblemindedness, and one of the advantages of the scale here given is its ability to separate the two.
>
> (52)

This seems to be the only reference in Knox's writings to the idea of comparing test performance in white and black people drawn from the domestic population of the United States, as opposed to comparisons of the different national or "racial" groups of emigrants from Europe. Indeed, it would seem that Knox's own discourse about race did not encompass variations within the national population at all. This merely reflected the national discourse about race and immigration at the time, which focused on the supposed qualities of "old immigrants" from northern and western Europe compared with those of "new immigrants" from southern and eastern Europe, essentially ignoring the situation of both black and Native American people (see, for example, King 2000:59–81). Even so, the last excerpt is striking, not because it asserts the existence of differences in test performance between white and black people but because of the explanation that it offers.

As soon as translations of Binet and Simon's scale had become available in the United States, researchers had begun to use it to make comparisons of black and white participants, typically finding poorer performance in black participants than in whites of the same age (see Morse 1913 for an early example). Eugenicists such as Charles Davenport interpreted such findings in terms of genetic differences in intelligence, a common view at the time. Lewis Terman (1916:90–92) described two brothers from a Portuguese family, M.P. and C.P., as examples of "borderline deficiency" and commented:

> It is interesting to note that M. P. and C. P. represent the level of intelligence which is very, very common among Spanish-Indian and Mexican families of the Southwest and also among negroes. Their dullness seems to be racial, or at least inherent in the family stocks from which they come. The fact that one meets this type with such extraordinary frequency among Indians, Mexicans, and negroes suggests quite forcibly that the whole question of racial differences in mental traits will have to be taken up anew and by experimental methods. The writer predicts that when this is done there will be discovered enormously significant racial differences in general intelligence, differences which cannot be wiped out by any scheme of mental culture.
>
> (91–92)

Of course, Knox himself shared the view that intelligence was largely inherited. In the same article in which he made reference to racial differences, he provided a highly pragmatic definition of intelligence:

> A man or woman who succeeds in life is mentally more energetic, better able to remember, more attentive, less open to evil suggestion, has better judgment and is less liable to brain fag than one who makes a failure of his opportunities. These qualities . . . constitute the thing we know as intelligence and *the quality and quantity of this that we possess is largely determined by heredity.*
>
> (1915a:52; emphasis added)

Nevertheless, Knox was perhaps the first person to argue that black people performed less well on conventional intelligence tests not because they were less intelligent but simply because they were poorly educated.

THE CAUSES OF MENTAL DEFICIENCY

During his first year at Ellis Island, Knox had claimed that physical and mental defects were inherited according to Mendelian principles (e.g., Knox 1913a). Within a few months, however, his position had altered. This was prompted by the realization that some emigrants showed mental disorders that were the result of the process of immigration itself, a point that had also been made by Thomas Salmon (1913b).

In July 1913 Knox published an article in the *Medical Record* concerning psychogenetic disorders in detained emigrants. As he explained, these disorders

> are thus termed because one or more distinct psychic experiences stand out as of special etiological importance in definite relation to their course. These experiences in this condition are either of a strongly pleasant or strongly unpleasant nature, especially affective to the patient possessing them. A characteristic of all psychogenetic disturbances . . . is that they usually disappear very soon after the psychic irritant which produced them is removed or successfully counteracted.
>
> (Knox 1913d:59)

Knox emphasized that many conditions were the result of "psychic experience," and he then cited the German psychiatrist Emil Kraepelin on the subject:

> Kraepelin has said that immigration stations afford excellent clinical facilities for the study of these disorders, and judging from the cases I have seen and from mistakes which are being made by lay-workers from various schools for the feeble-minded who are not aware of the importance of eliminating functional [i.e., psychogenetic] psychoses when dealing with conditions suggesting mental defect, I am inclined to agree with this learned neurologist.
>
> (61)

Knox gave the example of a female emigrant who had appeared to be suffering from dementia praecox (schizophrenia). The woman's condition had arisen following her arrival at Ellis Island, and it had disappeared once she had been hospitalized. Knox inferred that her condition had arisen from "the change of environment, involuntary confinement, strange surroundings, customs and people" (61). Knox (1917e) later concluded that dementia praecox could be either a mainly organic disease or a problem of psychic adjustment, and this view was undoubtedly encouraged by his experience of examining and treating this particular emigrant.

In his July 1913 paper Knox stressed that emigrants in whom psychogenetic disorders could be attributed to strong emotional shock subsequent to their landing at Ellis Island were not liable to be deported under the immigration laws. However, their condition might well give rise to poor performance on psychological tests. Knox concluded his article by directly attacking the approach to assessing emigrants that Goddard and his assistants had taken: "Immigrants suffering from psychogenetic disorders should not be examined for defectiveness while in this state, and lay-workers with no knowledge of medicine, psychiatry, or neurology, cannot detect these conditions but would call such a patient 'stupid' or rate him as 'seven years old on the Binet'" (61).

That September Knox elaborated on the idea that mental deficiency could arise as a temporary condition resulting from a number of physical causes:

> I wish to add one note of caution, and that is to be certain that the case of moronism is of congenital origin, and not a simple transient condition due to anemia and toxemia, as in uncinariasis [hookworm], to pellagra, to other toxines, to hypothyroidism or disturbances of other internal secretions, and lastly, and by far the most important, to psychogenetic depressions. These transient conditions, which may simulate true congenital moronism or feeblemindedness, are in the main curable, and it would be unjust to certify and deport such a person. It is therefore very essential that all such examinations be conducted by persons with medical training.
>
> (1913f:566)

Around the same time Knox had written another paper, "Subnormal Mentality in Immigrants," that was not published until March 1914. In this paper Knox confidently asserted that "all feeble-mindedness (not ignorance) is due to agenesis corticalis, that is, there are brain cells entirely missing, malformed or atypical in inherent or resistive and nutritive qualities" (1914d:142). He went on to discuss the probable causes of congenital and acquired mental deficiency, and he noted that the latter might be cured or at least improved. However, on this occasion he did not acknowledge that the notion of "curing" mental deficiency should raise doubts about whether the person should be deported.

The following January his article "Mental Defectives" discussed both the prenatal and the postnatal factors that appeared to predispose people to mental deficiency (1914a). Even so, his recommendations with regard to how society might deal with mental defectives were mainly aimed at reducing the opportunities for mentally defective people to gain access to the United States and subsequently reproduce:

> 1. Restricted immigration. . . . 2. Public education and eugenic laws. 3. Incarceration in self supporting institutions of all known defectives. 4. All children should be examined mentally when entering school and at the end of every year thereafter until their education is completed. 5. The eradication and prevention of infectious diseases both acute and chronic, protozoon and bacterial. 6. Sensible asexualization in properly selected cases.
>
> (221)

In March 1914 Knox published a paper in which he reproduced the scale of performance tests from his article in the *Journal of the American Medical Association* but then warned of the pitfalls that might be encountered if the intelligence of emigrants were evaluated simply on the basis of their achievement in psychological tests (Knox 1914e). On the one hand, he emphasized the range of conditions that might lead to poor test performance:

> Many of us, I believe, look upon deficiency in all cases as being due to heredity, or at least to tangible physical conditions with consequent organic or toxic change, whereas it may be due in any given case to conditions existing purely and solely in the psyche, caused by impressional stimuli that, having a peculiar and intense affective value for that particular individual, may be at the bottom of the whole trouble; until the exact percept can be unearthed, little headway will be made toward a successful termination of the affair. The lesson therefore is that the final disposition of all defectives, delinquents, and others, should be made on the advice of psychiatrists as well as psychologists.
>
> Another kind of pitfalls [sic] are sometimes seen by the staff at Ellis Island, and these are the transient disorders that arise as a result of recent psychic shock, such as incidents of the voyage of an unpleasant nature, during which the alien can do practically nothing that requires mentation. These recent psychic shocks are to the conscious mind what the repressed ones are to the subconscious, and the psychogenic depressions, etc., are to the former as the hysterias, psychasthenias, and neurasthenias are to the latter.
>
> (527)

On the other hand, the results of psychological testing might be misleading and needed to be interpreted with great care. As acting assistant surgeon Bernard Glueck noted:

One must have been actually engaged in the work among immigrants to adequately appreciate the importance of taking into consideration the mental state under which the alien is laboring upon arrival to our shores. The state of apprehension, anxiety, and severe fatigue, from which many of them suffer on arrival, must be reckoned with if our data on which to base a diagnosis are to be dependable.

(1913:764)

Knox made it clear that Goddard and his assistants from the Vineland Training School were the particular target of his criticisms because of their failure to take account of the emigrant's context and personal history when interpreting their test results:

Any one willing to do so may see . . . that the study of defectives is an infinitely complex problem, not one to be delegated to workers with mechanical tests who have no knowledge of the newer psychiatry, although performance tests are instruments of immense value when they are in the hands of people who are qualified to use them intelligently. . . .

The most remarkable mistakes that I have observed, in a way, were made by a young lady who came to Ellis Island armed with a bundle of tests which originated in work that had been done on school children, and of course were not applicable to illiterate aliens. The discoveries that she made were wonderful to contemplate. One was that you could detect defective aliens merely by looking at them whereupon she proceeded to stand on the inspection line and "tally" the defectives as they passed. Some of the "tallied" ones she proceeded to examine by her tests, after which she turned them over to the staff to be certified and was much disappointed to think that the latter would not do as she suggested. Here another remarkable detail comes out, namely, that by accident even, she did not detect even one defective during her sojourn at Ellis Island. There are on record at Ellis Island thirty-six individuals who Miss X, as I shall call her, averred were feebleminded or imbecile. These were all examined in detail by members of the staff and were in every case discharged, either as normal or too bright to certify under the law, or because their enfeeblement was only apparent and due to physical infirmities, such as defective vision.

(1914e:527–28)

Of course, one condition that might lead to poor test performance in emigrants was the very process of immigration itself. Eugene Mullan made this point in his survey, *Mentality of the Arriving Immigrant*:

In order to diagnose mental disease and mental deficiency in an immigrant at an immigration station a knowledge of the mental ability and conduct of the normal or average immigrant at the time of arrival is necessary. Normal aliens at the time of landing are in a peculiar mental state. Many of them have come from rural districts where opportunities have been meager; they have undergone a long voyage, perhaps suffering many hardships; they are anxious to land and to meet relatives. Therefore, their mental condition has been partly shaped by all these circumstances; and if they are questioned or given mental tasks to perform at the time of arrival it is to be expected that their replies and general behavior will not be the same as would be obtained under other conditions.

(1917b:5)

OPTIMIZING THE CONDITIONS OF EXAMINATION

In addition to taking into account the "peculiar mental state" of arriving emigrants when interpreting the results of psychological testing, the physicians could do a great deal to alleviate the emigrants' distress. Although he had only been at Ellis Island for a few months, Knox stated these requirements in January 1913:

In making tests on these people [emigrants] the following conditions should be fulfilled:

1. The interpreter should have a pleasant and kindly manner; he must be accurate in his statements and convey the exact thought and intent of the alien and he must be unbiased, impartial and above all else intelligent. The interpreter, like the examiner, should have special training.

2. A quiet, well-ventilated room should be used for the examination.

3. The condition of the alien should be taken into consideration; for instance, after ten days of sea-sickness, fatigue and excitement he could not be expected to do himself justice. Rest, food and reassurance are to be prescribed here in generous quantities.

(1913a:106)

Later that year, having introduced his new tests for detecting mentally deficient emigrants Knox he commented:

The line they draw between normal and defective illiterates is well marked, but, as in using other tests of these individuals, the general rules as to rest, nourishment, fresh air, and pleasing environment for the performance of the tests must be followed and, of course, physicians must operate these tests, else, psychosed, toxic, functional, and temporarily defective individuals will be interpreted as organic congenital feebleminds, which, after all, are the principal ones to be considered from an eugenic viewpoint.

(1913e:523–24)

Most of Knox's comments, like this one, focused on the kind of environment in which emigrants should be tested. Elsewhere, he gave the following instructions:

Select a quiet, well lighted and ventilated room, with a temperature of not over 68 degrees Fahrenheit. There must be no disturbing or distracting elements and the room must not have an official air, in fact it should look as much like a "den" in a private house as possible. Only those concerned in the examination should be present, that is, the interpreter and the examiners and in the case of children or timid people, a relative. The subject must have had good food and a bath previously and he must be mentally as tranquil as possible. The interpreter should be kindly disposed towards the alien and understand him thoroughly and be understood by him.

(1914b:129)

The idea that "only those concerned in the examination should be present" is a reminder that Goddard had relied on results that had been obtained in the presence of "many interested observers of every test" (1912b:111). Knox made similar proposals in his article in *Scientific American*:

All conditions should favor the one undergoing the examination; the room should be quiet and well ventilated, the temperature should be not over 70; there should not be over three persons present, if the subject does not understand English an interpreter should be used that he thoroughly understands; the examiner and the interpreter should be calm, patient, and kind, the subject should be encouraged and never told that he is wrong. He should previously have had a good meal, and if possible a bath and sleep. Allowance must always be made for fear and mental stress under which the subject may be laboring, and two or more separate examinations on different days may be necessary to accurately determine the upper limit of his ability.

(1915a:53)

As Ezra Sprague remarked: "Is there any wonder that many apparently below par mentally on the first examination, give, after a night's rest combined with quiet and good food, a normal mental reaction? Even the feeble-minded frequently show some improvement" (1914:466).

Apart from the purely physical environment, however, Knox later referred to the qualities that were needed in the examining physician:

In diagnosing mental enfeeblement in the higher and more refined grades, the most important test after all is the "human test," or the ability of one human being to take the measurement of another by conversing and associating with him. This intuitive ability can be very highly developed in persons of strong personality and physique. The physique is necessary; since it is well known that, all things being equal, the subjects of examination will divulge themselves more readily and more truthfully to the examiners possessed of generous proportions than to others. The ability to take this mental measure must be founded on the experience of having seen and examined many positive cases and the examiner must be a broadminded, big souled man with a keen insight into the frailties and shortcomings of the human race in general, including himself.

(1914a:216; for similar wording see Knox 1914b:127)

He added: "It is very evident that at the conclusion of this examination the physician is in a good position to give his subject a mental rating, provided of course that he tempers the tests with plenty of every day common sense" (Knox 1914b:130).

At the same time on at least one occasion Knox was markedly insensitive toward an emigrant. On November 9, 1915, an eighteen-year-old girl and her fifteen-year-old brother arrived at Ellis Island from Italy. Their father had emigrated to the United States in 1910 and was living and working as a lamplighter in Buffalo, New York. He submitted an affidavit that he had the means to support the children, and an immigration officer in Buffalo had testified that there was no danger of their becoming a public charge. However, the girl became distressed, and on November 19 she was transferred to the hospital at Ellis Island. Later that day assistant surgeons Knox, Kempf, and Treadway certified that she was "afflicted with [a] psychopathic personality which affects [her] ability to earn a living."

The children appeared before a board of special inquiry at Ellis Island on December 2, and Knox was called to testify as a witness before the board. His testimony was similar to what he had told a previous board on May 14, 1914 (see chapter 7).

Psychopathic personality implies a condition of individual constitutionality that is inherited, or at least existing in the make-up of the individual, which predisposes that individual to the development of insanity. That is, people who have a psychopathic personality are more liable to go insane than a normal individual. They may be said to possess the rudiments of insanity, that is, certain traits of character near insanity, actually are insanity. I might illustrate, giving the psychopathic personality we will say of maniacal depression. These individuals are very highly strung, always trying to do something which they never quite succeed in doing; in talking they take about 100 words to say what an individual would put into half a dozen. That in brief is a picture of what I mean by psychopathic personality of that stamp. That is, the psychopathic personality of that certain type of insanity, and with dementia praecox there is another type of psychopathic personality. An individual who is very secluded and does not confide in anybody, is opposed to the opposite sex and shuns them, who is addicted to excessive masturbation, we will say, and other symptoms of that nature. That man has a psychopathic personality. If he meets with adversity, if he gets into an environment he cannot adjust himself to he is going insane. The ones generally become insane who get into an adverse environment.[1]

As Margot Canaday (2004:56) of the University of Minnesota commented in her doctoral thesis, Knox ignored the fact that he was giving testimony about an eighteen-year-old woman, he used only male pronouns in his statement, and he made no attempt to link the perversions that he alleged to be typical of the psychopathic personality to the facts of the case.

The board determined that both children should be deported as people likely to become a public charge, but their father appealed to the Bureau of Immigration, arguing that his daughter's continued detention constituted an environment that was adverse to her medical condition. In the face of the recommendations of the immigration staff at Ellis Island, the assistant secretary at the Department of Labor in Washington, D.C., Louis Freeland Post, resolved that the boy should be allowed to enter the United States and that the girl should be admitted temporarily under security of a bond. The requisite bond was then issued by the Southwestern Surety Insurance Company of Denison, Oklahoma, and the children were transferred to the care of their father on December 17.

This was not, however, the end of the story. On November 20, 1916, another immigration inspector reported that the family had moved to a neighboring apartment in Buffalo and that the daughter had married another Italian immigrant. The inspector commented that she "appeared to be enjoying good health,

---

1. The documents relating to this case may be found in the records of the Immigration and Naturalization Service, Record Group 85, Accession 60A600, box 804, file 53999/811, National Archives, Washington, D.C.

promptly and cheerfully answered all questions asked, and appeared to possess a fair amount of intelligence." Nevertheless, the assistant commissioner of immigration at Ellis Island was outraged and wrote forthwith to the commissioner-general for immigration:

> This is another instance showing the inadvisability of permitting aliens, who are found to be inadmissible, temporarily to enter the country. To forestall complications bound to arise if she remains here long enough to give birth to a child, which would be a United States citizen, I feel that deportation should be ordered at once; otherwise you will have in the country not only a potentially insane person, but probably numerous offspring, mentally defective.

Although this view found some support among the commissioner-general's staff, Post decided that the woman should be admitted unconditionally and that the bond filed on her behalf should therefore be canceled.

THE DEMISE OF ELLIS ISLAND

By this time the importance of Ellis Island as an immigration station was in decline. Emigration to the United States had fallen markedly after the outbreak of World War I in Europe in September 1914. In the fiscal year that ended June 30, 1914, the total number of emigrants examined at ports of entry was nearly 1.5 million. The next year it was less than one third of that number, and the figure was reduced further in the subsequent two years. It dropped to less than 250,000 per year after the United States entered the war in April 1917.

From that point Ellis Island was also in decline as a key location for the development of mental tests. In May 1917 the United States imposed a literacy test on emigrants older than sixteen. Knox (1914d) had predicted that a literacy test would prevent 90 percent of alien mental defectives from entering the country for the next ten years, and, indeed, in the years that followed, the proportion of emigrants identified as mentally deficient declined to less than 20 per 100,000. As Surgeon Walter Treadway (1925) suggested, this might indicate that "those mentally defective persons who are unable or slow in acquiring a reading knowledge would be deterred from seeking admission and would be excluded from embarkation by steamship companies" (139). It could also mean that some tests that had been used to identify mentally deficient emigrants had been tapping their knowledge of reading and other verbal skills rather than their intelligence.

In 1924 Congress determined that the responsibility for screening emigrants would be delegated to the U.S. embassies or consulates in the emigrants' countries of origin, and quotas based upon the U.S. census of 1890 were established that restricted the numbers of immigrants. This clearly reduced the role of Ellis Island, and in 1943 the immigration reception was moved back to New York City. The facilities at Ellis Island continued to be used as a detention center for deportees, but in 1954 they were closed completely, and the buildings fell into disrepair. Nevertheless, Ellis Island became part of the Statue of Liberty National Monument in 1965. During the 1980s the main building was restored to appear as it had in 1918–24, and it was reopened as the Ellis Island Immigration Museum in 1990. As I was writing this book, the displays included examples of Knox's tests loaned by his family and by the Archives of the History of American Psychology at the University of Akron in Ohio.

~~~~~~~

In his published writings, Knox made a number of important prescriptions with regard to the appropriate conditions in which to carry out the mental testing of emigrants and with regard to the appropriate interpretation of the test results. Similar proposals were made in articles by other physicians at Ellis Island (see, for example, Mullan 1917b:6), so it is clear that they shared Knox's concerns. Indeed, Knox's advice remains relevant to the practice of mental testing nearly a hundred years later. Quite apart from the particular tests that he devised at Ellis Island, Knox made important contributions as a pioneer of intelligence testing. Nevertheless, as I explain in the next chapter, Knox left Ellis Island and the Public Health Service in May 1916, and he subsequently exhibited no further interest in the development of intelligence tests.

9

AFTER ELLIS ISLAND

O n May 4, 1916, Howard Knox resigned his commission in the Public Health Service. Several factors may have contributed to his decision. On the one hand, by this point most of Knox's contribution had been excised from the *Manual of the Mental Examination of Aliens,* and he seems subsequently to have ascribed the responsibility for this to the intervention of Claude Lavinder. On the other hand, in April 1916 Knox was being considered for promotion to the grade of passed assistant surgeon, and it is conceivable that his application for promotion turned out to be unsuccessful.

The most immediate circumstance was that at the beginning of May 1916 Knox had remarried: Indeed, he resigned his post while he and his new wife, Maka Harper, were taking a short honeymoon. Maka had been born on September 14, 1896. She was the youngest of a family of nine children from the village of Seneca in Oconee County, South Carolina, where her father was the postmaster. Her older brother Charles was married to the sister of Knox's first wife (Marion Henderson), and it was at their home in Laurel, Maryland, that Maka and Knox had first met. Howard and Maka Knox went on to have three children, Howard, Carolyn, and Robert, and their marriage lasted until Knox's death in 1949.

Figure 9.1 shows Knox toward the end of his time at Ellis Island. After the honeymoon Knox returned to Ellis Island and worked until the end of May. He then took the balance of the leave that was owing to him until his resignation from the Public Health Service formally took effect on August 10. At the beginning of

9.1 Howard Knox in a 1916 Oldsmobile, spring 1916, location unknown. (Courtesy the late Carolyn Knox Whaley)

June, Knox returned to Ashtabula, Ohio, where he had spent the first nine years of his life and where he still had relatives. He attempted to set up a private general practice there, but this venture proved unsuccessful. In the meantime, however, Knox had received an invitation from the superintendent of the State Village for Epileptics in Skillman, New Jersey, to take up the post of acting clinical director. (The State Village was replaced in 1953 by the New Jersey Neuro-Psychiatric Institute, which was later renamed the North Princeton Developmental Center. Following the general move to community care for people with developmental disabilities, it was closed in 1998.)

IN SKILLMAN

Knox may well have met the superintendent, David Fairchild Weeks, through his contacts in the eugenics movement. Weeks himself had been carrying out research, initially with Charles Davenport, to demonstrate the genetic basis of epilepsy (Davenport and Weeks 1911; Weeks 1912; Woods, Meyer, and Davenport 1914). Today it is generally acknowledged that some cases of epilepsy that have no identifiable cause may have a genetic origin; even so, in the vast majority of patients epilepsy is instead symptomatic of underlying neurological damage, such as that resulting from head injuries, tumors, or strokes (Chadwick 1993). There was, however, an alternative line of research open to Knox at the State Village for Epileptics.

Only a few years before, a psychologist at Skillman, Wallace Wallin, had measured the intelligence of epileptic patients according to his own translation of Binet and Simon's (1908) scale. Of 333 patients, he found that 5.7 percent had a mental age of one or two years, that 27.3 percent had a mental age between three and seven years, and that 61.5 percent had a mental age between eight and twelve years. Wallin concluded that "the Binet-Simon scale offers an ingenious but simple, practicable, objective and rapid device for estimating and classifying defectives" (Wallin 1912:379–80). In fact, modern research suggests that epilepsy has relatively little effect on the intelligence of either children or adults (Leitner 2000; Vingerhoets 2006), and Wallin's findings are more likely to have reflected the effect of the patients' institutionalization rather than any intellectual impairment resulting from their epilepsy.

Nevertheless, Knox ignored research on the genetic basis of epilepsy and on the mental ability of epileptic patients. Instead, he became interested in the hypothesis that epilepsy had a bacterial origin. In January 1917 he published a case report of an epileptic patient who had died as a result of an intestinal hemorrhage (Knox 1917a). Although Knox had not been allowed to carry out an autopsy, he had taken a sample of the patient's blood just before his death. Knox then prepared cultures from the blood sample and identified a form of streptococcus, suggesting that the patient's death had resulted from a bacterial infection. He presented the case to illustrate the difficulty of diagnosing such diseases in people with chronic conditions. However, in February and March Knox published three articles in successive issues of the *New York Medical Journal* on the role of bacteremia (presence of bacteria in the blood) in epilepsy.

In the first article Knox (1917b) described the results of tests that he had carried out on blood samples obtained from twenty-five epileptic patients either during or immediately following their seizures. In nine of these blood samples he found an unusual form of bacterium that he called "Streptobacillus epilepticus." Subsequent work indicated that it was common in patients who had grand mal seizures (now known as tonic-clonic seizures, typified by violent contractions and loss of consciousness) but absent in nonepileptic individuals and that the subcutaneous injection of a suspension of the organism in salt solution elicited positive skin reactions in 31 of 35 epileptic patients but not in Knox himself. He argued that this bacterium might be responsible for provoking epileptic seizures in people whose nervous systems had been weakened by trauma or disease.

In the second article Knox (1917c) coined the term *leptin* to refer to preparations of organisms obtained from the blood and intestinal flora of people with epilepsy. He described a similar streptobacillus that he had found in the feces of people with epilepsy, and once again a suspension of the organism elicited positive skin reactions in the majority of epileptic patients whom he injected. He then carried out a clinical trial with twenty-five patients who had grand mal seizures. They received subcutaneous injections of the suspension on roughly a weekly basis for two months, and most showed improvements in their condition. He concluded that systemic immunization with leptin would prove beneficial in the treatment of epilepsy.

In his third article Knox (1917d) described a general therapeutic approach to epilepsy. He emphasized that treatment should begin with a detailed personal history, a thorough physical examination, and a wide range of laboratory tests. He described a variety of procedures both for the treatment of seizures and for use in the longer term. Nevertheless, he asserted: "I believe that systemic immunization from the use of the specific antigens contained in leptin . . . is the most effective means at hand at the present time for the eradication of the seizures and episodes, and for the prevention of progressive deterioration" (1917d:409).

This work seems to have left no mark on medical science whatsoever. It is true that epilepsy is sometimes induced by bacterial infections such as those causing meningitis and tuberculosis. However, the classification of bacteria has evolved considerably in the last ninety years, and Knox's hypothesis of a "Streptobacillus epilepticus" has found no supporters. Moreover, modern clinicians have access to a huge arsenal of drugs with which to treat epilepsy without resorting to vaccination. Finally, the term *leptin* is now used to refer to a hormone involved in the regulation of appetite (it derives from the Greek *leptós*, or thin). A resistance to this hormone seems to be responsible for a tendency for epileptic patients to gain weight (see Hamed 2007). Even so, as an intriguing footnote, it has recently been claimed that the administration of leptin might reduce the frequency of epileptic seizures (Diano and Horvath 2008; Harvey 2003).

IN BAYONNE

Knox spent five months at the State Village for Epileptics from mid-July to mid-December 1916, but his new wife disliked living there. Consequently, in December he made a fresh attempt to set up a private practice, this time in Bayonne, a city in Hudson County, New Jersey. This had formerly been a resort town with farms, boatyards, and fisheries that attracted visitors from New York and farther afield. From the beginning of the twentieth century, however, it had rapidly become industrialized. Between the 1910 and 1920 censuses of the United States, Bayonne's population expanded from 55,545 to 76,754, an increase of nearly 40 percent. These new inhabitants obviously needed more doctors and more hospitals.

Initially, Knox practiced from the family home, but later he was able to obtain a house and an office on opposite sides of Avenue C in Bayonne. He also worked at a small private hospital, the Swiney Sanitorium, which had been opened along the street by Dr. Merrill Swiney in 1912. Howard and Maka Knox's first child, Howard Andrew Jr., was born in February 1917, and their second child, Carolyn, was born in February 1919. In April 1921 Knox produced his last medical publication. This was a note to protest unnecessary and unsuccessful surgery in the treatment of conditions affecting the ear, nose, throat, and mouth (Knox 1921). It had been prompted by two cases in which Knox had been summoned—albeit too late—to deal with the complications of surgical intervention that he construed as (to say the least) overenthusiastic.

IN NEW HAMPTON

In 1922 the Knoxes bought a summer home in New Hampton, part of Lebanon Township in Hunterdon County, New Jersey, which was and remains today a small community on the south bank of the Musconetcong River. Hunterdon County, in the western central part of the state, was then a remote rural region devoted mainly to farming. Knox was still only in his thirties, but the family had by this time become reasonably affluent. He would certainly have been gainfully employed during the influenza pandemic that affected many cities across the United States between September 1918 and March 1919 (Crosby 2003), but he had also acquired private clients over a wide stretch of the East Coast.

With the birth of their third child, Robert, in August 1924, Knox endeavored to retire to New Hampton, and he had a small cottage, Musconetcong Lodge, built nearby for his mother. However, the only local physician died shortly thereafter, and Knox took on the limited local practice. According to the 1934 edition of the *American Medical Directory,* the population of New Hampton was just 132, and Knox's specialty was internal medicine (American Medical Association 1934:1040). Ruth Brooks (personal communication), one of his former patients, recollected that his office was in his home, a small stone structure on a hillside overlooking the river. Figure 9.2 shows Howard and Maka Knox in their garden at New Hampton.

Knox remained in New Hampton for the rest of his life. He was an active member of the Musconetcong Valley Presbyterian Church, and he was a contribut-

9.2 Howard and Maka Knox in their garden at New Hampton, New Jersey, date unknown. (Courtesy the late Carolyn Knox Whaley)

ing editor for the church newspaper, the *Parish Visitor,* writing articles and poetry under the soubriquet "O. D. K." (for "Old Doc Knox"). His writings have a home-spun philosophy and humor that is reminiscent of Garrison Keillor's (1985) *Lake Wobegon Days.* For instance, the following narrative appeared in the issue dated August 28, 1925, when "Old Doc Knox" was in reality just forty years old:

JUDGE: (*to bootlegger who is about to be tried for plying his trade*): Your name?
BOOTLEGGER: Joshua, sir.
JUDGE: Are you the Joshua that made the sun stand still?
BOOTLEGGER: No, sire, I am the Joshua that made the moon shine.

It is reported that a very light sentence was meted out to the culprit. Quick wit and a sense of humor have saved many a delicate situation. Any fool can fight but it takes a wise man to avoid one.

O. D. K.

On July 27, 1949, Howard Knox died of arteriosclerosis in the Jersey City Medical Center. An obituary ran in the *New York Times* the next day, a sign of the deceased's accomplishments and reputation:

> Dr. Howard Andrew Knox of New Hampton, N.J., former superintendent of Ellis Island Hospital, New York Harbor, died in the Jersey City Medical Center early yesterday after a two-day illness, at the age of 64.
>
> Born in Romeo, Mich., Dr. Knox was graduated from the Medical School of Dartmouth College in 1908 and from the Army Medical School as a first lieutenant in 1910. He subsequently served two years in the Mexican campaign.
>
> From 1912 to 1916 he served with the Public Health Service on Ellis Island and then for eight years had an office in Bayonne, N.J. Dr. Knox went to New Hampton, near Washington, N.J., in 1925 and practiced general medicine there. He had been a Mason for more than forty years.

A more detailed obituary appeared in the *Hunterdon County Democrat* a week later:

> Dr. Howard Andrew Knox, a resident of New Hampton since 1925, and a specialist in heart and rheumatic diseases, died Wednesday, July 27, 1949, at 3 a.m. in Jersey City Medical Center, where he had been a patient for two days. He was 64.
>
> A former superintendent of the Ellis Island Hospital, New York Harbor, and a veteran Army physician, he served the U.S. Public Health Service for four years before coming to Hampton.
>
> He graduated from Dartmouth College Medical School in 1908, and was appointed to the Army Medical College, from which he was graduated as a lieutenant in 1910.
>
> He served two years in the Mexican campaign as an examining physician. In 1916 he entered private practice in Bayonne and served on the hospital staff in that city until his transfer to Hampton.
>
> He was an elder in the Musconetcong Valley Presbyterian Church and was a 40-year Mason, a member of the Odd Fellows, the American Medical Association and the Hunterdon County Medical Association.
>
> Private funeral services were held Friday in the Ford Funeral Home, Washington, and interment followed in Musconetcong Valley Cemetery. Rev. James Gillespie officiated.
>
> Surviving are his wife, Mrs. Maka Harper Knox, two sons, Robert of Easton and Howard of Washington, and one daughter, Mrs. W. H. Whaley of Atlanta, Ga. He was the son of the late Howard P. and Jennie Mahaffey [sic] Knox.

This seems to have been used as the basis for another obituary that was published the following October in the *Journal of the Medical Society of New Jersey* and a notice that appeared the same month in the *Journal of the American Medical Association*. All these obituaries were unsigned, and their author or authors are unknown. Among other things, they illustrate the limitations of obituaries as historical evidence. First, Knox was never superintendent of the Ellis Island Hospital, merely an assistant surgeon. Second, he had worked at the Swiney Sanitorium, not the Bayonne City Hospital. Third, he may well have been a Mason for forty years, but the Grand Lodge of New Jersey has no record of his membership.

Most intriguing of all is the idea that Knox "served two years in the Mexican campaign," a claim that was subsequently repeated and elaborated by others. In 1970 Philip Hunter DuBois of Washington University in St. Louis published *A History of Psychological Testing,* which he illustrated with pencil drawings that he had produced from photographic portraits of key individuals. However, he was not able to find suitable photographs of some, including "Knox, the inventive doctor at Ellis Island who served in the United States Army during the Mexican campaign and later went into private practice in New Jersey" (xi). Subsequently, Alan Morton Kraut (1988) maintained that "Knox . . . had a colorful military career as a medical officer with General John J. Pershing in Mexico on the trail of Pancho Villa" (Kraut 1994:73).

As Kraut's comment implies, the expression "the Mexican campaign" usually refers to the U.S. expeditionary force led by General John Joseph Pershing in 1916–17 to attempt to capture the Mexican revolutionary leader Francisco "Pancho" Villa. Knox had of course served for more than two years (October 1908 to April 1911) with the U.S. Army. In addition, he had seen active service with the Coast Artillery Corps during the maneuvers in Galveston, Texas. The latter had indeed been prompted by unrest in Mexico, although in Knox's case this period of field duty had lasted for barely six weeks and was restricted to Galveston itself. During this time Pershing was in the Philippines, where he was governor of the Moro Province. He was also an infantry officer and would have had no dealings with the Coast Artillery Corps.

Pershing did take field hospitals on his expedition to Mexico (Braddy 1966:9), but Knox's whereabouts can be accounted for elsewhere during the entire period of the campaign from March 1916 to February 1917. In particular, Knox had set up private practice in Bayonne before the campaign was concluded, so DuBois's chronology was certainly faulty. In any case, after Knox resigned from the Army Medical Corps in April 1911, the surgeon general of the U.S. Army had been adamant that he was not to be reinstated, and this decision remained on file in Washington, D.C., for the rest of Knox's life. In short, it is extremely unlikely that Knox ever met Pershing during his military career, and one can certainly be confident that Knox had no involvement in the Mexican campaign whatsoever.

~~~~~~

His obituaries show that Knox was remembered as a veteran, as a general physician, and for his work on behalf of his local community. However, by the time of his death in 1949 his contribution to intelligence testing had been forgotten, both by his family and by his profession. Nevertheless, if Knox considered that he had left nothing of significance to the development of intelligence testing, he was quite mistaken. The final part of this book examines the legacy of the work that he carried out at Ellis Island.

PART IV

THE LEGACY

10

DEVELOPING PERFORMANCE SCALES

Although Howard Knox worked at Ellis Island for only four years (May 1912 to May 1916), he and his colleagues produced a remarkable array of diverse psychological tests. These are summarized in table 10.1, together with the publications in which they were first described. They were made available just as interest in the measurement of intelligence and appreciation of the limitations of strictly verbal tests were increasing. It is therefore not surprising that Knox's tests were widely borrowed and adapted in the test batteries subsequently devised to measure intelligence during the next thirty years. Before I consider how they were borrowed and adapted, I need to mention certain technical developments in intelligence testing that had occurred while Knox was at Ellis Island.

THE INTELLIGENCE QUOTIENT

In devising his "scale . . . for estimating mental defect," Knox (1914b, 1914c) had followed the example of Binet and Simon (1908). Different test items in the scale were structured according to the age at which normal children would be expected to pass them (see tables 6.1 and 6.2). The age at which any particular child passed all or most items indicated their mental age, and mental deficiency was measured according to the difference between their chronological age and their mental age. However, this regarded mental deficiency as tantamount to mental

TABLE 10.1 THE PSYCHOLOGICAL TESTS DEVELOPED AT ELLIS ISLAND

Test	Original Source
Visual Comparison Test	Knox 1913e
Diamond Frame Test	Knox 1913e
Geographical Puzzle	Knox 1913f
Cube Imitation Test	Knox 1913f
Imbecile Test	Knox 1913g
Moron Test	Knox 1913g
Casuist Test	Knox 1914a
Construction Blocks Test	Knox 1914a
[Feature] Profile Test (Kempf)	Knox 1914a
Ship Test (Glueck)	Knox 1914c
Triangle Form Board (Gwyn)	Knox 1914c
Diagonal Form Board (Kempf)	Knox 1914c
Inkblot Imagination Test	Knox 1914c

retardation, an idea that had already been called into question both by Binet and Simon (1905b:192) and by de Sanctis (1911). Even among those who accepted the notion of mental deficiency as mental retardation, some had begun to argue that a particular number of years of mental deficiency did not have the same significance in children of different chronological ages. In particular, several German authors argued that a given number of years of mental deficiency was less serious in the case of an older child than in the case of a very young child (see Peterson 1926:223–24).

This led one German psychologist, William Stern (1914:42, 80–84), to propose that one should instead calculate a "mental quotient" by dividing a child's mental age by his or her chronological age. He remarked: "This quotient shows what fractional part of the intelligence normal to his age a feeble-minded child attains" (80). Stern analyzed data from a previous study of 228 children who had been suspected of being mentally deficient. He discovered that the children who had been eventually classified as imbeciles tended to have mental quotients between 0.61 and 0.70, that those classified as morons tended to have mental quotients between 0.71 and 0.80, and that those classified as not being deficient tended to have mental quotients between 0.81 and 0.90.

When Terman and his colleagues (1915) subsequently presented the Stanford revision of Binet and Simon's scale, they argued that mental age should be expressed as a *percentage* of chronological age: In other words, Stern's mental quotient should be multiplied by one hundred. Terman et al. called this index an "intelligence quotient" or "IQ." Terman had been influenced by Henry Goddard and other American researchers into believing that intelligence was a single trait rather than a collection of diverse capabilities. Henry Lee Minton (1988:49) observed that this belief was reflected in Terman's decision to capture an individual's intelligence in a single score. Even so, the idea of an age-scaled intelligence quotient is problematic when applied to adults, as there is relatively little increase in test performance beyond the age of sixteen. As Stern (1914:84) had noted, this means that age-scaled quotient measures decline during adolescence, and they should strictly be used only during childhood while intellectual development is still taking place.

Edmund Burke Huey was apparently the first person to suggest an alternative method for calculating a single measure of intelligence (Coxe 1916; Yerkes 1915), although he was not able to publish his proposal before his death in 1913. Rather than assessing children simply as having passed or failed different subtests in Binet and Simon's scale, one could score the accuracy of their responses on each subtest and add up a total points score. The performance to be expected at a particular age could then be expressed as a certain number of points. This idea was taken up by Robert Mearns Yerkes (pronounced "Yer-keez") at Harvard University. Yerkes was a biological psychologist, but in 1913 he was appointed on a half-time basis as director of psychological services and research in the Psychopathic Department at the Boston State Hospital. His role there was to advise on the development of ways of assessing the intellectual abilities of mentally ill patients (J. Reed 1987).

Working with James Winfred Bridges, a graduate student at Harvard, and Rose Standish Hardwick, an assistant psychologist at the hospital, Yerkes devised a way of scoring a person's performance on the subtests of Binet and Simon's scale out of a maximum score of one hundred (Yerkes and Bridges 1914). This could then be expressed as a percentage of the mean score that would be obtained by normal individuals of a similar age to derive a "coefficient of intellectual ability" (Yerkes, Bridges, and Hardwick 1915). This soon came to be regarded as an alternative (point-scaled) intelligence quotient, although it was realized at the time that conceptually it was quite a different measure from the age-scaled intelligence quotient (see, for instance, Pintner 1923:78).

To use a specific example, on the one hand, a ten-year-old boy would have an age-scaled IQ of 80 if he performed at the same level as normal *eight*-year-old children. On the other hand, a ten-year-old boy would have a point-scaled IQ of 80 if he performed at 80 percent of the level of normal *ten*-year-old children. As I said, Knox (1914c) had followed Binet and Simon (1908) in structuring his scale so that items appropriate for different ages were grouped together. However, when Knox's colleague Eugene Mullan developed his own battery, he followed Yerkes and Bridges in assigning points to each subtest and adding together a total score out of a possible maximum of one hundred (see E. H. Mullan 1917b:125–26).

Yerkes continued to look for ways of improving his point scale and began to write a book on mental testing. He investigated the kinds of tests being used by the U.S. Army and Navy, and on March 7, 1916, he wrote to "Doctor Herbert Knox, Ellis Island, New York," to request copies of available articles bearing on the use of psychological tests at the immigration station. Knox forwarded the request to the surgeon general of the Public Health Service. In his cover note Knox commented that his reprints "are fragmentary in nature and some are misleading." Instead, he suggested that Yerkes "be invited to come to Ellis Island and go over the manuscripts now in the possession of Surgeon Lavinder [i.e., the draft chapters for the *Manual of the Mental Examination of Aliens*] and in addition see the mental examinations as they are actually conducted." This idea met with the surgeon general's approval, and on April 10 Surgeon Ezra Sprague, acting chief medical officer, duly wrote to Yerkes to invite him to visit Ellis Island. Whether Yerkes took up this invitation is not known, but in any case Knox resigned his commission with the Public Health Service and left Ellis Island the following month.

PINTNER AND PATERSON'S SCALE OF PERFORMANCE TESTS

The first person to make extensive use of Knox's tests was Rudolf Pintner. He was an English psychologist who (following James McKeen Cattell and Charles Spearman) had worked for his doctorate in Wilhelm Wundt's laboratory in Leipzig. Pintner emigrated to the United States in 1912, and after a year at the University of Toledo, Ohio, he moved to Ohio State University in Columbus. Pintner's doctoral research had been concerned with the role of attention in the acquisition of reading, but he acquired many other interests in developmental and educational psychology. In collaboration with Donald Gildersleeve Paterson, an instructor at Ohio State, Pintner considered whether it was feasible to use Binet and Simon's (1908) scale with children who were deaf. At the time opinion on this matter was mixed. For instance, William Healy and Grace Fernald (1911) had insisted that Binet and Simon's scale was inappropriate for use with deaf children.

Nevertheless, researchers in the field of deafness were more sanguine. At that time one of the most influential people in the field was Alexander Graham Bell, the Scottish scientist and inventor who had emigrated to the United States in 1871. In 1880 Bell had been awarded a prize of fifty thousand francs by the Académie Française in Paris in recognition of his invention of the telephone. He used these funds to provide resources for research on deafness and to promote the dominant oralist approach to the education of deaf children. Adherents of this approach believed that deaf children should rely upon speech and lipreading for communication rather than upon the use of sign language. (In many schools in those days and, indeed, for many years after, the use of sign language in the classroom was harshly suppressed.)

The prize that Bell was awarded was named in honor of the Italian physicist Alessandro Volta, and Bell went on to use Volta's name for several of his own projects, including the Volta Bureau, a library of books and other resources on deafness that he established in Washington, D.C., in 1887. In 1890 Bell became the founding president of the American Association to Promote the Teaching of Speech to the Deaf (now the Alexander Graham Bell Association for the Deaf and Hard of Hearing). The association's journal was originally called the *Association Review,* but in 1908 it was adopted by the Volta Bureau, and in 1910 it was renamed the *Volta Review,* by which time it had become the preeminent scientific journal for research into deafness. From 1910 to 1911 the editor of the *Volta Review* was Frederick Kinney Noyes, who had studied English literature at Yale University before working as a reporter for the *New York Times.*

Noyes himself contributed short articles to the *Volta Review* on diverse topics from natural history, much in the style of the *National Geographic Magazine.* In 1911 he reprinted Edmund Huey's (1910a) translation of Binet and Simon's scale in the *Volta Review,* adding some introductory comments of his own. They included this statement: "While the following tests for feeble-mindedness were originally worked out for hearing children, they may readily be adopted for application to the deaf; or, at any rate, may serve to indicate the principles upon which a similar scale for such specialized uses might be based" (Huey 1911:26). Noyes was not an expert on deaf education, so it is unlikely that he made this remark without Bell's authority.

Despite this ringing endorsement, Pintner and Paterson (1915a) remained unconvinced. They therefore decided to administer Goddard's (1910b) translation of Binet and Simon's scale to twenty-two pupils aged eight to twenty at the Ohio State School for the Deaf. Usable data were obtained from eighteen pupils; they had an average chronological age of 12.50 years and an average mental age of 7.93 years, which suggested "an average amount of retardation" of 4.57 years. However, one child had a considerable amount of residual hearing, whereas three pupils seemed to be mentally defective. For the fourteen remaining pupils the "average amount of retardation" was 3.36 years, which led Pintner and Paterson to conclude that "the normal deaf child is during his school life about three years retarded as contrasted with the normal hearing child" (209–10).

Nevertheless, they had encountered several problems: "(1) Lack of comprehension, (2) Lack of environmental experience, (3) Difficulties due to the peculiar psychology of the deaf" (202). Even if the questions were administered in writing, many deaf children did not even understand that they were being asked questions, many questions referred to objects or events outside their experience, and many translations did not reflect how deaf children conceptualized physical or social interactions. Pintner and Paterson concluded that "the Binet-Simon Scale as it now stands cannot be applied satisfactorily to deaf children" and that the best tests for assessing deaf children would be performance tests. In particular, Pintner and Paterson referred to form boards, including "Knox's Imbecile Board," "Knox's Casuist Board," and "Knox's Feature Profile Board," and they concluded that a "Binet Scale for the deaf" would need to contain such tests (210).

One problem with these and most other tests was that they had been devised for use with individuals and would take a long time to administer to entire classes of schoolchildren. When Guy Whipple had compiled his *Manual of Mental and Physical Tests* in 1910, his model for test administration was the psychological laboratory, and he focused on individual tests in which the child was effectively in the position of an experimental subject. However, toward the end of 1913, William Henry Pyle of the University of Missouri had produced a similar book intended for teachers. This contained versions of eight of the mental tests and seven of the physical tests from Whipple's *Manual* that Pyle had adapted for group administration in the classroom. Pintner and Paterson examined these to see whether any would count as performance tests and hence be suitable for use with deaf children.

The only candidate seemed to be the "Substitution Test" (Pyle 1913:18–22). The child was presented with a table pairing each digit from one to nine with a different symbol, followed by a long random list of digits. The task was to write the appropriate symbol beside each of the digits in the list, working as quickly as possible. Corresponding to this "digit-symbol test" was a "symbol-digit test," in which the child had to work through a list of symbols, writing down the appropriate digit in each case. Pintner and Paterson (1915b) administered this test to 328 pupils at the Ohio State School for the Deaf, of whom 181 were in classes taught through the medium of speech and 147 were in classes taught (unusual for the time) through the medium of sign language.

In comparison with the norms provided by Pyle (which had in turn been borrowed from Whipple), these pupils showed an "average retardation" of 3.19 years. Pintner and Paterson observed that this was similar to the result that they had obtained using Binet and Simon's scale. They found no overall difference between children who were congenitally deaf and those who had become deaf since birth. However, the children taught through speech showed an "average retardation" of 2.60 years, whereas the children taught through sign language showed an "average retardation" of 4.35 years. Pintner and Paterson (1916) went on to explore the value of this test in a larger sample of deaf children. Even so, this kind of study would be criticized today for not excluding children with additional disabilities, since about 30 percent of deaf people have some other form of disability. Modern research suggests that, in terms of their IQs, deaf people with no additional disability show normal scores, but those with additional disabilities show impaired scores (Braden 1994:98). The implication is that deafness itself has no impact upon intelligence.

Since there appeared to be no other performance tests adapted for group administration, Pintner and Paterson turned their attention back to tests devised for individuals. They first tried out the Feature Profile Test with a sample of mentally deficient children (Pintner and Paterson 1915c). Pintner (1915) then considered Knox's Cube Imitation Test. He commented that "the test appeared to me, after first seeing it applied, to be an excellent one in many ways," but he felt that it needed to be extended and standardized "a little more adequately" (377). He made several changes to the procedure that Knox (1913f) had originally described. One was to prescribe that all the cubes (including the fifth cube, which was used for tapping) should be the same color, and he commented that he himself had used "the Binet black cubes" (377). The cubes should be placed on a table about two inches apart, and the sequences should be tapped at a rate of one tap per second. Finally, he specified a new series of twelve sequences that had been chosen to reflect roughly increasing levels of difficulty. To eliminate practice effects he allowed the examinee just one attempt at each sequence, and he provided no feedback on the correctness or otherwise of the examinee's responses.

The cubes in Knox's original test had been painted in different colors (red, blue, green, and yellow), and Pintner did not explain why he felt that all the cubes should be the same color. Nevertheless, it would be obvious to modern psychologists interested in human memory that remembering sequences of different colors or remembering sequences of different color names would provide an alternative and probably more effective method of remembering the spatial patterns tapped out by the examiner. A researcher at the Carnegie Institute of Technology (today part of Carnegie Mellon University) in Pittsburgh had collected introspections of participants who had been tested using Knox's original apparatus. Nearly all reported some kind of kinesthetic imagery (that is, imagery based upon imagined physical movements), but in most people this was accompanied either by visual imagery of the colors of the blocks or by auditory imagery of the color names (Rachofsky 1918).

Pintner's comment concerning "the Binet black cubes" is probably a reference to the five cubes that had been used in Binet and Simon's test of arranging weights (see tables 4.1 and 4.2). These cubes were in fact small boxes, 2.3 centimeters on each side. When Binet and Simon's scales were introduced into the United States, this test became widely used; indeed, Knox (1914c) included it in his own scale (see table 6.2). The materials were sold by C. H. Stoelting (the same company that marketed the Ellis Island tests) and were subsequently used in the Stanford revision of Binet and Simon's scale (Terman 1916:161, 236). Later, however, Stoelting produced a set of five black 3.5-centimeter cubes specifically for use in Pintner's version of the Cube Imitation Test, and these materials were listed in the company's catalog alongside the apparatus for Knox's tests.

Pintner collected data using his new procedure from 867 normal individuals (from five-year-olds to university students) and from 463 feebleminded children and adults. He discussed both the particular sequences and the number of sequences correctly performed by the normal examinees and showed how these measures could be used to produce alternative estimates of mental age. Pintner concluded that his standardized version of the Cube Imitation Test could make a useful contribution to a performance scale that could be used with normal children or with mentally deficient adults.

Pintner's work had influenced one of his colleagues at Ohio State, Thomas Harvey Haines, who was also the clinical director of the Ohio Bureau of Juvenile Research (which later became part of the Ohio Youth Commission). He had found that both the Stanford revision of Binet and Simon's scale and Yerkes and Bridges' (1914) Point Scale were useful in assessing the intelligence of delinquent boys and girls (Haines 1915b). However, he had found a group of children whose scores on the Point Scale were rather better than those on the Stanford-Binet scale. To try to resolve this he administered another series of tests to the same children, including some of Healy and Fernald's (1911) performance tests, and found that the latter tests differentiated these children both from those who were unequivocally defective and from those who were unequivocally of normal intelligence (Haines 1915a).

At around the same time Haines was asked to advise on the assessment of intelligence in children at the Ohio State School for the Blind. He observed that many tests adopted by Yerkes and Bridges from Binet and Simon's original scale were inappropriate for use with blind children. Haines therefore tried to find analogous tasks that could be used in a point scale of intelligence for administration to blind people. He eventually produced a list of twenty-two tasks and weighted them so that they yielded a total score out of a maximum of one hundred. In particular, he devised an analog of Pintner's version of the Cube Imitation Test:

The subject was asked to place his left hand (if right-handed), with palm upward, upon his thigh. He was asked to hold the hand comfortably relaxed, but with the fingers reasonably spread out. The examiner took the index finger as point *one* of the Knox cube test, and the little finger as point *four*. Of course nothing was said of this to the subject. The subject was told that the examiner would touch the subject's fingertips with the rubber end of a lead pencil. Then the examiner would put the pencil into the subject's right hand and ask him to touch the fingertips of his left hand in the same way the examiner had done (Haines 1916b:146; see also Haines 1916a).

At this time Haines seems to have had no direct knowledge of the Ellis Island tests. In contrast, Pintner and Paterson had become familiar with Knox's work, albeit only through his article in the *Journal of the American Medical Association* (Knox 1914c). This enabled them to assemble a scale containing a total of fifteen performance tests (Pintner and Paterson 1917). Six of these were from Ellis Island:

Casuist Test
Diagonal Form Board
Feature Profile Test
Ship Test
Triangle Form Board
Pintner's version of the Cube Imitation Test

Pintner and Paterson had obtained C. H. Stoelting's versions of the Diagonal Test, Ship Test, and Triangle Test, but they constructed their own versions of the Casuist Test and the Feature Profile Test before they became commercially available. They also included six tests taken from other sources:

The Healy Frame Test (Healy and Fernald 1911)
A modified version of Healy and Fernald's (1911) Mare-and-Foal Picture Form Board
The Seguin Form Board as standardized by Sylvester (1913)
A substitution test similar to Pyle's but taken from a series of tests devised by Robert Woodworth and Frederic Lyman Wells (1911)
A picture completion test devised by William Healy (1914), in which identical pieces, each one-inch square and each showing a different object, were to be fitted into the appropriate blank spaces in a pictured scene
An adaptation board devised by Henry Goddard (1912a, 1915). This consisted of a plain wooden board with a hole in each corner, one hole slightly wider than the other three, together with a circular block that just fitted the wider hole. The task was to remember which hole the block fitted after the board had been rotated from left to right, from top to bottom, and diagonally.

Finally, Pintner and Paterson added three tests of their own devising:

A two-figure form board devised by Pintner, in which nine square, rectangular, or triangular pieces had to be assembled to fit a square hole and a cross-shaped hole

A five-figure form board devised by Paterson, in which eleven pieces were to be assembled to fit five larger holes

A manikin test in which six pieces representing a torso, two arms, two legs, and a head were to be assembled to make a complete figure, or manikin (literally, a little man)

Pintner and Patterson showed how performance on their tests could be mapped to an age scale similar to that used by Binet and Simon and subsequently by Terman and Childs (1912a). An outcome on a given test was assigned to a particular mental age if 75 percent of all normal children of the corresponding chronological age achieved that outcome. Each individual was then classified as having a mental age equivalent to the median of the mental ages achieved across the different tests. (The median of a set of scores is the score that falls in the middle when they are ordered from the lowest to highest.) Nevertheless, Pintner and Paterson also showed how performance could be mapped to a point scale similar to that devised by Yerkes, Bridges, and Hardwick (1915) and how it could be expressed in terms of percentiles of the relevant age group.

Pintner and Paterson's Scale of Performance Tests was intended to be administered to individuals, but Pintner continued to pursue the goal of constructing a group performance scale. In September 1919 he published a "non-language group intelligence test" containing six tasks, which included two substitution tests and a new task modeled on the Cube Imitation Test. In the latter the examiner pointed to four dots in a line on a blackboard, and the examinees drew lines among dots printed on sheets of paper to copy the examiner's moves. As in Pintner's version of the Cube Imitation Test, twelve sequences of increasing difficulty were used. Pintner (1924) reviewed a variety of studies that had used his nonlanguage group test, and he concluded that it provided a reliable and valid way of assessing nonverbal aspects of intelligence. However, he warned that the scores obtained by the same individuals on verbal and nonverbal tests were not highly correlated and that the two kinds of test were measuring different aspects of intelligence.

Pintner (1923:125) suggested that it would be useful to derive a short version of the Scale of Performance Tests that included both the Casuist Test and his own version of the Cube Imitation Test. It also combined the Manikin Test and the Feature Profile Test into a single test where the former was used with younger children and the latter was used with older individuals. (This combination, the Manikin and Feature Profile Test, was subsequently used by many other researchers and practitioners.) However, he formally published this short version of the scale only some years later with the help of Gertrude Howell Hildreth, who was a psychologist at the Lincoln School at Teachers College, Columbia University (Hildreth and Pintner 1937).

Early in 1917 both Lewis Terman and Robert Yerkes had submitted separate research proposals to the General Education Board of the Rockefeller Foundation; they were seeking grants to develop their respective work on intelligence testing. In May the board replied that it was thinking of supporting a joint bid from the two researchers and encouraged them to collaborate (Minton 1988:54–55, 61). However, these plans were overtaken by international events. On April 6 the U.S. Congress had endorsed a proposal from President Woodrow Wilson that the United States declare war on Germany, and for both Terman and Yerkes (who had taken up a new post at the University of Minnesota) this led to the suspension of most of their professional activities.

Yerkes happened to be the current president of the American Psychological Association, and he called a meeting of the association's council for April 21. It approved the creation of a network of committees to enable psychologists to make specialist contributions to the war effort. In 1916 Walter Dill Scott, professor of psychology at Northwestern University, had been given leave of absence to serve as director of the new Bureau of Salesmanship at the Carnegie Institute of Technology in Pittsburgh. Scott became chair of the Committee on the Classification of Personnel, which proceeded to apply techniques from the field of vocational selection to the assessment of military officers. His work played an important part in the development of psychotechnics, the use of psychological techniques to control the behavior of workers in industrial contexts.

Yerkes himself became the chair of the Committee on the Psychological Examination of Recruits, the goal of which was to develop a series of mental tests for the selection and training of recruits to the U.S. Army. Binet and Simon (1908:94) had originally suggested that their scale would be useful in enabling the military to exclude "young people whose intellectual weakness renders them incapable of learning and understanding the theory and drill of arms and of submitting to regular discipline." Moreover, as early as February 1916 Yerkes had written to the War Department to suggest the use of mental testing in military recruitment (J. Reed 1987).

Financial support for Yerkes's initiative came from the Committee on Provision for the Feeble-Minded. Edward Johnstone, the superintendent of the Vineland Training School, had established this committee in 1910 to promote the public's awareness of mental deficiency. Initially, its activities were restricted to New Jersey, but in 1915 it became a national organization with its headquarters in Philadelphia (Zenderland 1998:228–31). Yerkes appointed to the Committee on the Psychological Examination of Recruits Henry Goddard, Lewis Terman, and Guy Whipple, together with Walter Van Dyke Bingham, who in 1915 had set up the division of applied psychology at the Carnegie Institute of Technology; Thomas Haines of Ohio State University; and Frederic Wells, who was an assistant in pathological psychology at the McLean Hospital in Waverley, Massachusetts.

Yerkes himself documented the work of this committee at the time (see Yerkes 1918a, 1918b, 1919, 1921). Its work was, however, usefully summarized more recently by Henry Minton (1988:62–76), and the following is based largely on his account. The committee's initial meeting was held at the Vineland Training School from May 28 to June 9, 1917. The first problem to be addressed was the one that Pintner had already faced in the field of deaf education: that most existing tests had been devised for administration to individuals and would take far too long to administer to large numbers of recruits. Like Pintner, the committee considered the possibility of adapting such tests for administration to groups.

Terman gave the committee an account of the work of his student, Arthur Sinton Otis, who had just developed a group scale for schoolchildren in grades four through eight. This was based upon the Stanford revision of Binet and Simon's scale but merely required simple written responses. Unlike the Stanford-Binet scale, however, it generated a point-scaled IQ. Curiously, the published description of Otis's scale made no reference to the work of either Pyle or Pintner and Paterson, who had also been interested in developing tests for group administration. Otis seems to have been more influenced by earlier classroom tests of reading and spelling (see Otis 1918a, 1918b). Nonetheless, his scale was adopted as the model for the committee's work.

An initial test battery was assembled, and members of the committee spent the next two weeks collecting data from personnel at military camps around the country. The committee reconvened from June 25 to July 7, and the members revised the tests in light of their findings. They then administered the revised battery to four thousand personnel at four different installations. The results encouraged them to present a plan to the surgeon general of the U.S. Army proposing the psychological examination of new recruits. At the end of July the surgeon general authorized a full trial of the revised test across four army cantonments, covering five thousand officers and eighty thousand troops. The outcome was again successful, and on December 24, 1917, a testing program was implemented for all newly appointed officers and all drafted and enlisted men.

The final version of the group test, which consisted of verbal and arithmetical problems, was known as Examination Alpha. The committee also produced a separate test for illiterate and foreign-born examinees, Examination Beta. This consisted of a series of performance tests that could be administered mainly through the use of pantomime, such as solving mazes or matching symbols to digits. Both Alpha and Beta were standardized by administering them to more than 650 men along with the Stanford revision of Binet and Simon's scale, and the results were used to classify examinees into five categories from A to E (Young 1924). A rating of A was indicative of officer material, but a rating of E was indicative of mental deficiency.

The necessity of using group tests in both Examination Alpha and Examination Beta ruled out procedures that required individual administration, which obviously included the Ellis Island tests. However, the committee also developed the Army Performance Scale, which was designed to be administered to individuals. Men who were deemed to be literate were to be given Examination Alpha; those who obtained a rating of E on Examination Alpha were to be given Examination Beta; and those who obtained a rating of E on Examination Beta were to be given either the Stanford revision of Binet and Simon's scale or the Point Scale developed by Yerkes, Bridges, and Hardwick (1915). Illiterate or foreign-born men were to be given Examination Beta, and those who obtained a rating of E were to be given the Army Performance Scale.

Clarence Stone Yoakum had joined Yerkes's team from the University of Texas, and after the war he became a professor of applied psychology at the Carnegie Institute of Technology. In 1920 Yoakum and Yerkes published a manual for the administration of all three army mental tests. The Performance Scale contained ten tests, including the Ship Test, the Manikin and Feature Profile Test, and an adapted version of the Cube Imitation Test. The apparatus for the latter test was described as follows: "Four 1-inch cubes fastened 2 inches apart to a wooden base. Both cubes and base are painted a dark red.... A fifth cube of the same size unattached and similarly painted" (Yoakum and Yerkes 1920:104–105). The procedure involved ten sequences of broadly increasing difficulty that were tapped out at a rate of one cube per second. Yoakum and Yerkes provided detailed accounts of the procedures to be followed for administering these tests to both English-speaking and non-English-speaking participants but did not acknowledge the people who had originally been responsible for devising the tests.

The army mental testing program was terminated soon after the armistice in November 1918, by which time 1.75 million men had been tested. The program attracted a good deal of public interest and was frequently mentioned in press reports. Indeed, in March 1919 the chief medical officer at Ellis Island prompted the surgeon general of the Public Health Service to write to the surgeon general of the U.S. Army to request information about the army's mental tests. (In March 1916 Yerkes had written to Knox to find out about his tests and had been invited to Ellis Island to see the tests being used. This request suggests that Knox's seniors had little idea of the impact of his tests, but it did rather neatly close the loop on the relationship between Yerkes and the Ellis Island physicians.)

Yerkes assembled the formal report of the program, which was published in 1921. It acknowledged Knox's (1914c) article in the *Journal of the American Medical*

Association as the original source for the Ship Test, the Feature Profile Test, and the Cube Imitation Test (Yerkes 1921:400). Yerkes gave credit to Stanley David Porteus for the maze tests used in Examination Beta and in the Army Performance Scale (401). Porteus had devised a procedure consisting of a series of increasingly complex mazes when he had been the head teacher of a special school in Melbourne, Australia (Porteus 1915), and in 1918 he had replaced Henry Goddard as director of research at the Vineland Training School in New Jersey. The Porteus Maze Test became widely known in the United States, partly because selected mazes had been included in the army mental tests.

The report of the army mental testing program appeared to provide a unique insight into the nature of human intelligence, and newspapers and magazines widely reported its contents. Reporters tended to focus on the poor performance of drafted personnel and the major differences among different racial groups: 47 percent of white draftees and 89 percent of black draftees appeared to have mental ages of less than thirteen and hence would be classified as feebleminded (Yerkes 1921:790). At the time critics (in particular, the journalist Walter Lippmann and the psychologist William Chandler Bagley) cast doubt on the interpretations of the findings, for which Terman was mainly responsible (Minton 1988:100–106). Nevertheless, only many years later did other commentators such as Stephen Jay Gould (1981:201–14) point out major deficiencies in the way that the tests had actually been administered. Indeed, the results had not even been used systematically in the assignment of recruits (J. Reed 1987).

After the armistice Yerkes and Terman revived their joint application to the General Education Board of the Rockefeller Foundation, which awarded them $25,000 to develop intelligence tests for children in elementary schools. As Minton (1988:91) pointed out, before the war both men had focused solely on individual tests, Yerkes with his point scale (Yerkes, Bridges, and Hardwick 1915) and Terman with the Stanford revision of Binet and Simon's scale (Terman et al. 1915). Indeed, Terman (1919) had written a book, *The Intelligence of School Children*, specifically to encourage schoolteachers to use the Stanford-Binet scale in the assessment of their pupils.

However, Yerkes's and Terman's experience with the army mental tests had convinced both men that group tests provided the only means of evaluating large numbers of children. They adapted Examination Alpha and Examination Beta to produce a verbal scale and a nonverbal scale, each containing five tests, known collectively as the National Intelligence Tests. These were intended for children in grades three through seven, but Terman went on to derive another scale from the army mental tests, the Terman Group Test of Mental Ability, for those in grades seven through twelve. These tests became widely adopted in U.S. schools and had a major impact on educational practice (Minton 1988:92–96).

FRANCES GAW AND THE NATIONAL INSTITUTE OF
INDUSTRIAL PSYCHOLOGY

Frances Isabel Gaw had studied at the Harvard Graduate School of Education in 1920–21, and she then worked as an intern in psychology in the Psychopathic Department of the Boston State Hospital. By this time Thomas Haines was the director of psychological services and research at the hospital. He had been using performance tests at the Ohio Bureau of Juvenile Research before the war, and he seems to have encouraged their use with patients at the Boston State Hospital. William Healy chaired the board of trustees of the hospital and would likely have supported such work. The psychologists at the hospital assembled a series of performance tests drawn from Pintner and Paterson's Performance Scale and the Army Performance Scale and compiled a manual for their administration (although this seems to have been a document for purely internal use that was never formally published). The tests themselves included Pintner's version of the Cube Imitation Test, Diagonal Form Board, Feature Profile Test, and Triangle Form Board, as well as the full version of the Porteus Maze Test.

In 1922 Gaw decided to go to the United Kingdom to study for a Ph.D., and she enrolled initially at the University of Edinburgh. However, soon afterward she obtained a post with the Industrial Fatigue Research Board, and she moved to the University of London, where she was awarded her Ph.D. in 1926 (Ogilvie and Harvey 2000, 1:492). During World War I psychological research had been carried out in the United Kingdom on the working conditions and practices of munitions workers, and the Industrial Fatigue Research Board had originally been set up by the UK Medical Research Council in 1918 to continue this kind of research in peacetime conditions. However, it soon took on a much broader responsibility, and some of its work in the 1920s and 1930s was carried out in collaboration with the National Institute of Industrial Psychology (NIIP). The latter was a nonprofit organization founded in 1921 by Charles Samuel Myers, director of the psychological laboratory at the University of Cambridge. The aim of the NIIP, which became an influential body, was to apply psychology for the benefit of industry and commerce.

In 1923 Gaw published a brief paper in the NIIP's house journal that advocated the use of performance tests and tests of mechanical ability in vocational guidance, especially in advising children about future occupations after they had left school. She acknowledged that performance tests had been used at Ellis Island to evaluate emigrants who did not speak English, and she illustrated her argument with data obtained from forty-six children at London elementary schools and from twenty-seven children who lived on canal boats. Gaw was unable to say whether the latter children were developmentally normal, but their education would have been severely disrupted because of their traveling with their families around the country carrying freight along the canals.

The performance tests that Gaw had been using with English children were actually the ones contained in the series she had helped to devise at Boston State Hospital. In a subsequent article (Gaw 1925b), she provided more details of the tests, and she presented data from one hundred schoolchildren and thirty-four canal-boat children. The pattern of correlations among the schoolchildren's scores on the various performance tests suggested that most tests were measuring a common central mental capacity, and the correlations both with their IQs (measured by a short form of the Stanford-Binet scale) and with their teachers' estimates of their ability suggested that this central capacity could be identified as general intelligence.

On the Stanford-Binet scale the canal-boat children scored on average just below the borderline for mental deficiency. On the performance tests, however, they approached the level that would be expected of normal children attending a poor school. Among the schoolchildren the performance tests showed a much lower correlation with their teachers' estimates of their intelligence than did the Stanford-Binet scale; among the canal-boat children the performance tests showed a much lower correlation with their scores on tests of academic attainment than did the Stanford-Binet scale. Gaw concluded that the performance tests were measuring intelligence in a way that was less influenced by the children's schooling, and she inferred that they provided the best way of measuring intelligence in children from abnormal environments.

From this account it is not clear whether Gaw seriously intended all fourteen tests to be used as a "performance scale." She introduced her article by saying that her aims were simply "to analyse the qualities measured by a group of performance tests" and "to determine whether this group of tests is standardised satisfactorily for normal English elementary school children" (1925b:374). Moreover, she specifically concluded, on the basis of her findings, that, "with three or four possible exceptions, the performance tests here used are to a large extent, but in differing degrees, tests of some central mental capacity" (391). Indeed, she declared that, if one were aiming to measure this capacity, some tests were decidedly better than others.

She provided a fuller account of her test battery in a report written for the Industrial Fatigue Research Board (Gaw 1925a). This was presented as a formal test manual, with descriptions of the tests, directions for administering them, and norms for ages eight to sixteen. Here she was quite unambiguous:

> It should be emphasized that this series of tests has been arranged as a scale, and that it is intended that the complete series or a prescribed part of it be

used. . . . Like all other tests, those constituting this series are based on the principle, familiarized by the Binet scale, of sampling a number of different abilities, and amalgamating the total results. To do this, it is essential to give a number of different tests and to combine the results in a prescribed way just as in the Binet scale.

(1925b:11–12)

In her previous accounts (Gaw 1923, 1925a) Gaw had not cited Howard Knox's work. In this report she explicitly cited Knox's (1914c) article in the *Journal of the American Medical Association* as the source for "Knox's (1914) scale, based on results obtained with immigrants at Ellis Island, New York. Various formboards, as well as other types of performance tests, are included in this scale" (1925a:8). However, she did not identify any tests in her own battery as originating in Knox's scale.

Gaw's research encouraged others in the NIIP to use the Cube Imitation Test and other performance tests in their work. Frank Maynard Earle, Angus Macrae, and colleagues (1929) found that children's scores on Pintner's version of the Cube Imitation Test were correlated with those on a group test of intelligence consisting predominantly of verbal subtests. They tested 125 boys at elementary school and 100 boys at secondary school and found correlation coefficients of 0.33 and 0.45, respectively. The latter figure increased to 0.51 when the effects of age were statistically controlled (27–29). These results suggest that that an age-scaled version of the Cube Imitation Test would provide a useful estimate of intelligence in normal children.

Earle, Marion Milner, and colleagues (1929) tested six hundred children on performance tests and conventional intelligence tests in a battery that included Pintner's version of the Cube Imitation Test. Based on the correlations among the scores, they argued that the tests divided into those measuring spatial relations and those measuring verbal skills. However, some, including the Cube Imitation Test, did not appear to be much influenced by either factor. Earle, Milner, and colleagues concluded that there was no one factor underlying all performance tests; hence the tests could not, on their own, be regarded as a satisfactory measure of intelligence. Both reports identified Howard Knox as the originator of the Cube Imitation Test but cited none of his publications. Instead, Pintner's procedure was followed.

THE ARTHUR POINT SCALE OF PERFORMANCE TESTS

Mary Grace Arthur was an educational psychologist who worked for the child guidance clinic in St. Paul, Minnesota, and who was awarded her Ph.D. by the

University of Minnesota in 1924. Because of the number of children with reduced language or reading capability that she encountered in her work, she argued that it would be desirable to have a performance scale specifically for use with children aged five to fifteen (Arthur 1925). She selected eight tests from earlier scales; these included Pintner's version of the Cube Imitation Test, the Seguin Form Board, Pintner's Two-Figure Form Board, the Casuist Test, Manikin and Feature Profile Test, Mare-and-Foal Picture Form Board, and Healy's Picture Completion Test. Arthur correctly identified the person who had devised each test, but she cited Pintner and Paterson's (1917) book as the source. She also used a block design task that had been devised by Samuel Calmin Kohs (1920). Kohs was a member of the faculty at Reed College in Portland, Oregon, and the psychologist assigned to the Portland Court of Domestic Relations. His test required examinees to assemble sixteen colored blocks to match one of seventeen different designs.

Arthur borrowed normative data from previously published sources, she presented tables for determining point-scaled IQs, and she described her own experience of using the new "point performance scale" at her clinic. She considered that the scale was broadly satisfactory, but she suggested that the reliability of the Cube Imitation Test would be enhanced if it were given both at the beginning and at the end of the test session and if the average from the two administrations were recorded. She adopted this modification when she restandardized the scale using a sample of eleven hundred normal schoolchildren (Arthur 1928). She also added the Porteus Maze Test.

Arthur observed that the order of difficulty of the twelve sequences in the Cube Imitation Test was not exactly the same as Pintner (1915) had previously suggested, and she reordered them when she published her scale as a formal clinical instrument (Arthur 1930, 1933). This contained two parallel or equivalent forms so that the scale could be administered to the same examinee on separate occasions to assess any decline or recovery in performance. However, both forms used the same procedure for the Cube Imitation Test: it was administered twice using the same twelve sequences at the beginning and end of the test session, and the average score from the two trials was recorded. Arthur (1943) retained this arrangement when she published a second edition of the scale's manual. She noted in passing that her examinees had tended to do better on the second administration of the Cube Imitation Test than they had on the first (10).

This was a potentially damaging finding, because it implied that the Cube Imitation test was vulnerable to the effects of practice. Thus a parallel or equivalent form of the scale that used the same twelve sequences in the Cube Imitation Test would tend systematically to overestimate the examinee's intelligence. (See Richardson 2005 for a fuller discussion of the practice effects obtained in the Cube Imitation Test.) Nevertheless, Arthur (1947) developed a revised parallel form of her performance scale that contained a different procedure for the Cube Imitation Test. This used eighteen new sequences, and it involved a different apparatus containing four black one-inch cubes attached two inches apart to a plain wooden board. This was depicted by Anne Anastasi (1954) in the first edition of her influential textbook, *Psychological Testing,* but her accompanying text incorrectly identified it as Knox's original apparatus (240, 242).

PAUL SQUIRES'S UNIVERSAL SCALE OF INDIVIDUAL PERFORMANCE TESTS

Paul Chatham Squires was a student working for his Ph.D. at Princeton University between 1923 and 1925. His supervisor, Carl Campbell Brigham, had been involved in the development of the Army Mental Tests. He had published a book based on the findings, in which he argued for the innate intellectual superiority of the descendants of emigrants from "Nordic" countries (e.g., Britain, Germany, and Norway) over those of emigrants from "Alpine" countries (e.g., Poland and Russia) or "Mediterranean" countries (e.g., Greece or Italy) (Brigham 1923). Although his book was influential at the time, Brigham later completely retracted his statements regarding the idea of racial differences in intelligence (Brigham 1930).

Squires submitted his thesis in May 1925; it was accepted and published as a book the following year. He defined the task that he had set himself as follows: "There is an urgent demand in the field of mental measurement for a scale of individual performance tests that completely dispenses with the use of language, that differentiates within the upper as well as within the lower ranges of mentality, and that may be applied to any individual whatever irrespective of his race, nationality, or culture" (Squires 1926:iii). The scale that he devised contained fourteen performance tests to be administered to individual examinees through the medium of pantomime alone, with performance scored using the point-scale method. However, only one of the fourteen tests was related in any way to those devised at Ellis Island.

As I mentioned earlier in this chapter, the cubes in Knox's (1913f) original version of the Cube Imitation Test were painted in different colors, so examinees could carry out the task by remembering sequences of colors or color names. To eliminate this possibility Pinter (1915) advocated using cubes of the same color. However, Squires wanted to present examinees with an apparatus that provided even more sensory cues and was also more attractive than mere blocks of wood. He therefore constructed a xylophone consisting of four metal tubes of varying lengths; the tubes themselves were painted in different colors, and varying numbers of rings were painted around their middles. The examiner tapped out sequences of two to twelve taps using a mallet, and the examinee then had to imitate this sequence, cued by the location, length, appearance, and pitch of the tubes. The procedure was repeated using backward recall (that is, requiring the examinee to tap sequences in the reverse order of that in which they had been presented) (13–19, 66–69).

Squires presented data from fifty students of Princeton University and fifty students from the Training School at Vineland, New Jersey. His Universal Scale was never widely used, but other test developers imitated his xylophone. Stanley Porteus used a similar apparatus in cross-cultural research on Australian Aborigines (1931:391–97). Many years later the McCarthy Scales of Children's Abilities (McCarthy 1972) included the Tapping Sequence Test, which uses a four-note xylophone. This too was developed as a task that would be more attractive and thus more motivating than the original Cube Imitation Test (Kaufman and Kaufman 1977:7, 24).

WILLIAM HEALY AND AUGUSTA BRONNER

In 1914 William Healy, director of the Juvenile Psychopathic Institute in Chicago, appointed a new assistant director, Augusta Fox Bronner. She had just completed her Ph.D. at Columbia University under the supervision of Edward Thorndike on the relationship between mental deficiency and delinquency in adolescent girls; contrary to widely held opinions, she argued that mental deficiency was not a major factor in juvenile delinquency (Bronner 1914). In 1917 a number of philanthropists established a clinic for delinquent children in memory of the first judge of the Boston juvenile court, Harvey Humphrey Baker. Healy was appointed as the first director of the Judge Baker Foundation (now the Judge Baker Children's Center), and Bronner was appointed as assistant director with responsibility for psychological testing. In the 1920s the foundation expanded to provide services to a wide variety of children and their families, and Healy and Bronner became generally recognized as authorities on psychological assessment.

In 1927, with assistance from two of their colleagues, Gladys Lowe and Myra Shimberg, Bronner and Healy published A Manual of Individual Mental Tests and Testing. This provided detailed descriptions and interpretations of 126 individual tests. Of the Ellis Island tests, they included the Casuist Test, Cube Imitation Test, Diagonal Form Board, Feature Profile Test, Ship Test, and Triangle Form Board. In each case the apparatus, procedure, and norms were taken from Pintner and Paterson's 1917 book, although Knox's (1914c) paper in the Journal of the American Medical Association was sometimes cited. Elsewhere in their book Bronner, Healy, and colleagues briefly described six "performance scales":

Army Performance Scale

Arthur Performance Scale

Gaw Performance Scale

Knox Scale

Pintner-Paterson Performance Scale

Universal Performance Scale

(1927:242–45)

With regard to the "Knox Scale," Bronner and colleagues commented, "The first performance scale was used by Knox to test immigrants at Ellis Island" (1927:243), and they cited Knox's paper in the *Journal of the American Medical Association*. Strictly speaking, however, this is incorrect, since the "Scale . . . for estimating mental defect" that Knox presented in that article contained verbal tests taken from Binet and Simon's 1908 scale, not just performance tests (see table 6.2). Knox had, of course, presented a scale that consisted solely of performance tests (or, as he called it, a "performing test examination") in a previous article in the *Journal of Heredity* (Knox 1914b; see table 6.1), but that was not cited by Bronner and colleagues or by subsequent commentators.

～～～～～

By the late 1920s many of the Ellis Island tests had become well established among the range of instruments available to the developers and users of intelligence tests. Moreover, these tests were explicitly linked to the name of Howard Knox, who was recognized as the progenitor of performance scales. Nevertheless, the tests themselves were known mainly through Pintner and Paterson's scale and through the Army Mental Tests. Even among experts in the field, few people seemed to consult, let alone reference, Knox's original writings. As I will explain in the next chapter, the Ellis Island tests continued to be used (in two instances, even into the twenty-first century). However, Knox's own role in the development of performance scales was gradually lost from the collective memory of physicians and psychologists.

11

BORROWING THE ELLIS ISLAND TESTS

Although Howard Knox had written various popular accounts of the work at Ellis Island, formal descriptions of his tests were published mainly in medical journals. Initially, therefore, the Ellis Island tests were not well known to psychologists. For instance, for ten years, from 1911 to 1920, Frank Nugent Freeman, director of the School of Education at the University of Chicago, wrote brief annual surveys of the latest developments in mental testing for the *Psychological Bulletin*. His review for 1914 listed one of Knox's papers (Knox 1913g), and Freeman's review for 1919 referred in passing to the "Knox Cube Test," although he cited the study by Rachofsky (1918) rather than any of Knox's own publications. Otherwise, Freeman wholly ignored the work at Ellis Island, including what probably was the most important article presenting the "scale . . . for estimating mental defect," the one in the *Journal of the American Medical Association* (Knox 1914c).

Nevertheless, the publication of Pintner and Paterson's (1917) *A Scale of Performance Tests* and of Yoakum and Yerkes' (1920) manual, *Army Mental Tests*, brought many of Knox's tests to the attention of psychologists. During the next twenty years this proved to have two major consequences, one positive and the other negative. On the one hand, both researchers and practitioners began to adopt the Ellis Island tests for use in ways that Knox himself had scarcely imagined. His tests were widely used in clinical, educational, experimental, neuropsychological, and cross-cultural research, eventually in countries around the world. On the other hand, these two books tended to be quoted as the immediate source of the tests in question, and the original contribution of Knox and his colleagues at Ellis Island was gradually forgotten.

To take just one example, Buford Jeannette Johnson was a psychologist at the Bureau of Educational Experiments (now the Bank Street College of Education) in New York City. From 1919 to 1923 she carried out an ambitious investigation into the relationship between children's mental and physical growth. As one aspect of this investigation, with the help of two assistants, Louise Schriefer and Dorothy Seago, Johnson administered Pintner and Paterson's (1917) Scale of Performance Tests to more than four hundred children aged two to ten at several public and private schools in New York City. Not all the children completed all the tests, but Schriefer also gave eighty-six children the Stanford revision of Binet and Simon's scale.

Johnson (1925:92–107) published a book with the results obtained from the entire sample of children three years after she and Schriefer (1922) reported the results from the subsample that had received the Stanford-Binet scale. Johnson and Schriefer found that the children's scores on the different performance tests varied in terms of how closely the scores were correlated with their IQs according to the Stanford-Binet scale, but the researchers concluded that the following would constitute a useful series of performance tests: the Mare-and-Foal Picture Form Board, Seguin Form Board, Pinter and Paterson's Two-Figure and Five-Figure Form boards, the Casuist Test, Manikin Test, Ship Test, and Cube Imitation Test. The last was described as the "Knox Cube Test," but otherwise neither account mentioned Knox and his work.

Myrtle Raymaker Worthington (1926) carried out a similar investigation. She worked at the Institute for Juvenile Research in Chicago (where William Healy had been the director until 1917). She assembled a battery of eleven "commonly used performance tests" to see how well children's scores matched their mental ages on the Stanford revision of Binet and Simon's scale. The tests included Sylvester's (1913) version of the Seguin Form Board, the Healy Frame Test, Mare-and-Foal Picture Form Board, Pintner's (1915) version of the Cube Imitation Test, and the Ship Test, together with Healy's (1914) Picture Completion Test and the Porteus Maze Test. She identified the originator of each test, and she cited Knox's (1914c) article in the *Journal of the American Medical Association* as the source for both the Cube Imitation Test and the Ship Test, although in both cases she followed Pintner and Paterson's (1917) procedure and norms.

Worthington gave these tests, together with the Stanford revision of Binet and Simon's scale, to 539 children aged three to 16 who had been referred for assessment because of possible mental deficiency or behavioral problems. Four tests, including the Seguin Form Board and Porteus Maze Test, showed high correlations with the children's mental ages on the Stanford-Binet scale. Nevertheless, the remaining tests did not. Some, including the Ship Test, could not be adequately standardized for very young children or for teenagers. Others, including the Cube Imitation Test, showed only moderate correlations with the children's mental ages. Worthington concluded that the tests were assessing "special" (that is, specific) mental abilities and should not be used as measures of general intelligence.

DREVER AND COLLINS'S "SERIES OF NON-LINGUISTIC TESTS"

One reason why Pintner and Paterson (1917) had developed their Scale of Performance Tests was to assess the intelligence of deaf children in a way that was less contaminated by their impaired comprehension of spoken language. Pintner and Paterson did subsequently use their scale to compare deaf and hearing children, but it is curious that they never published their findings. Instead, in his 1923 textbook *Intelligence Testing*, Pintner (1923:318) merely referred to an unpublished manuscript whose contents he summarized in a single bare statement: "In all comparisons of deaf and hearing in the tests of the Pintner-Paterson Performance Scale the deaf fall below the hearing." Indeed, the only published evidence he could offer for differences in intelligence between deaf and hearing came from his and Paterson's work using Pyle's (1913) Substitution Test (Pintner and Paterson 1915b, 1916).

Other researchers were skeptical of this conclusion. James Drever was director of the George Combe Psychological Laboratory at the University of Edinburgh in Scotland. (He was appointed to the chair in psychology there when it was established in 1931.) Drever and his colleague, Mary Collins, developed their own series of "non-linguistic tests for deaf and normal children" (Drever and Collins 1928). This included Kohs's Block Design Test, Pintner's version of the Cube Imitation Test, the Manikin and Feature Profile Test, Pintner's Two-Figure Form Board, Healy's Frame Test, and Healy's Picture Completion Test. Knox was correctly identified as the originator of the Cube Imitation Test and the Feature Profile Test, and his 1914 article in the *Journal of the American Medical Association* was cited as the source. Nevertheless, for both tests Drever and Collins based their procedure on Pintner and Paterson's (1917) account.

They initially tested four hundred deaf and hearing children and used the resulting data to derive provisional norms for these tests. They also compared the performance of the deaf and hearing children. Contrary to Pintner's (1923) position, they concluded that "no significant retardation [in deaf children] as yet has been indicated" (Drever and Collins 1928:20). Drever and Collins's book, *Performance Tests of Intelligence*, proved to be quite influential in the United Kingdom, and they provided more extensive norms in subsequent editions.

A few years later Drever and Collins advised on the choice of tests to be included in an evaluation of the intelligence of a representative sample of Scottish schoolchildren. This project set out to include all children born on four different days in 1926 and was carried out from September 1935 to November 1937. In addition to the Stanford revision of Binet and Simon's scale, the tests included the Seguin Form Board, Manikin Test, Healy's Picture Completion Test, Pintner's version of the Cube Imitation Test, and Kohs's Block Design Test. The results were published in 1939 by the researcher appointed to the project, Agnes Miller Macmeeken.

Macmeeken described the Cube Imitation Test as "Knox Cube Imitation" but otherwise did not mention Knox. She seems to have followed Drever and Collins's suggested procedure for this and other tests. Her preliminary analysis of the data suggested that the children's scores on the performance tests were highly correlated with their mental ages on the Stanford revision of Binet and Simon's scale. However, a more detailed comparison of the respective distributions of scores suggested that "the Performance tests were giving play to an adaptive type of intelligent process which the Binet test was failing to reach" (140).

Godfrey Hilton Thomson was the professor of education at the University of Edinburgh, and he conducted more detailed analyses of Macmeeken's data. He confirmed that the children's scores on the performance tests were highly correlated with their mental ages, but he found that the best predictors of mental age were Kohs's Block Design Test and Healy's Picture Completion Test (Thomson 1940:28). He also used the technique known as factor analysis to investigate the more general constructs that might underlie the relationships among the children's scores on the different performance tests. He found two independent factors: One was concerned mainly with the accuracy of the children's responding and seemed to represent general intelligence, whereas the other was concerned with the speed of their responses in tasks where performance was timed. Thomson did refer to the "Knox Cube Imitation Test" but made no mention of Knox himself.

HARRIET BABCOCK'S TEST OF MENTAL EFFICIENCY

In 1918 Lewis Terman had published an article that advocated the use of vocabulary tests as measures of intelligence. In these tests the examinees are presented with lists of words and are required to provide a brief definition for each word. Terman had found that the correlation coefficient between performance on a vocabulary test and mental age according to the Stanford revision of Binet and Simon's scale was 0.91 in the case of 631 schoolchildren and 0.81 in the case of 482 "miscellaneous adults" (hoboes, prisoners, delinquent youths, and businessmen). He concluded that "a mental age based on vocabulary score alone would not be far wrong in a large per cent. of cases" (454). Subsequent work also indicated that performance on such tests was often intact in neurological patients who showed impaired performance on other kinds of task.

In her doctoral research at Columbia University, Harriet Babcock (1930) suggested that these findings could be used to assess patients' previous level of functioning and therefore their amount of mental deterioration:

> The results of intelligence tests when given to mentally deteriorated subjects . . . show that for a long time after mental mal-functioning begins, old learning lasts practically unimpaired, except possibly for slowness of response, while ability to fixate new impressions shows weakness in varying degrees according to the degree of deterioration.
>
> . . . Mental deterioration instead of being a retrogression to some earlier developmental level, has qualitative differences which distinguish the person of high intellectual level who is deteriorated, from one whose intelligence was always inferior. These differences are shown in interests, in the data to which one spontaneously attends, and especially in the vocabulary. Words when once learned are not quickly forgotten, and remain as indications of the ability a person once had, since some kinds of words cannot be learned by persons of inferior intelligence, and the type of word one can learn is highly correlated with intelligence as measured by the criterion of ability in school and college work.
>
> (5)

Babcock constructed a battery of tests that either were timed or else required the processing of new information. They were drawn from a variety of sources and included what Babcock called the "Knox Cube Test." The latter combined the sequences used in Pintner's version of the Cube Imitation Test with those used in the Army Performance Scale and used the set of dark red cubes from the latter. Nevertheless, Knox's own work using the test was not mentioned.

Babcock administered this battery of tests together with a vocabulary test to 264 normal individuals and 75 neurological patients. She used the performance of the normal individuals to construct norms and used the difference between a person's score and the norm for people of their own intellectual level as an index of "mental efficiency." Comparisons with the patients' clinical records suggested that negative values of this index provided a measure of their mental deterioration. Babcock's work attracted a good deal of attention among psychologists working with neurological and psychiatric patients, and some years later a revised version of her test battery was published commercially (Babcock and Levy 1940).

Babcock (1933) attempted to apply the same methods to the measurement of mental deterioration in patients suffering from dementia praecox (schizophrenia). A reviewer objected that Babcock's claims with regard to the relative vulnerability to mental deterioration of vocabulary and other skills were not well founded and that she had not taken sufficient care in the identification of patients to be included in her study (M. B. Jensen 1934). However, the idea that vocabulary tests provide a convenient measure of a patient's previous level of functioning persisted for many years (e.g., Milberg, Hebben, and Kaplan 1986). In fact, patients with dementing diseases have been found to be impaired on vocabulary tests (Nelson and McKenna 1975). Today tests of *reading* ability are generally considered to be better indicators of previous ability than tests of vocabulary.

Babcock (1932) also turned her attention to the original Army Performance Scale. This was distinctive because it had been standardized on a large number of adults. As a result, it was by this time increasingly used in clinical contexts in the assessment of adult patients. However, Babcock observed that it had become common "to omit tests from the scale either to save time or because of the belief that they are standardized too low and do not do justice to the subject's intelligence" (533). She tested 259 hospital patients on the Stanford revision of Binet and Simon's scale and a short version of the Army Performance Scale. This consisted of just six tests, including the Ship Test, Manikin and Feature Profile Test, and Cube Imitation Test. Yet again, however, Knox's original work was not mentioned. Babcock found that these last tests often gave much higher estimates of mental age than did the Stanford-Binet, and she concluded that short versions of the Army Performance Scale were unsuitable for clinical use.

OTHER PERFORMANCE SCALES OF THE 1930S

Babcock's findings did not dissuade Ethel Letitia Cornell and Warren Winfred Coxe (1934) of the New York State Education Department from developing another short battery based on the Army Performance Scale. The Cornell-Coxe Performance Ability Scale contained seven tests, but, of the original Ellis Island tests, only the Feature Profile Test was retained. It was used for some years, but it was also criticized on a number of technical grounds (see, for example, Hildreth 1935). For instance, although the scale supposedly consisted of tests that were "capable of presentation by non-verbal methods" (Cornell and Coxe 1934:11), examiners were actually required to give oral instructions averaging about a hundred words for each of the tests (Mahan 1935).

Harry Amoss was inspector of auxiliary classes in the Ontario Department of Education in Canada. In 1936 he published the Ontario School Ability Examination, which was devised as a performance scale suitable for use with children who were deaf, who were language impaired, or whose first language was not English. The tests had been taken from several different sources such as the Stanford revision of Binet and Simon's scale, Pintner and Paterson's (1917) Scale of Performance Tests, and Drever and Collins's (1928) series of nonlinguistic tests. They included the Healy Frame Test and a version of the Cube Imitation Test (which Amoss variously referred to as the "Knox Cube" and the "Knox Blocks"). The last test used red enameled one-inch cubes (taken from another of the tests) placed two inches apart. The examiner presented nineteen sequences, depending on the examinee's mental level, of four to eight taps.

Raymond Bernard Cattell (no relation to James McKeen Cattell) was an English psychologist who obtained his doctorate from King's College, London, in 1929. He taught at the University of Exeter for a few years, but in 1932 he was appointed director of the child guidance clinic for the city of Leicester in the East Midlands of England. In 1936 he published A Guide to Mental Testing, which was intended for use by clinical, educational, and industrial psychologists. He referred to Arthur's Performance Scale and Drever and Collins's series of nonlinguistic tests, but his account of the Ellis Island tests seems to have been based on those given by Pintner and Paterson (1917) and by Bronner, Healy, Lowe, and Shimberg (1927). It was reproduced in two postwar editions of his book, essentially unchanged. Cattell moved to the United States in 1937, where he became well known for his writings on intelligence but notorious for his hereditarian and eugenicist views.

RACE, ETHNICITY, AND PERFORMANCE TESTING

In the United States the eugenics movement reached the peak of its popularity and influence during the 1920s. Nevertheless, that influence rested on a remarkably weak evidence base. To try to remedy the situation, Charles Davenport carried out an investigation into the effects of intermarriage between ethnic groups (or, as he put it, "race crossing") in Jamaica. Davenport's academic standing had been strengthened in 1921, when the Eugenics Record Office merged with the Station for Experimental Evolution at the Carnegie Institution of Washington, D.C., to form the Department of Genetics with Davenport as director (French, Demerec, and Corner 1956).

Davenport appointed a research assistant, Morris Steggerda, who was given the job of examining a hundred black people, a hundred white people, and a hundred people of mixed race (whom they referred to as "hybrids" or "browns"). Although the investigation was concerned mainly with "anthropometric" (physical) measurements, Steggerda also administered a battery of psychological tests, including the Army Examination Alpha, Cube Imitation Test, Manikin Test, and

Moron Test. For the Cube Imitation Test Steggerda used Knox's original apparatus with cubes of different colors; he also used the twelve sequences described by Pintner and Paterson (1917), except that in error he administered the sequences in reverse (that is, using the mirror images of the correct sequences).

Davenport (1928) provided an informal account of the preliminary findings in a popular magazine, and the following year Davenport and Steggerda (1929) published a full account as a book. They cited Knox's (1914c) article in the *Journal of the American Medical Association* as the source of the Cube Imitation Test and the Moron Test. In general they found that the white participants tended to achieve higher scores than did the black participants. On the performance tests the participants of mixed race tended to produce intermediate but more variable scores; on the Army Examination Alpha, however, the participants of mixed race tended to produce lower scores than did either the white or the black participants. Davenport interpreted these findings in hereditarian terms; in particular, he concluded, "a population of hybrids will be a population carrying an excessively large number of intellectually incompetent persons" (238).

Performance tests became popular in cross-cultural research of this nature because they seemed to offer a way of assessing intelligence that was "culture-free" or "culture-fair" (see Anastasi 1954:255–68; 1985). However, many other researchers were not disposed to interpret differences between cultural or ethnic groups in hereditarian terms. For instance, Franklin Cressy Paschal, a psychologist at the University of Arizona, and Louis Robert Sullivan, an anthropologist from the American Museum of Natural History in New York City, carried out a study of Mexican families in Tucson. To minimize the role of linguistic factors, they decided to use performance tests and after a pilot study selected six tests from Pintner and Paterson's Scale.

They administered these tests to all nine-year-old and twelve-year-old Mexican children in Tucson (204 nine-year-olds and 211 twelve-year-olds). Their scores tended to be below those appropriate for their ages according to the norms provided by Pintner and Paterson (1917), but Paschal and Sullivan (1925) ascribed this to problems that they had encountered in communicating the task demands to the children. The children's scores were also closely related to their socioeconomic status and were higher in children born in Mexico than in those born in Tucson, suggesting that more recent emigrant families were of higher status. The test battery included Pintner's version of the Cube Imitation Test, but the original work of Knox and his colleagues at Ellis Island was not mentioned.

Otto Klineberg was a Canadian student who qualified in medicine at McGill University. In 1925 he went to New York to study for a Ph.D. in psychology under the supervision of Robert Woodworth at Columbia University. He carried out four studies of black, white, and Native American children, in each case using four to twelve of the tests in Pintner and Paterson's scale. Klineberg published his results in 1928. He found that any differences in performance across different groups of children tended to arise in measures of their speed of responding rather than in measures of the accuracy of their responding. He argued that this was more likely to be the result of environmental rather than racial differences (107).

For instance, the scores obtained by Native American participants at Haskell Institute in Lawrence, Kansas ("perhaps the largest and most important Indian school in the country"[72]), tended to be higher than those obtained by children living on the Yakima Reservation in Washington State whose education was more limited. Moreover, those children who had lived on a reservation before coming to the institute performed less well than those who had never lived on a reservation. Similarly, the scores obtained by black children who attended a junior high school in Harlem tended to be higher than those obtained by black children living in rural communities in West Virginia, and black children who had come to New York from the South performed less well than those who had always lived in New York.

Although Klineberg referred to "the Knox cube test," he cited only Pintner and Paterson's manual as the source of his tests, and he otherwise made no mention of Knox and his colleagues at Ellis Island. Klineberg subsequently became an eminent social psychologist and was the first professor of social psychology at Columbia University. In 1954 his research findings were cited in the proceedings leading to the U.S. Supreme Court decision in *Brown v. Board of Education* (347 U.S. 483; Lambert 1992).

In the 1920s children in the United States were often assigned to grades based on their scores on a group test that was largely dependent on language ability. Olive Peckham Lester (1929), a psychologist at the University of Buffalo, studied twenty-six children at a local public school who had had to repeat the first grade because of their performance on just such a test. She gave them six performance tests (including a version of the Cube Imitation Test) and the Stanford revision of Binet and Simon's scale. Of the six performance tests, their scores on the Cube Imitation Test showed the lowest correlation with their mental ages according to the Stanford–Binet but the highest correlation with their teacher's ratings of their ability.

Of the twenty-six children, eight came from English-speaking families, and the other eighteen came from Polish-speaking families. Lester did not cite any of the work by Knox and his colleagues, but Knox's (1914c) choice of ethnic groups had implied that mental deficiency was likely to be more common in Polish immigrants. Lester found indeed that the children from Polish-speaking families had produced lower scores on the entrance test than the children from English-speaking families. However, the two groups had similar mental ages according to the Stanford-Binet, and the children from Polish-speaking families actually obtained higher scores on the Healy Frame Test, the Kohs Block Design Test, and the Cube Imitation Test. Lester argued that children from immigrant families should be classified on entry to elementary school on the basis of their scores on the Stanford-Binet and selected performance tests.

Robert Yerkes, who had been involved in the development of the Army Mental Tests, was by background a biological psychologist, and in 1924 he was appointed to a chair at Yale University, where he set up a laboratory for primate research. In 1930 one of Yerkes' colleagues, Henry Wieghorst Nissen, went to French Guinea in Africa to begin a naturalistic study of chimpanzees (Nissen 1931). During his stay, and apparently at Yerkes's suggestion, Nissen took the opportunity to carry out a study of fifty indigenous children using performance tests mainly taken from Pintner and Paterson's scale and the Army Performance Scale.

To help make sense of the results on his return to the United States, Nissen recruited Solomon Machover from the Psychiatric Clinic of the Court of General Sessions of New York County, and Elaine Flitner Kinder from the Letchworth Village for mentally deficient people in Thiells, New York. They summarized their findings as follows:

> Comparison of the tests on which our subjects did well with those on which they did poorly shows that the difficulty of the tests for our subjects increases as the content and activities involved are more closed related to the particularized experience of a civilized environment and, conversely, that those tests which are rooted in the basic, less differentiated experience common to all races in all environments are handled with relative ease and yield the highest scores in terms of the norms obtained with the standardization groups.
>
> (Nissen, Machover, and Kinder 1935:353)

In particular, the children performed relatively well on the Cube Imitation Test (except that they showed a systematic tendency to reverse the pattern that the examiner had tapped out, which was discounted in the scoring) but poorly on the Feature Profile Test and the Ship Test. Nissen, Machover, and Kinder made no mention of Knox or the work at Ellis Island.

Nissen and his colleagues had encountered some basic practical problems. They were more candid about these in a talk that they had given to the New York Branch of the American Psychological Association the previous year. This had been duly reported in a popular magazine, *Science News Letter*, on April 14, 1934. For one thing, there was uncertainty about the children's ages:

> In order to arrive at some sort of estimate of intelligence quotient, or the children's "brightness for their age," it was necessary to guess at the chronological age of the youngsters. No records were kept by the tribe, and although the tribal

chief and the parents were questioned, they could not help much. Consequently, a combined estimate by the examiner, the interpreter, and a white mechanician attached to the laboratory was used.

Ultimately, Nissen and his colleagues resorted simply to classifying the children into a younger group whose ages were thought to be between five and nine years and an older group whose ages were thought to be between ten and thirteen. More fundamentally, however, the children often seemed at a total loss as to how they should make sense of the examiner's requests: "All sorts of difficulties were encountered, but chief amongst them was that the children, although apparently of normal brightness, simply could not comprehend what they were to do with many of the tests."

Martin Laurence Fick was a psychologist with the National Bureau for Educational and Social Research in Pretoria, South Africa. He constructed a short battery of performance tests to compare intelligence in children from different racial groups. This included Pintner's version of the Cube Imitation Test and a series of form boards that had been devised by David Shakow and Grace Kent (1925) at the Worcester State Hospital in Massachusetts. At the time people in South Africa were classified by law into four groups:

European (people descended mainly from white settlers)
Native (people descended from the precolonial inhabitants of southern Africa)
Indian (people who came or whose families came from the Indian subcontinent)
Colored (people of mixed race)

Fick (1937) gave his battery to 645 European children, 532 Native children, 180 Colored children, and 94 Indian children. The scores of the European children were higher than those of the other three groups: Only 13.2 percent of the Native children, 20.1 percent of the Colored children, and 36.4 percent of the Indian children reached the median score obtained by European children of the same age.

In a subsequent analysis Fick (1939) focused on the twelve-year-old children whom he had tested, including 133 of the Native children and 74 of the European children. He tested a further 180 twelve-year-old Native children and then compared the combined sample with the twelve-year-old European children in terms of their mental ages. Fick insisted that his test battery was culturally fair for Native children since the role of linguistic factors had been minimized (33). He inferred from his results that the mental ages of Native children were consistently four to five years behind those of European children (12, 16). He also argued that there was little difference between children from urban and rural areas, and he concluded that the mental ages of the Native children were relatively unaffected by schooling or exposure to an urban environment (12–15, 37–40). However, Fick's conclusions soon came in for severe criticism.

While he was in high school, Simon Biesheuvel had emigrated with his family to South Africa from the Netherlands. After obtaining his Ph.D. in James Drever's department at the University of Edinburgh in 1933, Biesheuvel worked initially at the University of Stellenbosch and then at the University of the Witwatersrand. While at the latter institution, Biesheuvel began to write a critical review of Fick's research. In 1940, following the outbreak of World War II in Europe, he was appointed head of the aptitude test section of the South African Air Force, which was based at the Waterkloof Air Force Station at Lyttelton in the Transvaal (now the town of Centurion in Gauteng Province) in the north of South Africa. His review of Fick's work turned into a book that he completed in 1941, and the book was eventually published in 1943.

Biesheuvel's critique of Fick's research took account of the wider social, political, and historical context in which it had been carried out. Biesheuvel agreed that performance tests were less contaminated than were other measures of intelligence by the extrinsic effects of the specific cultural milieu in which they were used. However, he claimed that Fick had failed to allow for the different responses of African and European children to the test situation itself (Biesheuvel 1943:20, 60–61). In particular, Biesheuvel argued that performance on tests like the Cube Imitation Test would depend upon the examinee's attitude toward being tested and that African children would be less motivated to devote their attention wholeheartedly to copying the precise actions of a European tester (204–205). He concluded that the tests that Fick had used had not been genuinely culture fair (210–11, 221). In later life Biesheuvel went on to become an eminent figure in the field of personnel psychology. An unbylined obituary published shortly after his death in 1991 described him as "the most influential psychologist in the history of psychology in South Africa" ("Professor Simon Biesheuvel" 1991:683).

Consistent with Biesheuvel's position, subsequent research with children from diverse ethnic minorities around the world (such as Native American tribes, Aboriginal communities in Australia, Berbers in North Africa, and Polynesian communities in New Zealand) confirmed that their scores on performance tests depended on their contact with white culture (including being educated in Western educational systems) rather than on their race or ethnicity (Brooks 1976; Havighurst and Hilkevitch 1944; Kearney 1966:258–60; Lahy 1940; McIntyre 1976).

DAVID WECHSLER AND THE WECHSLER INTELLIGENCE SCALES

By the 1930s performance tests had become widely accepted, not only as essential tools for the assessment of intelligence in people of limited linguistic capability but also as highly desirable tools to complement the use of verbal tests in the assessment of intelligence in people of normal linguistic capability. Herbert Spencer Conrad worked at the Institute of Child Welfare (now the Institute of Human Development) at the University of California, Berkeley. In 1931 he listed twenty-four characteristics that he felt were "requisites of a general intelligence test." George Frank later summarized the six most important of these requisites as follows:

A good general intelligence test should:

(1) be a point scale with a definite zero point,
(2) provide scores on scales made up of equal units or should be scales so as to be converted into equal parts,
(3) include an adequate sample of tasks,
(4) measure general intelligence as well as specific aspects of intelligence,
(5) be reliable and valid, and
(6) measure verbal and non-verbal factors separately but equally.

(1983:13)

The first scale that included separate measurements of intelligence using verbal and performance tests was devised during the next eight years by David Wechsler and eventually published in 1939. However, the process whereby Wechsler arrived at his scale had begun back in 1916.

That year Wechsler entered Columbia University to work for a master's degree. His research topic was the memory disorder seen in Korsakoff psychosis, a complication of long-term alcoholism. He assessed five patients with this condition at Bellevue Hospital in New York City with regard to their memory spans for spoken digits, their memory spans for spoken concrete words, their performance on Howard Knox's (1913f) original Cube Imitation Test, and their performance on Eugene Mullan's (1917b) modified version of the latter test. Knox had allowed for the possibility of giving examinees several attempts at copying the sequences in his test; Mullan allowed only one attempt per sequence, but he tested his examinees using both four and five cubes. Whether each sequence was tested once or several times turned out to be a crucial difference between these tasks.

All but one of Wechsler's patients showed normal performance on digits and words in comparison with published norms and performance similar to that of twelve normal participants on Mullan's version of the Cube Imitation Test. In contrast, all but one patient performed less well than the normal participants on Knox's original Cube Imitation Test. Closer examination of the data revealed that the patients had not benefited from repeated presentations of the same sequences in several trials. In his master's thesis, Wechsler (1917) concluded that many patients with Korsakoff psychosis had normal memory spans but that they were impaired in the learning of new material that exceeded their memory spans. Oliver Louis Zangwill (1943, 1946), a British psychologist, subsequently found that this was characteristic of patients with memory impairment from brain damage, and in the 1970s it was recognized as the earliest empirical evidence to support a theoretical distinction between short-term memory (measured by span tasks) and long-term memory (measured by learning during several trials).

Corwin Boake (2002) of the University of Texas–Houston Medical School summarized the subsequent course of Wechsler's career, and the following is based largely on his account. After completing his master's thesis, Wechsler worked at a U.S. Army camp on Long Island, where he scored Examination Alpha protocols, and he then enlisted in the army himself. In the summer of 1918, he was trained as a psychological examiner at the School for Military Psychology, one of several specialist training schools that had been established at Camp Greenleaf, part of Fort Oglethorpe in Georgia. He was then assigned to Camp Logan near Houston, where he carried out individual psychological examinations using the Army Mental Tests in combination with the Stanford revision of Binet and Simon's scale and Yerkes's point scale. After the armistice the army sent Wechsler to the United Kingdom for further training with Karl Pearson and Charles Spearman at the University of London.

Wechsler then worked for two years in France on the psychophysiology of emotions. He chose this as the topic for a doctorate, which he undertook at Columbia University from 1922 to 1925. After working for several years as a psychologist at a child guidance bureau, he was appointed to the position of chief psychologist in the psychiatric division of Bellevue Hospital in 1932. He immediately noted that the Stanford revision of Binet and Simon's scale was of limited use in this context, partly because it had been standardized on children and was of questionable validity when administered to adults, but also because it was relatively insensitive in identifying special abilities or selective disabilities of the sort that might be found in clinical patients. He suggested that Examination Alpha from the army mental tests would be more useful (Wechsler 1932).

Using Examination Alpha as his starting point, Wechsler evaluated a variety of tests that might be useful for administration to adults in clinical settings, and he included the more promising of the tests in a single instrument that became known as the Wechsler-Bellevue Intelligence Scale. The tests were subsumed within separate verbal and performance scales that yielded separate point-scaled verbal and performance IQs as well as an overall or "full-scale" IQ. As it was published in 1939, the Wechsler-Bellevue Scale had the structure shown in table 11.1. In constructing his scale, Wechsler had borrowed freely from previous

TABLE 11.1 THE STRUCTURE OF THE WECHSLER-BELLEVUE INTELLIGENCE SCALE

Verbal Scale	Performance Scale
Information	Picture Completion
Comprehension	Picture Arrangement
Similarities	Object Assembly
Arithmetic	Block Design
Digits	Digit Symbol
Vocabulary (alternate)	

instruments. As he explained: "Our aim was not to produce a set of brand new tests but to select, from whatever source available, such a combination of them as would meet the requirements of an effective adult scale" (Wechsler 1939:78). In most cases (but not all) Wechsler cited the immediate source for each test (79–103). (Several authors have provided more detailed explanations of the pedigrees of the tests. See Boake 2002; Frank 1983:9–13; Tulsky, Saklofske, and Zhu 2003.)

Of the six verbal tests, four (Information, Comprehension, Similarities, and Arithmetic) had counterparts in Army Examination Alpha. Five (Comprehension, Similarities, Arithmetic, Digits, and Vocabulary) had counterparts in Binet and Simon's (1905b, 1908) scales and also in the Stanford revision of their 1908 scale. Although Terman (1918) had expressed confidence in the use of vocabulary tests as measures of intelligence, Wechsler had been concerned that "the number of words a man acquires must necessarily be influenced by his educational and cultural opportunities" (1939:101). As a result, he added Vocabulary to the scale only as an afterthought when most of the normative data had been collected. Because of this Wechsler proposed that it should be used merely as an alternate test if the administration of another verbal test was disrupted. However, he soon became convinced of the value of this test, and later versions of his scale included Vocabulary along with the other tests that constituted the verbal scale.

Wechsler was less sure about Digits (85–87). This was a conventional test of immediate memory (or "memory span") for spoken digits but with one amendment. When Terman (1916:207–209) had revised Binet and Simon's (1908) scale, he had adopted a suggestion made by Otto Bobertag (1911) that examinees should be assessed on their ability to repeat sequences of digits both forward (that is, in the order of presentation) and backward (that is, in the reverse order). Wechsler's Digits Test followed the same pattern, using the total of the forward digit span and the backward digit span as the measure of performance. He used this method of scoring for two reasons. The first was that both measures showed relatively little variation in normal adults: most could recall sequences of five to eight digits forward and sequences of four to six digits backward. Adding the two together yielded a somewhat greater range of scores. The second reason for combining them into one score was to avoid giving too much weight to what was, after all, just a test of rote memory.

The five performance tests all had counterparts in either Army Examination Beta or the Army Performance Scale. Picture Completion required the identification of missing details, as in Binet and Simon's (1908) scale (see table 4.2). (For example, one picture showed a pig without a tail.) It is therefore different from Healy's (1914) Picture Completion Test, in which missing pieces were to be fitted into blank spaces in a pictured scene. Picture Arrangement required the rearrangement of a series of pictures to tell a simple story, as in a comic strip. (One item that Wechsler used had actually been taken from a comic strip in the *New Yorker*.) Block Design was based on the test of the same name that had been devised by Samuel Kohs (1920), and Digit Symbol was similar to the Substitution Test that had been devised by Robert Woodworth and Frederic Wells (1911).

None of these performance tests was related to those that had been devised by Howard Knox and his colleagues at Ellis Island. Indeed, Wechsler rejected form boards and picture form boards in general because they typically did not discriminate between people (and especially adults) of average intelligence: "Our experience over a long period with the commonly used formboards, had convinced us that whatever their merit when administered to children, they were generally ill adapted for testing adults. Most of the standardized formboards are much too easy for the average adult, and at the high levels have very little discriminative value" (1939:99). Nevertheless, one test developed at Ellis Island, the Feature Profile Test, was incorporated into one of the performance tests in the Wechsler-Bellevue Scale.

To be more specific, Object Assembly consisted of three puzzles: a Manikin, a Feature Profile, and a Hand (Wechsler 1939:98). Wechsler had devised the third puzzle himself. It consisted of a hand from which the fingers and part of the palm had been cut away. However, the Manikin and Feature Profile tasks were based on their counterparts in Pintner and Paterson's (1917) Scale of Performance Tests. The manikin had been redrawn to make its features more human in appearance, and the feature profile had also been altered in a number of respects: "It is a profile of a woman's head instead of a man's, the ear is divided into two instead of four parts, and a piece has been cut out of the base of the skull" (Wechsler 1939:98). Wechsler cited Pintner and Paterson's book as the source of these tasks and made no mention of Knox and his colleagues.

The Wechsler-Bellevue Scale received favorable reviews (see Tulsky 2003), and by 1946 it was the second most widely used test in psychological clinics across the United States after the Stanford revision of Binet and Simon's scale (Louttit and Browne 1947). During World War II Wechsler devised an alternative version, the Wechsler Mental Ability Scale, for use in screening recruits for the U.S. Army, rather as the Army Mental Tests had been used in World War I. The verbal tests were used with recruits who understood sufficient English, and the performance tests were used with those who did not (Altus 1945). After the war a revised version of this scale was published as the Wechsler-Bellevue Intelligence Scale, Form II (Wechsler 1946). The latter in turn evolved into the Wechsler Intelligence Scale for Children (WISC) (Wechsler 1949), and the original Wechsler-Bellevue Scale evolved into the Wechsler Adult Intelligence Scale (WAIS) (Wechsler 1955). Both the WAIS and the WISC went through several subsequent revisions.

David Wechsler died in 1981. Later editions of the WAIS and the WISC were developed by teams of researchers, but Wechsler continued to be credited as the sole author. The team responsible for the third edition of the WAIS altered its broad structure by changing the status of Object Assembly (see Tulsky, Saklofske, and Zhu 2003). They retained the three original puzzles (the Manikin, Feature Profile, and Hand) and added two puzzles to increase the range of possible scores. However, they shared concerns about the validity of Object Assembly that Wechsler had expressed (1939:99–100), so they demoted it to an alternate test that could be used if the administration of some other performance test was disrupted. Object Assembly was eventually dropped completely from the fourth edition of the WISC in 2003 and from the fourth edition of the WAIS in 2008.

THE DEMISE OF PERFORMANCE SCALES

The success of the Wechsler-Bellevue Intelligence Scale was not surprising, since it met all the key criteria put forward by Conrad (1931) as the "requisites of a general intelligence test" and in addition provided clinicians with a sensitive tool for interpreting the different patterns or profiles of intellectual abilities and disabilities seen in their patients. However, a corollary of its success was a marked decline in the use of previous scales that contained only performance tests. For instance, surveys of the tests that were used in psychological clinics across the United States found that Arthur's point scale was the third most widely used test in 1935, while it was ranked just fifteenth in 1946; even more marked, Pintner and Paterson's scale was the sixth most widely used test in 1935, but it was ranked only fifty-four in 1946 (Louttit and Browne 1947). A few of Pintner and Paterson's tests continued to be used on an individual basis immediately after World War II. Of the tests that predated the work of Knox and his colleagues at Ellis Island, these included the Seguin Form Board, Healy and Fernald's (1911) construction puzzles, and the Mare-and-Foal Picture Form Board. Of the Ellis Island tests themselves, only the Casuist Test, Feature Profile Test, and Cube Imitation Test appear to have survived as practical tools.

Except for the Cube Imitation Test, this phenomenon was short-lived. Grace Helen Kent neatly summarized the situation in 1950. She was best known for the word-association norms that she had published with Aaron Joshua Rosanoff when working with psychiatric patients at Kings Park State Hospital on Long Island in 1910. She then worked at the Government Hospital for the Insane in Washington, D.C., and at the state psychiatric hospital in Warren, Pennsylvania. She returned to Washington to study for a Ph.D. at George Washington University from 1912 to 1915 (Ogilvie and Harvey 2000, 1:690). She then obtained a position at the School of Pedagogy at New York University, where she devised her own form boards and picture puzzles for use with mentally deficient children (Kent 1916a, 1916b). As she noted, "It would seem that they should be especially helpful in the study of children of foreign parentage, and possibly in the examination of immigrants at Ellis Island" (Kent 1916b:42).

From 1920 to 1922 Kent was employed as a psychologist at the Pineland State Training School for mentally deficient people in Columbia, South Carolina, and from 1922 to 1926 she worked at the Worcester State Hospital in Massachusetts (where Howard Knox had been briefly employed after he graduated from Dartmouth College in 1908). There Kent met David Shakow, a student who was taking a break between his undergraduate and graduate studies at Harvard University. Kent and Shakow developed a new series of smaller, lighter form boards that were more convenient to carry to the numerous clinics that were held at diverse locations around the eastern half of the state (Shakow and Kent 1925). These were the form boards that Fick (1937, 1939) later used with South African children. (Shakow himself went on to have a highly distinguished career in clinical psychology.)

Kent, who had been born in 1875, was still working as a clinical psychologist and writing about psychological tests well into her seventies, when she was employed at the State Hospital at Waterbury, Vermont. She was familiar with performance tests and had used them throughout her professional career. In 1950, however, she published a textbook on mental tests for use with children in which she was highly critical in her evaluation of both previous and existing tests. In particular, she concluded, "The sub-tests of the Pintner-Paterson series [which included six of the original Ellis Island tests] are either obsolete or obsolescent, and those that remain in use will probably be superseded within a generation" (44). Although this prediction was broadly accurate, there were two exceptions: a version of the Feature Profile Test survived until 2008 in the Object Assembly

Test of Wechsler's intelligence scales, and the Cube Imitation Test continued to be used in research and practice around the world after 1950.

THE CUBE IMITATION TEST

Table 11.2 summarizes the many variants of the Cube Imitation Test. This section briefly describes the versions developed since World War II, but further details can be found in the literature review on which the following account is based (Richardson 2005).

Papua New Guinea is located on the eastern half of the island of New Guinea in the southwestern Pacific Ocean. In the 1950s both the northern part of the country (the Trust Territory of New Guinea) and the southern part (Territory of Papua) were administered by Australia, the former under a mandate from the League of Nations after World War I, the latter on behalf of the United Kingdom. Young men from the indigenous population were recruited into the Pacific Islands Regiment of the Australian Army, and Australian psychologists included a version of the Cube Imitation Test in a battery for screening recruits from Papua and New Guinea (Ord 1971:16, 94). During the 1960s the original battery was extended to yield the New Guinea Performance Scales, which were used in both cross-cultural studies and educational testing. George Kearney (1966), a student working for a Ph.D. at the University of Queensland in Australia, adapted these scales for administration through mime alone as the Queensland Test, and this contained a different version of the Cube Imitation Test.

Johannes Theodorus Snijders and Anna Wijnanda Maria (Nan) Snijders-Oomen (1958) of the University of Groningen in the Netherlands published a scale of nonverbal tests that included a version of the Cube Imitation Test. This scale was published in four successive editions in Dutch, German, French, and English and was sold in Europe, South Africa, and the United States. Subsequently, Johannes Jacobus Fredericus Schroots and Robbert Jan van Alphen de Veer (1976) of the Nederlands Instituut voor Praeventieve Geneeskunde (the Netherlands Institute for Preventive Medicine) in Leyden developed the Leidse Diagnostische Test (Leyden Diagnostic Test) for assessing children with learning difficulties. This included a subtest called *natikken* (copy tapping) based on Arthur's (1947) version of the Cube Imitation Test.

In 1977 Ronald Lou Trites, a neuropsychologist at the Royal Ottawa Hospital in Canada, published a manual combining a widely used battery of tests used to evaluate brain functioning, the Halstead-Reitan Neuropsychological Test Battery, with a variety of other tasks, including a version of the Cube Imitation Test based on that of Arthur (1947). Hallgrim Kløve of the University of Bergen produced a

TABLE 11.2 VARIATIONS OF THE CUBE IMITATION TEST

Source	Color of Cubes	Spacing of Cubes (cm)	Number of Sequences
Knox 1913f	red, blue, green, yellow	10.0	5
Pintner 1915	black	5.0	12
Yoakum and Yerkes 1920	dark red	5.0	10
Arthur 1928	black	5.0	12
Drever and Collins 1928	black	5.0	12
Babcock 1930	red	5.0	14
Amoss 1936	red	5.0	19
Goodenough, Maurer, and Van Wagenen 1940	red	2.5	5
Arthur 1947	black	5.0	18
Snijders and Snijders-Oomen 1958	green	5.0	15
Levinson 1960	brown	5.0	18
Kearney 1966	black	4.2	15
Ord 1968, 1971	red	4.0	12
Schroots and van Alphen de Veer 1976	red	5.0	12
Trites 1977	black	5.0	18

(continues on next page)

TABLE 11.2 VARIATIONS OF THE CUBE IMITATION TEST *(continued)*

Source	Color of Cubes	Spacing of Cubes (cm)	Number of Sequences
Manual Nevropsykologisk Testbatteri, n.d.	unpainted wood	5.0	18
M. H. Stone and Wright 1980	black	5.0	16 or 22

Source: Adapted from Richardson 2005:188.

Norwegian adaptation of the Halstead-Reitan Battery, and this too included a version of the Cube Imitation Test (*Manual Nevropsykologisk Testbatteri*, n.d.). The procedure and the accompanying norms were taken from Arthur's (1947) manual, but new data were provided from young and older adults for comparative purposes.

Benjamin Drake Wright and Mark H. Stone (1979) of the University of Chicago devised a new version of "Knox's Cube Test" consisting of a "Senior Form" of twenty-two sequences for use with adults and a "Junior Form" of sixteen sequences for children. This was commercially published by C. H. Stoelting, the company that had originally distributed the Ellis Island tests (M. H. Stone and Wright 1980). Wright and Stone had used the results of earlier studies to calculate age-related norms, but this was criticized because it had involved pooling results obtained with varying materials, procedures, and subject populations (Dean 1985; Sattler 1985). More recently, Stone (2002) published a revised version of the test that included new norms based on more than three thousand people aged three to eighty-four.

All these versions of the Cube Imitation Test followed Pintner's (1915) suggestion that the cubes should be identical, and some used apparatus based directly upon Pintner's. Nevertheless, a wide variety of procedures have been used, and the cubes themselves have been presented in a variety of colors, as table 11.2 shows. Boris Mayer Levinson (1960), a child psychologist at Yeshiva University in New York, used four brown cubes attached to a thin board, and in the last few years an apparatus of this description (whose origins are uncertain) has been exhibited at the Ellis Island Immigration Museum.

Eugene Mullan (1917b) had modified the Cube Imitation Test by, among other things, adding a fifth cube. In 1932 Edith Atwood Davis of the Institute of Child

Welfare (now the Institute of Child Development) at the University of Minnesota replaced the four blocks with a row of five squares of gray paper attached to a white board. However, the test-retest reliability of this procedure proved to be poor. In the late 1950s Doreen Kimura, a research student at the Montreal Neurological Institute (part of McGill University), used a row of five black cubes and sequences in which the tester tapped all five cubes once in a random order. She assessed some of her participants using both immediate testing and after a five-second delay (Kimura 1960:41). Some years later she described her procedures in more detail in a manual of neuropsychological tests (Kimura 1997:65–67).

In Knox's original version of the Cube Imitation Test, the cubes were painted different colors, which might have prompted the participants simply to remember sequences of colors or sequences of color names. In fact, even when cubes of the same color are used, about a third of the participants report that they have mentally labeled the cubes in some way and have remembered the sequences of labels that corresponded to the sequences of tapped cubes (Reymert and Hartman 1933; Richardson 2005). Mark Stone (2002:38) suggested that the most commonly used labels were 1, 2, 3, 4; a, b, c, d; and f, a, c, e (the names of spaces in the treble clef). Contrary to what one might expect, this strategy does not seem to lead to improved performance (Inglis 1957; Richardson 2005), but it certainly changes the basic nature of the task.

A few years after Doreen Kimura had completed her Ph.D., another research student at the Montreal Neurological Institute, Philip Michael Corsi, considered using her version of the Cube Imitation Test. However, he was concerned that, even with this more difficult task, participants might still try to remember the sequences using verbal labels. He therefore constructed a new apparatus that contained nine black cubes arranged in an irregular manner in two dimensions on a black rectangular board. Corsi (1972) used this apparatus to measure "spatial span" (analogous to the verbal digit span). Similar tasks have subsequently been used in both clinical and experimental research (see Berch, Krikorian, and Huha 1998 for a review) and in published test batteries (Kaplan, Fein, Morris, and Delis 1991; Wechsler 1987, 1999), and some of these have been adapted for administration on the display screen of a computer.

Today Corsi's procedure is generally known as the Corsi Blocks Test. The use of a second spatial dimension seems to render this a wholly spatial task that cannot be performed by mentally labeling the cubes (Vecchi and Richardson 2001). It is therefore perhaps not surprising that the Corsi Blocks Test has generally superseded the Cube Imitation Test in clinical research and practice. Nevertheless, versions of the Cube Imitation Test are still being used, even in the twenty-first century. Arthur's 1947 version was the most widely used in North America until the 1980s, but since then Stone and Wright's version has become more prevalent.

Pintner's version is still used in India, perhaps because of the use of Raymond Cattell's (1936) manual in colonial times. The version in the Queensland Test has continued to be used in Australia, and in continental Europe the versions devised by Snijders and Snijders-Oomen, by Schroots and van Alphen de Veer, and by Kløve are still used by both researchers and practitioners.

One might also note the similarities between certain versions of the Cube Imitation Test and some modern electronic games. Most obviously, Pintner's version of the test, with its row of identical black cubes, is formally similar to an arcade game called "Touch-Me," which was first produced by the video game company Atari in 1974. The console contained four large black buttons in a single row that were lit up in a particular sequence, each accompanied by a different sound. The player's task was to respond by pushing the buttons in the same sequence. This then prompted the invention of a hand-held game called "Simon" (after the children's game "Simon Says"), which was produced by the Milton Bradley Company in 1977. This contained four colored buttons arranged in a circle; once again, the buttons lit up in a particular sequence, each accompanied by a different sound, and the player's task was to respond by pushing the buttons in the same sequence. Atari produced a similar hand-held game called "Touch Me" the following year. In both games the buttons were colored red, blue, green, and yellow, just like the cubes in Knox's original version of the Cube Imitation Test. However, Ralph Henry Baer, one of the inventors of "Simon," told me that he was not aware of Knox's Cube Imitation Test (personal communication).

~~~~~~~~

The Cube Imitation Test has survived for nearly a hundred years, and variants of the test are still used in many countries. The Feature Profile Test also survived until 2008, albeit buried within the WAIS as an optional test. Many other Ellis Island tests were widely used during the 1920s and 1930s, but after World War II they were superseded, just as Grace Kent (1950) had predicted, and the name of Howard Knox was forgotten. Even so, performance tests remain a key part of the Wechsler scales and other tests of intelligence. So what, exactly, do they measure?

12

WHAT DO PERFORMANCE TESTS MEASURE?

The idea of a performance test has been around for roughly a hundred years. Howard Knox first used the term in his own writings in September 1913 (Knox 1913e), but at that point it seems already to have been in common use in discourse about intelligence and intelligence testing. Since his work at Ellis Island there have been different views about what performance tests actually measure. This chapter considers the ways in which the phrase "performance test" has been used and then discusses three kinds of contemporary evidence to suggest that the distinction between verbal and performance tests may not be straightforward.

THE MEANING OF "PERFORMANCE TEST"

In Chapter 5 I mentioned that the term *performance test* originally was intended to refer to any test that relied on the measurement of overt performance, but its usage became more refined. In 1946 Grace Arthur provided the following succinct definition of *performance tests*:

> Performance tests might be any tests requiring overt response. In practice, they have come to mean tests which can be given without the use of language, either oral or written, or abstract symbols such as words or numbers by either the

subject or the examiner. A *performance scale* is a battery of performance tests, the scores of which can be combined in such a way as to yield a total score that can be translated into an I.Q. or . . . some other index of brightness.

(447)

Arthur pointed out that the scale described by Knox (1914c) in the *Journal of the American Medical Association* was not a performance scale because it included many verbal tests. This is correct, but the scale that Knox had described a month earlier in the *Journal of Heredity* (1914b) was indeed a performance scale, according to Arthur's definition. It did not include the Inkblot Imagination Test, which was not a performance test because it demanded verbal instructions from the examiner and verbal responses from the examinee. It did, however, include all the performance tests that were developed at Ellis Island, except the Triangle Form Board and the Diagonal Form Board, which were subsequently added as "make-up tests for adults."

However, the expression "performance test" gradually took on additional connotations. This is evident from the following explanation, which was given by Frances Gaw:

Performance tests can be defined as short mental problems, which may be presented and must be solved in non-verbal terms. Thus performance tests are designed (1) to measure intelligence primarily, and (2) to do so without making demands on the subject's ability to use language. His response, therefore, is almost of necessity manual, and it follows that the problem presented in a performance test is largely of a concrete nature.

(1925a:3)

In Gaw's definition, there is a subtle shift from "a test that does not require the use of language for its administration" to "a task that does not involve the use of language in its execution," and it is clearly invalid to infer that the latter description holds simply because the former is true.

THE STRUCTURE OF THE WECHSLER INTELLIGENCE SCALES

Whether language is involved in the execution of performance tests or not, are they measuring the same thing as verbal tests? In earlier chapters I mentioned the dispute between Charles Spearman and Edward Thorndike as to whether human intelligence was better regarded as a central trait or factor or as a loose collection of different abilities. This dispute continued unabated well into the 1930s (Deary, Lawn, and Bartholomew 2008; R. M. Thorndike 1990:64–75). Knox would have been aware of the debate's significance for the eugenics movement, because the issue of whether intelligence was a "unit character" had been a major discussion topic at the Eugenics Research Association's second annual meeting in June 1914, which Knox had attended. He did not address this issue in his writings, but he seems to have held the view that intelligence was a unit character: He regarded performance tests as a different way of measuring intelligence when verbal tests were inappropriate, thus effectively siding with Spearman in the dispute.

Most developers and users of performance tests between the two world wars seem to have made similar assumptions. Nevertheless, David Wechsler's position was different. Although he acknowledged Spearman's theoretical distinction between general intelligence and specific traits, he claimed that this was essentially a "psychomathematical" (statistical) artifact rather than a substantive property of intelligence itself (Wechsler 1939:8). Instead, he proposed, "the entity or quantity which we are able to measure by intelligence tests is not a simple quantity. Certainly it is not something which can be expressed by one single factor alone" (11). Wechsler suggested that apparent disparities in a patient's performance on different tests in the Wechsler-Bellevue Intelligence Scale—and, most notably, the difference between verbal IQ and performance IQ—might well be of clinical significance (137–40).

Corwin Boake (2002) maintained that Wechsler's original distinction between verbal IQ and performance IQ was based mainly upon the origins of the relevant tests: The verbal scale was mostly derived from Army Examination Alpha, and the performance scale was mostly derived from Army Examination Beta and the Army Performance Scale. Even so, Wechsler was clearly of the opinion that the distinction between verbal IQ and performance IQ reflected different kinds of psychological functioning, and he made this explicit in later editions of his test manual:

> The most obviously useful feature of the Wechsler-Bellevue scales is their division into a Verbal and Performance part. . . . Its a priori value is that it makes possible a comparison between a subject's facility in using words and symbols and his ability to manipulate objects, and to perceive visual patterns. . . . Differences between verbal and performance test scores, particularly when large, have a special interest for the clinician because such discrepancies are frequently associated with certain types of mental pathology.
>
> (Wechsler 1944:146)

An empirical distinction between verbal IQ and performance IQ received support from studies that used the technique of factor analysis to investigate the relations among test scores on the Wechsler Adult Intelligence Scale (WAIS) (Canavan, Dunn, and McMillan 1986; Maxwell 1960). A similar pattern emerged in the revised version of the Wechsler Intelligence Scale for Children (WISC), except that Digit Span (as it was now called) seemed to define a third factor that was distinct from both verbal IQ and performance IQ (A. R. Jensen and Reynolds 1982).

Analyses carried out on the revised version of the WAIS also indicated that Digit Span defined a third factor variously characterized as "attention/concentration" and "freedom from distractibility" (Atkinson et al. 1989; Crawford 1992; Crawford et al. 1989). The third edition of the WISC (Wechsler 1991) included additional tests that had initially been intended to clarify this third factor. In fact, they revealed a fourth factor that seemed to measure the examinee's speed of information processing (Tulsky, Saklofske, and Zhu 2003). A similar structure appeared in analyses of the WAIS scores that had been obtained by certain groups of clinical patients (Spreen and Strauss 1998:99). The multifactorial structure of the WAIS was acknowledged in its third edition (Wechsler 1997). Like the third edition of the WISC, this included a number of additional tests and provided separate measures of verbal comprehension, perceptual organization, working memory, and processing speed, as well as verbal IQ, performance IQ, and full-scale IQ.

These developments have prompted debate about exactly what the performance tests in the Wechsler intelligence scales are measuring. Some writers have suggested that they measure "fluid" intelligence, originally defined by Raymond Cattell (1943) as the ability to adapt to new situations (as opposed to "crystallized" intelligence, or the ability to use existing skills and knowledge). Nevertheless, this interpretation is not supported by empirical research (Keith 1997), and it has been rejected by modern proponents of Cattell's theoretical framework. They argue that Wechsler's performance tests measure visual processing ability or processing speed, and this leads the Cattell camp to reject the verbal/ performance dichotomy altogether as a theory of human intelligence. Indeed, despite the additional tests that have been included in more recent editions of the Wechsler intelligence scales, the Cattell camp claims that the scales provide only incomplete measures of the full range of human intellectual abilities (see chapter 2 in Flanagan, McGrew, and Ortiz 2000). The same argument was made by Howard Gardner (1983) and Robert Jeffrey Sternberg (1985), each of whom put forward a theory in which intelligence was seen as a complex system of discrete components or domains.

The team that was responsible for developing the third edition of the WAIS produced a comprehensive guide to help clinicians interpret their test results.

The lead members of the team suggested that the traditional verbal and performance IQ scores were less diagnostically useful than the four new factor-derived scores (Verbal Comprehension, Perceptual Organization, Working Memory, and Processing Speed). Moreover, just six of the thirteen tests in the scale could be used to obtain a General Ability Index, which, they claimed, would be more useful than the traditional full-scale IQ (Tulsky, Saklofske, and Zhu 2003). Like the traditional IQ measures, these new scores were measured on a scale with a mean of 100 and a standard deviation of 15.

On the face of it, such models appear to favor a multifactorial view of intelligence of the sort proposed by Edward Thorndike. Even so, in the Wechsler intelligence scales the full-scale IQ score and the General Ability Index represent Spearman's idea of a central trait, or general intelligence, and this is also included in modern versions of Cattell's framework (Flanagan, McGrew, and Ortiz 2000:91–94, 106–107). One commentator has summarized the current position as follows: "The long-standing argument over general intelligence versus multiple abilities has given rise to a broad acceptance of a hierarchical model in which abilities are nested under a higher order general factor, each level having a substantial amount of explanatory power" (Daniel 1997:1039).

THE ROLE OF LINGUISTIC PROCESSING IN PERFORMANCE TESTS

Earlier, it was pointed out that one could not assume that the execution of a test did not involve the use of language simply because the administration of the test did not involve the use of language. This point can be illustrated by reference to the Cube Imitation Test, which Knox described as "one of the most valuable single performance tests" (1913f:564). Even when cubes of the same color are used, about a third of examinees who are given this task report that they have mentally labeled the cubes in some way and have simply remembered the sequences of labels that corresponded to the sequences of tapped cubes. Psychologists today would prefer to demonstrate the use of linguistic processing in a particular task by using some kind of objective procedure rather than merely accepting their participants' subjective reports of how they have gone about the task.

One commonly used procedure is "articulatory suppression": requiring participants to repeat irrelevant sounds aloud while they are carrying out the task. (The choice of speech sounds seems to be unimportant so long as they are familiar: researchers have, for example, used the word *the,* the greeting "hi-ya," or reciting "one, two, three.") The findings obtained using this procedure are clear and consistent. First, it is well established that articulatory suppression impairs performance in tests of digit span (see, for example, Chincotta and Underwood

1997). This is consistent with the notion that articulatory suppression interferes with some kind of speech-based representation in memory that is used to rehearse and maintain the sequences of digits to be remembered.

In contrast, articulatory suppression appears to have no effect on performance in the Corsi Blocks Test (Smyth, Pearson, and Pendleton 1988; Vandierendonck et al. 2004; Vecchi and Richardson 2001). This is consistent with the suggestion that the use of a second spatial dimension renders the Corsi Blocks Test a wholly spatial task that does not rely upon any speech-based representation in memory. Nevertheless, articulatory rehearsal does impair performance in the Cube Imitation Test (Richardson 2005; Vecchi and Richardson 2001). This is consistent with participants' self-reports in suggesting that the execution of the Cube Imitation Test can—and sometimes does—involve some kind of speech-based representation in memory.

In short, it cannot be assumed that the execution of a performance test does not involve the use of language. Rather, this has to be demonstrated empirically for each individual test (and it appears not to be true in the case of the Cube Imitation Test). It may indeed be true that the execution of form boards, picture form boards, and construction tests does not involve the use of language, but there seems to be no direct experimental evidence on this matter. Nevertheless, there does exist indirect, correlational evidence.

THE ROLE OF LANGUAGE PREFERENCE

In Chapter 11, I mentioned that the scores obtained on performance tests by people from ethnic minorities depended upon their contact and their engagement with the dominant white culture. This process might in principle be influenced by testees' general life experience or more specifically by their education or their use of language. The researchers who collected normative data for the third edition of the WAIS had asked their participants about these three different aspects of their acculturation to U.S. society, and the results can be used to examine the role of education and language as predictors of test performance.

Josette Garess Harris, David Scott Tulsky, and Maria Teresa Schultheis (2003) identified 151 participants who had been born outside the United States, whose first language was not English, but who were fluent in English on both their own assessment and that of the person who had administered the WAIS to them. Harris and her colleagues expressed the participants' U.S. experience as the proportion of their lives during which they had been resident in the United States, and the researchers expressed the participants' U.S. education as the proportion of their education that they had received in the United States. The participants' language preference was measured according to their answers to the following four questions:

What language do you prefer to use when speaking?
What language do you prefer to use when thinking?
What language do you prefer to use when reading?
What language do you prefer to use when writing?

The answer to each question was coded as English, 0; another language, 1; equal preference, 0.5. An overall language preference score between 0 and 4 was obtained by summing their scores on the four questions, so that lower scores reflected a stronger preference for English.

Harris and her colleagues then carried out a series of multiple regression analyses to see whether the three aspects of acculturation predicted the participants' factor-derived scores on the WAIS. Verbal Comprehension is measured by three verbal tests (Vocabulary, Similarities, and Information), and Harris and her colleagues found that the participants' Verbal Comprehension scores were predicted strongly by their language preference, less strongly by their U.S. education, and not at all by their U.S. experience. The regression coefficient for language preference was −5.2; since this was being measured on a scale from 0 to 4, this means that the participants who had an exclusive preference for English tended to obtain scores on Verbal Comprehension that were (5.2 × 4.0) = 20.8 IQ points higher than the scores obtained by the participants who had an exclusive preference for another language, even though the latter were regarded as fluent English speakers. Participating in an intelligence test seems to require particular communication skills that are not necessarily part of the ordinary repertoire of even fluent English speakers.

Even more surprising, Harris and her colleagues found remarkably similar results for the participants' scores on Perceptual Organization and Processing Speed, both of which are measured by performance tests. The regression coefficients were −4.9 and −4.0, respectively. This means that the participants who had an exclusive preference for English tended to obtain Perceptual Organization scores that were (4.9 × 4.0) = 19.6 IQ points higher and Processing Speed scores that were (4.0 × 4.0) = 16.0 IQ points higher than those obtained by the participants who had an exclusive preference for another language. In other words, language preference seems to be an important predictor of participants' scores on the performance tests in the Wechsler intelligence scales, and this is indirect evidence that the execution of such tests involves linguistic processing.

In addition to this theoretical conclusion, these results have important implications for clinical practice, as Harris and her colleagues explained in the following way:

> Our data suggest that when testing someone who is bilingual, it is important to assess acculturation. The examinee's self-reported preferred language is a key variable for planning assessment strategies and other decision making. If the examinee does not indicate a preference for English, then his/her scores may be affected, and, as the individual diverges from the sample upon which the test was developed, the norms may become less meaningful. The examiner should take these factors into account when deciding how to test the individual and how to interpret scores.
>
> (377–78)

How, exactly, should examiners take such factors into account when testing people whose first language is not English and who express a clear preference for their first language? Harris and her colleagues suggested that, for those who had emigrated to the United States following the completion of their formal education or whose residency in the United States had been relatively brief, it might be more appropriate to administer versions of the Wechsler intelligence scales that had been developed and standardized in their countries of origin. As Harris and colleagues noted,

> An examiner or assistant who speaks the language of the examinee and is trained in the basic theory and methods of assessment can be used for this purpose. However, it remains the responsibility of the clinician to ensure that the translation or adaptation has been developed according to established guidelines and standards, and that the normative sample is relevant and representative of the examinee.
>
> (385)

The Wechsler intelligence scales have indeed been translated into the languages of many other countries, and in most cases appropriate local norms exist. Moreover, according to the data analyzed by Harris and her colleagues, time spent in the United States does not itself predict any of the scores obtained on the WAIS by people whose first language is not English. Nevertheless, time spent away from their native countries might well lead to a process of "de-culturation," which means that the local norms will be inappropriate. More fundamentally, Harris and her colleagues did not demonstrate an equivalence between the two situations: it remains to be shown that immigrants to the United States who have a strong preference for their first language achieve scores on translated versions of the Wechsler intelligence scales that are similar to those obtained on the U.S. versions of those scales by immigrants who have a strong preference for English.

～～～～～

A subtle but invalid shift in the meaning of "performance test" encouraged test developers to assume that the execution of such tests did not involve the use of language. This assumption is untrue in the case of at least one performance test, the Cube Imitation Test, and its validity in the case of other performance tests is thus in doubt. Analyses of later versions of the Wechsler intelligence scales suggest that the performance tests included in these scales measure diverse capacities such as visual processing ability or processing speed, although these can also be regarded as reflecting some underlying central trait, or general intelligence. Finally, language preference appears to be an important predictor of the performance of immigrants to the United States on both verbal and performance tests.

Nearly a century after the work of the Ellis Island physicians, how to test the intelligence of immigrants in a fair and accurate manner remains a serious practical problem, whether the tests are administered in English or in the immigrants' first language. In other words, and notwithstanding their usefulness in other settings, performance tests did not solve the problem that they were supposed to address: providing a way of identifying mental deficiency that was not contaminated by differences in language and culture.

13

AN APPRAISAL

~~~~~~~~~~~~~~~~~~~~~~~~~~~~~~~~

In this concluding chapter I examine Howard Knox's life and work from a number of different points of view. What can one say about Knox's involvement in and commitment to the development of intelligence tests? What role did Knox himself play in devising the Ellis Island tests, and how much were they subsequently used? Did Knox really succeed in finding a way of differentiating between moronism and ignorance? Was Knox himself a eugenicist or a racist? Finally, I describe the neglect and rediscovery of the Ellis Island tests in the second half of the twentieth century, a process that has culminated in a reevaluation of the contribution of Knox and his colleagues to intelligence testing.

KNOX'S INVOLVEMENT IN INTELLIGENCE TESTING

At the beginning of this book I described Knox's early life and his time as a medical student at Dartmouth College in New Hampshire. His early influences are clear: the principal of his high school in Willimantic, Arthur Petersen, had encouraged him to seek a college education, and his stepfather, Leander Blackwell, despite apparently never having practiced as a physician himself, had inspired the young Knox to study medicine. (The exact nature of his mother's influence is less clear, but she was both physically and emotionally close to him until her death in 1929). I went on to describe what initially seemed to be a promising career, first in the Medical Reserve Corps of the U.S. Army and subsequently in the Army Medical Corps itself.

As I have commented elsewhere (Richardson 2001), the information that we have about Knox's brief military career raises many more questions than it answers. The assessments submitted by his superior officers always spoke highly of his professional ability and his performance of duty. Knox's own subsequent writings suggest someone who was professionally highly competent, as well as someone who could be compassionate toward other human beings. (However, he was capable of being remarkably insensitive, as when he testified about young emigrants before the boards of special inquiry at Ellis Island.)

By April 1911 Knox seems to have reached a key point in his military career, but this was also the point at which he lost the support of his superior officers. The precise nature of his transgressions is not at all apparent from his military records. I have discussed several possible explanations, but the issue is unlikely ever to be resolved. As I concluded, whatever the reason, Knox was not sufficiently well regarded by his superiors for them either to discourage him from resigning his commission or to permit his subsequent readmission to the Army Medical Corps. Nevertheless, a year later he was offered new employment in the U.S. Public Health and Marine Hospital Service, and thus it was that he came to work at the immigration station on Ellis Island.

This appointment enabled Knox to make a significant contribution to medical science, but in a rather different field from that in which he had originally expected to work. Indeed, he would never have made that contribution if he had been allowed to resume his commission in the Army Medical Corps. However, the immediate corollary to this is that his arrival at Ellis Island was a matter of accident rather than one of design. Certainly, nothing in Knox's background—his upbringing, his education, or his previous employment as a physician—indicated that he had any interest whatsoever in the development of psychological tests. Nevertheless, he appears to have entered into his work on mental testing with enthusiasm and commitment.

Although he devoted considerable time and energy to developing, publicizing, and popularizing the Ellis Island tests, Knox appears to have completely turned his back on the world of intelligence testing and seems not to have kept in touch with his colleagues from Ellis Island after he resigned his commission in the Public Health Service. As one of Knox's children put it to me, his father adopted an attitude of "closing the door" on successive episodes in his life. He did keep copies of the Ellis Island tests in the family home, but he did not treat them with any reverence or respect. On the contrary, he allowed his children to play with them as mere toys. That his contribution to intelligence testing was gradually forgotten may have been just what he wanted.

Accordingly, the first point to acknowledge is that Knox's involvement in mental testing lasted only four years (specifically, from May 1912 to May 1916). His contribution cannot be considered to be on a par with the work of Francis Galton, Alfred Binet, Henry Goddard, Lewis Terman, Robert Yerkes, and David Wechsler, whose names I listed at the outset of this book and who devoted much of their intellectual lives to research into intelligence and intelligence testing. Rather, Knox was just a small-town or army doctor who became caught up in questions of his day and who made some significant and influential contributions in seeking to address those questions.

WHO DEVISED THE ELLIS ISLAND TESTS?

During the time that he spent at Ellis Island, Knox published sixteen articles in several different learned journals. Indeed, in a period of just eight months, from September 1913 to April 1914, Knox published six articles that described a diverse range of thirteen new tests of intelligence. This in itself would be a highly impressive feat for an academic researcher, not simply for the time but even by the standards of today's publish-or-perish culture. Nevertheless, it is even more impressive for a mere assistant surgeon, someone who was on the bottom rung of the career scale and whose main duty was to inspect the thousands of emigrants arriving at Ellis Island every day of the year.

But where, exactly, should the credit for devising the Ellis Island tests lie? In addition to Knox's having taken responsibility both for presenting the tests in learned medical journals and for publicizing them elsewhere, there are other reasons for concluding that he was largely responsible for devising the tests themselves. Harry Hollingworth of Columbia University had written a letter of introduction for Walter Dill Scott of Northwestern University, so that Scott could visit Knox's testing rooms and see "the ingenious tests you have yourself devised." And in an article published in January 1914, Knox's superior officer, Surgeon Ezra Sprague, mentioned that he had tried using the de Sanctis tests, Binet and Simon's scale, the Seguin Form Board, and Healy and Fernald's construction puzzles. However, he continued, Howard Knox "had recently introduced other performance tests" (466).

In *Scientific American* Knox (1915a) in turn credited Sprague with the idea of a scale for measuring intelligence: "The idea of using a graduated scale with performance tests for determining the intelligence of aliens, and especially illiterates, upon whom no real honest work had ever before been done, was original with Surgeon Ezra K. Sprague of the Public Health Service, and to him much honor is due for the present efficient methods at Ellis Island" (53). Moreover, Knox explicitly recognized the contributions of his colleagues (particularly those of Bernard Glueck, Matthew Gwyn, and Grover Kempf) (Knox 1914a, 1914b). It is worth quoting the acknowledgment from his article in the *Journal of the American Medical Association*:

> The officers who participated equally with me in this work and through whose painstaking and untiring efforts much valuable data has been obtained are Surgeon M. K. Gwyn, P. A. Surgeon R. E. Ebersole, P. A. Surgeon E. H. Mullin [sic], Assistant Surgeons G. A. Kempf and W. L. Treadway, and Dr. Bernard Gluek [sic] of the Government Hospital for the Insane at Washington, D.C.
>
> (Knox 1914c:747)

At the same time the Public Health Service was evidently content for Knox to arrange for the tests to be sold by a commercial test publisher and, indeed, content to buy copies of the tests to be used at Ellis Island. Some illustrations in the *Manual of the Mental Examination of Aliens* (1918), a government publication, show examples of C. H. Stoelting's products.

Nonetheless, we might ask how original the Ellis Island tests really were. Citation practices in the medical literature of 1912–16 were quite different from those of today, and Knox's articles typically give little clue as to where the ideas for his tests came from. The one truly original example is the Cube Imitation Test. It seems to have been devised as a nonverbal analog of tests of digit span, which had been used since the 1880s (Richardson 2007) and had been included in Binet and Simon's scales. It is, however, quite unlike any earlier procedure, and it was used throughout the twentieth century in educational, cross-cultural, and neuro-psychological research (see Richardson 2005 for a review). However, all the other tests are probably best described as multiple variations on existing themes. Many were based on the tests described by Healy and Fernald (1911), but the Inkblot Imagination Test is probably the most obvious example of Knox adapting existing materials and procedures to his own purposes.

Also, Knox went about using the Ellis Island tests in a fairly traditional way. Indeed, he never seems to have questioned Binet and Simon's basic methodology. Performance on different tasks or items was scored on a simple pass/fail basis, and an emigrant's intelligence was assessed by comparing her scores on an appropriate selection of tests with those to be expected from normal children of different ages. This yielded an estimate of what Binet had called mental level but which, following Goddard, Knox and his colleagues called mental age. It was left to Eugene Mullan (1917b) to introduce the notion of a point-scale to Ellis Island.

HOW MUCH WERE THE TESTS SUBSEQUENTLY USED?

Knox and his colleagues can be credited with devising thirteen different tests. Three were used extensively in the interwar period: the Cube Imitation Test, Feature Profile Test, and Ship Test. This was mainly because they had been included both in Pintner and Paterson's *A Scale of Performance Tests* (1917) and in Yoakum and Yerkes's *Army Mental Tests* (1920). Three other tests were perhaps less widely used: the Casuist Test, Diagonal Form Board, and Triangle Form Board. Nevertheless, they would still have been familiar to researchers and practitioners of the era because they had been included in Pintner and Paterson's scale, although not in the Army Mental Tests.

However, the remaining tests—the Construction Blocks Test, Diamond Frame Test, Geographical Puzzle, Imbecile Test, Inkblot Imagination Test, Moron Test, and Visual Comparison Test—were rarely used. None of these tests was included in either Pintner and Paterson's scale or the Army Mental Tests. In addition, many other form boards and tests requiring visual comparisons became available and were more familiar to psychologists. (Indeed, in the case of the Inkblot Imagination Test, more extensive alternatives already existed.) In a study of 116 normal children from a wide variety of schools, Dorothy Ruth Morgenthau (1922), a research student at Columbia University, found that the Diamond Frame Test and Moron Test were neither reliable nor correlated with mental age as measured by the Stanford revision of Binet and Simon's scale. To be fair, this was partly because they had been intended simply to detect people who were mentally deficient rather than to measure the full range of intelligence.

The Construction Blocks Test, in which participants assembled five wooden cubes to make various structures, was particularly neglected. (This was described as the "Block Test" in C. H. Stoelting's leaflet advertising the Ellis Island tests but as an "Imitation Test" in various editions of the publisher's catalog.) One reason for its neglect is that a test with a similar name became widely used. Edgar Arnold Doll, who was Henry Goddard's assistant at the Vineland Training School, described the "Painted Cube Construction Test" at the annual meeting of the American Psychological Association in New York in December 1916 (Doll 1917). Yoakum and Yerkes (1920:105–107) described an easier version of this task in *Army Mental Tests*. This became widely known as the Cube Construction Test and was used by many researchers who developed their own performance scales

(Babcock 1932; Cornell and Coxe 1934; Drever and Collins 1928; Gaw 1925a, 1925b). It is different from Knox's Construction Blocks Test and has no connection with Ellis Island, although one Italian researcher mistakenly referred to the task as the "'cubi di costruzione' di Knox-Pintner" (the Knox-Pintner "construction cubes") (Reda 1950:459).

DIFFERENTIATING BETWEEN MORONISM AND IGNORANCE

Knox (1913f) stated that the key problem facing the physicians at Ellis Island was to differentiate between moronism and ignorance. This was the original purpose of the performance tests, and he claimed that as a result of developing their tests "it is probably now possible to say in every case whether an alien is defective or whether he is simply ignorant" (564). This raises the issue of whether Knox's confidence in the tests was justified. (The editorial commentary to his article in the *Journal of Heredity* stated that the tests were used to "determine exact mentality" [Knox 1914b:122].) Tests today are mainly evaluated in terms of two properties: their reliability and their validity.

An instrument is reliable to the extent that it yields the same measurement when used on repeated occasions and is therefore not subject to measurement error. This was a concern of the Ellis Island physicians', particularly because an emigrant's test performance might be adversely affected by his experience of the voyage across the Atlantic. Any emigrant who was suspected of being mentally deficient was tested on several occasions over two or more days under conditions designed to alleviate any residual distress. However, the physicians did not publish any formal evidence of the reliability of their tests in mentally normal individuals. Studies such as Morgenthau's (1922) suggested that some tests were of doubtful reliability, but this could have been addressed by more careful standardization of the test procedures, as in the case of Pintner's (1915) version of the Cube Imitation Test.

An instrument is valid to the extent that it measures what it purports to measure. This can be addressed in a number of different ways. The Ellis Island physicians confined themselves to a consideration of the consistency among the results of different tests. This could be regarded as an early way of evaluating their construct validity: whether the tests reflect different ways of measuring the same underlying trait or construct (that is, intelligence). It would have been more convincing if Knox and his colleagues had obtained evidence of their criterion validity: whether the tests yielded the same result as some independent measure or criterion. When the Army Mental Tests were devised, this was assessed by comparing the results of literate examinees with their scores on the Stanford revision of Binet and Simon's scale. However, Knox and his colleagues collected no evidence of this sort.

Evaluating the reliability and validity of intelligence tests was becoming standard practice among psychologists when Knox was working at Ellis Island, but his background in conventional medicine seems to have led him to attach little importance to such matters. Thus claims that the Ellis Island tests could determine the "exact mentality" of emigrants were quite simply inappropriate. Another issue is whether the tests measure "native ability," uncontaminated by linguistic or cultural knowledge (Knox 1913g:1017). Knox was probably the first proponent of "culture free" or "culture fair" tests, an idea that psychologists did not pick up until the 1920s. Can the claim that performance tests are culture free or culture fair be sustained?

In chapter 11, I mentioned Simon Biesheuvel's (1943) suggestion that performance tests were not strictly culture fair because non-Western children were less motivated to respond to the demands of a Western tester. Knox (1913g) referred to the problem of motivation in introducing the Imbecile Test. He claimed that the test was valuable in itself, but, he added: "This test is also used as an encouragement test at Ellis Island in working with suspected higher defectives, that is, it is given to them at the beginning of the performance test examination to inspire confidence, and to reassure them as to their ability to perform the more difficult performance tests suitable to their mental measure" (1018). However, on this account it is unclear whether the performance tests were measuring the emigrants' intelligence or their motivation to perform the tests.

I also mentioned in chapter 11 that the scores obtained on performance tests by children from diverse ethnic minorities depended upon their contact with white culture (including being educated in Western educational systems) rather than upon their race or ethnicity. In effect, these tests are measuring the extent to which children have acquired the particular aptitudes and skills that Western culture values. It follows from this that the very idea of a culture-free or culture-fair test is simply a chimera, because different cultures vary in the extent to which they value the kinds of skills that are measured by particular tests (Anastasi 1954:255–56; 1985). More fundamentally, intelligence tests are artifacts constructed within a specific culture, and they cannot be expected to transfer to different cultures from the one in which they were constructed.

This has been appreciated by researchers who adopt the approach of cultural psychology, which originated in the sociohistorical school of psychology developed in the 1920s and 1930s by the Russian researchers Lev Semeonovich Vygotski (Vygotsky), Aleksandr Romanovich Luria, and Aleksei Nicolaevich Leontiev (Leont'ev). Following the Marxist-Leninist thesis that human consciousness was the product of sociohistorical processes, they argued that psychological functions evolved at both the individual level and the societal level within each particular historical context. This kind of development was mediated by language and by other cultural artifacts that enabled successful adaptations to be passed on to later generations (Leontiev 1932; Luria 1928; Vygotski 1929). It follows from this account that the development of intelligence depends upon the activities and artifacts that happen to be valued within each specific culture. Curiously, however, the Russian psychologists did not apply this argument to the results of their own cross-cultural research.

Russian researchers were familiar with the scale developed by Binet and Simon (1908). Anna M. Schubert (who sometimes rendered her name in the Roman alphabet as "Shubert") was a psychologist who worked in St. Petersburg and later in Moscow. She had previously produced a Russian translation of the scale and used it to gather data from 229 children at an orphanage in Moscow (Terman, Lyman, et al. 1917:28, 84).) In 1929 she participated in two expeditions to study children in remote communities of Soviet central Asia (Shubert 1930). One expedition went to the Baikal region (now part of the Buryat Republic) to study children of the Tungus (now known as Evenks); the second went to Altai (in what is now Kazakhstan) to study children of the Oirots. The researchers observed the children in their everyday lives, but in some cases they also tried to measure the children's intelligence. The researchers used existing Russian tests and administered them to children who knew Russian. One test was Schubert's translation of the 1908 version of Binet and Simon's scale; the other was a battery of tests developed by Grigory Ivanovich Rossolimo, a neurologist at the University of Moscow. On both scales the children scored lower than expected on the basis of norms derived from children in Moscow. The researchers concluded that tests developed and standardized for use with urban European children were inappropriate for use with children living in other environments.

In addition, fifteen Tungus children received two of the "Pintner tests" (Bulanov [1930] 1993:59), and fifty-two Oirot children were given "the sixth, seventh, and eighth form boards" from the "Pintner-Petersen test" (Zaporozhets 1930:82), presumably the Triangle Form Board, Diagonal Form Board, and Healy Frame Test (see Pintner and Paterson 1917:24). Both groups of children tended to do better on these tests than on Binet and Simon's scale, and they showed much more enthusiasm and concentration. Nevertheless, they showed characteristic errors, and their level of performance was still less than that of Western children. The researchers ascribed this to "the artificiality and abstractness of the material" (Bulanov [1930] 1993:59), and they concluded that the tests were measuring specific skills rather than practical intelligence.

In response to extensive food shortages in the winter of 1928–29, Joseph Stalin, the Russian leader, imposed the collectivization of rural farms across the

Soviet Union. This prompted Luria to organize two expeditions to Uzbekistan and Kirgizia (now Kyrgyzstan) in 1931 and 1932 to investigate the intellectual abilities of peasant communities. He assumed that people in such communities would be intellectually inferior to those living in urban environments but that collectivization would lead to improvements in their thinking and other psychological processes through "the introduction of higher and more complex forms of economic life and the raising of the general cultural level" (Luria 1931:383; see also Luria 1932:241).

Given the findings of the two previous expeditions, the researchers eschewed established intelligence tests in favor of new tasks of their own devising. Even so, they viewed the results as suggesting that cross-cultural differences in test performance reflected different stages of intellectual development (Luria 1933, 1934). It was nevertheless thought to be undesirable to publish such research when the Soviet government was trying to encourage these communities to contribute to the national economy, and complete accounts did not appear until the 1970s (Luria 1976:58–80; 1979). Even then Luria did not consider the possibility that his results might simply have represented variations in the acquisition of the skills valued by urban culture.

Luria died in 1977, but by that time a number of studies had been published indicating that people from non-Western cultures would achieve higher performance on procedures that measured the intellectual skills that their everyday activities demanded. In a series of publications Michael Cole (1988, 1990, 1996) of the University of California at San Diego sought to reconcile these findings with the principles of the Russian sociohistorical school in a new approach that he called cultural psychology. The key point of this approach is that the development of psychological functions is historically contingent in that it is grounded in locally relevant practices and activities. It follows that it is inappropriate to use intelligence tests to compare people of different cultures, because the items that make up those tests were chosen to measure the skills valued by a specific culture (see, for example, Cole 1996:52–57, 66–67).

Patricia Marks Greenfield (1997) of the University of California at Los Angeles extended this analysis to propose that intelligence tests were items of symbolic culture. As a result, people from other cultures might simply not share the presuppositions about values, knowledge, and communication implicit in such tests. Indeed, even the idea of taking an intelligence test is both culture dependent and culture specific. This is well illustrated by certain episodes that were later recalled by Philip Cowen (1932:174). He had worked for the U.S. Immigration Service at Ellis Island when Knox was employed there by the Public Health Service.

I was some years at the work before mental and psychological examinations were intensified by the introduction of such tests as the Binet-Simon, jig-saw puzzles, etc. I had taken home with me a set of some of the mental and other tests one day to give them careful study. My daughter chanced to have at dinner a group of friends, nearly all school teachers, and as a game to while away an hour we submitted to the group these tests for immigrants, and they stumped most of them. One day a member of the medical staff passed my desk while I was speaking with one of his associates. He said to him: "You ought to see the new jig-saw puzzle they have downstairs; it beat me all right."

Even at this early stage in the development of mental tests, many Americans were clearly both familiar and comfortable with the idea of taking a test or solving a puzzle, and the same was probably true for emigrants from northern and western Europe. Jigsaw puzzles, in particular, had become popular with both children and adults on both sides of the Atlantic. This in itself caused a problem for Knox and his colleagues, because their tests would be not be valid for use with emigrants who already had experience of similar puzzles; as he acknowledged, "The author's imbecile test, in addition to being of value in diagnosticating adult imbeciles, is of value as a test for six year old normals, provided that in childhood they have not been in the habit of playing with similar contrivances" (Knox 1913g:1017).

Nevertheless, emigrants from southern and eastern Europe or from countries farther afield would be highly unlikely to have had similar experiences and hence might well be unfamiliar and uncomfortable with the idea of taking a test. These considerations alone would tend to explain why emigrants from the more developed countries in northern and western Europe would produce better results (and, conversely, be less likely to be identified as mentally deficient) than would emigrants from the less developed countries in eastern and southern Europe. As a consequence, Knox and his colleagues at Ellis Island would have been unable to differentiate between moronism and ignorance of the idea of taking a test.

WAS KNOX A EUGENICIST?

There is no evidence as to whether Knox held eugenicist views before he arrived at Ellis Island. However, it would not be surprising if he had, because such views were widely held at the time. Indeed, they went barely questioned until the 1920s (see Zenderland 1998:311–26). Even less surprising is that he held such views during his time at Ellis Island. Not only were they shared by most, if not all, of Knox's colleagues and superiors (see, for example, Gwyn 1914; Knight 1913; Stoner 1913; Williams 1914), but there were established links between the Public Health Service and the eugenics movement. Paul A. Lombardo and Gregory Michael Dorr (2006) discussed these links in detail and ascribed them to the medical curriculum of the University of Virginia in Charlottesville, the alma mater of many senior officers in the service. For many years public health issues taught with an explicitly eugenic and racist focus had dominated the curriculum there.

When Knox worked at Ellis Island, the main organization for promoting eugenic research in the United States was the American Breeders' Association, which in 1914 became the American Genetic Association (Kimmelman 1983). The surgeon general, Rupert Blue, and his assistant surgeons general, William Rucker and Leland Cofer, were all active members of the association; both Blue and Rucker served on its eugenics committee, and both Rucker and Cofer wrote articles for its official publication, the *Journal of Heredity*. In a public demonstration of support for the eugenics movement, Blue had issued a "eugenic certificate" confirming the fitness of a prospective bridegroom whom Rucker and his colleagues had examined, the *New York Times* reported in October 1913.

In comparison, Knox himself seems to have done little to advance the cause of eugenics. He used his own article in the *Journal of Heredity* and his paper for the meeting of the Eugenics Research Association as opportunities to publicize the work at Ellis Island rather than to advocate eugenicist principles. His article in the journal had a clearly eugenicist subtitle ("How the Public Health Service Prevents Contamination of Our Racial Stock . . .") (Knox 1914b:122), as did his article in *Scientific American* ("A Progressive Series of Standardized Tests . . . to Protect Our Racial Stock") (Knox 1915a:52), but these may have been added by overenthusiastic editors. However, Knox does seem to have accepted membership in the Eugenics Research Association and to have had a cordial relationship with Harry Laughlin, the superintendent of the Eugenics Record Office.

It should, of course, be acknowledged that the work of Knox and the other physicians at Ellis Island was explicitly and effectively racist, insofar as it targeted emigrants from eastern and southern Europe. Knox's (1914c) article in the *Journal of the American Medical Association* contained normative data from Italian, "Hebrew," Polish, and Russian children and adults. None of the physicians even seems to have considered the idea of collecting comparable data in order to evaluate emigrants from France, Germany, or Scandinavia. Evidently, the risk of admitting feebleminded emigrants from those countries was considered to be much less or nonexistent.

At the same time, it should be acknowledged that the eugenics movement was a broad church that accommodated people with widely varying views. Some aligned themselves with "positive eugenics," aimed at encouraging the reproduction of healthy and talented individuals, rather than "negative eugenics," which aimed to curtail the reproduction of supposedly disadvantaged individuals. One proponent of positive eugenics was Alexander Graham Bell, who was a member of the Board of Scientific Directors of the Eugenics Record Office. In December 1912 he wrote to Charles Davenport to suggest that the office was giving too much attention to "cacogenics" (the breeding of weak offspring) rather than to eugenics (the breeding of strong offspring):

> The appropriations approved at the first meeting of the Board related exclusively to undesirable characteristics (feeble-mindedness, insanity, defective and criminalistic immigrants, and cancer)—*cacogenics* not eugenics! Why not vary a little from this programme and investigate the inheritance of some desirable characteristics.
>
> A good subject for investigation would be the family history of persons who have lived to extreme old age in full possession of their faculties. Other subjects of a desirable character will readily suggest themselves, if we aim to make eugenics instead of cacogenics the distinguishing feature of our work.
>
> It is the fostering of desirable characteristics that will *advance* the race; whereas the cutting off of undesirable characteristics simply prevents deterioration. (Emphasis in original)

Bell expressed similar views in an article entitled "How to Improve the Race," which he published in the *Journal of Heredity*:

> The simple process of promoting the marriages of the desirable with the desirable will, through the mixture of the descendants with the rest of the population, inaugurate an improvement of the whole race; and the movement will advance with accelerated velocity as we have more and more potent individuals of the desirable class. This process continued through a number of successive generations would ultimately result in the establishment of a prepotent stock within the desirable class, and then the improvement would be very marked indeed. . . .
>
> This should be the chief object of eugenics; and it is to be regretted that the efforts of eugenists have been mainly directed to the diminution of the undesirable class.
>
> So much has this been the case that the very word "eugenics" is suggestive to most minds of hereditary disease and objectionable abnormalities; and of an attempt to interfere, by compulsory means, with the marriages of the defective and undesirable. This relates to cacogenics ("badly born") rather than to eugenics ("well born").
>
> (Bell 1914:6)

(When he referred to "the race," Bell clearly meant the human race. Like some other eugenicists, Bell did not relate his ideas to ethnic divisions within society.)

In his very first publication on the subject of mental deficiency, Knox characterized it as a social problem, both among emigrants and in the indigenous population of the United States: "There are hundreds of minors in reformatories that should be in training-schools for the feeble-minded, and if delinquents and prostitutes were regarded as mental defectives in the eyes of the law and appropriate means taken to inhibit procreation, the social problem would be practically settled, at least for our great-grandchildren" (Knox 1913a:105).

Similarly, when he later made the Ellis Island tests available through C. H. Stoelting Company, his aim was to provide a means to identify mentally deficient individuals within the United States. Knox wrote the following statement to accompany descriptions of the tests in the publisher's catalog:

> Our ability to live in peace and happiness with our fellow-beings, or free from restraint, depends to a great extent upon our ethical perception. In order to properly protect society from the mentally-deficient, who are more or less morally deficient, it is of the greatest importance that these endividuals [sic] be discovered early in their careers, preferably in the school-room, so that corrective training may be early administered, or when this holds out no hope of success, that other steps be taken to protect society from their activities.

He had previously indicated that the "other steps" could extend to "sensible asexualization [e.g., vasectomy] in properly selected cases" (Knox 1914a:221).

Nevertheless, like Bell, Knox did not specifically link his accounts to race or ethnicity. When he presented "A Diagnostic Study of the Face," Knox compared the facial characteristics of black and white people, but he made no comments about their relative intellectual capabilities (Knox 1913c). Moreover, as I suggested in chapter 8, Knox was the first person to argue that black people performed less well on intelligence tests not because they were less intelligent but simply because they were poorly educated (see Knox 1915a). Indeed, it is hard to find generalizations about the capacities of different racial or ethnic groups in Knox's writings. The only example of pejorative stereotyping that I have found in his publications was directed against Spaniards and Mexicans:

> The dull, stupid immigrant is not so entirely because of his previous environment and opportunities. The environment and opportunities are the same now as they have been for countless centuries because of the immigrant's inability to change them. This country is as it is simply because it has been improved by men from prosperous northern European countries, which countries were pros-

perous simply because of the type of men who inhabited them. The civilization in Mexico is in its present state because of the nature of the people who settled there. It must be remembered that the form of government is the same there as in our own land and the natural resources are even greater. These factors are not to be blamed for the pitiable condition of the class of people that are coming to our shores at this time. They are simply undesirables and can never be assimilated to our advantage.

(Knox 1914b:127)

Moreover, Knox certainly was not opposed to immigration per se: in his talk to the Mississippi Valley Medical Association, he positively welcomed the prospect of "the mixture of the blood of races and peoples gathered together from all parts of the earth" (Knox 1915b:496).

Except for a brief exchange of correspondence with Harry Laughlin regarding the idea of writing a book about the Ellis Island tests, there is no evidence that Knox had any involvement with the eugenics movement after he left the Public Health Service. While he was working at the State Village for Epileptics in Skillman, New Jersey, he did not take the opportunity to work with the superintendent, David Weeks, who was an associate of Charles Davenport's, on the possibility of a genetic basis of epilepsy; instead, Knox pursued the notion that it had bacterial (and therefore environmental) origins. In contrast, Goddard, Terman, and Yerkes all continued to work actively with the eugenics movement to campaign (among other things) for a reduction in the level of immigration to the United States. The movement had its most pronounced influence in the 1920s, well after Knox had left Ellis Island. In particular, Laughlin used the testimony of Terman and Yerkes to influence the congressional committee on immigration and naturalization to propose severe quotas under the 1924 Immigration Act (Gelb et al. 1986).

THE NEGLECT OF THE ELLIS ISLAND TESTS

Use of the Ellis Island tests progressively declined after World War II, with the exceptions that the Cube Imitation Test is still used in many countries and that the Feature Profile Test was until recently included in the Wechsler intelligence scales. Paralleling with this decline was a progressive neglect of the Ellis Island tests in accounts of the history of psychological testing.

For example, the first edition of Anne Anastasi's widely used book, *Psychological Testing* (1954) included one brief reference to Knox's (1914c) article in the *Journal of the American Medical Association* and mentioned in this connection only the

Cube Imitation Test and the Ship Test. She mistakenly ascribed the Casuist Test and Feature Profile Test to Pintner and Paterson (1917) (Anastasi 1954:240–43). Even this brief account was removed from later editions of the book, although a passing reference to Knox was reinstated in the last edition published before Anastasi's death in 2001 (Anastasi and Urbina 1997:260). The brief account of Knox's work in Philip DuBois's *History of Psychological Testing* (1970) included illustrations of the Casuist Test and Feature Profile Test (52–53, 56) and correctly attributed both to Knox (1914c).

The first modern critique of mental testing was published by Leon Judah Kamin of Princeton University in *The Science and Politics of I.Q.* (1974). His main concern was to refute the idea that scores on intelligence tests were heritable. Instead, he argued that intelligence tests were an instrument of oppression against the poor, foreign-born, and racial minorities. However, Kamin's first chapter, "The Pioneers of I.Q. Testing in America" (pp. 5–13), refers only to the work of Henry Goddard, Lewis Terman, and Robert Yerkes. Moreover, Kamin's account in chapter 2, "Psychology and the Immigrant" (pp. 15–32), conflates Goddard's four excursions to Ellis Island in 1911–13 into a single visit and then skips to the development of the Army Mental Tests. Kamin did not mention Knox, Knox's colleagues, or the notion of performance tests.

The Mismeasure of Man (1981) by Stephen Jay Gould of Harvard University was a broader attack on biological determinism that encompassed nineteenth-century endeavors to measure the size and volume of the cranium and the brain as well as mental testing. Nevertheless, Gould's fifth chapter, "The Hereditarian Theory of IQ," refers only to Binet, Goddard, Terman, and Yerkes (147–233). Gould describes Goddard's visits to Ellis Island (165–68) but makes no mention of the physicians who were actually working there. Regarding the Army Mental Tests, he remarked: "Literate recruits would be given a written examination, called the Army Alpha. Illiterates and men who had failed Alpha would be given a pictorial test, called the Army Beta. Failures in Beta would be recalled for an individual examination, usually some version of the Binet scales" (194). However, Gould does not explain either the origins or the implications of the distinction between the two tests, nor does he refer to the Army Performance Scale. Again, Gould makes no mention of Knox, his colleagues, or the idea of performance tests.

In 1990 Robert Mann Thorndike of Western Washington University (the grandson of Edward Lee Thorndike) published *A Century of Ability Testing*. In one chapter, "The Army Testing Program and Its Legacy," he refers to the work of the Committee on the Psychological Examination of Recruits:

> The work of the committee ultimately resulted in five equivalent forms of an examination for literate recruits (Form Alpha), which came to be called the Army

Alpha. For those recruits who did not speak English, could not read, or got low scores on Form Alpha, the committee provided a "performance" test known as Form Beta (the Army Beta). Form Beta was modeled on a test developed by Rudolph [sic] Pintner and Donald Paterson (1915, 1917) for use with deaf subjects. It employed a variety of form boards and mazes, including some of those developed in Australia by Porteus (1915). Administration of the test required no use of language. Instructions were given in pantomime. For those who still appeared mentally unfit to serve in the army, the plan was to examine them with the Stanford-Binet.

(45)

This account conflates Examination Beta (a group test) with the Army Performance Scale (which was designed for individual administration and did include "a variety of form boards" as well as the Porteus Maze Test). Illiterate or foreign-born recruits who obtained the lowest rating on Examination Beta were of course given the Army Performance Scale, not the Stanford-Binet.

Thorndike does not mention the work of the Ellis Island physicians in connection with the development of the Army Mental Tests. Nine pages later, however, he writes the following under the heading "Mental Testing and Immigration Policy":

As early as 1913 the American Medical Association, in response to concern that the mental quality of immigrants was dropping, editorialized that "inspection by experts at the port of entry will result in a much larger percentage of defective immigration being detained" (AMA, 1913, p. 209). The experts were to be medical men who would administer a battery of physical and psychological tests to screen out the mentally unfit. As part of this program, Knox published a nonverbal test in 1914 to be used with immigrants (cited in DuBois, 1970). Mullan (1917) reported on a small-scale study that was conducted under the auspices of the U.S. Surgeon General to determine if various tests could detect immigrants who were mentally unfit. A wide variety of tests, many of school-related subjects, was given to 293 immigrants on their second day at Ellis Island. . . . The concern with denying admission to those of low mental ability was definitely an item of governmental attention, and research had started on a test-oriented response to the problem before the research program that led to the Army Alpha had begun.

(54)

This description of Mullan's (1917b) "small-scale study" is inaccurate insofar as it was intended to be a survey of mentally normal immigrants rather than a trial to detect mentally deficient ones. Moreover, the cursory reference to Knox's work is misleading. Thorndike had misread DuBois's (1970) brief account, which clearly stated that Knox "had developed a series of tests requiring imitation and other action but no language responses" (52–53), not just a single "nonverbal test." Although Thorndike is correct to point out that the development of the Ellis Island tests preceded that of the Army Mental Tests, he failed to spot that the Ellis Island tests were actually the direct inspiration for Examination Beta and the Army Performance Scale.

In *The Definition of a Profession* (1992) JoAnne Brown of Johns Hopkins University argues that the pioneers of the mental testing movement expropriated the discourse of medicine and engineering in order to gain professional and public acceptability and authority. It should be acknowledged that Brown's primary focus is on the educational applications of intelligence tests. Nevertheless, her more specific assertion that psychologists took over the language of medicine to make the idea of mental testing respectable contains a serious flaw. It ignores who many of the people responsible for developing the early performance tests of intelligence were: physicians rather than psychologists, and the physicians never saw themselves as being anything else. For them the diagnosis of mental deficiency was an inherently medical task, not a psychological one.

More important, Knox and his colleagues repeatedly insisted that diagnoses of mental deficiency should only be made by people with medical training, since only they would be able to differentiate between a persistent "genetic" state of mental deficiency and the various transient conditions that might temporarily result in poor test performance. These latter conditions could be the result of a variety of physical causes or recent distressing events, such as an uncomfortable transatlantic voyage and the process of arriving at Ellis Island (Knox 1913f, 1914e; see also Glueck 1913; Mullan 1917b:5). Conversely, psychologists or other "layworkers from various schools for the feeble-minded" would be unaware of the importance of eliminating purely psychogenetic causes of mental deficiency that were in principle curable (Knox 1913d:59).

Because of her concentration on the educational applications of intelligence tests, Brown considers immigration as an issue only in connection with the schools system, not the state more generally. Once again, however, her account of the origins of mental testing is mainly concerned with the work of Goddard, Terman, and Yerkes. Her book appears to contain no mention at all of Knox, the work at Ellis Island, or performance tests. Brown's account, like those of Kamin and Gould, assumes that Yerkes and his colleagues directly inherited the ideas of Binet and Goddard, with no intervening agency. (Thorndike does at least acknowledge the roles of Pintner and Paterson.) This fails to explain why Pintner, Yerkes, and later researchers dedicated so much attention to the development of performance tests.

According to the version of events told by Kamin, Gould, and Brown, the distinction between verbal and nonverbal tests was a purely technical idea without any precedent that had somehow just occurred to those developing the Army Mental Tests. This has become such a canonical account that it has been uncritically adopted wholesale by other writers on the history of intelligence testing (for example, Kaufman 2000). It has even been exported to other countries. Nikolas Rose of Brunel University in the United Kingdom discusses the role of psychology as an agent of political control in his book, *Governing the Soul* (1989). He cites Kamin's book as the most influential account of the "prehistory of intelligence testing in the United States," and he refers to the military use of mental testing during World War I: "By the end of the war they appeared to have achieved considerable success. The famous alpha and beta group tests of intelligence had been developed—the former required ability to read, the latter was nonverbal—and by 1918 their use had been extended to the whole army" (18).

THE REDISCOVERY OF THE ELLIS ISLAND TESTS

Nevertheless, there have been modest attempts to rediscover the work of the physicians at Ellis Island. These were initially prompted by a wave of articles and books in the early 1980s that referred to the results of Henry Goddard's various visits to the immigration station (see Gelb 1986 for references). In 1988 Alan Morton Kraut of American University published an article on the role of the Ellis Island physicians in detecting physical illness, mental illness, and mental deficiency in emigrants that briefly refers to the tests that Knox had devised. In a later book on the subject Kraut (1994:72–75) gives a similar account in which he also refers to the misgivings expressed by Knox and his colleagues with regard to Goddard's use of Binet and Simon's scale in assessing the intelligence of emigrants.

In 1998 Leila Zenderland of California State University at Fullerton published a detailed biography of Goddard in which she evaluates his role in the early days of American intelligence testing. She devotes a section (263–81) to Goddard's work at Ellis Island, she quotes extensively from the publications of the Ellis Island physicians, and she cites the original sources for several of Knox's performance tests. However, Zenderland's account of Knox's work is fairly brief (271–72) and to some extent overshadowed by references to the work of Knox's colleague, Eugene Mullan (1917a, 1917b). Moreover, she fails to make a link between the Ellis Island tests and later instruments such as the Army Performance Scale (285).

In *Science at the Borders* (2003) Amy Lauren Fairchild of Columbia University construes the medical inspection of emigrants as part of their induction into an industrial society. It is certainly true that one responsibility of the Public Health

Service physicians was to identify individuals who might become a burden on society, and it is equally true that a broad, though perhaps superficial, analogy can be made between the examination of emigrants at Ellis Island and a purely mechanical process. Stephen Graham (1914) was a British journalist who in 1913 crossed the Atlantic in steerage with a party of Russians émigrés to experience the life of an immigrant in the United States. He described his arrival at Ellis Island as follows:

> Once more it was "Quick march!" and hurrying about with bags and baskets in our hands, we were put into lines. Then we slowly filed up to a doctor who turned our eyelids inside out with a metal instrument. Another doctor scanned faces and hands for skin diseases, and then we carried our ship-inspection cards to an official who stamped them. We passed into the vast hall of judgment, and were classified and put into lines again, this time according to our nationality. It was interesting to observe at the very threshold of the United States the mechanical obsession of the American people. This ranging and guiding and hurrying and sifting was like nothing so much as the screening of coal in a great breaker tower.
>
> (44)

(When coal is extracted from a mine, it is taken to the top of a breaker tower to be crushed, and the resulting lumps fall through a series of screens to be sorted according to their size.) There is little evidence that the physicians at Ellis Island saw their role as one of acculturating emigrants to the norms and conventions of an industrial workforce, and it is equally unlikely that the emigrants perceived the physicians as having such a role, given the brief contact that they had with them. Indeed, Surgeon Ezra Sprague (1913:422) estimated that "the average time expended on each alien during a fairly busy day" was just six seconds.

To be sure, intelligence tests themselves can be seen as devices for screening and classifying people for their roles in an industrial society. It is therefore rather odd that Fairchild gives only a brief account of the use of mental testing in the examination of emigrants (101–104). She cites one of Knox's (1913a) early papers in which he criticized Goddard and his colleagues for trying to use tests such as those in Binet and Simon's scale, because they assumed a particular culture and language. However, she does not cite any of Knox's other writings and does not mention the development of performance tests at Ellis Island. Fairchild does report Mullan's (1917b:123–24) comments on the role of cultural factors in the interpretation of pictures, with specific reference to the picture called "Last Honors to Bunny." Even so, she apparently is unaware that Mullan used this test in a survey of mentally normal emigrants, not as a screening test to detect mentally deficient ones.

Recently, Stephen Murdoch, a journalist in Santa Barbara, California, published a popular account of the history of intelligence testing, *IQ: A Smart History of a Failed Idea* (2007). After three chapters in which he describes the work of Galton and Cattell, Binet and Simon, Goddard and (briefly) Terman, he provides just seven pages on the assessment of emigrants at Ellis Island. Murdoch cites a combination of primary and secondary sources, although of Knox's publications he cites only the 1914 article in the *Journal of the American Medical Association*. Murdoch spots that the scale reported in this article was a mixture of verbal and performance tests, as Grace Arthur had noted sixty years earlier. Indeed, this leads Murdoch to an overly critical conclusion: "In hindsight, these hodgepodge testing devices seem to have been developed haphazardly—school questions originally devised to cull out the retarded were thrown together with children's toys" (65).

This comment is unfair. Knox was quite clear about the nature of performance tests and had published a scale consisting only of performance tests just a week earlier (Knox 1914b). Later researchers such as Pintner and Yerkes understood the nature of Knox's achievement (even if they did not always acknowledge his contribution explicitly). Indeed, a serious limitation of the accounts of the Ellis Island tests provided by Kraut, Zenderland, Fairchild, and Murdoch is that they were written from a mainly historical perspective without fully acknowledging the scientific importance of these tests themselves. Whereas the earlier writings by Kamin, Gould, and Brown ignored the work at Ellis Island completely, these more recent accounts do locate that work at essentially the correct point in the historical narrative about the development of intelligence tests. Nevertheless, they do not explain why the work at Ellis Island was of any lasting scientific importance. To do so, the expertise of historians needs to be complemented by the expertise of scientists and, more specifically, of psychologists.

KNOX'S CONTRIBUTION TO PSYCHOLOGICAL TESTING

Corwin Boake (2002) of the University of Texas–Houston Medical School reviewed the early history of intelligence tests from Galton through Binet and Simon and on to Wechsler. In one section Boake briefly describes the development of performance tests at Ellis Island. He cites four of Knox's publications and then shows how the Ellis Island tests were adopted by Pintner and Paterson (1917) and later in the Army Mental Tests and other performance scales, culminating in the Performance Scale of the Wechsler-Bellevue Intelligence Scale. Boake also quotes David Wechsler as claiming that he had conceived the idea "that an intelligence scale, combining verbal and nonverbal tests, would be a useful addition to the psychometrist's armamentarium" as early as 1918 when he was administering individual verbal and performance tests to soldiers who had failed both Examination

Alpha and Examination Beta in the Army Mental Tests. Boake makes it clear that the Ellis Island tests provided a key point of reference for subsequent test developers and were the ultimate source of Wechsler's insight.

In chapter 12, I mentioned that the team responsible for the third edition of the WAIS produced a guide to help clinicians interpret their results, and I referred to the study by Josette Harris, David Tulsky, and Maria Schultheis (2003) concerning the assessment of intelligence in people who are not native speakers of English. In reviewing the historical evidence, Harris and her colleagues give a detailed account of the line-inspection procedure at Ellis Island as well as a short but accurate summary of Knox's tests, citing both his 1914 article in the *Journal of the American Medical Association* and his 1915 article in *Scientific American*. Another chapter in the guide links the Ellis Island tests to those found in the Army Mental Tests and later performance scales, again culminating in the Performance Scale of the Wechsler-Bellevue (Tulsky, Saklofske, and Ricker, 2003). Finally, the guide concludes with short biographies of many pioneers in intelligence testing, including Howard Knox (Tulsky and Chiaravalloti 2003).

In 2003, I published an article that contained a preliminary sketch of Knox's life and work, and in this book I have built on that initial account. I have placed Knox in his personal context by describing his boyhood, education, army career, and later life (chapters 1, 2 and 9). I have placed Knox in his historical context by referring to the public and political concern in the early years of the twentieth century regarding the admission of mentally deficient emigrants (chapters 3 and 4). I have placed Knox and his colleagues in their scientific context by examining the process by which they engaged with debates about the nature and measurement of intelligence, as well as their attempts to publicize and popularize the results of their research (chapters 5, 6, 7, and 8). I have considered the various ways in which the Ellis Island tests were exploited and their impact on the subsequent course of mental testing (chapters 10 and 11). I have explained that the measurement of intelligence in emigrants remains an important practical issue to this day (chapter 12). Finally, in this chapter I have tried to give an objective assessment of Knox's contribution to the development of intelligence tests.

~~~~~~~~

For just four years, between 1912 and 1916, Knox was not just a conscientious physician and government employee; he was also a highly prolific scientist at the forefront of developments in the construction of intelligence tests. I have tried to demonstrate that the research carried out by Knox and his colleagues at Ellis Island constitutes the key link between the ideas of Binet and Goddard and the later research of Pintner and Yerkes. Knox may have closed the door on mental testing in May 1916 as far as his own life was concerned, but his attempts to popularize his work suggest that at the time he intended it to have a lasting significance. His claim that performance tests measure some "native ability," uncontaminated by linguistic or cultural knowledge, cannot be sustained; the issue of what performance tests actually measure has still to be resolved; and how to measure intelligence among non-English-speaking emigrants remains a serious problem. Verbal tests do remain the most common tools for assessing intelligence, and they are sometimes treated uncritically, especially by those who lack proper training in their administration and their interpretation. Nevertheless, it is thanks to Knox that psychologists have a much broader view of the nature of intelligence and of how it can be measured and, in particular, that today they tend to take it for granted that any adequate measure of intelligence must include both verbal and performance tests. In consequence, Howard Andrew Knox should now be recognized as a major figure in the history of intelligence testing.

REFERENCES

PUBLICATIONS OF HOWARD A. KNOX

Knox's publications are listed chronologically.

Knox, H. A. 1911. Filariasis at Fort Hancock, New Jersey. *Military Surgeon* 28 (June): 659–60.

———. 1913a. The moron and the study of alien defectives. *Journal of the American Medical Association* 60 (January 11): 105–106.

———. 1913b. Some practical psychotherapy. *Journal of the American Medical Association* 60 (March 1): 657–59.

———. 1913c. A diagnostic study of the face. *New York Medical Journal* 97 (June 14): 1225–31.

———. 1913d. Psychogenetic disorders: Cases seen in detained immigrants. *Medical Record* 84 (July 12): 58–61.

———. 1913e. Two new tests for the detection of defectives. *New York Medical Journal* 98 (September 13): 522–24.

———. 1913f. The differentiation between moronism and ignorance. *New York Medical Journal* 98 (September 20): 564–66.

———. 1913g. A test for adult imbeciles and six year old normals. *New York Medical Journal* 98 (November 22): 1017–18.

———. 1914a. Mental defectives. *New York Medical Journal* 99 (January 31): 215–21.

———. 1914b. Tests for mental defects. *Journal of Heredity* 5 (March): 122–30.

———. 1914c. A scale, based on the work at Ellis Island, for estimating mental defect. *Journal of the American Medical Association* 62 (March 7): 741–47.

———. 1914d. Subnormal mentality in immigrants. *Medical Review of Reviews* 20 (March): 142–49.

———. 1914e. Psychological pitfalls: Report of cases. *New York Medical Journal* 99 (March 14): 527–29.

———. 1914f. A comparative study of the imaginative powers in mental defectives. *Medical Record* 85 (April 25): 748–51.

———. 1915a. Measuring human intelligence: A progressive series of standardized tests used by the Public Health Service to protect our racial stock. *Scientific American,* January 9: 52–53, 57–58.

———. 1915b. Mentally defective aliens: A medical problem. *Lancet-Clinic* 113 (May 1): 491–96.

———. 1915c. A broader view of mental deficiency in aliens. *New York Medical Journal* 102 (October 9): 751–56.

———. 1915d. *Apparatus and Supplies for "A Scale for Estimating Mental Defects."* C. H. Stoelting Company, Chicago.

———. 1915e. *Alien Mental Defectives: A Collection of Papers Descriptive of the Tests and Methods Employed by the United States Public Health Service, Ellis Island, N.Y.* Chicago: C. H. Stoelting.

———. 1917a. Fatal streptococcemia in an epileptic due to hemolyzing short chain streptococci. *New York Medical Journal* 105 (January 20): 101–103.

———. 1917b. Research in epilepsy, with report of twenty-five cases. Part 1: Bacteriemia. *New York Medical Journal* 105 (February 17): 308–10.

———. 1917c. Research in epilepsy. Part 2: Leptin. *New York Medical Journal* 105 (February 24): 344–47.

———. 1917d. Research in epilepsy. Part 3: Therapy. *New York Medical Journal* 105 (March 3): 406–409.

———. 1917e. A brief statement of the treatment of the psychopathic personalities observed in those who develop dementia praecox. In M. P. E. Groszmann, ed., *The Exceptional Child*, 648–51. New York: Charles Scribner's.

———. 1921. A protest against thoughtless radicalism in surgery of the nose, throat and mouth. *Journal of the Medical Society of New Jersey* 18 (April): 117–18.

OBITUARIES OF HOWARD A. KNOX

Dr. Howard A. Knox. 1949. *Journal of the Medical Society of New Jersey* 46:489.

Dr. Howard A. Knox. 1949. *New York Times*, July 28.

Dr. Howard A. Knox died in hospital. 1949. *Hunterdon County Democrat*, August 4.

Howard Andrew Knox. 1949. *Journal of the American Medical Association* 141:344.

OTHER SOURCES

Adams, A. 1996. *Architecture in the Family Way: Doctors, Houses and Women, 1870–1900.* Montreal: McGill-Queen's University Press.

Adityanjee, Y. A. Aderibigbe, D. Theodoridis, and W. V. R. Vieweg. 1999. Dementia praecox to schizophrenia: The first 100 years. *Psychiatry and Clinical Neurosciences* 53: 437–48.

Aikens, H. A., and E. L. Thorndike, with the assistance of E. A. Hubbell. 1902. Correlations among perceptive and associative processes. *Psychological Review* 9:374–82.

Altus, W. D. 1945. The differential validity and difficulty of subtests of the Wechsler Mental Ability Scale. *Psychological Bulletin* 42:238–49.

American Medical Association. 1914. *American Medical Directory.* 4th ed. Chicago: American Medical Association.

———. 1934. *American Medical Directory.* 13th ed. Chicago: American Medical Association.

Amoss, H. 1936. *Ontario School Ability Examination: A Performance Test Prepared More Especially for Use Among Children Who Are Deaf, Whose Native Tongue Is Other Than English or Who for Any Reason Are Lacking in Language Facility.* Toronto: Ryerson Press.

Anastasi, A. 1954. *Psychological Testing.* New York: Macmillan.

———. 1985. Some emerging trends in psychological measurement: A fifty-year perspective. *Applied Psychological Measurement* 9:121–38.

Anastasi, A., and S. Urbina. 1997. *Psychological Testing.* 7th ed. Upper Saddle River, N.J.: Prentice Hall.

Arthur, G. 1925. A new point performance scale. *Journal of Applied Psychology* 9:390–416.

———. 1928. The re-standardization of a point performance scale. *Journal of Applied Psychology* 12:278–303.

———. 1930. *Clinical Manual.* Vol. 1 of *A Point Scale of Performance Tests.* New York: Commonwealth Fund.

———. 1933. *The Process of Standardization.* Vol. 2 of *A Point Scale of Performance Tests.* New York: Commonwealth Fund.

———. 1943. *Clinical Manual.* Vol. 1 of *A Point Scale of Performance Tests.* 2nd ed. New York: Commonwealth Fund.

———. 1946. Performance tests. In *Encyclopedia of Psychology.* Edited by P. L. Harriman, 447–53. New York: Philosophical Library.

———. 1947. *A Point Scale of Performance Tests, Revised Form II.* New York: Psychological Corp.

Atkinson, L., J. J. Cyr, N. C. S. Doxey, and G. M. Vigna. 1989. Generalizability of WAIS-R factor structure within and between populations. *Journal of Clinical Psychology* 45: 124–29.

Babcock, H. 1930. An experiment in the measurement of mental deterioration. *Archives of Psychology* 18 (117): 1–105.

———. 1932. The short Army Performance Scale in clinical practice. *Journal of Applied Psychology* 16:532–48.

———. 1933. *Dementia Praecox: A Psychological Study.* New York: Science Press.

Babcock, H., and L. Levy. 1940. *Test and Manual of Directions: The Revised Examination for the Measurement of Efficiency of Mental Functioning.* Wood Dale, Ill.: C. H. Stoelting.

Bair, J. H. 1902. The practice curve: A study in the formation of habits. *Psychological Review Monograph Supplements* 5 (19): 1–70.

Baldwin, J. M., J. M. Cattell, and J. Jastrow. 1898. Physical and mental tests. *Psychological Review* 5:172–79.

Baumgarten-Tramer, F. 1943. Zur Geschichte des Rorschachtests [On the history of the Rorschach test]. *Schweizer Archiv für Neurologie und Psychiatrie* 50:1–13.

Baynes, E. H. 1915. *Wild Bird Guests: How to Entertain Them.* New York: E. P. Dutton.

Beardsley, T. 2000. Principals lay down academic groundwork for WHS. *(Willimantic, Conn.) Chronicle,* August 5, Album sec.

Bell, A. G. 1914. How to improve the race. *Journal of Heredity* 5:1–7.

Benjamin, L. T. Jr. 2003. Harry Hollingworth and the shame of applied psychology. In D. B. Baker, ed., *Thick Description and Fine Texture: Studies in the History of Psychology,* 38–56. Akron, Ohio: University of Akron Press.

———. 2004. Meet me at the fair: A centennial retrospective of psychology at the 1904 St. Louis World's Fair. *APS Observer* 17, no. 3 (July), www.psychologicalscience.org/observer/getArticle.cfm?id=1603.

Benjamin, L. T., Jr., A. M. Rogers, and A. Rosenbaum. 1991. Coca-Cola, caffeine, and mental deficiency: Harry Hollingworth and the Chattanooga trial of 1911. *Journal of the History of the Behavioral Sciences* 27:42–55.

Berch, D. B., R. Krikorian, and E. M. Huha. 1998. The Corsi block-tapping task: Methodological and theoretical considerations. *Brain and Cognition* 38:317–38.

Biesheuvel, S. 1943. *African Intelligence.* Johannesburg: South African Institute of Race Relations.

Binet, A. 1903. *L'étude expérimentale de l'intelligence* [The experimental study of intelligence]. Paris: Schleicher.

———. 1909. *Les idées modernes sur les enfants* [Modern ideas about children]. Paris: Flammarion.

———. 1911. Nouvelles recherches sur la mesure du niveau intellectuel chez les enfants d'école [New research on the measurement of intellectual level in schoolchildren]. *L'Année Psychologique* 17:145–210.

Binet, A., and V. Henri. 1896. La psychologie individuelle [Individual psychology]. *L'Année Psychologique* 2:411–65.

Binet, A., and T. Simon. 1905a. Application des méthodes nouvelles au diagnostic du niveau intellectuel chez des enfants normaux and anormaux d'hospice et d'école primaire [Application of new methods to the diagnosis of intellectual level in normal and subnormal children in institutions and primary schools]. *L'Année Psychologique* 11:245–336.

———. 1905b. Méthodes nouvelles pour le diagnostic du niveau intellectuel des anormaux [New methods for the diagnosis of the intellectual level of subnormals]. *L'Année Psychologique* 11:191–244.

———. 1908. Le développement de l'intelligence chez les enfants [The development of intelligence in children]. *L'Année Psychologique* 14:1–94.

———. 1911. La mesure du développement de l'intelligence chez les jeunes enfants [The measurement of the development of intelligence in young children]. *Bulletin de la Société Libre pour l'Étude Psychologique de l'Enfant*, nos. 70 and 71:187–248.

———. 1912. *A Method of Measuring the Development of the Intelligence of Young Children.* Trans. C. H. Town. Lincoln, Ill.: Courier.

———. 1916. *The Development of Intelligence in Children (The Binet-Simon Scale).* Edited by H. H. Goddard. Translated by E. S. Kite. Baltimore: Williams and Wilkins.

Boake, C. 2002. From the Binet-Simon to the Wechsler-Bellevue: Tracing the history of intelligence testing. *Journal of Clinical and Experimental Neuropsychology* 24:383–405.

Bobertag, O. 1911. Über Intelligenzprüfungen (nach der Methode von Binet und Simon) [Concerning intelligence tests (after the method of Binet and Simon)]. *Zeitschrift für angewandte Psychologie* 5:105–203.

Bond, E. D. 1950. *Thomas W. Salmon: Psychiatrist.* New York: W. W. Norton.

Boody, B. M. 1926. *A Psychological Study of Immigrant Children at Ellis Island.* Mental Measurement Monographs 3. Repr., New York: Arno, 1970.

Braddy, H. 1966. *Pershing's Mission in Mexico.* El Paso: Texas Western Press.

Braden, J. P. 1994. *Deafness, Deprivation, and IQ.* New York: Plenum.

Bravais, A. 1846. Analyse mathématique sur les probabilités des erreurs de situation d'un point [Mathematical analysis of the probabilities of point location errors]. *Mémoires Présentés par Divers Savants à l'Académie Royale des Sciences de l'Institut de France* 9:255–332.

Brigham, C. C. 1923. *A Study of American Intelligence.* Princeton, N.J.: Princeton University Press.

———. 1930. Intelligence tests of immigrant groups. *Psychological Review* 37:158–65.

Bronner, A. F. 1914. A research on the proportion of mental defectives among delinquents. *Journal of Criminal Law and Criminology* 5:561–68.

Bronner, A. F., W. Healy, G. M. Lowe, and M. E. Shimberg. 1927. *A Manual of Individual Mental Tests and Testing.* Judge Baker Foundation Publications 4. Boston: Little, Brown.

Brooks, I. R. 1976. Cognitive ability assessment in two New Zealand ethnic groups. *Journal of Cross-Cultural Psychology* 7:347–56.

Brown, J. 1992. *The Definition of a Profession: The Authority of Metaphor in the History of Intelligence Testing, 1890–1930*. Princeton, N.J.: Princeton University Press.

Brown, W. 1910. Some experimental results in the correlation of mental abilities. *British Journal of Psychology* 3:296–322.

Bulanov, I. 1930. Findings from a study of the behavior of the Tungus child. *Journal of Russian and East European Psychology* 31 (1993):45–60.

Burdette, L. 1904. Description of the heating, lighting, and ventilation of the Lying-In Hospital, New York. *American Journal of Nursing* 4:344–47.

Bureau of Public Health and Marine Hospital Service. 1903. *Book of Instruction for the Medical Inspection of Immigrants*. Washington, D.C.: Government Printing Office.

Burt, C. 1909. Experimental tests of general intelligence. *British Journal of Psychology* 3:94–177.

Butt, A. W. 1930. *Taft and Roosevelt: The Intimate Letters of Archie Butt, Military Aide*. 2 vols. New York: Doubleday, Doran.

Canaday, M. 2004. The straight state: Sexuality and American citizenship, 1900–1969. Ph.D. diss., University of Minnesota.

Canavan, A. G. M., G. Dunn, and T. M. McMillan. 1986. Principal components of the WAIS-R. *British Journal of Clinical Psychology* 25:81–85.

Cattell, J. M. 1886. The time taken up by cerebral operations. *Mind* 11:220–42.

———. 1890. Mental tests and measurements. *Mind* 15:373–80.

Cattell, J. M., and L. Farrand. 1896. Physical and mental measurements of the students of Columbia University. *Psychological Review* 3:618–48.

Cattell, R. B. 1936. *A Guide to Mental Testing for Psychological Clinics, Schools, and Industrial Psychologists*. London: University of London Press.

———. 1943. The measurement of adult intelligence. *Psychological Bulletin* 40:153–93.

Chadwick, D. 1993. Seizures, epilepsy, and other episodic disorders. In J. Walton, ed., *Brain's Diseases of the Nervous System*, 697–739. 10th ed. Oxford: Oxford University Press.

Chermayeff, I., F. Wasserman, and M. J. Shapiro. 1991. *Ellis Island: An Illustrated History of the Immigrant Experience*. New York: Macmillan.

Chincotta, D., and G. Underwood. 1997. Digit span and articulatory suppression: A cross-linguistic comparison. *European Journal of Cognitive Psychology* 9:89–96.

Cole, M. 1988. Cross-cultural research in the sociohistorical tradition. *Human Development* 31:137–52.

———. 1990. Cultural psychology: A once and future discipline? In *Nebraska Symposium on Motivation 1989*. Vol. 37, *Cross-Cultural Perspectives*. Edited by J. J. Berman, 279–335. Lincoln: University of Nebraska Press.

———. 1996. *Cultural Psychology: A Once and Future Discipline*. Cambridge, Mass.: Harvard University Press.

Conrad, H. S. 1931. The measurement of adult intelligence, and the requisites of a general intelligence test. *Journal of Social Psychology* 2:72–86.

Cornell, E. L., and W. W. Coxe. 1934. *A Performance Ability Scale: Examination Manual.* New York: World Book.

Corsi, P. M. 1972. Human memory and the medial temporal region of the brain. Ph.D. diss., McGill University, Montreal.

Cowen, P. 1932. *Memories of an American Jew.* Repr., New York: Arno, 1975.

Coxe, W. W. 1916. Grading intelligence by years and by points. *Journal of the American Institute of Criminal Law and Criminology* 7:341–65.

Craig, S. C. 2006. The evolution of public health education in the U.S. Army, 1893–1966. *Army Medical Department Journal* (April–June): 7–17.

Crawford, J. R. 1992. Current and premorbid intelligence measures in neuropsychological assessment. In J. R. Crawford and D. M. Parker, eds., *A Handbook of Neuropsychological Assessment,* 21–49. Hove, U.K.: Erlbaum.

Crawford, J. R., K. M. Allan, D. W. Stephen, D. M. Parker, and J. A. O. Besson. 1989. The Wechsler Adult Intelligence Scale-Revised (WAIS-R): Factor structure in a UK sample. *Personality and Individual Differences* 10:1209–12.

Crosby, A. W. 2003. *America's Forgotten Pandemic: The Influenza of 1918,* new ed. Cambridge: Cambridge University Press.

Daniel, M. H. 1997. Intelligence testing: Status and trends. *American Psychologist* 52: 1038–45.

Darwin, C. 1859. *On the Origin of Species by Means of Natural Selection, or The Preservation of Favoured Races in the Struggle for Life.* London: John Murray.

——. 1871. *The Descent of Man, and Selection in Relation to Sex.* 2 vols. London: John Murray.

Davenport, C. B. 1910. *Eugenics: The Science of Human Improvement by Better Breeding.* New York: Henry Holt.

——. 1928. Race crossing in Jamaica. *Scientific Monthly* 27:225–38.

Davenport, C. B., and M. Steggerda. 1929. *Race Crossing in Jamaica.* Washington, D.C.: Carnegie Institute of Washington.

Davenport, C. B., and D. F. Weeks. 1911. A first study of inheritance in epilepsy. *Journal of Nervous and Mental Disease* 38:641–70.

Davis, E. A. 1932. Knox Cube Test and digit span. *Journal of Genetic Psychology,* 40: 234–37.

Dean, R. S. 1985. Review of Knox's Cube Test. In J. V. Mitchell Jr., ed., *The Ninth Mental Measurements Yearbook,* 1:793–94. Lincoln: University of Nebraska, Buros Institute of Mental Measurements.

Dearborn, G. V. 1897. Blots of ink in experimental psychology. *Psychological Review* 4:390–91.

——. 1898. A study of imaginations. *American Journal of Psychology* 9:183–90.

Deary, I. J., G. Der, and G. Ford. 2001. Reaction times and intelligence differences: A population-based cohort study. *Intelligence* 29:389–99.

Deary, I. J., M. Lawn, and D. J. Bartholomew. 2008. A conversation between Charles Spearman, Godfrey Thomson, and Edward L. Thorndike: The International Examinations Inquiry meetings 1931–1938. *History of Psychology* 11:122–42.

Decroly, O. 1908. Les tests de Binet et Simon pour la mesure de l'intelligence [Binet and Simon's tests for the measurement of intelligence]. *Archives de Psychologie* 6:27–130.

Delabarre, E. B. 1899. Report on the effects of *Cannabis Indica*. *Psychological Review* 6:153–54.

Delabarre, E. B., and J. A. Popplestone. 1974. A cross-cultural contribution to the *cannabis* experience. *Psychological Record* 24:67–73.

Denis, D. J. 2001. The origins of correlation and regression: Francis Galton or Auguste Bravais and the error theorists? *History and Philosophy of Psychology Bulletin* 13:36–44.

de Sanctis, S. 1906. Types et degrés d'insuffisance mentale [Types and degrees of mental deficiency]. *L'Année psychologique* 12:70–83.

———. 1911. Mental development and the measurement of the level of intelligence. *Journal of Educational Psychology* 2:498–507.

Diano, S., and T. L. Horvath. 2008. Anticonvulsant effects of leptin in epilepsy. *Journal of Clinical Investigation* 118:26–28.

Doll, E. A. 1917. The Painted Cube Construction Test. *Journal of Educational Psychology* 8:176–78.

Drever, J., and M. Collins. 1928. *Performance Tests of Intelligence: A Series of Non-linguistic Tests for Deaf and Normal Children.* Edinburgh: Oliver and Boyd.

DuBois, P. H. 1970. *A History of Psychological Testing.* Boston: Allyn and Bacon.

Earle, F. M., A. Macrae, and others. 1929. *Tests of Mechanical Ability.* Report No. 3. London: National Institute of Industrial Psychology.

Earle, F. M., M. Milner, and others. 1929. *The Use of Performance Tests of Intelligence in Vocational Guidance.* Report No. 53. London: Medical Research Council, Industrial Fatigue Research Board.

Ellenberger, H. 1954. The life and work of Hermann Rorschach. *Bulletin of the Menninger Clinic* 18:173–219.

Ellis Island & Statue of Liberty. 2010. New York: American Park Network.

Extra fingers and toes. 1916. Editorial. *Journal of Heredity* 7:320–24.

Faden, R. R., and T. L. Beauchamp with N. M. P. King. 1986. *A History and Theory of Informed Consent.* New York: Oxford University Press.

Fairchild, A. L. 2003. *Science at the Borders: Immigrant Medical Inspection and the Shaping of the Modern Industrial Labor Force.* Baltimore: Johns Hopkins University Press.

Fancher, R. E. 1998. Alfred Binet, general psychologist. In G. A. Kimble and M. Wertheimer, eds., *Portraits of Pioneers in Psychology,* 3:67–83. Washington, D.C.: American Psychological Association.

Feeble-mindedness and immigration. 1913. Editorial. *Journal of the American Medical Association* 60:129.

Fenton, S. 1996. Counting ethnicity: Social groups and official categories. In R. Levitas and W. Guy, eds., *Interpreting Official Statistics*, 143–65. London: Routledge.

Fick, M. L. 1937. The educability of Native children of the Transvaal compared with other groups on the basis of intelligence tests. In E. G. Malherbe, ed., *Educational Adaptations in a Changing Society*, 448–56. Capetown: Juta.

———. 1939. *The Educability of the South African Native*. Research Series No. 8. Pretoria: South African Council for Educational and Social Research.

Flanagan, D. P., K. S. McGrew, and S. O. Ortiz. 2000. *The Wechsler Intelligence Scales and Gf-Gc Theory: A Contemporary Approach to Interpretation*. Boston: Allyn and Bacon.

Folks, H. 1913. Letter to William G. McAdoo. March 13. Record Group 90, box 36, file 219, National Archives, College Park, Md.

Foster, M. H. 1914. Methods of examination of illiterates for mental defectiveness. *Journal of the American Medical Association* 62:1068–71.

Frank, G. 1983. *The Wechsler Enterprise: An Assessment of the Development, Structure, and Use of the Wechsler Tests of Intelligence*. Oxford, U.K.: Pergamon.

Freeman, F. N. 1911. Tests. *Psychological Bulletin* 8:21–24.

———. 1914. Tests. *Psychological Bulletin* 11:253–56.

———. 1919. Tests. *Psychological Bulletin* 16:374–81.

French, C. S., M. Demerec, and G. W. Corner. 1956. Biological research in the Carnegie Institution of Washington. *AIBS Bulletin* 6 (2): 17–19.

Freud, S. 1910. The origin and development of psychoanalysis. *American Journal of Psychology* 21:181–218.

Galton, F. 1869. *Hereditary Genius: An Inquiry into Its Laws and Consequences*. London: Macmillan.

———. 1883. *Inquiries into Human Faculty and Its Development*. London: Macmillan.

———. 1885. On the Anthropometric Laboratory of the late International Health Exhibition. *Journal of the Anthropological Institute* 14:205–21.

———. 1888. Co-relations and their measurement, chiefly from anthropometric data. *Proceedings of the Royal Society of London* 45:135–45.

Gardner, H. 1983. *Frames of Mind: The Theory of Multiple Intelligences*. New York: Basic.

Gaw, F. 1923. The use of performance tests and mechanical tests in vocational guidance. *Journal of the National Institute of Industrial Psychology* 1:333–37.

———. 1925a. *Performance Tests of Intelligence*. Report No. 31. London: Medical Research Council, Industrial Fatigue Research Board.

———. 1925b. A study of performance tests. *British Journal of Psychology* 15:374–92.

Geddings, Henry Downes. 1906. Letter to Surgeon General. November 16. Public Health and Marine Hospital Service, Record Group 90, box 36, file 219. National Archives, College Park, Md.

Gelb, S. A. 1986. Henry H. Goddard and the immigrants, 1910–1917: The studies and their social context. *Journal of the History of the Behavioral Sciences* 22:324–332.

Gelb, S. A., G. E. Allen, A. Futterman, and B. Mehler. 1986. Rewriting mental testing history: The view from the *American Psychologist*. *Sage Race Relations Abstracts* 11 (2): 18–31.

Gillham, N. W. 2001. *A Life of Sir Francis Galton: From African Exploration to the Birth of Eugenics*. New York: Open University Press.

Glueck, B. 1913. The mentally defective immigrant. *New York Medical Journal* 98: 760–66.

Goddard, H. H. 1908a. The Binet and Simon tests of intellectual capacity. *Training School* 5 (10): 3–9.

———. 1908b. The grading of backward children. *Training School* 5 (9): 12–14.

———. 1910a. Four hundred feeble-minded children classified by the Binet method. *Journal of Psycho-Asthenics* 15:17–30. Reprinted in *Pedagogical Seminary* 17:387–97.

———. 1910b. A measuring scale for intelligence. *Training School* 6:146–55.

———. 1911a. The bearing of heredity upon educational problems. *Journal of Educational Psychology* 2:491–97.

———. 1911b. Two thousand normal children measured by the Binet measuring scale of intelligence. *Pedagogical Seminary* 18:232–59.

———. 1912a. The Adaptation Board. *Psychological Bulletin* 9:79–80.

———. 1912b. The feeble minded immigrant. *Training School* 9:109–13.

———. 1912c. Feeble-mindedness and immigration. *Training School* 9:91–94.

———. 1912d. The form board as a measure of intellectual development in children. *Training School* 9:49–52.

———. 1912e. *The Kallikak Family: A Study in the Heredity of Feeble-Mindedness*. New York: Macmillan.

———. 1914. *Feeble-Mindedness: Its Causes and Consequences*. New York: Macmillan.

———. 1915. The Adaptation Board as a measure of intelligence. *Training School* 11: 182–88.

———. 1917a. The mental level of a group of immigrants. Abstract. *Psychological Bulletin* 14:68–69.

———. 1917b. Mental tests and the immigrant. *Journal of Delinquency* 2:243–77.

———. 1933. In the beginning. *Understanding the Child* 3 (2): 22–26.

Goodenough, F. L., K. M. Maurer, and M. J. Van Wagenen. 1940. *Minnesota Preschool Scale*. Minneapolis: Educational Test Bureau.

Gould, S. J. 1981. *The Mismeasure of Man*. New York: W. W. Norton.

Graham, S. 1914. *With Poor Immigrants to America*. London: Macmillan.

Greenfield, P. M. 1997. You can't take it with you: Why ability assessments don't cross cultures. *American Psychologist* 52:1115–24.

Grob, G. N. 1966. *The State and the Mentally Ill: A History of Worcester State Hospital in Massachusetts, 1830–1920*. Chapel Hill: University of North Carolina Press.

Groszmann, M. P. E. 1917. *The Exceptional Child*. New York: Charles Scribner's.

Gwyn, M. K. 1914. The Healy puzzle picture and defective aliens. *Medical Record* 85:197–99.

Haeckel, E. H. P. A. 1866. *Generelle Morphologie der Organismen: allgemeine Grundzüge der organischen Formen-Wissenschaft, mechanisch begründet durch die von Charles Darwin reformirte Descendenz-Theorie* [General Morphology of Organisms: General Features of the Science of Organic Forms, Mechanically Justified Through the Theory of Evolution Revised by Charles Darwin]. Berlin: Reimer.

Hafner, A. W., ed. 1993. *Directory of Deceased American Physicians 1804–1929*. Vol. 1. Chicago: American Medical Association.

Haines, T. H. 1915a. Diagnostic values of some performance tests. *Psychological Review* 22:299–305.

———. 1915b. Point scale ratings of delinquent boys and girls. *Psychological Review* 22:104–109.

———. 1916a. Mental measurements of the blind. *Psychological Monographs* 21 (1, whole no. 89): 1–86.

———. 1916b. A point scale for the mental measurement of the blind. *Journal of Educational Psychology* 7:143–49.

Hall, G. S. 1904. *Adolescence: Its Psychology and Its Relations to Physiology, Anthropology, Sociology, Sex, Crime, Religion and Education*. 2 vols. New York: Appleton.

Hall, P. F. 1913. The recent history of immigration and immigration restriction. *Journal of Political Economy* 21:735–51.

Hamed, S. A. 2007. Leptin and insulin homeostasis in epilepsy: Relation to weight adverse conditions. *Epilepsy Research* 75:1–9.

Harris, J. G., D. S. Tulsky, and M. T. Schultheis. 2003. Assessment of the non-native English speaker: Assimilating history and research findings to guide clinical practice. In D. S. Tulsky, D. H. Saklofske, G. J. Chelune, R. K. Heaton, R. J. Ivnik, R. Bornstein, A. Prifitera, and M. F. Ledbetter, eds., *Clinical Interpretation of the WAIS-III and the WMS-III*, 343–90. San Diego: Academic.

Hart, J. M. 1987. *Revolutionary Mexico: The Coming and Process of the Mexican Revolution*. Berkeley: University of California Press.

Harvey, J. 2003. Novel actions of leptin in the hippocampus. *Annals of Medicine* 35:197–206.

Havighurst, R. J., and R. R. Hilkevitch. 1944. The intelligence of Indian children as measured by a performance scale. *Journal of Abnormal and Social Psychology* 39:419–33.

Healy, W. 1910. The individual study of the young criminal. *Journal of the American Institute of Criminal Law and Criminology* 1:50–62.

———. 1914. A pictorial completion test. *Psychological Review* 21:189–203.

Healy, W., and G. M. Fernald. 1911. Tests for use in practical mental classification. *Psychological Monographs* 13 (2, whole no. 54): 1–53.

Heiser, V. 1936. *An American Doctor's Odyssey: Adventures in Forty-Five Countries*. New York: Grosset and Dunlap.

Hildreth, G. 1935. Review of *A Performance Ability Scale: Examination Manual* by E. L. Cornell and W. W. Coxe. *Psychological Bulletin* 32:850–52.

Hildreth, G. H., and R. Pintner. 1937. *Manual of Directions for Pintner-Paterson Performance Tests, Short Scale*. New York: Teachers' College Press.

History of Franklin, Jefferson, Washington, Crawford & Gasconade Counties, Missouri. 1970. Indexed ed. Cape Girardeau, Mo.: Ramfire Press. Originally published in 1888.

Hobhouse, H. 2002. *The Crystal Palace and the Great Exhibition: Art, Science and Productive Industry. A History of the Royal Commission for the Exhibition of 1851*. London: Athlone Press.

Hoelzel, N. J., and C. F. Hoelzel. 2000. *Blackwell, Missouri and Beyond: A Pictorial History 1800–1997*. Rev. ed. De Soto, Mo.: Jefferson County Historical Society.

Hollingworth, H. L. 1912. The influence of caffeine on mental and motor efficiency. *Archives of Psychology* 3 (22): 1–166.

———. 1927. *Mental Growth and Decline: A Survey of Developmental Psychology*. New York: Appleton.

Huey, E. B. 1908. *The Psychology and Pedagogy of Reading, with a Review of the History of Reading and Writing and of Methods, Texts, and Hygiene in Reading*. New York: Macmillan.

———. 1910a. The Binet scale for measuring intelligence and retardation. *Journal of Educational Psychology* 1:435–44.

———. 1910b. Retardation and the mental examination of retarded children. *Journal of Psycho-Asthenics* 15:31–43.

———. 1911. Binet's scale for measuring intelligence. *Volta Review* 13:26–30.

———. 1912. The present status of the Binet scale of tests for the measurement of intelligence. *Psychological Bulletin* 9:160–68.

Inglis, J. 1957. An experimental study of learning and "memory function" in elderly psychiatric patients. *Journal of Mental Science* 103:796–803.

Itard, E. M. [J. M. G. Itard] 1801. *De l'éducation d'un homme sauvage, ou Des premiers développements physiques et moraux du jeune sauvage de l'Aveyron* [The Education of a Feral Man, or The First Physical and Moral Development of the Feral Boy of Aveyron]. Paris: Goujon fils.

Jensen, A. R., and C. R. Reynolds. 1982. Race, social class and ability patterns on the WISC-R. *Personality and Individual Differences* 3:423–38.

Jensen, M. B. 1934. Review of *Dementia Praecox: A Psychological Study* by Harriet Babcock. *American Journal of Psychology* 46:523–24.

Johnson, B. J. 1925. *Mental Growth of Children in Relation to Rate of Growth in Bodily Development: A Report of the Bureau of Educational Experiments, New York City*. New York: E. P. Dutton.

Johnson, B., and L. Schriefer. 1922. A comparison of mental age scores obtained by performance tests and the Stanford Revision of the Binet-Simon Scale. *Journal of Educational Psychology* 13:408–17.

Jonas, S., ed. 1989. *Ellis Island: Echoes from a Nation's Past*. New York: Aperture Foundation.

Kamin, L. J. 1974. *The Science and Politics of I.Q.* Potomac, Md.: Lawrence Erlbaum.

Kaplan, E., D. Fein, R. Morris, and D. C. Delis. 1991. *WAIS-R NI manual.* San Antonio: Psychological Corp.

Karpman, B. 1948. The myth of the psychopathic personality. *American Journal of Psychiatry* 104:523–34.

Kaufman, A. S. 2000. Tests of intelligence. In R. J. Sternberg, ed., *Handbook of Intelligence,* 445–76. Cambridge: Cambridge University Press.

Kaufman, A. S., and N. L. Kaufman. 1977. *Clinical Evaluation of Young Children with the McCarthy Scales.* New York: Grune and Stratton.

Kearney, G. E. 1966. Some aspects of the general cognitive ability of various groups of Aboriginal Australians as assessed by the Queensland Test. Ph.D. diss., University of Queensland.

Keillor, G. 1985. *Lake Wobegon Days.* New York: Viking.

Keith, T. Z. 1997. Using confirmatory factor analysis to aid in understanding the constructs measured by intelligence tests. In D. P. Flanagan, J. L. Genshaft, and P. L. Harrison, eds., *Contemporary Intellectual Assessment: Theories, Tests, and Issues,* 373–402. New York: Guilford.

Kent, G. H. 1916a. A graded series of colored picture puzzles. *Journal of Experimental Psychology* 1:242–46.

———. 1916b. A graded series of geometrical puzzles. *Journal of Experimental Psychology* 1:40–50.

———. 1950. *Mental Tests in Clinics for Children.* New York: Van Nostrand.

Kent, G. H., and A. J. Rosanoff. 1910. A study of association in insanity. *American Journal of Insanity* 67:37–96, 317–90.

Kerner, J. 1890. *Kleksographien.* Stuttgart: Deutsche Verlage-Anstalt.

Kimmelman, B. A. 1983. The American Breeders' Association: Genetics and eugenics in an agricultural context, 1903–13. *Social Studies of Science* 13:163–204.

Kimura, D. 1960. Visual and auditory perception after temporal-lobe damage. Ph.D. diss., McGill University, Montreal.

———. 1997. *Neuropsychology Test Procedures.* Rev. ed. Montreal: DK Consultants.

King, D. 2000. *Making Americans: Immigration, Race, and the Origins of the Diverse Democracy.* Cambridge, Mass.: Harvard University Press.

Kinney, D. G. 1990. Reopening the gateway to America. *Life,* September, 27–38.

Kirkpatrick, E. A. 1900. Individual tests of school children. *Psychological Review* 7:274–80.

Klebaner, B. J. 1958. State and local immigration regulation in the United States before 1882. *International Review of Social History* 3:269–95.

Klineberg, O. 1928. An experimental study of speed and other factors in "racial" differences. *Archives of Psychology* 15 (93): 1–111.

Knight, C. P. 1913. The detection of the mentally defective among immigrants. *Journal of the American Medical Association* 60:106–107.

Kohs, S. C. 1920. The Block-design Tests. *Journal of Experimental Psychology* 3:357–76.

Kraut, A. M. 1988. Silent travelers: Germs, genes, and American efficiency, 1890–1924. *Social Science History* 12:377–94.

———. 1994. *Silent Travelers: Germs, Genes, and the "Immigrant Menace."* New York: Basic.

Krueger, F., and C. Spearman. 1907. Die Korrelation zwischen verschiedenen geistigen Leistungsfähigkeiten [The correlations among different measures of intelligence]. *Zeitscrift für Psychologie* 44:50–117.

Kuhlmann, F. 1912. *A Revision of the Binet-Simon System for Measuring the Intelligence of Children* (Journal of Psycho-Asthenics Monograph Supplement no. 1). Faribault, MN: Minnesota School for the Feeble-Minded.

———. 1913. The results of grading thirteen hundred feeble-minded children with the Binet-Simon tests. *Journal of Educational Psychology* 4:261–68.

Lahy, B. 1940. Mesure de l'intelligence pratique des membres d'une tribu berbère du Moyen-Atlas [Measurement of the practical intelligence of the members of a Berber tribe in the Middle Atlas]. *Journal de Psychologie Normale et Pathologique* 37–38: 394–411.

Lambert, B. 1992. Otto Klineberg, who helped win '54 desegregation case, dies at 92. *New York Times,* March 10.

Lavinder, C. H., A. W. Freeman, and W. H. Frost. 1918. *Epidemiologic Studies of Poliomyelitis in New York City and the North-Eastern United States During the Year 1916.* Public Health Bulletin No. 91. Washington, D.C.: Government Printing Office.

Leander Blackwell, M.D. 1904. *Journal of the American Medical Association,* 42:479.

Lebensohn, Z. M. 1973. In memoriam: Bernard Glueck, Sr., 1884–1972. *American Journal of Psychiatry* 130:326.

Leitner, Y. 2000. Cognitive deficits in adolescents and children with epilepsy. *International Journal of Adolescent Medicine and Health* 12 (Suppl. 1): S25–S40.

Leontiev, A. N. [A. N. Leont'ev] 1932. Studies on the cultural development of the child: III. The development of voluntary attention in the child. *Journal of Genetic Psychology* 40:52–83.

Lester, O. P. 1929. Performance tests and foreign children. *Journal of Educational Psychology* 20:303–9.

Levinson, B. M. 1960. A research note on the Knox Cubes as an intelligence test for aged males. *Journal of Gerontology* 15:85–86.

Lombardo, P. A., and G. M. Dorr. 2006. Eugenics, medical education, and the Public Health Service: Another perspective on the Tuskegee syphilis experiment. *Bulletin of the History of Medicine* 80:291–316.

Louttit, C. M., and C. G. Browne. 1947. The use of psychometric instruments in psychological clinics. *Journal of Consulting Psychology* 11:49–54.

Lovie, P., and A. D. Lovie. 1996. Charles Edward Spearman, F.R.S. (1863–1945). *Notes and Records of the Royal Society of London* 50:75–88.

Luria, A. R. 1928. The problem of the cultural behavior of the child. *Journal of Genetic Psychology* 35:493–506.

———. 1931. Psychological expedition to central Asia. *Science* 74:383–84.

———. 1932. Psychological expedition to central Asia. *Journal of Genetic Psychology* 40:241–42.

———. 1933. The second psychological expedition to central Asia. *Science* 78:191–92.

———. 1934. The second psychological expedition to central Asia. *Journal of Genetic Psychology* 44:255–59.

———. 1976. *Cognitive Development: Its Cultural and Social Foundations.* Edited by M. Cole. Translated by M. Lopez-Morillas and L. Solotaroff. Cambridge, Mass.: Harvard University Press.

———. 1979. *The Making of Mind: A Personal Account of Soviet Psychology.* Edited by M. Cole and S. Cole. Cambridge, Mass.: Harvard University Press.

Macmeeken, A. M. 1939. *The Intelligence of a Representative Group of Scottish Children.* Publications of the Scottish Council for Research in Education No. 15. London: University of London Press.

Mahan, H. C. 1935. Review of *Cornell-Coxe Performance Ability Scale* by E. L. Cornell and W. W. Coxe. *Journal of Applied Psychology* 19:499–501.

Manual Nevropsykologisk Testbatteri: Batteri I, Voksne (over 15 år) [Neuropsychological Test Battery Manual: Battery I, Adults (Over 15 Years)]. n.d., Bergen, Norway: NeuroTest A/S.

Manual of the Mental Examination of Aliens. 1918. Washington, D.C.: Government Printing Office.

Maxwell, A. E. 1960. Obtaining factor scores on the Wechsler Adult Intelligence Scale. *Journal of Mental Science* 106:1060–62.

McCarthy, D. 1972. *Manual for the McCarthy Scales of Children's Abilities.* New York: Psychological Corp.

McGovern, T., and B. Smith. 2006. *American Coastal Defenses 1885–1950.* Oxford, U.K.: Osprey.

McIntyre, L. A. 1976. An investigation of the effect of culture and urbanisation on three cognitive styles and their relationship to school performance. In G. E. Kearney and D. W. McElwain, eds., *Aboriginal Cognition: Retrospect and Prospect,* 231–56. Canberra: Australian Institute of Aboriginal Studies.

McKee, S. H. 1919. The work of a stationary hospital in the field. *Canadian Medical Association Journal* 9:49–51.

Milberg, W. P., N. Hebben, and E. Kaplan. 1986. The Boston Process Approach to neuropsychological assessment. In I. Grant and K. H. Adams, eds., *Neuropsychological Assessment of Neuropsychiatric Disorders,* 65–86. New York: Oxford University Press.

Military personnel file of Howard A. Knox. 1908–12. AGO 1392370. National Archives, Washington, D.C.

Minton, H. L. 1988. *Lewis M. Terman: Pioneer in Psychological Testing.* New York: New York University Press.

Montessori, M. 1912. *The Montessori Method: Scientific Pedagogy as Applied to Child Education in "the Children's Houses."* Translated by A. E. George. New York: Stokes.

Moreno, B. 2004. *Encyclopedia of Ellis Island*. Westport, Conn.: Greenwood.

Morgenthau, D. R. 1922. Some well-known mental tests evaluated and compared. *Archives of Psychology* 7 (52): 1–54.

Morse, J. 1913. A comparative study of white and colored children by the Binet tests. *Psychological Bulletin* 10:170–71.

Mullan, E. H. 1917a. Mental examination of immigrants: Administration and line inspection at Ellis Island. *Public Health Reports* 31:733–46.

———. 1917b. *Mentality of the Arriving Immigrant*. Public Health Bulletin No. 90. Washington, D.C.: Government Printing Office.

Mullan, F. 1989. *Plagues and Politics: The Story of the United States Public Health Service*. New York: Basic.

Murdoch, S. 2007. *IQ: A Smart History of a Failed Idea*. Hoboken, N.J.: John J. Wiley.

National Geographic Society. 1975. *We Americans*. Washington, D.C.: National Geographic Society.

Nelson, H. E., and P. McKenna. 1975. The use of current reading ability in the assessment of dementia. *British Journal of Social and Clinical Psychology* 14:259–67.

The new immigration law. 1907. Editorial. *American Journal of International Law* 1:452–58.

Nissen, H. W. 1931. A field study of the chimpanzee. *Comparative Psychology Monographs* 8 (1): 1–122.

Nissen, H. W., S. Machover, and E. F. Kinder. 1935. A study of performance tests given to a group of native African Negro children. *British Journal of Psychology* 25:308–55.

Norsworthy, N. 1906. The psychology of mentally deficient children. *Archives of Psychology* 1 (1): 1–111.

Ogilvy, M., and J. Harvey, eds. 2000. *The Biographical Dictionary of Women in Science: Pioneering Lives from Ancient Times to the Mid-20th Century*. 2 vols. New York: Routledge.

Ord, I. G. 1968. The P.I.R. Test and its derivatives. *Australian Psychologist* 2:137–46.

———. 1971. *Mental Tests for Pre-literates*. London: Ginn.

Otis, A. S. 1918a. An absolute point scale for the group measurement of intelligence: Part II. *Journal of Educational Psychology* 9:333–48.

———. 1918b. An absolute point scale for the group measurements of intelligence: Part I. *Journal of Educational Psychology* 9:239–61.

Parezo, N. J., and D. D. Fowler. 2007. *Anthropology Goes to the Fair: The 1904 Louisiana Purchase Exposition*. Lincoln: University of Nebraska Press.

Paschal, F. C., and L. R. Sullivan. 1925. Racial influences in the mental and physical development of Mexican children. *Comparative Psychology Monographs* 3 (serial no. 14): 1–76.

Pearson, K. 1896. Mathematical contributions to the theory of evolution: III. Regression, heredity, and panmixia. *Philosophical Transactions of the Royal Society of London, Series A* 187:253–318.

Peterson, J. 1926. *Early Conceptions and Tests of Intelligence*. New York: World Book.

Pintner, R. 1915. The standardization of Knox's cube test. *Psychological Review* 22:377–401.

———. 1919. A non-language group intelligence test. *Journal of Applied Psychology* 3:199–214.

———. 1923. *Intelligence Testing: Methods and Results.* New York: Henry Holt.

———. 1924. Results obtained with the Non-language Group Test. *Journal of Educational Psychology* 15:473–83.

Pintner, R., and D. G. Paterson. 1915a. The Binet Scale and the deaf child. *Journal of Educational Psychology* 6:201–10.

———. 1915b. A class test with deaf children. *Journal of Educational Psychology* 6:591–600.

———. 1915c. The factor of experience in intelligence testing. *Psychological Clinic* 9:44–50.

———. 1916. Learning tests with deaf children. *Psychological Monographs* 20 (4, whole no. 88): 1–23.

———. 1917. *A Scale of Performance Tests.* New York: Appleton.

Polk's Medical Register and Directory of the United States and Canada, 7th rev. ed. 1902. Detroit: R. L. Polk.

Popplestone, J. A., and M. W. McPherson. 1999. *An Illustrated History of American Psychology,* 2nd ed. Akron, Ohio: University of Akron Press.

Porteus, S. D. 1915. Motor intellectual tests for mental defectives. *Journal of Experimental Pedagogy* 3:127–35.

———. 1931. *The Psychology of a Primitive People: A Study of the Australian Aborigine.* London: Edward Arnold.

The problem of the feeble-minded among immigrants. 1913. Editorial. *Journal of the American Medical Association* 60:209–10.

Professor Simon Biesheuvel. 1991. Obituary. *International Journal of Psychology* 26:683.

Pyle, W. H. 1913. *The Examination of School Children: A Manual of Directions and Norms.* New York: Macmillan.

Rachofsky, L. M. 1918. Speed of presentation and ease of recall in the Knox Cube Test. *Psychological Bulletin* 15:61–64.

Reda, G. C. 1950. Osservazioni sui "cubi da costruzione" di Knox-Pintner in babini di diverse eta [Observations on the Knox-Pintner construction cubes in children of different ages]. *Archivio di Psicologia, Neurologia, e Psichiatria* 11:459–75.

Reed, A. C. 1912a. The medical side of immigration. *Popular Science Monthly* 80:383–92.

———. 1912b. Scientific medical inspection at Ellis Island. *Medical Review of Reviews* 18:541–44.

———. 1913. The relation of Ellis Island to the public health. *New York Medical Journal* 98:172–75.

Reed, J. 1987. Robert M. Yerkes and the mental testing movement. In M. M. Sokal, ed., *Psychological Testing and American Society 1890–1930,* 75–94. New Brunswick, N.J.: Rutgers University Press.

Reeves, P. 2000. *Ellis Island: Gateway to the American Dream.* New York: Crescent.

Reitan, R. M. 1966. A research program on the psychological effects of brain lesions in human beings. In N. R. Ellis, ed., *International Review of Research in Mental Retardation*, 1:153–218. New York: Academic.

"Resolutions Adopted by the Board of Managers of the State Charities Aid Association, February 16, 1912." Record Group 90, box 36, file 219, National Archives, College Park, Md.

Reymert, M. L., and M. L. Hartman. 1933. A qualitative and quantitative analysis of a mental test. *American Journal of Psychology* 45:87–105.

Richardson, J. T. E. 2001. A physician with the Coast Artillery Corps: The military career of Dr. Howard Andrew Knox, pioneer of psychological testing. *Coast Defense Journal* 15 (4): 88–93.

———. 2003. Howard Andrew Knox and the origins of performance testing on Ellis Island, 1912–1916. *History of Psychology* 6:143–70.

———. 2005. Knox's cube imitation test: A historical review and an experimental analysis. *Brain and Cognition* 59:183–213.

———. 2007. Measures of short-term memory: A historical review. *Cortex* 43:635–50.

Roberts, R. R. 1988. *Encyclopedia of Historic Forts: The Military, Pioneer, and Trading Posts of the United States*. New York: Macmillan.

Rorschach, H. 1921. *Psychodiagnostik: Methodik und Ergebnisse eines wahrnehmungsdiagnostischen Experiments (Deutenlassen von Zufallsformen)*. [Psychodiagnostics: Methods and Results of a Perceptual Diagnostic Experiment (Interpretation of Accidental Forms)]. Bern, Switzerland: Bircher.

Rose, N. 1989. *Governing the Soul: The Shaping of the Private Self*. London: Routledge.

Rosenzweig, S. 1944. A note on Rorschach pre-history. *Rorschach Research Exchange* 8:41–42.

———. 1992. *Freud, Jung, and Hall the King-Maker: The Historical Expedition to America, with G. Stanley Hall as Host and William James as Guest*. St. Louis: Rana House Press.

Rybakov, F. E. 1910. *Atlas dlya ekspiremental'no-psikhologicheskogo issledovaniya lichnosti* [Atlas for the Experimental Psychological Investigation of Personality]. Moscow: Sytin.

Salmon, T. W. 1905. The diagnosis of insanity in immigrants. In *Annual Report of the Public Health and Marine-Hospital Service*, 271–78. Washington, D.C.: Government Printing Office.

———. 1911. Insanity and the immigration law. *New York State Hospitals Bulletin* 4:379–98.

———. 1913a. Immigration and the mixture of races in relation to the mental health of the nation. In W. A. White and S. E. Jelliffe, eds., *The Modern Treatment of Nervous and Mental Diseases*, 1:241–86. Philadelphia: Lea and Febiger.

———. 1913b. Mental diseases. In M. J. Rosenau, *Preventive Medicine and Hygiene*, 298–312. New York: Appleton.

Sanford, E. C. 1896. The Philadelphia meeting of the American Psychological Association. *Science* 3:119–24.

Sass, H., and A. R. Felthous. 2008. History and conceptual development of psychopathic disorders. In A. R. Felthous and H. Sass, eds., *International Handbook of Psychopathic Disorders and the Law*, 1:7–30. Hoboken, N.J.: John J. Wiley.

Sattler, J. M. 1985. Review of Knox's Cube Test. In J. V. Mitchell Jr., ed., *The Ninth Mental Measurements Yearbook*, 1:794–95. Lincoln: University of Nebraska, Buros Institute of Mental Measurements.

Schroots, J. J. F., and R. J. van Alphen de Veer. 1976. *Leidse Diagnostische Test: Deel 1. Handleiding* [Leyden Diagnostic Test. Vol. 1, Manual]. Amsterdam: Swets and Zeitlinger.

Seashore, C. E. 1908. *Elementary Experiments in Psychology*. New York: Henry Holt.

Séguin, É. 1843. *Hygiène et éducation des idiots* [Hygiene and education of idiots]. Paris: Baillière.

———. 1846. *Traitement moral, hygiène et éducation des idiots et des autres enfants arriérés ou retardés dans leur développement, agités de mouvements involontaires, débiles, muets non-sourds, bègues, etc.* [Moral treatment, hygiene, and education of idiots and other children who are backward or retarded in their development, agitated by involuntary movements, feebleminded, dumb but not deaf, stammerers, etc.]. Paris: Baillière.

Seguin, E. 1856. Origin of the treatment and training of idiots. *American Journal of Education* 2:145–152.

Shakow, D., and G. H. Kent. 1925. The Worcester formboard series. *Pedagogical Seminary and Journal of Genetic Psychology* 32:599–611.

Sharp, S. E. 1899. Individual psychology: A study in psychological method. *American Journal of Psychology* 10:329–91.

Shubert, A. M. [A. M. Schubert] 1930. The experience of pedological-pedagogical expeditions to study the peoples of far-off regions. *Journal of Russian and East European Psychology* 31 (1993): 13–18.

Siegler, R. S. 1992. The other Alfred Binet. *Developmental Psychology* 28:179–90.

Sillitoe, K., and P. H. White. 1992. Ethnic group and the British census: The search for a question. *Journal of the Royal Statistical Society: Series A* 155:141–63.

Smith, B. W. 1993. Coast artillery maneuvers, Galveston Texas, 1911. *Coast Defense Journal* 7 (3): 57–58.

Smith, D. C. 1994. Military medicine. In J. E. Jessup and L. B. Ketz, eds., *Encyclopedia of the American Military: Studies of the History, Traditions, Policies, Institutions, and Roles of the Armed Forces in War and Peace*, 1575–1626. New York: Charles Scribner's.

Smyth, M. M., N. A. Pearson, and L. R. Pendleton. 1988. Movement and working memory: Patterns and positions in space. *Quarterly Journal of Experimental Psychology* 40A:497–514.

Snijders, J. T., and N. Snijders-Oomen. 1958. *Niet-verbaal intelligentieonderzoek van horen-den en doofstommen: Snijders-Oomen Niet-Verbale Intelligentieschaal S.O.N.* [Examination of nonverbal intelligence in hearing and deaf-mute people: Snijders-Oomen Nonverbal Intelligence Scale S.O.N.]. Groningen: Wolters.

Sokal, M. M. 1987. James McKeen Cattell and mental anthropometry: Nineteenth-century science and reform and the origins of psychological testing. In M. M. Sokal, ed., *Psychological Testing and American Society*, 21–45. New Brunswick, N.J.: Rutgers University Press.

Spearman, C. 1904. "General intelligence," objectively determined and measured. *American Journal of Psychology* 15:201–92.

Sprague, E. K. 1913. Medical inspection of immigrants. *Survey* 30:420–22.

——. 1914. Mental examination of immigrants. *Survey* 31:466–68.

Spreen, O., and E. Strauss. 1998. *A Compendium of Neuropsychological Tests: Administration, Norms, and Commentary.* 2nd ed., New York: Oxford University Press.

Squires, P. C. 1926. *A Universal Scale of Individual Performance Tests.* Princeton, N.J.: Princeton University Press.

Stern, W. 1914. *The Psychological Methods of Testing Intelligence.* Educational Psychology Monographs, No. 13. Translated by G. M. Whipple. Baltimore: Warwick and York.

[Sternberg, G. M.] 1893. *Report of the Surgeon-General of the Army to the Secretary of War for the Fiscal Year Ending June 30, 1893.* Washington, D.C.: Government Printing Office.

Sternberg, R. J. 1985. *Beyond IQ: A Triarchic Theory of Human Intelligence.* Cambridge: Cambridge University Press.

Stewart, R. W. 2004. *American Military History.* Vol. 1, *The United States Army and the Forging of a Nation, 1775–1917.* Washington, D.C.: U.S. Army, Center of Military History.

Stone, J. 1996. Ethnicity. In A. Kuper and J. Kuper, eds., *The Social Science Encyclopedia,* 260–63. 2nd ed. London: Routledge.

Stone, M. H. 2002. *Knox's Cube Test—Revised: A Manual for Clinical and Experimental Uses.* Wood Dale, Ill.: C. H. Stoelting.

Stone, M. H., and B. D. Wright. 1980. *Knox's Cube Test—Revised.* Chicago: C. H. Stoelting.

Stoner, G. W. 1913. Insane and mentally defective aliens arriving at the Port of New York. *New York Medical Journal* 97:957–60.

Stuart, R. M., and A. B. Paine. 1896. *Gobolinks, or Shadow-Pictures for Young and Old.* New York: Century.

Sylvester, R. H. 1913. The form board test. *Psychological Monographs* 15 (4, whole no. 65): 1–56.

Terman, L. M. 1906. A study of some of the intellectual processes of seven "bright" and seven "stupid" boys. *Psychological Seminary* 13:307–73.

——. 1911. The Binet-Simon scale for measuring intelligence: Impressions gained by its application. *Psychological Clinic* 5:199–206.

——. 1916. *The Measurement of Intelligence.* Boston: Houghton Mifflin.

———. 1917. Feeble-minded children in the public schools of California: The menace of feeble-mindedness. *School and Society* 5:161–65.

———. 1918. The vocabulary test as a measure of intelligence. *Journal of Educational Psychology* 9:452–66.

———. 1919. *The Intelligence of School Children.* Boston: Houghton Mifflin.

———. 1930. Trails to psychology. In C. Murchison, ed., *A History of Psychology in Autobiography,* 2:297–331. New York: Russell and Russell.

Terman, L. M., and H. G. Childs. 1912a. A tentative revision and extension of the Binet-Simon measuring scale of intelligence. *Journal of Educational Psychology* 3:61–74.

———. 1912b. A tentative revision and extension of the Binet-Simon measuring scale of intelligence: Part II. Supplementary tests. I: Generalization test: Interpretation of results. *Journal of Educational Psychology* 3:133–43.

———. 1912c. A tentative revision and extension of the Binet-Simon measuring scale of intelligence: Part II. Supplementary tests, continued. *Journal of Educational Psychology* 3:198–208.

———. 1912d. A tentative revision and extension of the Binet-Simon measuring scale of intelligence: Part III. Summary and criticisms. *Journal of Educational Psychology* 3:277–89.

Terman, L. M., and M. A. Merrill. 1937. *Revised Stanford-Binet Scale.* Boston: Houghton Mifflin.

Terman, L. M., G. Lyman, G. Ordahl, L. Ordahl, N. Galbreath, and W. Talbert. 1915. The Stanford revision of the Binet-Simon scale and some results from its application to 1000 non-selected children. *Journal of Educational Psychology* 6:551–62.

———. 1917. *The Stanford Revision and Extension of the Binet-Simon Scale for Measuring Intelligence.* Baltimore: Warwick and York.

Thomson, G. H. 1940. *An Analysis of Performance Test Scores of a Representative Group of Scottish Children.* Publications of the Scottish Council for Research in Education No. 16. London: University of London Press.

Thorndike, E. L. 1903. *Educational Psychology.* New York: Lemcke and Buechner.

Thorndike, E. L., W. Lay, and P. R. Dean. 1909. The relation of accuracy in sensory discrimination to general intelligence. *American Journal of Psychology* 20:364–69.

Thorndike, R. M., with D. F. Lohman. 1990. *A Century of Ability Testing.* Chicago: Riverside.

Tobias, P. V. 1996. Race. In A. Kuper and J. Kuper, eds., *The Social Science Encyclopedia,* 711–15. 2nd ed. London: Routledge.

[Torney, G. H.] 1909. *Report of the Surgeon-General U.S. Army to the Secretary of War 1909.* Washington, D.C.: Government Printing Office.

———. 1910. *Report of the Surgeon-General U.S. Army to the Secretary of War 1910.* Washington, D.C.: Government Printing Office.

———. 1911. *Report of the Surgeon General U.S. Army to the Secretary of War 1911.* Washington, D.C.: Government Printing Office.

Town, C. H. 1912. The Binet-Simon scale and the psychologist. *Psychological Clinic* 5:239–44.

Treadway, W. L. 1925. *Mental Hygiene with Special Reference to the Migration of People*. Public Health Bulletin No. 148. Washington, D.C.: Government Printing Office.

The trend of the science of eugenics. 1914. *Survey* 32:388.

Trevelyan, B., M. Smallman-Taynor, and A. D. Cliff. 2005. The spatial structure of epidemic emergence: Geographical aspects of poliomyelitis in north-eastern USA, July–October 1916. *Journal of the Royal Statistical Society A* 168:701–22.

Trites, R. L. 1977. *Neuropsychological Test Manual*. Ottawa: Royal Ottawa Hospital.

Tuddenham, R. D. 1966. The nature and measurement of intelligence. In L. Postman, ed., *Psychology in the Making: Histories of Selected Research Problems*, 469–525. New York: Alfred A. Knopf.

Tulsky, D. S. 2003. Reviews and promotional material for the Wechsler-Bellevue and Wechsler Memory Scale. In D. S. Tulsky et al., eds., *Clinical Interpretation of the WAIS-III and the WMS-III*, 579–602. San Diego: Academic.

Tulsky, D. S., and N. D. Chiaravalloti. 2003. Pioneers in the assessment of intelligence and memory. In Tulsky et al., *Clinical Interpretation of the WAIS-III and the WMS-III*, 533–78.

Tulsky, D. S., D. H. Saklofske, and J. Ricker. 2003. Historical overview of intelligence and memory: Factors influencing the Wechsler scales. In Tulsky et al., *Clinical Interpretation of the WAIS-III and the WMS-III*, 7–41.

Tulsky, D. S., D. H. Saklofske, and J. Zhu. 2003. Revising a standard: An evaluation of the origin and development of the WAIS-III. In Tulsky et al., *Clinical Interpretation of the WAIS-III and the WMS-III*, 43–92.

Unrau, H. D. 1984. *Statue of Liberty National Monument: Ellis Island. Historical Resource Study (Historical Component)*. 3 vols. Washington, D.C.: National Park Service, U.S. Department of the Interior.

Vandierendonck, A., E. Kemps, M. C. Fastame, and A. Szmalec. 2004. Working memory components of the Corsi blocks task. *British Journal of Psychology* 95:57–79

Vecchi, T., and J. T. E. Richardson. 2001. Measures of visuospatial short-term memory: The Knox cube imitation test and the Corsi blocks test compared. *Brain and Cognition* 46:291–94.

Vingerhoets, G. 2006. Cognitive effects of seizures. *Seizure* 15:221–26.

Vygotski, L. S. [L. S. Vygotsky] 1929. [Studies on the cultural development of the child:] II. The problem of the cultural development of the child. *Journal of Genetic Psychology* 36:415–34.

Wallin, J. E. W. 1911. A practical guide for the administration of the Binet-Simon scale for measuring intelligence. *Psychological Clinic* 5:217–38.

———. 1912. Eight months of psycho-clinical research at the New Jersey State Village for Epileptics, with some results from the Binet-Simon testing. *Epilepsia* 3:366–80.

————. 1962. Reminiscences from pioneering days in psychology, with a few personality portraits. *Journal of General Psychology* 67:121–40.

Wechsler, D. 1917. A study of retention in Korsakoff psychosis. *Psychiatric Bulletin of the New York State Hospitals* 2:403–51.

————. 1932. Analytic use of the Army Alpha Examination. *Journal of Applied Psychology* 16:254–56.

————. 1939. *The Measurement of Adult Intelligence.* Baltimore: Williams and Wilkins.

————. 1944. *The Measurement of Adult Intelligence.* 3rd ed. Baltimore: Williams and Wilkins.

————. 1946. *The Wechsler–Bellevue Intelligence Scale, Form II. Manual for Administering and Scoring the Test.* New York: Psychological Corp.

————. 1949. *Wechsler Intelligence Scale for Children: Manual.* New York: Psychological Corp

————. 1955. *Manual for the Wechsler Adult Intelligence Scale.* New York: Psychological Corp.

————. 1987. *Wechsler Memory Scale–Revised.* San Antonio: Psychological Corp.

————. 1991. *Wechsler Intelligence Scale for Children: Third Edition.* San Antonio: Psychological Corp.

————. 1997. *Wechsler Adult Intelligence Scale, Third Edition: Administration and Scoring Manual.* San Antonio: Psychological Corp.

————. 1999. *Wechsler Memory Scale—Third Edition.* San Antonio: Psychological Corp.

Weeks, D. F. 1912. The heredity of epilepsy analyzed by the Mendelian method. *Proceedings of the American Philosophical Society* 51:178–90.

Whipple, G. M. 1910. *Manual of Mental and Physical Tests.* Baltimore: Warwick and York.

Williams, L. L. 1914. The medical examination of mentally defective aliens: Its scope and limitations. *American Journal of Insanity* 71:257–68.

Wilson, J. G. 1911. Some remarks concerning diagnosis by inspection. *New York Medical Journal* 94:94–96.

Wissler, C. 1901. The correlation of mental and physical tests. *Psychological Review: Monograph Supplements* 3 (6): 1–62.

Wolf, T. H. 1973. *Alfred Binet.* Chicago: University of Chicago Press.

Woods, F. A., A. Meyer, and C. B. Davenport. 1914. Studies in human heredity. *Journal of Heredity* 5:547–55.

Woodworth, R. S. 1910. Racial differences in mental traits. *Science* 31:171–86.

Woodworth, R. S., and F. L. Wells. 1911. Association tests. *Psychological Monographs* 13 (5, whole no. 57): 1–85.

Worthington, M. R. 1926. A study of some commonly used performance tests. *Journal of Applied Psychology* 10:216–27.

Wright, B. D., and M. H. Stone. 1979. *Best Test Design.* Chicago: MESA Press.

Yerkes, R. M. 1915. A point scale for measuring mental ability. *Proceedings of the National Academy of Sciences of the United States of America* 1:114–17.

———. 1918a. Measuring the mental strength of an army. *Proceedings of the National Academy of Sciences of the United States of America* 4:295–97.

———. 1918b. Psychology in relation to the war. *Psychological Review* 25:85–115.

———. 1919. The measurement and utilization of brain power in the Army. *Science* 49:221–26, 251–59.

———, ed. 1921. *Psychological Examining in the United States Army*. Memoirs of the National Academy of Sciences. Vol. 15. Washington, D.C.: Government Printing Office.

Yerkes, R. M., and J. W. Bridges. 1914. The point scale: A new method for measuring mental capacity. *Boston Medical and Surgical Journal* 171:857–66.

Yerkes, R. M., J. W. Bridges, and R. S. Hardwick. 1915. *A Point Scale for Measuring Mental Ability*. Baltimore: Warwick and York.

Yew, E. 1980. Medical inspection of immigrants at Ellis Island, 1891–1924. *Bulletin of the New York Academy of Medicine* 56:488–510.

Yoakum, C. S., and R. M. Yerkes, eds. 1920. *Army Mental Tests*. New York: Henry Holt.

Young, K. 1924. The history of mental testing. *Pedagogical Seminary* 31:1–48.

Zangwill, O. L. 1943. Clinical tests of memory impairment. *Proceedings of the Royal Society of Medicine* 36:576–80.

———. 1946. Some qualitative observations on verbal memory in cases of cerebral lesion. *British Journal of Psychology* 37:8–19.

Zaporozhets, A. 1930. The mental development and psychological characteristics of Oirot children. *Journal of Russian and East European Psychology* 31 (1993): 78–91.

Zenderland, L. 1998. *Measuring Minds: Henry Herbert Goddard and the Origins of American Intelligence Testing*. Cambridge: Cambridge University Press.

INDEX

and Marine Hospital Service, 31, 45, 46; assigned to Ellis Island, xxv, 46, 69, 70, 92, 153, 251; criticizes Binet and Simon's scale, 78, 97, 171; on conditions of examination, 180–82; devises performance tests, xxv, 107–13, 115–21, 197–98, 252; on importance of facial signs, 87–88, 169; on psychogenetic disorders, 176–79; on causes of mental deficiency, 177–78, 266; popularizes work at Ellis Island, xxxi, 142–57, 251; on method of examination, 114–15; divorced by Gladys Barnett Knox, 138; on cultural demands of Binet and Simon's scale, 171; devises performance scale, 121–32, 151–52, 197–98, 217; attitude towards eugenics, 259–60, 262–63; on literacy test, 184; on racial stereotyping, 262–63; on make-up tests, 125–31, 152–53; litigation brought by father, 139–41; criticizes Goddard, 179; addresses second annual meeting of Eugenics Research Association, 146, 148–49, 150; addresses Mississippi Valley Medical Association, 150; on intelligence tests in industry, 174; on intelligence in black people, 174–75, 176, 262; acknowledges contributions of others, 253; marketing Ellis Island tests, 157–58; on dementia praecox, 156–57; marries Maka Harper, 186; resigns from Public Health Service, 186; in private practice in Ashtabula, 187; in Skillman, New Jersey, 187–89; on causes of epilepsy, 188–89; in Bayonne, New Jersey, 189–90, 193; on unnecessary surgery, 190; in New Hampton, New Jersey, 190–91; death, 192; obituaries, 192–94; appraisal, 250–71
Knox, Howard Andrew, Jr. (son of Howard Andrew Knox), xxvii, 186

Knox, Howard Reuben (father of Howard Andrew Knox), xxvii, 3–4, 139–41, 192
Knox, Jennie Mahaffy (mother of Howard Andrew Knox), xxvii, 3–8, 12, 16, 19, 24, 26, 27, 192
Knox, Maka Harper (wife of Howard Andrew Knox), xxvii, 186, 189, 190, 191
Knox, Marion Henderson (wife of Howard Andrew Knox), xxvii, 12, 16, 19, 29, 30
Knox, Robert (son of Howard Andrew Knox), xxvii, 186, 190
Knox, Ruth (putative daughter of Howard Andrew Knox), xxvii, 30
Knox, Violet (daughter of Howard Andrew Knox), xxvii, 16
Kohs, Samuel Calmin, 214, 233
Kohs Blocks Test, 214, 220, 221, 227, 233
Korsakoff psychosis, 230–31
Kraepelin, Emil, 149, 156, 157, 176
Kraut, Alan Morton, 193, 267, 269
Kuhlmann, Frederick, 66

La Garde, Louis Anatole, 19, 24–25, 29
language, to describe people of limited intelligence, xxviii-xxx
language preference, role in performance tests, 246–249
"Last Honors to Bunny," 171–72, 268
Laughlin, Harry, Dr., 92, 153
Laughlin, Harry Hamilton, 150, 167, 260, 263
Lavinder, Claude Hervey, 163–66, 167, 186, 200
Leontiev (Leont'ev), Aleksei Nicolaevich, 256–57
leptin, 189
Lester, Olive Peckham, 226–27
Levinson, Boris Mayer, 237, 238
line inspection, 40–42, 76, 80, 90, 118, 123, 168–69; see also diagnosis by inspection